Understanding the Theory, History, and Practice

T0307104

THE CHALLENGE OF BIBLE TRANSLATION

COMMUNICATING GOD'S WORD TO THE WORLD

GLEN G. SCORGIE, MARK L. STRAUSS, STEVEN M. VOTH

GENERAL EDITORS

Essays in Honor of Ronald F. Youngblood

ZONDERVAN®

ZONDERVAN.com/
AUTHORTRACKER
follow your favorite authors

ZONDERVAN®

The Challenge of Bible Translation

Requests for information should be addressed to:

Zondervan, *Grand Rapids, Michigan 49530*

Library of Congress Cataloging-in-Publication Data

The challenge of Bible translation : communicating God's word to the world / Glen G. Scorgie, Mark L. Strauss, and Steven M. Voth, general editors.
p. cm.
Includes bibliographical references and index.
ISBN-10: 0-310-24685-7
ISBN-13: 0-310-24685-5
1. Bible—Translating. I. Scorgie, Glen G. II. Strauss, Mark L. III. Voth, Steven M.
BS449 .C43 2003
220.5—dc21

2003000027

This edition printed on acid-free paper.

Printed in the United States of America

CONTENTS

PART 3: THE PRACTICE OF BIBLE TRANSLATION

THE CHALLENGE OF BIBLE TRANSLATION

CONTRIBUTORS

Kenneth L. Barker (Ph.D., Dropsie College for Hebrew and Cognate Learning), Executive Director, NIV Translation Center, International Bible Society (Retired)

D. A. Carson (Ph.D., Cambridge University), Research Professor of New Testament, Trinity Evangelical Divinity School

Charles H. Cosgrove (Ph.D., Princeton Theological Seminary), Professor of New Testament Studies and Christian Ethics, Northern Baptist Theological Seminary

Kent A. Eaton (Ph.D., University of Wales, Lampeter), Associate Professor of Pastoral Ministries and Associate Dean, Bethel Seminary San Diego

Dick France (Ph.D., University of Bristol), formerly Principal, Wycliffe Hall, Oxford (Retired)

David Noel Freedman (Ph.D., Johns Hopkins University), Professor of History, Endowed Chair of Hebrew Biblical Studies, University of California, San Diego

Andreas J. Köstenberger (Ph.D., Trinity Evangelical Divinity School), Professor of New Testament and Greek and Director of Ph.D. and Th.M. Studies, Southeastern Baptist Theological Seminary

David Miano (B.A., State University of New York at Buffalo), Ph.D. Candidate and Associate Instructor, University of California, San Diego

Douglas J. Moo (Ph.D., University of St. Andrews), Blanchard Professor of New Testament, Wheaton College Graduate School

Glen G. Scorgie (Ph.D., University of St. Andrews), Professor of Theology, Bethel Seminary San Diego

Moisés Silva (Ph.D., University of Manchester), formerly Professor of New Testament, Westminster Theological Seminary and Gordon-Conwell Theological Seminary

James D. Smith III (Th.D., Harvard University), Associate Professor of Church History, Bethel Seminary San Diego, Lecturer at the University of San Diego, and Associate Pastor, College Avenue Baptist Church

John H. Stek (Drs., Free University, Amsterdam), Emeritus Professor of Old Testament, Calvin Theological Seminary

Mark L. Strauss (Ph.D., Aberdeen University), Associate Professor of New Testament, Bethel Seminary San Diego

Ronald A. Veenker (Ph.D., Hebrew Union College—Jewish Institute of Religion), Professor of Religious Studies, Western Kentucky University

Steven M. Voth (Ph.D., Hebrew Union College—Jewish Institute of Religion), Translation Consultant, United Bible Societies

Larry Lee Walker (Ph.D., Dropsie College for Hebrew and Cognate Learning), formerly Professor of Hebrew and Old Testament, Beeson Divinity School (Retired)

Bruce K. Waltke (Ph.D., Harvard University), Emeritus Professor of Biblical Studies, Regent College, and Professor of Old Testament, Reformed Theological Seminary, Orlando

Walter W. Wessel (Ph.D., Edinburgh University), Emeritus Professor of New Testament, Bethel Seminary San Diego (Deceased)

Herbert M. Wolf (Ph.D., Brandeis University), Professor of Old Testament, Wheaton College and Graduate School (Deceased)

ABBREVIATIONS

Bible Versions

AMP	Amplified Bible
ASV	American Standard Version
BER	New Berkeley Version (also MLB)
BOL	Book of Life: A Messianic Jewish Version
CEV	Contemporary English Version
ESV	English Standard Version
GNB	Good News Bible (also TEV)
GNC	God's New Covenant
GW	God's Word
HCSB	Holman Christian Standard Bible
ISV	International Standard Version
JB	Jerusalem Bible
JNT	Jewish New Testament (Stern)
KJV	King James Version
JPS	The Holy Scriptures: Jewish Publication Society
LB	Living Bible
MLB	Modern Language Bible (also BER)
NAB	New American Bible
NASB	New American Standard Bible
NCV	New Century Version
NEB	New English Bible
NET	New English Translation
NJB	New Jerusalem Bible

NIV	New International Version
NIVI	NIV Inclusive Language Edition (Britain)
NIrV	New International Reader's Version
NKJV	New King James Version
NL	New Life Version
NLT	New Living Translation
NRSV	New Revised Standard Version
NVI	Nueva Versión Internacional
PHILLIPS	The New Testament in Modern English, J. B. Phillips
REB	Revised English Bible
RSV	Revised Standard Version
RV	Revised Version
RVR	Reina Valera Revisada
TEV	Today's English Version (also GNB)
TNIV	Today's New International Version
TNK	Tanakh: A New Translation of the Holy Scriptures According to the Traditional Hebrew Text (Jewish Publication Society)

Other Abbreviations

AGJU	Arbeiten zur Geschichte des antiken Judentums und des Urchristentums
AThR	*Anglican Theological Review*
BAG(D)	Bauer, Arndt, Gingrich (2d ed.: and Danker). *Greek-English Lexicon of the New Testament and Other Early Christian Literature*
BDAG	Bauer, Danker, Arndt, and Gingrich (3d ed.). *Greek-English Lexicon of the New Testament and Other Early Christian Literature*
BDB	Brown, Driver, and Briggs. *A Hebrew and English Lexicon of the Old Testament*
BDF	Blass, Debrunner, and Funk. *A Greek Grammar of the New Testament and Other Early Christian Literature*
BECNT	Baker Exegetical Commentary on the New Testament
BETL	Bibliotheca ephemeridum theologicarum lovaniensium

BFBS	British and Foreign Bible Society
BHS	*Biblia Hebraica Stuttgartensia*
Bib	*Biblica*
BIOSCS	*Bulletin of the International Organization for Septuagint and Cognate Studies*
BKAT	Biblischer Kommentar, Altes Testament
BZAW	Beihefte zur ZAW
BZNW	Beihefte zur ZNW
CBMW	Council on Biblical Manhood and Womanhood
CBT	The Committee on Bible Translation (for the NIV)
CBQ	*Catholic Biblical Quarterly*
CRC	Christian Reformed Church
CT	*Christianity Today*
EBC	Expositor's Bible Commentary
ETS	Evangelical Theological Society
ExpTim	*Expository Times*
FBA	Forum of Bible Agencies
HALOT	Koehler, Baumgartner, and Stamm. *The Hebrew and Aramaic Lexicon of the Old Testament*
HAT	Handbuch zum Alten Testament
HNTC	Harper's New Testament Commentaries
IBHS	Waltke and O'Connor. *An Introduction to Biblical Hebrew Syntax*
ICC	International Critical Commentary
IJAL	*International Journal of American Linguistics*
IVP	InterVarsity Press
JBC	*Journal of Biblical Counseling*
JBL	*Journal of Biblical Literature*
JETS	*Journal of the Evangelical Theological Society*
JTS	*Journal of Theological Studies*
JSNT	*Journal for the Study of the New Testament*
JSNTSup	JSNT Supplement Series
JSOT	*Journal for the Study of the Old Testament*

JSOTSup	JSOT Supplement Series
LCL	Loeb Classical Library
LXX	Septuagint
NAE	National Association of Evangelicals
NIB	*The New Interpreter's Bible*
NICNT	New International Commentary on the New Testament
NIDOTTE	*New International Dictionary of Old Testament Theology and Exegesis*
Notes	*Notes on Translation*
NovTSup	Novum Testamentum Supplements
NPNF	*Nicene and Post-Nicene Fathers*
NT	New Testament
NTS	*New Testament Studies*
NYBS	New York Bible Society
NYBSI	New York Bible Society International
OT	Old Testament
PNTC	Pillar New Testament Commentary
SIL	Summer Institute of Linguistics
SNT	Studien zum Neuen Testament
SNTG	*Studies in New Testament Greek*
SNTSMS	Society for New Testament Studies Monograph Series
TDNT	Kittel and Friedrich. *Theological Dictionary of the New Testament*
TDOT	Botterweck and Ringgren. *Theological Dictionary of the Old Testament*
TLOT	*Theological Lexicon of the Old Testament*
TWOT	*Theological Wordbook of the Old Testament*
TynBul	*TyndaleBulletin*
UBS	United Bible Societies
VT	*Vetus Testamentum*
VTSup	Vetus Testamentum Supplements
WUNT	Wissenschaftliche Untersuchungen zum Neuen Testament
ZAW	*Zeitschrift für die alttestamentliche Wissenschaft*
ZIBBC	Zondervan Illustrated Bible Backgrounds Commentary
ZNW	*Zeitschrift für die neutestamentliche Wissenschaft und die Kunde der älterern Kirche*

ca.	circa (around, about, approximately)
cf.	*confer,* compare
ch(s).	chapter(s)
diss.	dissertation
ed(s).	editor(s), edited by
e.g.	for example
esp.	especially
et al.	and others
etc.	and the rest
f(f).	and the following one(s)
ibid.	in the same place
idem	the same
i.e.	that is
lit.	literally
p(p).	page(s)
passim	here and there
s.v.	under the word
trans.	translator, translated by
v(v).	verse(s)
rpt.	reprinted
x	number of times a form occurs

Old Testament Books

Gen	Genesis
Exod	Exodus
Lev	Leviticus
Num	Numbers
Deut	Deuteronomy
Josh	Joshua
Judg	Judges
Ruth	Ruth
1–2 Sam	1–2 Samuel

New Testament Books

Matt	Matthew
Mark	Mark
Luke	Luke
John	John
Acts	Acts
Rom	Romans
1–2 Cor	1–2 Corinthians
Gal	Galatians
Eph	Ephesians

OLD TESTAMENT BOOKS NEW TESTAMENT BOOKS

1–2 Kgs	1–2 Kings
1–2 Chr	1–2 Chronicles
Ezra	Ezra
Neh	Nehemiah
Esth	Esther
Job	Job
Ps/Pss	Psalms
Prov	Proverbs
Eccl	Ecclesiastes
Song	Song of Songs
Isa	Isaiah
Jer	Jeremiah
Lam	Lamentations
Ezek	Ezekiel
Dan	Daniel
Hos	Hosea
Joel	Joel
Amos	Amos
Obad	Obadiah
Jonah	Jonah
Mic	Micah
Nah	Nahum
Hab	Habakkuk
Zeph	Zephaniah
Hag	Haggai
Zech	Zechariah
Mal	Malachi

Phil	Philippians
Col	Colossians
1–2 Thess	1–2 Thessalonians
1–2 Tim	1–2 Timothy
Titus	Titus
Phlm	Philemon
Heb	Hebrews
Jas	James
1–2 Pet	1–2 Peter
1–2–3 John	1–2–3 John
Jude	Jude
Rev	Revelation

DEDICATORY PREFACE

"Great men seem to us men of great boldness; in reality they are more obedient than others."

—A. G. Sertillanges, *The Intellectual Life*

This volume of essays on the challenge of Bible translation is presented in honor of Ronald F. Youngblood, a leading evangelical voice and an outstanding teacher, scholar, editor, and Bible translator. It is a modest work to honor a great person whose entire direction in life—and significant achievements along the way—has been the natural product of his lifelong obedience to the higher purposes of his Lord.

Ron was born in Chicago, Illinois, in 1931, nurtured in modest circumstances, and drawn to faith in Jesus Christ at a young age. During his teen years he moved with his family to the small town of Chesterton, Indiana. In due course he attended nearby Valparaiso University and upon graduation in 1952 married Carolyn Johnson, with whom he has enjoyed the blessing of a half century of mutually supportive partnership. After Valparaiso the Youngbloods traveled to the West Coast, where Ron enrolled in the Bachelor of Divinity program at Fuller Seminary (1952–55) and was formatively influenced by E. J. Carnell, William Sanford La Sor, and David Hubbard. Ron's emerging aptitude and passion for Old Testament research led the Youngbloods back across America to the Dropsie College for Hebrew and Cognate Learning in Philadelphia, Pennsylvania, where Ron earned his Ph.D. in 1961. Always learning, he subsequently invested an academic year (1967–68) on an archaeological fellowship at the Hebrew Union College in Jerusalem. Over the years he has become a savvy traveler and explorer of ancient things in the Middle East.

At the same time Ron has always been committed to the welfare of the church. This was signaled early on through his ordination to the gospel ministry in 1958 at Oxford Circle Baptist Church in Philadelphia. His direct contributions to congregational life since then have included regular pulpit ministry, lay teaching, and periodic interim pastorates. One literary legacy of this dimension of his vocation is a collection of his sermons titled *Special-Day Sermons: Outlines and Messages* (1973, 1978, 1989).

Ronald Youngblood has been closely and continuously associated with Bethel Seminary for his entire academic career of over forty years. In 1961 he was hired to teach Old Testament at Bethel Seminary in St. Paul, Minnesota, and did so with distinction until 1978. Even while subsequently serving for much briefer periods at Wheaton College Graduate School (1978–81) and Trinity Evangelical Divinity School (1981–82), he maintained his Bethel association on an annual basis as an adjunct professor. In 1982 he accepted the Old Testament professorship at Bethel Seminary West, Bethel's new campus in San Diego, California. Ron's presence added, and continues to add, considerable credibility to this school (now known as Bethel Seminary San Diego), and Southern California has been home for the Youngbloods ever since. It serves as his base for consultations, lectureships, and short-term teaching ministries literally around the world.

Unquestionably, Ron Youngblood has been gifted with a brilliant mind. He has an encyclopedic memory, an enviable aptitude for languages, and an astonishing editorial efficiency and accuracy. Yet for all of that, he has never been one of those stereotypical ivory-tower scholars who thinks (in the words of Adolf Harnack) that he has discharged his duties by treating the gospel "in the recondite language of learning and burying it in scholarly folios."[1] He has always loved the church and respected the laity too much to treat the gospel in such a manner. He represents the democratic instinct of the evangelical tradition at its very best. It is no accident that C. S. Lewis and Billy Graham are among those he most admires.

Ron has made a very significant contribution to biblical scholarship through his many Old Testament publications. There is no scandal to his evangelical mind. Space limitations require that only a few of his scholarly publications be highlighted here. His first book, *Great Themes of the Old Testament* (1968), has enjoyed perennial appeal and is still in print under a new title *The Heart of the Old Testament* (2d ed., 1998). Two of his smaller books, *Faith of Our Fathers* (1976) and *How It All Began* (1980), were blended into *The Book of Genesis: An Introductory Commentary* (2d ed., 1999). In this work he demonstrated a judicious "conservationist" perspective while taking full account of the historical origins and literary genre of Genesis. His research on biblical beginnings also qualified him to edit a related work, *The Genesis Debate: Persistent Questions about Creation and the Flood* (1986), in which two opposing views were fairly presented.

The breadth of Ron's Old Testament scholarship is reflected in additional publications on *Exodus* (1983, 1999), *Themes from Isaiah* (1983), and especially in his extensive work on First and Second Samuel for volume 3 of the Expositor's Bible Commentary (1992), work that was later adapted for inclusion in the two-volume *Zondervan NIV Bible Commentary* (1994).

Ron has also been an outstanding editor over the years. He served for a remarkably long run of twenty-two crucial years (1976–98) as the editor of the *Journal of the Evangelical Theological Society (JETS)*. In this capacity he helped to fortify the scholarly reputation of the Evangelical Theological Society and contributed to the intellectual credibility of the evangelical tradition generally. He has always been an irenic advocate of a high view of Scripture, and during his tenure as *JETS* editor he selected and published a collection of *JETS* articles known as *Evangelicals and Inerrancy* (1984). Certainly no less significant were his labors as an associate editor for the *NIV Study Bible* (1985)—work that continues to this day (he was associate editor for a revised edition published in October 2002)—and as general editor of *Nelson's New Illustrated Bible Dictionary* (1995). In 1996 this latter volume won the Evangelical Christian Publishers Association Gold Medallion Award for reference books.

It is for Ron as a person that those of us privileged to know him feel the most affection. His exceptional sense of humor has often brought relief to stultifying committee meetings, diffused tension at other times, and always reminded us that it is unwise to take ourselves too seriously. And there are some paradoxical features of his temperament that endear him to us as well. He oscillates, for example, between statesmanship on significant matters to occasional goofiness over lunch at the local Burger King. He can be a creature of rather parochial lunchtime habits while at home but then immediately get on an airplane for another of his adventures to the Caribbean, Europe, Africa, Asia, or the Middle East. A largehearted and generous man, his frugality is legendary.

His accomplishments have been considerable, to say the least, yet he remains a genuinely humble person who encourages younger colleagues and students and rejoices in the accomplishments of others. His heart truly is set on the bigger picture of kingdom advance and the interests of his Savior. And by drawing on the resources of his faith in Jesus Christ, Ron has developed an unusual joy in living and a buoyancy of spirit that are contagious to everyone around him. This joy has remained resilient, even in the midst of anxieties and experiences of loss.

Nothing has been closer to Ron's heart over the years than the challenge of finding ways to faithfully communicate the Bible's meaning through the symbols and words of diverse and changing cultures. This significant dimension of

Ron's vocation began in 1970. Arthur Lewis, his Old Testament colleague at Bethel College, was working on a translation team reporting to the newly organized Committee on Bible Translation (CBT), and Dr. Lewis arranged for Ron to join the team. Ron's administrative efficiency and exceptional gifts for editing and translating became progressively evident, and in 1976 he was invited to join the CBT (initially as a "nonmember" member) during its pressured run to meet a 1978 deadline for publication of the complete New International Version. He has been an integral part of the CBT ever since and played an active editor-translator role in the development of the first revised edition of the NIV (1984). He also served as executive editor of the New International Reader's Version: New Testament (1995, 1998), a Bible designed for youthful readers and adult readers with more limited vocabularies (e.g., those for whom English is a second language). More recently he played a significant role in the development of the Today's New International Version (TNIV), a version designed to reflect more recent developments in English-language meanings. The TNIV New Testament was published in 2002; the Old Testament portion is projected to release in 2004.

Ron continues as an active member of the International Bible Society's Committee on Bible Translation. He seems most alive when he is hunkered down with his closest friends and colleagues in the painstaking collaborative work of Bible translation. In addition to this significant hands-on work, he chairs the board of directors of the International Bible Society, the official sponsor of the NIV and an organization with a vision for Bible translation and distribution that extends well beyond the English-speaking world.

Ron's great passion for the task of correctly handling the word of truth (2 Tim 2:15) will be part of his legacy to the next generation of evangelical scholars and colleagues. He has enriched our lives by his mentoring and friendship and by his faithfulness to Scripture and to the vocation of a Christian scholar. It has been a special honor, inspiration, and delight for all of us to have been associated with him over the years.

—Glen G. Scorgie, Mark L. Strauss, and Steven M. Voth

Notes

1. Adolf von Harnack, Preface to *What is Christianity?* trans. Thomas Bailey Saunders (Philadelphia: Fortress, 1986), vi.

INTRODUCTION AND OVERVIEW

Glen G. Scorgie

From Alexandria to Ukarumpa

The twin-engine Cessna descended through a break in the clouds and circled a hillside community before landing on a dirt airstrip nearby. We had arrived in the mile-high town of Ukarumpa in the highlands of Papua New Guinea. Encircled by protective fencing, the town is home to over a thousand international residents and their local assistants. Their modest but well-maintained houses cover the slopes. Near the end of the day conservatively dressed people can be seen striding along the roads, shoulders hunched in earnestness as they lug laptops and tote bags of important paperwork home for the evening. An air of quiet diligence pervades the scene.

All around is coffee-growing country, but the town of Ukarumpa exists for a different purpose. Founded in the 1950s, owned and operated by the Summer Institute of Linguistics (SIL—also known as Wycliffe Bible Translators), an evangelical parachurch organization, it is probably the world's largest installation for the purpose of linguistic research and Bible translation. The linguistic techniques, computer software, and technical support employed here are state-of-the-art. Fact-gathering visits to tribal situations are kept brief and to a minimum out of respect for fragile indigenous cultures. An impressive number of translation projects have already been completed, and personnel here are working in no less than 175 different languages.

Ukarumpa may be exceptional, but it is not an oddity. Rather, it is a notable example of a much larger enterprise going on for many years just below the radar screen of public awareness. This work is really as old as the Greek Septuagint version of the Hebrew Bible prepared in the Egyptian city of Alexandria prior to the birth of Jesus Christ. It is as venerable as the New Testament itself, in which, as former missionary Andrew Walls puts it, "the very words of Jesus come to us in Greek dress."[1] It is as ancient as Jerome's fourth-century Latin Vulgate version that monopolized the mind of the Western church for over a millennium.

But the challenge of Bible translation as we know it today is fueled to a considerable extent by evangelical Protestant passion to get the transforming Word of God out into the hands and hearts of the people of the world. The evangelical tradition is nothing if it is not Bible-centered,[2] so it continues to resonate with the sentiments of Protestant Reformer Martin Luther, who said, "I should prefer all my books to perish that only the Bible might be read, for other books take up our attention and make us neglect [it]."[3] And evangelicals exude an almost boundless confidence in the spiritual power of these same Scriptures, a confidence memorably expressed by Charles Spurgeon when he said, "The word of God is like a lion. You don't have to defend a lion. All you have to do is let the lion loose, and the lion will defend itself."

The evangelical view leads first, then, to the conviction that Bible translation is a vitally important endeavor. But what exactly is the challenge of Bible translation all about? As with translation endeavors generally, the goal of Bible translation is to transfer the meaning of a biblical text from its source language to some other receptor language so that *communication* occurs. Everything else about the translation business—all the linguistic expertise and scholarly apparatus, the lexicons, and the software—is little more than scaffolding. The key point is that communication is not just a matter of proclaiming something. It requires that the message sent out be received—and not only received but received in such a way that the reader (or viewer or listener) actually "gets it." In Bible translation, faithfulness to the original meaning of a text is important, but it is not enough. The other critical test is what it enables its readers to understand. Translation is all about communication, and communication is by its very nature dialogical. It cares about its source *and* it cares about its audience. It is about what *actually transfers* from a point of origin to a destination. Every undergraduate is familiar with Bishop George Berkeley's philosophical question, "If a tree falls in the forest and no one is around, does it make a sound?" In a similar vein we might well ask, "If a translation is published but fails to communicate, is it really a translation?"

Particularly in these days of fuzzy thinking and epistemological malaise, it is important to affirm something else about Bible translation: Not only is it highly desirable; it is also *possible*. It is thoroughly Christian to hold that the divinely inspired Word first communicated through Hebrew and Greek language (and the ways of viewing life that those languages reflected) can now be meaningfully conveyed through other human languages as well. It is a great grace—and one to be celebrated by Christians—that divinely revealed truth is portable between linguistic systems and equally potent in its new dress. Meaningful communication need not be confined within the locus of any linguistic system, including the loci of the original biblical languages.

The Christian faith carries within itself the grounds for affirming the possibility of interlinguistic transfer and successful Bible translation. It does so through its heuristic paradigms of Pentecost and the Incarnation. Certainly this is at least part of what was symbolically proclaimed at Pentecost when an international audience in Jerusalem reported that every one of them was able to hear and understand the apostolic gospel in his or her own tongue (Acts 2:11). It was Luke's way of affirming that Babel was not to be God's final and fateful verdict on the human race. And Christian hopefulness about Bible translation does not depend on this alone. It is grounded as well in the Incarnation itself. The paradigm of the Incarnation, the Word becoming flesh, is foundational to the translator's task. Andrew Walls again puts it so well: "There is a history of translation of the Bible because there was a translation of the Word into flesh."[4] Bible translators must be modest, but they also ought to be—if they are Christians—optimistic as well. Meaning can never be transferred between linguistic systems comprehensively (thus the modesty), but it can be transferred truly and substantially (thus the hopefulness). Historic Christianity affirms with the apostle Paul that "in Christ all the *fullness* of the Deity lives in bodily form" (Col 2:9, emphasis added). Christ's divinity was not lost or diminished through his assumption of our humanity. Christian translators rightly draw inspiration from the triumphs of Pentecost and the Incarnation.

The Incarnation is a Christian's ground for affirming that translation is possible. It may also be treated as a pointer to how translation ought to be conducted. The God who previously communicated in a variety of ways eventually chose, as his ultimate communication initiative, to become fully incarnate as a human being (Heb 1:1–2). God's truth was communicated with unprecedented clarity and depth as God *fully* embraced our humanity. The application of this principle to translation leads us to conclude that the more thoroughly the Bible is translated into the language and thought-constructs of a receptor group, the more powerfully and effectively its divine message can be expected to shine through. Just as the early church celebrated a Savior who was fully God and fully human, without compromise of either nature, we should expect by analogy that the most powerful translations for communicating divine truth will be the ones that are most thoroughly contextual (or "human") in form. Unlike ancient Docetism, incarnational Christianity enters fully and without fear into the world as it is.

Bible translation is both important and possible—yet it is also far from simple. Quite a few contributors to this volume refer to a famous Italian aphorism about all translators being "traitors." *Traitor* is a strong word, and these contributors deliberately use it to puncture naïveté about the business of translation. They use it as a way of humbly acknowledging that some things will become hidden through translation and that, realistically, good translation is more about minimizing such losses than escaping them altogether.

Today the complexity of the translation challenge is becoming more deeply appreciated. As a result the Christian public is undergoing a somewhat painful adjustment in thinking as it comes to understand that no two human languages ever match up exactly word for word in a convenient parallel-column sort of way. Translation is not as straightforward as converting Fahrenheit temperatures to Celsius or Roman numerals to regular numbers. Thus, one of the recurring themes in this volume is that translation is not an exact science. We should take this to mean that the fantasy of a one-for-one mechanical conversion process has finally been exposed for the falsehood it really is. Consequently, we should begin to think of translation method as different from the more rigid methodologies of the hard sciences and as demanding a wider breadth of competencies and sensitivities on the part of the translator. It is, after all is said and done, an art. Yet, for all of this there is still a rigor and a discipline to translation that is actually more demanding than the older model anticipated. As a result the challenge might better be described as a ***disciplined art*** of Bible translation.

In certain cases Christians who hold to a high view of Scripture find it difficult to adjust to this reality. By way of explanation, some of their more uncharitable opponents speculate that such persons are Fundamentalists, and as such are allergic to complexity and gravitate out of fear toward simplistic resolutions of issues. But the problem with this dismissive view is that not everyone who highly esteems Scripture and who struggles to embrace established principles of Bible translation is a Fundamentalist by viewpoint or temperament. There must be something else going on as well. Others propose that the problem lies in a linguistic naïveté widespread among conservative Christians, a naïveté that can be corrected through better information and education. This may well be the case in some instances, and the dissemination of accurate information can only help.

But perhaps conservative objections will prove resistant to such efforts, because they are actually rooted in something else, namely, some common conservative assumptions about biblical inspiration and inerrancy. According to the historic evangelical view, divine inspiration is more than a general influence over the biblical authors as a whole; inspiration extends to the micro-level of the very words found in the original text. This is an important doctrine for evangelicals, and it needs to be maintained. But at this point the reasoning of some (not all) conservative evangelicals begins to shift from defensible doctrine to questionable inference. Each individual word of Scripture, the questionable reasoning suggests, was specifically selected by God and delivered to us from above in a manner very similar to dictation. The words were sent down, one at a time, like crystal droplets. Each word is an autonomous integer, separate from the rest, and each is to be treasured like a sacred gem and cherished inviolate for all time.

When it comes to translation preference and practice, the implications of this way of thinking are predicable. Those who view Scripture this way (and not all evangelicals do, of course) favor attempts at word-for-word translation. Translations produced in this fashion are naively thought to retain all the precious original words, except that they are just in a different code now. The inclination is to assume that in every language there is a template of more or less exact equivalents to the inspired Hebrew and Greek words with which we started out. This is, of course, not the case at all. If evangelicals are to get beyond their current impasse over translation theory, they will need a more profound doctrine of biblical inerrancy—one that continues to respect the inspired words of the original text but also acknowledges that these words are mere instruments in the service of a higher purpose, namely, the communication of meaning.

Today there is a growing awareness of the strategic role that (usually anonymous) translators play. Most Christians do not understand the original languages, and therefore do not personally have access to the text of the Bible as it was originally written. For the most part they are dependent on translators to tell them what the Bible says. Translators are thus the first-line gatekeepers for the Word of God. Just as stock market investors need to be able to trust corporate executives and their auditors, the church must be able to trust its translators. When translators are, fairly or unfairly, suspected or accused of ulterior motives or deliberate distortion, there is a crisis of confidence. The current debates in the church over translational integrity requires that thoughtful clergy and laity gain information about what is going on in this field so they can determine for themselves where their confidence should be properly placed. The literature on translation (and Bible translation in particular) is substantial, but it is for the most part written for specialists and practitioners. Popular literature on the topic is still not extensive. This volume is a modest contribution toward a more accessible body of work on this important topic.

Admittedly, this book provides only a narrow window on the broad enterprise of Bible translation. While there are some references to translation in

Spanish and other languages—and certainly many of the principles articulated have wider application—the book focuses on English Bible translation. It is a familiar criticism that the disproportionately large and ever-increasing number of English Bible translations reflects both an intolerable inequity and patent Anglophone self-indulgence. While there may be, in certain restricted instances, a measure of truth to this criticism, the other reality is that the English language continues to change, probably more rapidly than some others, and English Bible translation must keep pace with these developments. Beyond this, there is also the fact that the potential usefulness of an English translation today far exceeds that of most other language translations—and probably equals the potential reach of many hundreds of smaller language translations put together. So both sides of this issue have to be weighed fairly. The spread of the English language around the world is truly phenomenal, and it just so happens that today Bibles in English have an almost unmatched potential to communicate globally.

The contributors to this volume, though not in lockstep, are generally united in their support of the translation theory of functional equivalence in its basic contours. The reader will soon discover that the influence of Eugene Nida has been significant for many of the contributors. Nida's views on translation, as found in such publications as *Toward a Science of Translating* (1964), *The Theory and Practice of Translation* (1974), and *From One Language to Another: Functional Equivalence in Bible Translating* (1986), provide the theoretical foundation for their ongoing enterprise. And, as Dick France points out in this volume, the influence of Nida is, if anything, even more profound among contemporary translators (like those in Ukarumpa) working outside the English-speaking world. Despite their general theological conservatism, such individuals seem comfortable with so-called "functional equivalence" translation philosophy and are evidently accustomed to bold ventures in it every day.

The majority of the contributors to this volume are leading international scholars in the field of biblical studies who also have a wealth of experience as Bible translators. This is a most welcome and distinctive characteristic of this group of writers. Most have been doing translation for years—and doing so with unsurpassed rigor and expertise. This is evident in the rich variety of illustrations they tumble out to explain their points and in the plethora of examples they use to buttress their arguments and confirm their statements. They are practitioners—even better, they are practitioners who understand theory. This may be the greatest strength of this book. A significant number of these same contributors have also served with Ronald Youngblood on the Committee on Bible Translation, so some of these essays function unintentionally as a kind of apologia for the New International Version (NIV).

Even those of us who are not experts in Bible translation can readily grasp the importance of accuracy (or faithfulness) as a translation ideal. The contributors to this volume readily agree, yet they widen our horizons by explaining that accuracy is not the only criteria by which a good translation should be measured. In different ways, they consistently speak of a second category of qualities that translators should aspire to achieve, namely, those (like clarity, naturalness, and readability) that pertain to audience sensitivity and are so essential to closing the communication loop between sender and receiver. Finally, the authors speak in different ways of a third category of qualities that are of a more aesthetic and affective nature. Such ideals as beauty, orality (suitability for public reading), and dignity are also important to a translation's popularity and durability. In short, there is more to a great translation than first meets the eye.

The eighteen essays have been organized into three sections that address, respectively, the theory, history, and practice of Bible translation. The first six essays (chapters 1–6) examine the competing theoretical approaches (or so-called philosophies) of translation and evaluate their respective merits. The second set of six essays (chapters 7–12) explores the history of Bible translation, with particular attention to English Bible translation and with special reference to the KJV and the NIV. The third set of essays (chapters 13–18) addresses the actual practice of translation and includes some illuminating case studies in translation.

The contributors to this volume have come together, not because of a uniform commitment to a particular philosophy of Bible translation, but because of their mutual appreciation for their friend Ronald Youngblood—an outstanding scholar, a gifted translator, and above all a person of Christian character and contagious joy. It is our hope that this volume will be not only a worthy recognition of his work but also a further contribution to the task for which he has shown such passion and ability—the disciplined art of Bible translation. The following chapter summaries are provided for the reader's convenience and as an aid to locating treatments of specific topics of interest.

Part 1: The Theory of Bible Translation

In chapter 1, Moisés Silva offers personal reflections on an old Italian complaint that translators are traitors in the sense that they always (and necessarily) fall short of conveying the *total* meaning of a text in one language into another. His personal struggle early on to translate into English all the rich nuances of Spanish, his own first language, convinced him that any "literal" word-for-word translation strategy will prove both impossible and ultimately unhelpful. As he points out, even so-called literal Bible translations like the ESV reflect countless interpretive decisions and departures from strict literalism. With literary sensitivity Silva explains that a faithful translator is obliged to convey in clear and readable form, not only the meanings of individual words and phrases, but something also of the structure, rhythm, and emotive elements of the original text. Ultimately the "accuracy" of a translation should be measured by the degree to which a translator has achieved all of these things. Silva sees the good translator, not as a traitor, then, but as someone who responsibly "transforms a text by transferring it from one linguistic-cultural context to another."

Kenneth Barker, longtime member of and spokesperson for the Committee on Bible Translation, which has among its many translation achievements the New International Version, sagely observes in chapter 2 that every group of Bible translators must establish at the very outset the type of translation they intend to produce. This in turn requires a conscious philosophical positioning of their translation project. After emphatically rejecting as naive the possibility of meaningful translation without at least some degree of interpretation, Barker acknowledges that a group of translators may choose to pursue a philosophy that leans either toward formal equivalence or toward dynamic equivalence. But he argues that it is also possible to adopt a balanced or mediating translation philosophy that combines the strengths of these respective options while avoiding the weaknesses inherent in their more extreme forms. Barker presents the NIV as an example of such optimal balance in its intentional pursuit of the four highly desirable translation characteristics of accuracy, clarity, beauty, and dignity.

D. A. Carson (chapter 3) begins by noting two opposing trends in recent years: (1) the virtual triumph of functional-equivalence theory across the scholarly disciplines relevant to Bible translation, and (2) the contrasting rise of what he calls "linguistic conservatism"—a popular movement with a strongly expressed preference for more direct and "literal" translation methods. By pointedly challenging a couple of representatives of this latter perspective, he builds his case for functional equivalence as the only responsible approach to Bible translation for a general readership. As he then points out, the ideological gulf between the practitioners of these two competing approaches is nowhere more evident than in the recent debate over gender-accurate language in Bible translation.

Carson devotes the remainder of his essay to sounding a caution on the limitations—and even risks, when taken to excess—of functional-equivalence theory. Responsible practitioners of functional equivalence will not make "reader response" the supreme criterion in translation decision, nor will they concede the skeptical assumption of an impassible dichotomy between message and meaning. He calls for limits on a variety of other factors as well, from the pursuit of comprehensibility and stylistic elegance at all costs to the dubious incorporation of opinionated study notes in the published text of Scripture.

In chapter 4 Mark Strauss addresses current issues in the gender-language debate. The chapter is essentially a response to various charges leveled by Vern Poythress and Wayne Grudem against recent gender-accurate Bible translations (see *The Gender-Neutral Bible Controversy: Muting the Masculinity of God's Word* [2000]). Strauss begins by listing a surprising number of important areas of agreement between the two sides—shared convictions about the nature of authoritative Scripture, the translation enterprise, and even gender language itself.

Strauss then moves on to critical areas of disagreement between the two camps. Most of these, he suggests, are rooted in different understandings of linguistics. Throughout this section Strauss repeatedly concedes that the gender-inclusive approach may in some cases sacrifice some of the nuances of the original text. But such losses, he insists, are unavoidable and "come with the territory" of translation work. He urges the opponents of gender-inclusive translation to be equally up-front about the dimensions of meaning they are compelled to sacrifice through their approach. At the very least there should be a cessation on both sides of emotive charges that the opposition is deliberately distorting the Word of God.

In chapter 5 the late Herbert Wolf, a longtime member of the Committee on Bible Translation, reflects from his own experiences on the communal dimensions of translation. He begins with a carefully nuanced acknowledgment that translators belong to larger communities and traditions that powerfully inform and shape (but—and here he shows his epistemological optimism—need never completely determine) their reading of the biblical text.

Wolf also sees great benefits in the fact that most recent translations of the Bible have been group projects—not least that group arrangements enable translators to pool strengths and purge idiosyncrasies; and here he speaks (as only an experienced translation practitioner can) of the humbling aspect of having one's work tested and improved by peers. He also sees translation as communal in the sense that it draws from related fields like archaeology and linguistics, a point he illustrates with fascinating insights from the field of rhetorical criticism. Finally, the potential readers of a translation also constitute a most relevant community, inasmuch as responsible translation decisions will always factor in readers' anticipated responses to the text.

In chapter 6 Charles Cosgrove reflects on the values that should inform and the approach that should characterize a Bible translation methodology compatible with the legitimate aspirations of postmodernism. The defining feature of such a legitimate postmodern approach, he suggests, is best encapsulated in the adjective *holistic*. Under this rubric he first considers translating the Bible as a *whole* (that is, as a canonical integrity), then translating the *whole* communicative effect of Scripture (that is, its genre and medium, as well as its language), and finally, translation as an activity of the *whole* people of God (the democratization of translation).

Cosgrove's first point—translating the Bible with canonical integrity—raises such difficult issues as whether the translation of the Old Testament should be guided in any way by how the New Testament purports to quote it. His second point affirms the postmodern trend to "challenge traditional distinctions between form and content and the hierarchy that subordinates one to the other." At the same time, he notes, the postmodern view is properly sensitive to the enormous challenge (and downright trickiness) of achieving holistic equivalence in any communication transfer between distinct cultural-linguistic systems. Finally, Cosgrove argues that "the democratizing or 'flattening' cultural effect of postmodernity—epitomized by the Internet" means that the age of officially authorized versions is permanently over. He anticipates such a future scenario with optimism, because he believes that the inevitable diffusion of translations will only make the fullest sense of Scripture more accessible to all.

Part 2: The History of Bible Translation

In chapter 7 Dick (R. T.) France provides a concise overview of the history of English Bible translation. He stresses throughout that English translation remains a never-ending challenge for two reasons: (1) manuscript resources continue to improve, and (2) the English language continues to change. After noting that ad hoc sections of the (Vulgate) biblical text were translated into English from as early as the seventh century, he describes the contributions of translation pioneers such as Wycliffe and Purvey in the fourteenth century and Tyndale and Coverdale in the sixteenth, and traces the development of English translation through a long list of works culminating in the Authorized Version of 1611—a Bible that "had no significant rival for 270 years." As France points out, certain continuities of language and style were deliberately preserved throughout this long history (an English translation tradition, if you will), one result of which is that certain echoes of William Tyndale's "vigorous, idiomatic" style persist even to the present. Particularly helpful is the care France takes to explain the motives behind these projects, the distinctive features of each translation, and the notable advances embodied in many of them. A flood of translations followed the publication of the Revised Version in 1885, and from this point the survey is necessarily more selective. Nonetheless, it is easy to see that readability and literary elegance have been among the keys to a translation's relative popularity and longevity.

The chapter concludes with a brief treatment of important contemporary issues in English Bible translation. On the topic of religious opposition to advances in translation, France notes candidly that "conservativism, in the sense of resistance to change, seems to affect people in matters of religion more readily than in other areas." Other topics include the determination of the most reliable manuscripts, the choice between literal and dynamic translation alternatives, the vexed issue of gender inclusiveness, and consideration of a translation's suitability for public reading.

Of all the Bibles in the English language, the King James Version is properly regarded as the most influential. Alister McGrath's *In the Beginning: The Story of the King James Bible and How It Changed a Nation, a Language, and a Culture* (2001) is a valuable recent study of the King James Version's magisterial contribution over a wide range of fields. In chapter 8 the late Walt Wessel reviews McGrath's book through the lens of an experienced Bible translator and makes insightful comparisons and connections between the KJV and the translation projects (most notably, the NIV) of which he had been a part in recent years.

Wessel begins by describing the KJV's powerful influence on his own life as he emerged from a German-speaking American community in the earlier decades of the twentieth century—an influence that proved difficult to shake years later when he engaged in Bible translation himself. We see Wessel's own values reflected in his applause for John Purvey's stated commitment to produce the second Wycliffite Bible of 1384 by translating sentences and other linguistic meaning-groups rather than in a wooden word-for-word way. We see them again in his support of Luther's insistence that a Bible translation "sound right" as well as prove accurate. Not surprisingly, Wessel is also intrigued by the innovative committee structure adopted by the translators of the KJV. Finally, he gently corrects McGrath's understanding of "literal translation," as well as his presumption that the eloquence of the KJV was purely accidental.

Kent Eaton (chapter 9) offers an engaging profile of James "Diego" Thomson (1788–1854), one of the most creative and effective promoters of Bible distribution in nineteenth-century Protestant missions. A Scottish-born agent of the British and Foreign Bible Society—and a consummate colporteur—Thomson is considered by some "the patriarch of Protestantism and public education in South America." His perambulatory missionary career, which began in 1816, spanned numerous countries of Central and South America, as well as Canada and Spain.

In his tireless efforts to sow the seed of the Scriptures in all soils, he displayed remarkable powers of persuasion and a gift for judicious ecumenical compromise.

Eaton's profile of Thomson underscores the point that good translation by itself does not automatically ensure that the Scriptures will be read and understood by the groups for which they were designed. Priority must also be given to the effective *delivery* of the Scriptures—something that requires attention to such things as publishing, literacy education, ecumenical cooperation, product promotion, aggressive colportage, and efficient physical distribution systems.

Dick France offers an overview of the history of Bible translation in English. Walt Wessel examines one great chapter of that history, the story of the King James Version; in chapter 10 John Stek focuses on another—the New International Version (1973; complete Bible 1978; rev. ed. 1984) and how it came to be. As a key participant in this story, Stek makes careful use of unpublished primary sources to narrate the development of the most popular English-language Bible on the market today. The chapter traces the genesis of the NIV to the initiatives of a layperson in the small (Dutch) Christian Reformed Church in America in the 1950s and records the growing confluence of energy for the project as the National Association of Evangelicals, then the New York Bible Society, and eventually Zondervan Publishing House joined the cause. The conscious positioning of this translation in relationship to other available English versions is made clear. It is worth noting that from the beginning all the actual translation work has been done by a vigilantly independent Committee on Bible Translation, whose steady efforts and periodically changing membership are carefully recorded here.

Under the title "That Fabulous Talking Snake" (chapter 11), Ronald Veenker offers a controversial reflection on the first three chapters of Genesis. The essay focuses on the identity of the unusual serpent in the Garden of Eden. Veenker points out that the seductive snake is nowhere explicitly equated with Satan in this narrative, even though this assumption about the snake's identity has prevailed in mainstream Christianity since the earliest centuries and been subsequently reinforced by influential Christian writers such as John Milton. Veenker suggests alternatively that the passage is about theodicy, not diabolical temptation, and that the snake is not Satan at all but an innocent animal made to speak so that, as a verbal and therefore patently intelligent creature, it can be held morally responsible and judged for its actions in opposition to the will of God.

Certainly not every reader will agree with Veenker about the snake, but the inference he draws from this discussion is one that even his opponents will likely concede. Translators should not presume to make explicit that which ought properly to remain enigmatic or merely implicit in the text. As he puts it, "It is important for the task of translation, and even annotation, that the scholar try as much as possible to free himself from leading the reader to his own personal perspective" on a matter.

David Noel Freedman and David Miano's article on textual criticism—"Slip of the Eye: Accidental Omission in the Masoretic Tradition" (chapter 12)—is an excellent reminder that many disciplines impinge on the task of translation. As the authors point out, "The first step in Bible translation is the determination of the text." The article deals with the phenomenon of haplography, a surprisingly common form of unintentional scribal error in the copying of ancient biblical manuscripts. Haplography occurs when a copyist's eye, in response to some form of repetitiveness in the manuscript, is tricked into passing over and omitting characters, words, or even whole lines. Freedman and Miano classify the various ways the fallible human eye can slip; using the first two chapters of Genesis as a case study, they provide rather compelling evidence that such "mechanical errors" occurred in the textual transmission of even the most important biblical manuscripts. The conventional wisdom in textual criticism has been that the shorter version of a text is the more reliable, because (so it is assumed) it is more pristine and free of agenda-driven embellishments. The authors challenge this conventional wisdom by concluding that often the longer alternative reading is more reliable, because it has been less truncated by haplography.

PART 3: THE PRACTICE OF BIBLE TRANSLATION

In chapter 13 Bruce Waltke offers a translation and exegesis of Agur's confession in Proverbs 30:1–6. He challenges the assumption that these verses express a bitter epistemological skepticism (vv. 1–4), which a more orthodox and faith-filled editor subsequently endeavored to contradict and correct (vv. 5–6). Instead, Waltke makes a case (strengthened by appeals to wisdom parallels in Job and Baruch) for reading these six verses as the unified work of a single author. Moreover, he argues, the skeptical tone of the first four verses is not an absolute skepticism but a humble acknowledgment that deep truth remains forever elusive to the human mind until it seeks and finds it in the inspired revelation embodied in Scripture. As such, Agur's confession constitutes "the most sustained argument in the Bible for the necessity of special revelation (through Israel's Scripture) to bridge the gulf between the infinite and the finite."

Waltke concludes that the best foundation for Bible translation lies precisely in this conviction that "the Bible is God's special revelation for humanity's salvation and that God inspired its words." Such a conviction certainly reinforces the urgency of the translation task, as well as the importance of translators handling the biblical text with care and reverence. Finally, the translator, inasmuch as he or she makes plain that which otherwise would remain enigmatic or unknown, is privileged to participate in God's work of moving people from darkness and despair to illumination and hope.

In chapter 14 Steven Voth offers an intriguing comparative analysis of how the Hebrew word *ṣedeq* has been translated for—and understood by—English-speaking and Spanish-speaking readers in recent centuries. As Voth points out, *ṣedeq* was translated for an English-speaking audience in the King James Version quite consistently as "righteousness" and for a Spanish-speaking audience by the magisterial Reina Valera Revisada as *justicia* (justice). While *ṣedeq* has a breadth of meaning well in excess of any single English or Spanish word, the KJV translators' decision to use "righteousness" moved Anglophone Christianity along a trajectory that prioritized personal morality to the relative neglect of other important nuances of *ṣedeq* and the biblical theology it embodies. Conversely, the Spanish decision to go with *justicia* (justice) sensitized that particular culture more to the social imperatives and communal obligations of Christianity and perhaps somewhat less to the call to personal sanctification.

The article considers historical factors that may have influenced these respective translation choices, and, even more important, it examines the profound impact of these word selections on English and Spanish readers' respective understandings of the gospel message. Ultimately, Voth argues, even the ways in which the Bible was able historically to challenge, sensitize, and transform these two cultures was profoundly affected. The article is a sobering reminder that ideological realities can intrude into the translation process, often unconsciously, yet with huge consequences for both churches and cultures.

In chapter 15 Andreas Köstenberger reviews the special challenges and opportunities faced by those endeavoring to translate the Gospel of John. As he does so, he discusses textual, background, ideological, exegetical, and stylistic considerations. Among the textual issues considered is whether the questionable account of the adulterous woman (7:53–8:11) should be retained in the English text—and if not, how its qualified status should be visually conveyed in the page layout. The many other issues addressed include the best rendering of Johannine references to time (for example, "the tenth hour"), and the fact that in John the conjunction *kai* has a considerably wider semantic range than the simple English word *and.*

The most important ideological consideration addressed is how to translate *hoi Ioudaioi* (in the KJV, consistently translated "the Jews") in ways that reflect complete translation integrity, sensitivity to the unique context of each Johannine usage of the term, and concern about the ever-present risk of contributing to the great evil of Christian anti-Semitism. At the end Köstenberger ranks nine leading English translations by their degree of apparent concurrence with the translation decisions he commends in this article. As it turns out, the NIV and ISV earn second place in the unofficial competition, with the recent TNIV taking top spot.

In chapter 16 Douglas Moo considers the special challenges of translating the term *sarx* (KJV, "flesh") in the Epistle to the Romans. This ubiquitous term is actually a "polymorphous concept"—one that has a number of quite distinct meanings, even in the apostle Paul's own usage. Moo suggests five basic senses of *sarx:* (1) the physical material that covers a body's bones, (2) the human body in its entirety, (3) human beings generally, (4) the human condition (as legitimately distinct from God), and (5) the state of human fallenness (in illegitimate opposition to God).

The fallible translator is under considerable pressure to determine in each instance which meaning of *sarx* the apostle had in mind. Much is at stake, since the potential meanings of the term range from those with neutral connotations to those with highly negative associations. A tempting response, therefore, and one followed by a number of more "direct" Bible translations, is to apply a simple word-for-word equation and let *sarx* come through consistently as "flesh." The problems with this option are (1) that it leaves the determination of meaning entirely to the reader, which is an abdication of the translator's responsibility, and (2) it only sets the reader up to confuse material reality (one meaning of *sarx*) with sinfulness (another meaning of *sarx*)—along the lines of the ancient Gnostic heresy. The TNIV actually uses twenty-eight different words or phrases to translate *sarx,* and Moo's own labors in translation make him appreciate these efforts, including even the use in some instances of the admittedly awkward term "sinful nature."

In chapter 17 James Smith III profiles two venerable traditions of interpreting and translating the word *hypostasis* in relation to faith in Hebrews 11:1. The first tradition (which Smith traces to John Chrysostom and finds reinforced in the West by the Vulgate's rendering of it as *substantia*) understands the term to refer to an objective "substance"—a divine gift through which the promised future has already become in part a reality. The second tradition, which he links to Martin Luther and the English translation pioneer William Tyndale, views it in the more subjective or psychological sense of "surety," or being sure. Smith sees the former tradition sustained by, among other translations, the KJV ("now faith is the *substance* of things hoped for"), and the latter extending into the present through versions like the NASB ("now faith is the *assurance* of things hoped for").

Nevertheless, he argues, the subjective "surety" tradition now prevails in modern English versions, and it is also being recommended by the United Bible Societies to translators around the world through the resource materials the UBS makes available to them. Smith considers this state of affairs regrettable, not only because it perpetuates a flawed interpretation of *hypostasis,* but also because (from a pastoral perspective) it fails to convey a healthy God-centered vision of faith as "participation in divine realities already present." The article concludes with a call for great vigilance against unwitting adherence to flawed traditions of translation.

Finally, Larry Walker (chapter 18) analyzes the use of capital letters in translating Scripture into English. Neither biblical Hebrew nor Aramaic employed capital letters at all, and New Testament Greek did not use them in the way that English does. Since English begins proper nouns (in contrast to common nouns) with a capital letter, the English Bible translator is obliged to decide through judicious interpretation which biblical words are proper nouns, and therefore treated as such, and which are not.

Walker provides an extensive set of comparative reference tables (twenty-eight in all) that lay out how the KJV, the NIV, and an assortment of other English Bible translations handle the capitalization of the more difficult nouns found in Scripture. These tables (and the commentary that accompanies them) survey references to deity, names of persons and places, titles of mythical beings, personifications, and terms connected to religious ceremonies. Walker's analysis is helpful in detecting capitalization trends over time, as well as the general tendencies of different translations. Some capitalization decisions, as he points out, are purely matters of style and preference. Others, like the translator's choice between "spirit" and "Spirit," can be of enormous significance.

Notes

1. Andrew F. Walls, *The Missionary Movement in Christian History* (Maryknoll, N.Y.: Orbis, 1996), 32.

2. See, for example, David Bebbington, *Evangelicalism in Modern Britain* (London: Unwin Hyman, 1989), 2–19; and Roger Olson, "The Future of Evangelical Theology," *Christianity Today* 42, no. 2 (9 February 1998): 40.

3. Cited in Hugh T. Kerr, ed., *A Compend of Luther's Theology* (Philadelphia: Westminster, 1966), 16.

4. Walls, *The Missionary Movement,* 26.

PART ONE

THE THEORY OF BIBLE TRANSLATION

1

ARE TRANSLATORS TRAITORS? SOME PERSONAL REFLECTIONS.[1]

Moisés Silva

During my student days, while looking over a Spanish theological journal, I happened to notice an article on a topic I knew would be of interest to one of my professors. When I brought it to his attention, he asked me whether I would be willing to translate the essay into English for him. Since Spanish is my mother tongue, he figured I'd be able to come up with a rough translation quite quickly. I thought so, too, but to my surprise, the project became a nightmare. I labored over virtually every sentence and felt burdened that at no point was I communicating in a truly satisfactory manner what I knew to be the "total" meaning of the Spanish. Possibly for the first time I sensed what factors may have motivated the old Italian complaint, *Traduttore traditore*—"A translator is a traitor."[2]

This incident was rather puzzling and troubling to me. True, I was unduly concerned over precision—my teacher needed only a general understanding of the article's main points (and I was too afraid of writing down something that might be misleading). It was also true that at that stage in my life, although I had served as an interpreter on a few occasions, I had little experience in the translation of written literature. But my inadequacy as a translator was not the real problem. What was disturbing to me was that I found it much easier to render Greek and Hebrew into English, even though my knowledge of those languages was almost infinitely inferior to my knowledge of Spanish! In a very important sense, my understanding of the latter (simply because it was a living language learned from infancy) was far greater than the understanding that *anyone* can have of an ancient language no longer spoken. Yet I struggled to express in English the meaning of a Spanish sentence in a way that I did not experience when translating a biblical text (naturally, I might struggle trying to figure out what the Greek and Hebrew meant, but that's a different question).

In truth, there is a simple solution to the mystery. The answer is twofold. First, the very fact that Spanish was a living language for me meant that I was much more conscious of its subtleties and connotations than I could be of comparable nuances in Greek and Hebrew. As a result, I was fully aware of my failure to reproduce such features in English, whereas in the case of the biblical languages, well, ignorance is bliss.[3] True, increased practice in translation develops one's skills in finding adequate equivalents, but it takes years of intensive work—to say nothing of the need for an inherent linguistic and literary gift—to become a truly competent translator. There is an important lesson here for the many students, and even professional scholars, who think that after two or three years of Greek they are qualified to translate the New Testament.

But I am more interested here in the second part of the answer. College and seminary courses in the biblical languages consist primarily of guiding the student in translating word-for-word.[4] If the resulting rendering violates English syntax or makes no sense at all, changes may be introduced, but as a rule these translations are stilted (sometimes barely intelligible to a layperson) and rarely express the thought of the original in the most natural way that the rich resources of the English language make available. Most of us have thus been led to believe that if we manage to represent the Greek and Hebrew words in as close a one-to-one correspondence as possible, we have succeeded in the task of translation. But who would consider successful a Spanish-to-English translation that had such renderings as "I have cold in the feet" (instead of "My feet are cold") or "He has ten years" (instead of "He is ten years old")—even though these sentences conform to English syntax and their meaning can be figured out?

Perhaps a fuller illustration from Spanish may be helpful. The *Larousse Gran Diccionario Español-Inglés, English-Spanish* (1991) has a foreword in both languages; presumably, the editor wrote it in Spanish and himself translated it into English. The Spanish of the last paragraph, if translated literally, would read like this: "We would sin of ingratitude if we did not mention finally the names of ... valuable collaborators without whose help the execution of our effort would have been much more arduous, and [we would sin] of immodesty if we did not beg our readers to have the courtesy of indicating to us the omissions and imperfections that we might have incurred, *errare humanum est,* so that we may emend them in future editions."[5]

Such a literal translation is not only too long, awkward, and complicated for acceptable English style, but it also reflects certain cultural elements that are out of place in an English-speaking society. Accordingly, the English foreword reads very businesslike: "Finally, we would like to express our gratitude to . . . , whose valuable assistance greatly facilitated the task. Since *errare humanum est,* we would also be grateful to readers for kindly bringing omissions and imperfections to our notice so that they may be corrected in future editions."

Admittedly, this is an extreme example, but the principle it illustrates needs to be appreciated. All successful translations of literature (for example, contemporary German novels) sound *natural,* as though they had originally been written in English (while also preserving a feel for the original cultural setting). Therefore, they are more easily read and understood than if they reflected the foreign syntax and word usage. (Incidentally, since the message communicates more clearly, one can argue that they are more accurate than literal renderings would be.) In contrast, one can hardly call accurate or faithful the KJV's word-for-word translation of Micah 1:11—"Pass ye away, thou inhabitant of Saphir, having thy shame naked: the inhabitant of Zaanan came not forth in the mourning of Beth-ezel; he shall receive of you his standing."

The preface to the recently released English Standard Version describes its philosophy of translation as "essentially literal" and as "word-for-word" (over against the thought-for-thought approach of some modern Bible versions).[6] Literalness in translation, however, is something of an illusion, and although the preface goes on to qualify these claims ("Every translation is at many points a trade-off between literal precision and readability"), the unwary reader can hardly suspect how many major syntactical transformations are adopted by the ESV. Here is a fairly word-for-word rendering of Hebrews 7:20–22 (but respecting the word order required by English):

> And according to which [= inasmuch as it was] not without an oath—for on the one hand the ones having become priests are without an oath, but he with an oath through the one saying to him, "The Lord swore and will not regret: 'You are a priest forever'"—according to so much Jesus became a guarantee of a better covenant.

Some versions (e.g., the NASB), while making this complex sentence a bit more understandable, retain the basic structure of the original. The ESV, however, renders it this way:

> And it was not without an oath. For those who formerly became priests were made such without an oath, but this one was made a priest with an oath by the one who said to him: "The Lord has sworn and will not change his mind, 'You are a priest forever.'" This makes Jesus the guarantor of a better covenant.

By (1) breaking up one long sentence into three, then (2) transforming a binary comparative structure (with a long parenthesis in the middle) into a set of independent clauses, and finally (3) adding quite a few items absent from the Greek ("it was," "formerly," "were made such," "was made," "This makes"), the ESV successfully clarifies the statement to modern readers and makes its meaning clear to them. But to call such a rendering *literal* (let alone word-for-word) is a fantasy.

It is not surprising that my illustration comes from the letter to the Hebrews. Although examples of this sort could probably be found in every book of the Bible, the author of Hebrews makes greater use of the stylistic resources of Greek than other New Testament writers do. And here precisely is part of our problem. Because most New Testament books (as well as Old Testament Hebrew narrative) are characterized by a fairly straightforward syntax, many of whose features can be paralleled in English syntax, we are lulled into thinking that literal renderings of the Greek text "work."[7] But just because a certain Greek syntactical pattern *can* be reproduced in English, that hardly means it *should,* as though such reproduction were the best or most faithful representation of the original.

Things are quite different in the translation of classical Greek literature generally. A recent and successful translator of Plato's dialogues, R. E. Allen, defends his method in a manner reminiscent of arguments in favor of literal Bible translations:

> Claims of fidelity presuppose that the underlying Greek text is fully understood, that is, interpreted, and that translations can be done in terms of this interpretation. Interpretive translations, like newspaper editorials, have their value; but they decide in advance issues on which students may reasonably differ and on which the English reader may be invited to make up his or her own mind. Some degree of interpretation, no doubt, is unavoidable, and a wholly neutral translation which preserved every ambiguity and all the overtones of connotation would require constant reference to the Greek in order to make sense of the English. Yet neutrality, no less than fidelity, remains an important value in translation. Let no man tell you what is in the text of Plato if you have means of finding out for yourself.[8]

He goes on to argue that a literal approach should be part of the translation process (while acknowledging that "literalness requires interpretation after all").

It soon becomes clear, however, that *literalness* for this classical scholar means something a little different from what it means to many biblical students. On the very first page of the translation, when Socrates says that a certain Meletus has brought an indictment against him, Euthyphro asks him what the charge is, to which Socrates replies, *ouk agennnē*—"not an ignoble one,"—but Allen renders it, "One that does him credit."[9] Or consider one of the statements by Socrates in his speech before the Athenians. Translated word-for-word (as much as English syntax allows), it reads: "And certainly and entirely, O Athenian men, this I ask of you and beg for." Allen's rendering: "So I must specifically ask one thing of you, Gentlemen."[10]

And yet, typical translations of classical Greek literature are even freer (though it is also true in classical studies that some scholars argue in favor of a very literal method of translating). As an illustration, take the beginning sentence of Thucydides' *History of the Peloponnesian War.* First I provide a literal rendering:

> Thucydides an Athenian wrote down the war of the Peloponnesians and Athenians, how they warred toward one another, beginning immediately [with] its establishment and expecting [it] to be both great and more worthy of note than those that had taken place before, judging that both were at their height for it in all preparation and seeing the other Greek[s] banding together to either [side], some on the one hand immediately, but some also intending [to do so].[11]

Here is Rex Warner's translation (1954; Penguin Books, 1972):

> Thucydides the Athenian wrote the history of the war fought between Athens and Sparta, beginning the account at the very outbreak of the war, in the belief that it was going to be a great war and more worth writing about than any of those which had taken place in the past. My belief was based on the fact that the two sides were at the very height of their power and preparedness, and I saw, too, that the rest of the Hellenic world was committed to one side or the other; even those who were not immediately engaged were deliberating on the courses which they were to take later.

For comparison, I also quote the earlier translation by Richard Crawley (Loeb Classical Library, 1910):

> Thucydides, an Athenian, wrote the history of the war between the Peloponnesians and the Athenians, beginning at the moment that it broke out, and believing that it would be a great war and more worthy of relation than any that had preceded it. This belief was not without its grounds. The preparations of

> both the combatants were in every department in the last state of perfection; and he could see the rest of the Hellenic race taking sides in the quarrel; those who delayed doing so at once having it in contemplation.

It should be pointed out that, as far as Thucydides' style is concerned, this is not an abnormally difficult example; much more complicated passages could readily be found. And of course, even these are child's play in comparison with the demands that Greek poetry places on translators. Here are the last lines of book 9 of the *Odyssey,* first in the Loeb translation by A. T. Murray (1919):

> And as soon as early Dawn appeared, the rosy-fingered, I roused my comrades, and bade them themselves to embark and to loose the stern cables. So they went on board straightway and sat down upon the benches, and sitting well in order smote the grey sea with their oars. Thence we sailed on, grieved at heart, glad to have escaped death, though we had lost our dear comrades.

Next is the poetic and highly regarded version by Robert Fitzgerald (1961):

> When the young Dawn with finger tips of rose
> touched the world, I roused the men, gave orders
> to man the ship, cast off the mooring lines;
> and filing in to sit beside the rowlocks
> oarsmen in line dipped oars in the grey sea.
> So we moved out, sad in the vast offing,
> having our precious lives, but not our friends.

The first time I taught extrabiblical Hellenistic Greek, I had a small group of advanced college students who had shown strong competence in two years of New Testament Greek. One of them was an unusually gifted student who, nevertheless, felt quite frustrated and discouraged because of the difficulties she was experiencing. How was it possible that she could do so well understanding and translating the Greek of the New Testament and yet feel so lost working with Epictetus? Almost all students I've taught since then have had a comparable reaction, even though the language of Epictetus is in fact relatively simple. How does one explain this phenomenon?

Part of the answer is that biblical students are dependent—to a much greater degree than they realize—on their familiarity with the contents of the New Testament. There is no shame in this. The main reason we understand *Time* magazine well is that we are very familiar with the historical context in which American English is spoken. The further removed we are from the context of a document (e.g., in time—say, Shakespeare—or in subject matter—legal documents), the greater our difficulties in making sense of it. A student's basic familiarity with the biblical subject matter and form of expression, over against an unfamiliarity with the concerns and phraseology of Hellenistic philosophers, has much to do with the frustrations he or she will experience moving from one to the other.[12]

But that explanation does not get to the heart of the linguistic problem. As already suggested, an exclusive (or nearly exclusive) acquaintance with the simple narrative of the Gospels or with the unassuming discourse of the Pauline letters, combined with the instinctive tendency (confirmed and encouraged by the instructor) to represent the text by means of one-to-one English correspondences whenever possible, creates a conception of the workings of the Greek language that is derived from an alien structure. On the other hand, intensive training translating clauses and sentences that *cannot* be rendered word-for-word and thus require restructuring would give students an entrée into the genius (i.e., the authentic character) of the foreign tongue. It would also help them see much more clearly that such restructuring could be the preferable method of rendering even when it may not appear "necessary." The point here is that a nonliteral translation, precisely because it may give expression to the genius of the target language (in this case English), can do greater justice to that of the source language (Greek).

For example, one of the distinctive features of Greek syntax is the frequent use of adverbial participles. Many of these can be rendered literally without violating English grammar, and the resulting translations are intelligible, yet even literal versions like the NASB and the ESV wisely resort to the use of conjunctions modifying finite verbs (indicative mood). Thus, "Having seen the star" becomes "*When they saw* the star" (Matt 2:10); "Titus, being a Greek," becomes "Titus, *though he was* a Greek" (Gal 2:3); "we will reap, not giving up," becomes "we will reap, *if we do not give up*" (6:9). An alternative way of restructuring the participial construction may be illustrated from Acts 8:27, where "He had come worshiping" becomes "He had come *to worship.*" Notice that all these translations reflect interpretative decisions. The last reference, for example, excludes the possible (though unlikely) interpretation that the Ethiopian eunuch was involved in worship during the course of his travel.

It is true, of course, that scholars are generally agreed about the proper way to render the participial clauses in these particular verses. But general agreement is not the same as total certainty. One could make the case, for instance, that the first three examples should be rendered as causal participles. While not many would be persuaded that such renderings are preferable, the truth remains that even literal English versions of the Bible (to echo Allen's objection quoted above) have decided "in advance issues on which students may reasonably differ and on which the English reader may be invited to make up his or her own mind." Again, one could complain that by changing the participles to finite verbs, these translations unnecessarily remove English readers one additional step from the original, thus preventing them from experiencing something of the "feel" of Greek style (a common argument against modernized versions of ancient texts).

Such objections, however, would not be valid grievances against the ESV. And by the same token, one should be cautious about using arguments of this sort to criticize functional-equivalence versions. There may indeed be instances where the NIV, for example, adds an excessive amount of information to the text. But defects in the application of a method are no argument against the method itself. So far as philosophy of translation is concerned, the NIV merely seeks to apply, in a more thorough and systematic way than "traditional" versions, the principles that all versions are using when they transform the syntactical structure of Greek participial clauses. Those principles are clarity and naturalness of expression.[13]

But there is an additional and serious problem with the argument that Bible versions should be more or less neutral with regard to texts where the interpretation is debatable. Or as it is usually put, "What is ambiguous in the original should be left ambiguous in the translation." The main flaw in this principle (whatever truth it may contain) is the assumption that typical English readers recognize an ambiguity when they see one. Take 1 Corinthians 5:5, which the ESV renders quite literally, "You are to deliver this man to Satan for the destruction of the flesh, so that his spirit may be saved in the day of the Lord." Some people object to the NIV rendering "sinful nature" instead of the literal "flesh" for various reasons, including their concern that the Greek word *sarx* is ambiguous, and that therefore the NIV immediately slants the text in a particular direction. But it would be delusion to think that the literal translation "flesh" does not slant the text for the average reader, who needs a book or a preacher to tell him or her what the options are (of course, a book or a preacher can clarify those options regardless of which version is being read). At least the NIV provides a footnote with the alternate renderings "his body" and "the flesh."

A different type of example is "your work of faith and labor of love and steadfastness of hope in our Lord Jesus Christ" (1 Thess 1:3). That is the basically word-by-word rendering of the ESV.[14] In contrast, the NIV interprets all the genitival constructions as follows: "your work *produced by* faith, your labor *prompted by* love, and your endurance *inspired by* hope in our Lord Jesus Christ" (my emphasis). Now one may legitimately ask whether adding the italicized phrases is the most faithful way to represent the text, but it would be naive to think that the average believer in the pew immediately recognizes the ambiguities inherent in the Greek genitive—let alone that he or she has the means to reach an informed opinion regarding the meaning without at least consulting other translations. But if in either case (with the NIV or the ESV) it is necessary to consult something or someone, then what harm has been done by providing a more intelligible rendering that represents, at the very least, a defensible understanding of the text?

A few years ago, Douglas R. Hofstadter, the author of influential works in the areas of cognition and creativity (e.g., *Gödel, Escher, Bach,* 1979), published a remarkable book on the art of translation.[15] The work is built on and around a brief poem, "A une Damoyselle malade" (To an ill damsel), written in the sixteenth century by Clément Marot. I reproduce the verse below. The middle column gives a very literal translation, which is not always intelligible. The right column provides a rendering that is still basically word-for-word but seeks to be more helpful (in an approach that approximates that of literal Bible versions).[16]

Ma mignonne	*My cute one*	*My darling,*
Je vous donne	*I give thee*	*I bid thee*
Le bon jour;	*The good day;*	*Good day;*
Le séjour	*The stay*	*Thy stay in bed*
C'est prison.	*It's prison.*	*Is like prison.*
Guérison	*Healing*	*Thy health*
Recouvrez,	*Recover,*	*Recover,*
Puis ouvrez	*Then open*	*Then open*
Votre porte	*Thy door*	*Thy door*
Et qu'on sorte	*And that one leaves*	*And go out*
Vitement,	*Quickly,*	*Quickly,*
Car Clément	*For Clément*	*For Clément*
Le vous mande.	*Informs it to thee.*	*Orders thee.*
Va, friande	*Go, dainty one*	*Go, you who likes to indulge*
De ta bouche,	*Of your mouth,*	*Your mouth,*
Qui se couche	*Who lies down*	*Who is lying down*
En danger	*In danger*	*In danger,*
Pour manger	*To eat*	*So that you might eat*
Confitures;	*Preserves;*	*Some preserves;*
Si tu dures	*If you last*	*If you remain a long time*
Trop malade,	*Too sick,*	*Very sick,*
Couleur face	*Color of face*	*Pale*
Tu prendras,	*You will take on,*	*You will become,*
Et perdra	*And will lose*	*And you will lose*

Líembonpoint.	*The stoutness.*	*Your plumpness.*
Dieu te doint	*God give you*	*May God grant you*
Santé bonne,	*Good health,*	*Good health,*
Ma mignonne	*My cute one.*	*My darling.*

The problem with a literal translation of the poem is that, even though it may convey fairly accurately its (cognitive) contents, it fails to reproduce its formal and emotive elements—*the very things that make the poem what it is.* The verse is made up of twenty-eight lines, each line consists of three syllables (with the stress on the last syllable), there are fourteen rhyming couplets (AA, BB, CC, etc.), and, interestingly, the units of sense are conveyed primarily by couplets composed of the non-rhyming lines (lines 2–3, 4–5, 6–7, etc.). Among other features, note that the first and last line are the same, and that the author has inserted his name in the middle.

Each of the seventeen chapters in Hofstadter's book includes several translations of the poem—almost ninety translations in all! Many of these are by the author himself, but he also includes efforts by a variety of acquaintances who were challenged to capture the various characteristics of the poem. Although some of the resulting translations cannot be taken too seriously, it is truly illuminating to see the great variety of legitimate renderings that are possible, depending on which features the translator decides to bring out. As an illustration, I reproduce only three of them for the reader's amusement.[17] Note that the first version retains the three-syllable lines but does not attempt to make them rhyme. The second translation (middle column) has rhyming couplets, but these are the ones that convey the sense units. In the last version, as in the original French, the units of sense are carried by the non-rhyming couplets.

My sweet maid,	*Lover mine,*	*Babe o' mine*
You I wish	*Here's a sign*	*Gal divine,*
A good day;	*Of my love,*	*Here's a kiss,*
Your sickbed	*Turtledove.*	*It ain't bliss*
Is a jail.	*You're not well,*	*Bein' sick.*
Total health	*I can tell.*	*Get up quick,*
Please regain,	*All cooped up,*	*Take a spin!*
Then unlatch	*Buttercup?*	*Don't stay in*
Your room's door	*How about*	*Where it's dark.*
And go out	*Going out?*	*For a lark,*
With full speed,	*Hit the town!*	*Go on out,*
For Clement	*Lose that frown,*	*Jump about—*
Does insist.	*Little pet!*	*Clem's command!*
Go, gourmande,	*Clem's all set*	*Hey, gourmande,*

Thou whose mouth
Lies abed
Under threat,
Off to eat
Fruit preserves;
If thou stay'st
Sick too long,
A pale shade
Wilt acquire,
And wilt lose
Thy round shape.
May God grant
Thee good health,
My sweet maid.

For some fun,
Honey bun.
In the mood
For some food?
Then let's munch,
Honeybunch.
If you stick
At home sick,
You'll get pale,
Nightingale.
Hope tonight
You're all right,
Feeling fine,
Lover mine.

You whose wish
Is a dish
Full of fruit,
You should scoot
From your bed,
And instead
Get some sun.
Come on, hon'—
Losin' weight
Makes your great
Figure flat.
Don't do that!
Just get fine,
Babe o' mine!

Notice that all three of these translations preserve the basic structure and rhythm of the poem (they also convey its emotive aspect much better than the literal translations above), but only by abandoning almost completely the notion of word-for-word equivalences.[18] A different but defensible approach would be to use an alternate poetic structure—say, a smaller number of longer lines—that might allow the translator to preserve features otherwise lost.[19] Another problem is that the last two renderings above use very colloquial and trendy language and thus take away from the dignified quality of the original. In the very nature of the case, there cannot be one definitive translation of the poem; several renderings are needed in order to capture its various features.

It should be obvious by now that "faithfulness" in translation is neither a simple concept to define nor an easy goal to achieve. Are we thus obligated to conclude that translators are traitors? I would prefer to say, *traduttore transmutore* (or even better, *traspositore*). The translator is someone who, like it or not, *transforms* a text by *transferring* it from one linguistic-cultural context to another. In such a process, it is inevitable that some things will be left behind and that others will be picked up along the way. The King James translators, for all their skill, failed to preserve countless features—both formal and semantic—that were present in the original Hebrew and Greek texts. By the same token, their mere use of seventeenth-century English ensured that, at virtually every turn, they would add features absent from the original. Yet this simple reality does not for a moment take anything away from their magnificent achievement. They responsibly interpreted the text, then transposed it to a different historical setting and thereby transmuted it into a form it did not have before. But that hardly means they betrayed the text. On the contrary, such a transformation made it possible for millions to hear and understand its message.

The kinds of language games played by Clément Marot in his little poem are seldom if ever to be found in the biblical text (even in its poetic sections), but the Bible consists of language all the same, and the fundamental challenges of translation are certainly no different. If the ideal of biblical translation were to represent the original as much as possible in a word-for-word manner, then there would be little room for variety. The multiplicity of modern Bible versions, while thought by many to be a great disadvantage for the church today, is instead reason for exultation. To be sure, the differences among these versions can create confusion; new problems have surfaced that still have not been solved. It remains true, however, that contemporary Bible readers, precisely because they are not bound to one or two versions, enjoy certain remarkable advantages over previous generations. For them, Scripture, read through different lenses, shines all the brighter.

Notes

1. It is a pleasure to offer this essay to Ron Youngblood—or Sangrejoven, as the translators of the *Nueva Versión Internacional,* in all good humor, like to refer to him. I am sure that they join me in gratitude to him for the amount of time and effort he devoted to the work of this Bible translation. Though he modestly minimized his competence in Spanish, time and again in the course of our meetings he showed the enviable skills of a good translator, namely, sensitivity to the meaning of the original text and a genuine feel for language. The extent of his contribution is difficult to overstate.

2. I haven't been able to trace the origin of this oft-quoted (and sometimes abused) expression. Remarks about the alleged impossibility of translation, especially when dealing with poetry, are legion. With regard to the Bible, this conception is ancient. Rabbi Judah is reported to have said, "If one translates a verse literally, he is a liar; if he adds thereto, he is a blasphemer and a libeler" (*b. Kiddushin* 49a; see *The Babylonian Talmud,* Seder Nashim 8: Kiddushin, ed. I. Epstein [London: Soncino, 1936], 246).

3. My experience thus illustrates a fundamental principle of the universe: The less one knows, the quicker one can form an opinion.

4. Note that in modern-language courses students are seldom asked to translate written texts into English.

5. "Pecaríamos de ingratitud si no mencionásemos por·último los nombres de ..., valiosas colaboradoras sin cuya ayuda la ejecución de nuestro empeño hubiese sido mucho más ardua, y de inmodestia si no rogásemos a nuestros lectores que tengan la amabilidad de indicarnos las omisiones e imperfecciones en que hubiéramos incurrido, *errare humanum est,* para enmendarlas en ediciones futuras."

6. I should emphasize that I consider the ESV a very useful work, and I was happy to make a minor contribution in reviewing one of the NT books.

7. I vividly recall a comment by one of my teachers (a man of extraordinary linguistic competence, I should add) to the effect that the Bible is eminently translatable, particularly in comparison with other ancient literature, such as Homer.

8. R. E. Allen, *The Dialogues of Plato,* vol. 1 (New Haven, Conn.: Yale Univ. Press, 1984), xii.

9. Ibid., 41 (*Euth.* 2a).

10. Ibid., 79 (*Apol.* 17c). The Greek reads, *kai mentoi kai pany, ō andres Athēnaioi, touto hymōn deomai kai pariemai.* The word *mentoi* is an asseverative particle, while *pany* is an adverb meaning "altogether" (often used with verbs in the sense "very, exceedingly," etc.). The combination of these two terms here appears to be unique and lends much emphasis to the statement; the phrase could be rendered, "And by all means," "And most certainly." H. N. Fowler's translation (for the Loeb series) is, "And, men of Athens, I *urgently* beg and beseech you" (my emphasis).

11. *Thoukydidēs Athēnaios xynegrapse [= synegrapse] ton polemon tōn Peloponnēsiōn kai Athēnaiōn, hōs epolemēsan pros allēlous, arxamenos euthys kathistamenou kai elpisas megan te esethai kai axiologōtaton tōn progegenēmenōn, tekmairomenos hoti akmazontes te ēsan es [= eis] auton amphoteroi paraskeuē tē pasē kai to allo Hellēnikon horōn xynistamenon [= synistamenon] pros hekaterous, to men euthys, to de kai dianooumenon.*

12. Ideally, students learning biblical Greek should do so only within the context of learning Hellenistic Greek generally (with at least a smattering of the late classical period). Of course, such a program would easily require a tripling of the time and effort nowadays devoted to the subject, and it would be virtually impossible to persuade students (or even faculty and administrators) that one needs to "waste time" with Plato and Polybius and Plutarch in order to understand the language of Paul. But can one imagine a person with two years of college French daring to translate (or write an exegetical commentary on) the plays of Molière?

13. As Martin Luther put it, "what is the point of needlessly adhering so scrupulously and stubbornly to words which one cannot understand anyway? Whoever would speak German must not use Hebrew style. Rather he must see to it—once he understands the Hebrew author—that he concentrates on the sense of the text, asking himself, 'Pray tell, what do the Germans say in such a situation?' Once he has the German words to serve the purpose, let him drop the Hebrew words and express the meaning freely in the best German he knows." See *Luther's Works,* ed. E. T. Bachmann (Philadelphia: Muhlenberg, 1960), 35:213–14. Quoted by Ernst R. Wendland, "Martin Luther, the Father of Confessional, Functional-Equivalence Bible Translation: Part 1," *Notes on Translation* 9/1 (1995): 16–36. This article includes many other insightful quotations.

14. Even the ESV, however, interprets the phrase *tēs elpidos tou kyriou hēmōn* (lit., "the hope of our Lord") by rendering it as an objective genitive, although theoretically it could also mean "the hope that our Lord gives."

15. *Le Ton Beau de Marot: In Praise of the Music of Language* (New York: Basic Books, 1997). This volume—which is partly autobiographical, interweaves a great variety of themes, and is highly idiosyncratic—runs to more than 600 pages and could have profited from some serious pruning (one is left with the impression that the author was determined to make some use of every illustration he had accumulated in his files). Nevertheless, those who persevere to the end will be greatly rewarded by the richness and insightfulness that characterize much of the material.

16. The change in pronouns in the middle of the poem from *vous* (respectful) to *tu* (familiar) would correspond formally to a change from *you* to *thou*. I have inverted these two, however, because modern English speakers tend to view *thou* as more respectful.

17. These translations are found respectively in the sections entitled Poems III (13b), IV (15b), and X (46b).

18. It is worth noting that literal translations are often said to use the notion of "formal correspondence," but in the case of poems (or other styles that make heavy use of such formal constraints as alliteration, meter, and rhyme), the distinctive *form* of the original gets lost. And we should remember that all standard translations of acrostic poems in the Bible (e.g., Ps 119, where the verses of each stanza begin with the same letter of the Hebrew alphabet) fail to preserve the acrostic, even though that is their most prominent formal feature.

19. One of the translations in Hofstadter's book (Poems XIII) is composed as a classical sonnet.

2

BIBLE TRANSLATION PHILOSOPHIES WITH SPECIAL REFERENCE TO THE NEW INTERNATIONAL VERSION[1]

Kenneth L. Barker

When translators set out to translate the Bible, among the first questions they must face are, What type of translation do we want to produce, and what translation philosophy, theory, method, or approach must we follow in order to achieve the desired results? To ask these questions, though, raises another question: What types of Bible translations are there? Bible translators and linguists speak primarily of two major types of translations. The first is referred to variously as formal or complete or literal or gloss equivalence. Here the translator pursues a word-for-word rendering as much as possible. The New American Standard Bible (NASB) and New King James Version (NKJV) are good examples of this approach.

Fortunately it is frequently possible to translate literally and still retain contemporary English idiom and excellent literary style. For example, "In the beginning God created the heavens and the earth" is a straightforward translation of the Hebrew text of Genesis 1:1, and it is also good English. So why change it? In fact, why not follow this more literal approach everywhere and all the time, with an absolute minimum of interpretation? Moisés Silva responds, "Translators who view their work as pure renderings rather than interpretations only delude themselves; indeed, if they could achieve some kind of noninterpretative rendering, their work would be completely useless."[2] Daniel Taylor reinforces the point: "All translation is interpretation, as George Steiner and others have pointed out. At every point, the translator is required to interpret, evaluate, judge, and choose."[3] Bob Sheehan correctly states that the "idea of a noninterpretive translation is a mirage."[4]

Several years ago I wrote about this very issue:

> Translation without interpretation is an absolute impossibility, for at every turn the translator is faced with interpretative decisions in different manuscript readings, grammar, syntax, the specific semantic possibilities of a Hebrew or Greek word for a given context, English idiom, and the like. For example, should a particular occurrence of the Hebrew word *ʾereṣ* be contextually nuanced as "earth," "land," or something else? ... In the very act of deciding, the translator has interpreted.[5]

Moisés Silva further indicates the following:

> A successful translation requires (1) mastery of the source language—certainly a much more sophisticated knowledge than one can acquire over a period of four or five years; (2) superb interpretation skills and breadth of knowledge so as not to miss the nuances of the original; and (3) a very high aptitude for writing in the target language so as to express accurately both the cognitive and the affective elements of the message.[6]

And biblical scholar Ephraim Speiser reminds us of the translator's challenge:

> The main task of a translator is to keep faith with two different masters, one at the source and the other at the receiving end.... If he is unduly swayed by the original, and substitutes word for word rather than idiom for idiom, he is traducing what he should be translating, to the detriment of both source and target. And if he veers too far in the opposite direction, by favoring the second medium at the expense of the first, the result is a paraphrase.[7]

Speiser concludes by declaring that a "faithful translation is by no means the same thing as a literal rendering."[8]

Unfortunately, then, it is often not possible to translate literally and retain natural, idiomatic, clear English. Consider the NASB rendering of Matthew 13:20: "The one on whom seed was sown on the rocky places, this is the man who hears the word and immediately receives it with joy." The NIV reads: "The one who received the seed that fell on rocky places is the man who hears the word and at once receives it with joy." Here the NASB is so woodenly literal that the result is a cumbersome, awkward, poorly constructed English sentence. The NIV, on the other hand, has a natural and smooth style without sacrificing accuracy.

The second major type of translation is referred to variously as dynamic or functional or idiomatic equivalence. Here the translator attempts a thought-for-thought rendering. The Good News Bible (GNB; also known as Today's English Version, TEV), the New Living Translation (NLT), God's Word (GW), the New Century Version (NCV), and the Contemporary English Version (CEV) are some of the examples of this approach to the translation challenge. Such versions seek to find the best modern cultural equivalent that will have the same effect the original message had in its ancient cultures. Obviously this approach is a much freer one.

At this point the reader may be surprised that the NIV has not been included as an illustration of either of these two major types of translations. The reason is that, in my opinion, it fits neither. After considerable personal study, comparison, and analysis, I have become convinced that, in order to do justice to translations like the NIV and the New Revised Standard Version (NRSV), scholars must recognize the validity of a third major category of translation, namely, the balanced or mediating type. To discuss this subject intelligently, we must have a working definition of formal equivalence and dynamic equivalence. Eugene Nida gives us important insight:

> Since "there are ... no such things as identical equivalents," ... one must in translation seek to find the closest possible equivalent. However, there are fundamentally two different types of equivalence: one which may be called formal and another which is primarily dynamic.
>
> Formal equivalence focuses attention on the message itself, in both form and content.... Viewed from this formal orientation, one is concerned that the message in the receptor language should match as closely as possible the different elements in the source language. This means ... that the message in the receptor culture is constantly compared with the message in the source culture to determine standards of accuracy and correctness.
>
> The type of translation which most closely typifies this structural equivalence might be called a "gloss translation," in which the translator attempts to reproduce as literally and meaningfully as possible the form and content of the original.... [Student] needs call for a relatively close approximation to the structure of the early ... text, both as to form (e.g., syntax and idioms) and content (e.g., themes and concepts). Such a translation would require numerous footnotes in order to make the text fully comprehensible.

> A gloss translation of this type is designed to permit the reader to identify himself as fully as possible with a person in the source-language context, and to understand as much as he can of the customs, manner of thought, and means of expression. For example, a phrase such as "holy kiss" (Romans 16:16) in a gloss translation would be rendered literally, and would probably be supplemented with a footnote explaining that this was a customary method of greeting in New Testament times.
>
> In contrast, a translation which attempts to produce a dynamic rather than a formal equivalence is based upon "the principle of equivalent effect." ... In such a translation one is not so concerned with matching the receptor-language message with the source-language message, but with the dynamic relationship ..., that the relationship between receptor and message should be substantially the same as that which existed between the original receptors and the message.
>
> A translation of dynamic equivalence aims at complete naturalness of expression and tries to relate the receptor to modes of behavior relevant within the context of his own culture; it does not insist that he understand the cultural patterns of the source-language context in order to comprehend the message. Of course, there are varying degrees of such dynamic-equivalence translations.... [Phillips, e.g.,] seeks for equivalent effect.... In Romans 16:16 he quite naturally translates "greet one another with a holy kiss" as "give one another a hearty handshake all around."
>
> Between the two poles of translating (i.e., between strict formal equivalence and complete dynamic equivalence) there are a number of intervening grades, representing various acceptable standards of literary translating.[9]

Edward L. Greenstein further describes the principle of dynamic equivalence as proposing a "three-stage translation process: analysis of the expression in the source language to determine its meaning, transfer of this meaning to the target language, and restructuring of the meaning in the world of expression of the target language."[10]

Two observations may be helpful at this point. First, it is instructive that the NIV retains "Greet one another with a holy kiss" in Romans 16:16. Second, it is significant that Eugene Nida seems to open the door for a mediating position between the two main translation philosophies, theories, or methods. In general terms, all Bible translation is simply "the process of beginning with something (written or oral) in one language (the source language) and expressing it in another language (the receptor language)."[11] A translation cannot be said to be faithful that does not pay adequate attention to both the source language and the receptor language.

A distinction must be made between dynamic equivalence as a translation principle and dynamic equivalence as a translation philosophy. The latter exists only when a version sets out to produce a dynamic-equivalence rendering from start to finish, as the GNB did. The foreword to the Special Edition Good News Bible indicates that word-for-word translation does not accurately convey the force of the original, so the GNB uses instead the "dynamic equivalent," the words having the same force and meaning today as the original text had for its first readers. Dynamic equivalence as a translation principle, on the other hand, is used in varying degrees by all versions of the Bible.[12] This is easily illustrated by a few examples, several of which were given to me about 1990 by former Old Testament professor (Calvin Theological Seminary) Dr. Marten Woudstra (now deceased).

- A literal rendering of the opening part of the Hebrew text of Isaiah 40:2 would read, "Speak to the heart of Jerusalem." Yet all English versions (including the KJV) see the need for a dynamic-equivalence translation here (e.g., the NIV has "Speak tenderly to Jerusalem").
- In Jeremiah 2:2 the KJV and the NASB read "in the ears of Jerusalem," but the NKJV and the NIV have "in the hearing of Jerusalem." Here the NKJV is just as "dynamic" as the NIV. That it did not have to be is clear from the NASB. Yet the translators wanted to communicate the meaning in a natural way to modern readers, which is precisely what the NIV also wanted to do.
- In Haggai 2:16 the NASB has "grain heap," but the KJV, NKJV, and NIV all use "heap" alone (which is all the Hebrew has). Here the formal-equivalent version, the NASB, is freer than the NIV.
- The KJV and the NKJV read "no power at all" in John 19:11, whereas the NIV has only "no power" (in accord with the Greek). Which version is following the formal-equivalence approach here, and which ones are following the dynamic approach?

One could continue ad infinitum with this kind of illustration. Suffice it to mention additionally that there is a book of over two hundred pages published as a glossary to the oddities of the KJV word use and diction.[13]

In a similar vein, Ron Youngblood has written the following:

> To render the Greek word *sarx* by "flesh" virtually every time it appears does not require the services of a translator; all one needs is a dictionary (or, better yet, a computer). But to recognize that *sarx* has differing connotations in different contexts, that in addition to "flesh" it often means "human standards" or "earthly descent" or "sinful nature" or "sexual impulse" or "person," etc., and therefore to translate *sarx* in a variety of ways is to understand that translation is not only a mechanical, word-for-word process but also a nuanced [I would have said contextually nuanced], thought-for-thought procedure. Translation, as any expert in the field will readily admit, is just as much an art as it is a science. Word-for-word translations typically demonstrate great respect for the source language ... but often pay only lip service to the requirements of the target language....
>
> When translators of Scripture insist on reproducing every lexical and grammatical element in their English renderings, the results are often grotesque.[14]

Because I have served on the executive committee of the NIV's Committee on Bible Translation (CBT) since 1975 and have been the chief spokesperson for the NIV, people often ask me, "What kind of translation, then, is the NIV? Where does it fit among all the others?" While these related questions have been dealt with generally in several publications and reviews, they are addressed specifically in only one published authoritative source dating back to the release of the complete NIV in 1978:

> Broadly speaking, there are several methods of translation: the concordant one, which ranges from literalism to the comparative freedom of the King James Version and even more of the Revised Standard Version, both of which follow the syntactical structure of the Hebrew and Greek texts as far as is compatible with good English; the paraphrastic one, in which the translator restates the gist of the text in his own words; and the method of equivalence, in which the translator seeks to understand as fully as possible what the biblical writers had to say (a criterion common, of course, to the careful use of any method) and then tries to find its closest equivalent in contemporary usage. In its more advanced form this is spoken of as dynamic equivalence, in which the translator seeks to express the meaning as the biblical writers would if they were writing in English today. All these methods have their values when responsibly used.

> As for the NIV, its method is an *eclectic* one with the emphasis for the most part on a *flexible use of concordance and equivalence,* but with a *minimum of literalism, paraphrase, or outright dynamic equivalence*. In other words, the NIV stands on *middle ground*—by no means the easiest position to occupy. It may fairly be said that the translators were convinced that, through long patience in seeking the right words, it is possible to attain a high degree of faithfulness in putting into clear and idiomatic English what the Hebrew and Greek texts say. Whatever literary distinction the NIV has is the result of the persistence with which this course was pursued.[15]

The CBT has also formulated certain guidelines in an unpublished document ("Translators' Manual," dated 29 November 1968):

1. At every point the translation shall be faithful to the Word of God as represented by the most accurate text of the original languages of Scripture.
2. The work shall not be a revision of another version but a fresh translation from the Hebrew, Aramaic, and Greek.
3. The translation shall reflect clearly the unity and harmony of the Spirit-inspired writings.
4. The aim shall be to make the translation represent as clearly as possible only what the original says, and not to inject additional elements by unwarranted paraphrasing.
5. The translation shall be designed to communicate the truth of God's revelation as effectively as possible to English readers in the language of the people. In this respect the Committee's goal is that of doing for our own times what the King James Version did for its day.
6. Every effort shall be made to achieve good English style.
7. The finished product shall be suitable for use in public worship, in the study of the Word, and in devotional reading.

The following statements appear later in this same document:

1. Translators should keep the principles of the translation constantly in mind and strive for accuracy, clarity, and force of expression.
2. Translators should do their work originally from the original language, but before the completion of their work representative translations and commentaries shall be consulted.
3. Certain notes of text variation, alternative translation, cross reference, or explanation will be put in the margin.

4. The purpose of the project is not to prepare a word-for-word translation nor yet a paraphrase.
5. Read the passages as a whole and aloud to check for euphony and suitability for public reading.

At the time of the NIV's publication I wrote this about the translation work:

> About two thousand years ago, when confronted with the prospect of translating Plato's *Protagoras* into Latin, Cicero declared, "It is hard to preserve in a translation the charm of expressions which in another language are most felicitous.... If I render word for word, the result will sound uncouth, and if compelled by necessity I alter anything in the order or wording, I shall seem to have departed from the function of a translator." Such is the dilemma of all translators! And the problem is particularly acute for those who attempt to translate the Bible, for it is the eternal Word of God. The goal, of course, is to be as faithful as possible in all renderings. But faithfulness is a double-edged sword, for true faithfulness in translation means being faithful not only to the original language but also to the "target" or "receptor" language. That is precisely what we attempted to produce in the New International Version—just the right balance between accuracy and the best contemporary idiom.[16]

In spite of that goal, I am certain that from time to time we will continue to be criticized—by some for being literal but not contemporary enough, and by others for being contemporary but not literal enough. Yet perhaps that fact in itself will indicate that we have basically succeeded.

All this clearly indicates that the CBT attempted to make the NIV a balanced, mediating version—one that would fall about halfway between the most literal and the most free. But is that, in fact, where the NIV fits? Many neutral parties believe so. For example, Steven Sheeley and Robert Nash state, "The NIV committees attempted to walk this fine line and, to their credit, usually achieved a good sense of balance between fidelity to the ancient texts and sensitivity to modern expression." They conclude, "Like any other modern translation of the Bible, the NIV should not be considered the only true translation. Its great achievement, though, lies in its readability. No other modern English translation has reached the same level and still maintained such a close connection to the ancient languages."[17]

A similar opinion is expressed in the "Report to General Synod Abbotsford 1995" by the Committee on Bible Translations appointed by General Synod Lincoln 1992 of the Canadian Reformed Churches. The members of the committee (P. Aasman, J. Geertsema, W. Smouter, C. Van Dam, and G. H. Visscher) thoroughly and carefully investigated the NASB, the NKJV, and the NIV. They indicated that the NIV "attempted to strike a balance between a high degree of faithfulness to the text and clarity for the receptor in the best possible English." They added that "it was frequently our experience that very often when our initial reaction to an NIV translation was negative, further study and investigation convinced us that the NIV translators had taken into account all the factors involved and had actually rendered the best possible translation of the three versions."[18] Similarly, when the committee questioned a passage as being too interpretive, upon closer examination it was often discovered that the NIV had produced a text that was accurate yet idiomatic.[19] They concluded that "the NIV is more idiomatic than the NASB and NKJV but at the same time as accurate as the NASB and NKJV."[20] (By the way, the General Synod Abbotsford 1995 of the Canadian Reformed Churches adopted these two recommendations—among others: [1] to continue to recommend the NIV for use in the churches, and [2] to continue to leave it in the freedom of the churches if they feel compelled to use other translations that received favorable reviews in the reports.)

Another neutral voice is that of Terry White in an article about how a Baptist General Conference church (Wooddale in Eden Prairie, Minnesota) endorsed the NIV as the best translation for their membership. The church appointed a task force to evaluate the NIV, the RSV, the NASB, and the NKJV. The NIV came out ahead in nine of ten areas evaluated (most readable, best scholarship used, best grammatically, best paragraphing, best concordances and supplemental writing, best for use by laity, best Old Testament, best New Testament, and best total Bible). A slight edge was given to the NASB as the most accurate rendering of the original texts. Nonetheless it was clear that the NIV had the best overall balance.[21]

Strictly speaking, then, the NIV is not a dynamic-equivalence translation. If it were, it would read "snakes will no longer be dangerous" (GNB) instead of "dust will be the serpent's food" (Isa 65:25). Or it would read in 1 Samuel 20:30 "You bastard!" (GNB) instead of "You son of a perverse and rebellious woman!" Similar illustrations could be multiplied to demonstrate that the NIV is an idiomatically balanced translation.

How was such a balance achieved? By having a built-in system of checks and balances. We called it the A–B–C–Ds of the NIV, using those letters as an alphabetic acrostic to represent *accuracy, beauty, clarity,* and *dignity*. We wanted to be *accurate,* that is, as faithful to the original text as possible (see our comments on the rendering of Genesis 1:1 at the beginning of this chapter). But it was important to be equally faithful to the target or receptor language—English in this case. So we did not want to make the mistake—in the name of *accuracy*—of creating "translation English" that would not be *beautiful* and natural. *Accuracy,* then, must be balanced by *beauty* of language. The CBT attempted to make the NIV read and flow the way any great English literature should. Calvin D. Linton (professor emeritus of English at George Washington University) has praised the *beauty* of the NIV as literature:

> The NIV is filled with sensitive renderings of rhythms, from the exultant beat of the Song of Deborah and Barak (Judg 5:1–31) to the "dying fall" of the rhythms of the world-weary Teacher in Ecclesiastes, with myriad effects in between. As a random sample, let the reader *speak* the following lines from Job (29:2–3), being careful to give full value to the difference between stressed and unstressed syllables:
>
> How I long for the months gone by,
> for the days when God watched over me,
> when his lamp shone upon my head
> and by his light I walked through darkness!
>
> It is better than the KJV![22]

At the same time we did not want to make the mistake—in the name of *beauty*—of creating lofty, flowery English that would not be *clear*. So *beauty* must be balanced by *clarity:* "When a high percentage of people misunderstand a rendering, it cannot be regarded as a legitimate translation."[23] If a translation is to be both *accurate* and *clear* (idiomatic), it cannot be a mechanical exercise; instead, it must be a highly nuanced process. Popular columnist Godfrey Smith wrote in *The Sunday Times* (London, England):

> I was won over by the way the new Bible [the NIV] handles Paul's magnificent [First] Epistle to the Corinthians [13:4]. "Charity suffereth long, and is kind; charity envieth not; charity vaunteth not itself, is not puffed up." So runs the old version [the KJV], but the word charity is a real showstopper. The new version puts it with admirable simplicity: "Love is patient, love is kind. It does not envy, it does not boast, it is not proud." The old thunder has been lost, but the gain in sense is enormous.[24]

My favorite illustration of lack of *clarity* is the KJV rendering of Job 36:33: "The noise thereof sheweth concerning it, the cattle also concerning the vapour." In the interest of *clarity* the NIV reads, "His [God's] thunder announces the coming storm; even the cattle make known its approach." Or consider the Lord's description of the leviathan in Job 41:12–14 (KJV): "I will not conceal his parts, nor his power, nor his comely proportion. Who can discover the face of his garment? or who can come to him with his double bridle? Who can open the doors of his face? His teeth are terrible round about." Again, in order to communicate *clearly* in contemporary English idiom, the NIV translates as follows:

> I will not fail to speak of his limbs,
> his strength and his graceful form.
> Who can strip off his outer coat?
> Who would approach him with a bridle?
> Who dares open the doors of his mouth,
> ringed about with his fearsome teeth?

The importance of *clarity* in Bible translations is obvious. Yet, the CBT did not want to make the mistake—in the name of *clarity*—of stooping to slang, vulgarisms, street vernacular, and unnecessarily undignified language. *Clarity,* then, must be balanced by *dignity,* particularly since one of our objectives was to produce a general, all-church-use Bible. Some of the dynamic-equivalence versions are at times unnecessarily undignified, as illustrated above in 1 Samuel 20:30.

Additional examples could be given. But the point is that when we produced the NIV, we wanted *accuracy,* but not at the expense of *beauty;* we wanted *beauty,* but not at the expense of *clarity;* and we wanted *clarity,* but not at the expense of *dignity*. We wanted all these in a nice balance. Did we succeed? Rather than be restricted to using descriptive terms like formal equivalence, dynamic equivalence, paraphrase, and the like, in answering this question, it may be more helpful to note the distinctions John Callow and John Beekman make between four types of translations: highly literal, modified literal, idiomatic, and unduly free. Their view can be diagrammed like this:[25]

Unacceptable	Acceptable		Unacceptable
highly literal	modified literal	idiomatic	unduly free

In their classification system the NIV, in my opinion, contains primarily modified literal and idiomatic renderings, though with a greater number of idiomatic ones. To sum up, there is a need for a new category in classifying translations—a classification I'd call a *mediating* position.

What, then, makes a good Bible translation? In my opinion, a good translation will follow a balanced or mediating translation philosophy. Donald Burdick puts it this way:

> A good translation is neither too much nor too little. It is neither too slavish a reproduction of the Greek [and Hebrew], nor is it too free in its handling of the original. It is neither too modern and casual, nor is it too stilted and formal. It is not too much like the KJV, nor does it depart too far from the time-honored beauty and dignity of that seventeenth-century classic. In short, the best translation is one that has avoided the extremes and has achieved instead the balance that will appeal to the most people for the longest period of time.[26]

An appropriate conclusion to this chapter is provided by Bible translation specialist Bruce Metzger:

> Translating the Bible is a never-ending task. As long as English remains a living language it will continue to change, and therefore new renderings of the Scriptures will be needed. Furthermore, as other, and perhaps still more, ancient manuscripts come to light, scholars will need to evaluate the history of the scribal transmission of the original texts. And let it be said, finally, alongside such developments in translating the Bible there always remains the duty of all believers to translate the teaching of Holy Writ into their personal lives.[27]

Notes

1. This chapter is adapted from a similar one in Kenneth L. Barker, *The Balance of the NIV: What Makes a Good Translation* (Grand Rapids: Baker, 1999), 41–55, 112–14. Appreciation is hereby expressed to the publisher for permission to use some of that material. I take great pleasure in presenting this chapter in honor of my dear friend and esteemed colleague, Dr. Ronald Youngblood, on the occasion of his retirement at age seventy. Ron and I have known each other since 1959. I have appreciated his valuable contributions to the New International Version (NIV), *The NIV Study Bible,* and the New International Reader's Version (NIrV)—all of them being projects I've had the enjoyable privilege of working on with him. God be praised!

2. Moisés Silva, *God, Language, and Scripture* (Grand Rapids: Zondervan, 1990), 134.

3. Daniel Taylor, "Confessions of a Bible Translator," *Books & Culture* (November/December 1995), 17.

4. Bob Sheehan, *Which Version Now?* (Sussex: Carey Publications, n.d.), 21.

5. Kenneth L. Barker, *The Accuracy of the NIV* (Grand Rapids: Baker, 1996), 16–17.

6. Silva, *God, Language, and Scripture,* 134.

7. E. A. Speiser, *Genesis,* Anchor Bible (Garden City, N.Y.: Doubleday, 1964), lxiii–lxiv.

8. Ibid., lxvi; see also Herbert M. Wolf, "Literal versus Accurate," in *The Making of the NIV,* ed. Kenneth L. Barker (Grand Rapids: Baker, 1991), 125–34, 165.

9. Eugene A. Nida, *Toward a Science of Translating* (Leiden: Brill, 1964), 159–60.

10. Edward L. Greenstein, "Theories of Modern Translation," *Prooftexts* 3 (1983): 9–39; quoted by J. T. Barrera, *The Jewish Bible and the Christian Bible,* trans. W. G. E. Watson (Grand Rapids: Eerdmans, 1998): 126.

11. R. Elliott, "Bible Translation," in *Origin of the Bible,* ed. Philip W. Comfort (Wheaton, Ill.: Tyndale, 1992), 233.

12. See Cecil Hargreaves, *A Translator's Freedom* (Sheffield: JSOT Press, 1993).

13. Melvin E. Elliott, *The Language of the King James Bible: A Glossary Explaining Its Words and Expressions* (Garden City, N.Y.: Doubleday, 1967); see also Edwin H. Palmer, "The KJV and the NIV," in *The Making of the NIV,* 140–54, 165.

14. Ronald Youngblood, "The New International Version was published in 1978—this is the story of why, and how," *The Standard* (November 1988): 18. For an example of such a "grotesque" rendering, see Bob Sheehan, *Which Version Now?* 19 (this latter work is available from International Bible Society in Colorado Springs, Colorado).

15. *The Story of the New International Version* (New York: The New York International Bible Society, 1978), 13 (italics mine).

16. Kenneth L. Barker, "An Insider Talks about the NIV," *Kindred Spirit* (Fall 1978): 7.

17. Steven M. Sheeley and Robert N. Nash Jr., *The Bible in English Translation* (Nashville: Abingdon, 1997), 44, 46.

18. "Report to General Synod Abbotsford 1995" from the Committee on Bible Translations appointed by Synod Lincoln 1992 of the Canadian Reformed Churches, 16.

19. See "Report to General Synod Abbotsford 1995," 169.

20. "Report to General Synod Abbotsford 1995," 63.

21. See Terry White, "The Best Bible Version for Our Generation," *The Standard* (November 1988): 12–14.

22. Calvin D. Linton, "The Importance of Literary Style," in *The Making of the NIV,* 30.

23. Eugene A. Nida and Charles R. Taber, *The Theory and Practice of Translation* (Leiden: Brill, 1982), 2.

24. Quoted in *A Bible for Today and Tomorrow* (London: Hodder & Stoughton, 1989), 19.

25. John Callow and John Beekman, *Translating the Word of God* (Grand Rapids: Zondervan, 1974), 23–24.

26. Donald W. Burdick, "At the Translator's Table," *The [Cincinnati Christian] Seminary Review* 21 (March 1975): 44.

27. Bruce M. Metzger, "Handing Down the Bible Through the Ages: The Role of Scribe and Translator," *Reformed Review* 43 (Spring 1990): 170.

3

THE LIMITS OF FUNCTIONAL EQUIVALENCE IN BIBLE TRANSLATION—AND OTHER LIMITS, TOO

D. A. Carson

Seventeen years ago I wrote an essay with a similar title: "The Limits of Dynamic Equivalence in Bible Translation."[1] At the time, the expression "dynamic equivalence" was still being used, though even then it was being superseded by "functional equivalence," which, doubtless, is a better label for the translation theory to which both expressions refer. The article was reprinted in various places[2] and (I am told) has served students in many courses on translation in several parts of the world. At the suggestion of the editors of this *Festschrift,* and with the permission of the journal in which the essay first appeared, I shall in this essay incorporate most of what I said seventeen years ago but cast it in rather different terms, and in any case bring some of the discussion up-to-date.

THE CHANGED CLIMATE OF DISCUSSION

The earlier draft was written at a time when the triumph of functional equivalence was largely applauded, even taken for granted in many circles. By and large, I concurred that the theory was fundamentally right and certainly useful. My essay was a modest attempt to offer a handful of warnings against abuses of the theory.[3] The most competent translators needed no guidance from me, of course, but some practitioners, picking up on some facets of the theory, were making decisions not demanded by the theory—decisions laden with problems that needed to be addressed. So when I spoke of the "limits" of functional (or dynamic) equivalence, I was not calling into question the significant gains that the theory had brought to Bible translators all around the world, but I was merely trying to curb some of the less informed enthusiasm with a modicum of critical reserve.

Today, however, the climate of discussion has changed—rather differently, perhaps, in two groups: on the one hand, professional translators, and on the other, ordinary Christians who, after all, support Bible translation, directly or indirectly. The changes in the climate may usefully be summarized in three observations, namely, developments in translation theory, the rise of linguistic conservatism, and the debate over gender-inclusive language.

Developments in Translation Theory

Translation theory has continued to develop. One of the standard works for Bible translators a quarter of a century ago,[4] for instance, was substantially eclipsed just over a decade later by the volume that became the "bible" of functional-equivalence theory.[5] Since then there have been dramatic developments in diverse contributing fields—sociolinguistics,[6] relevance theory,[7] text linguistics (discourse analysis),[8] the application of various elements of linguistic theory to the Greek and Hebrew,[9] and the bearing of narrative criticism on translation technique,[10] to mention but a few.[11]

Almost no one pretends that Bible translation can be reduced to an exact science; almost all vocational Bible translators are eclectic in their appeal to various linguistic developments, not in arbitrary ways, but in ways that recognize the complexities of the challenge and that appreciate the varied contributions on offer. As a result, the vast majority of experienced vocational Bible translators, at least in my experience in various parts of the so-called Third World, are remarkably sophisticated about their business. What this means in practice is that they are not naive about the strengths and weaknesses of any translation theory. Even if they have not formulated such matters themselves, their actual experience in the work of translation and their exposure to complementary—and even competing—theories tend to make them attentive to problems. Nevertheless, it is true to say that functional-equivalence theory has a dominant place in the thinking of Bible translators around the world, especially those who work in receptor languages remarkably different from either the Indo-European or Semitic languages in which most people in the West have been nurtured.

The Rise of Linguistic Conservatism

While these trends have been going on apace, in the last few years a linguistically conservative reaction has taken root in some circles deeply interested in interpreting the Bible accurately, though relatively few of the voices on this front are vocational translators. The common thesis in these contributions is that many modern English translations—I say *English,* because almost all the protests of which I'm aware have to do with English translations of the Bible, with very little awareness of the strengths and weaknesses of translations into other languages (strengths and weaknesses, by the way, that often shed light on the challenges of translation)—have become too sloppy, too paraphrastic, too inaccurate. What is needed, it is argued, is more "literal" translation (many linguists would prefer to speak of more "direct" translation).

The observations these critics make vary in quality. Ironically, however, the best points they offer *have already been made by exponents of functional equivalence themselves.*[12] These exponents are for the most part acutely aware of the dangers of functional-equivalence theory and hoist their own flags of warning; but they are also acutely aware of the dangers of more direct translation. The linguistically conservative critics of functional equivalence, however, cite the dangers as though they were insuperable objections to the theory (rather than features of which the functional-equivalence theorists are thoroughly aware), while not, on the whole, treating evenhandedly the plethora of problems associated with more direct translation—problems that helped call functional equivalence theory into being.[13] And in some cases, it must be said, the objections advanced by those critics who prefer more direct translation are linguistically naive.

Consider, for example, a recent essay by Raymond C. Van Leeuwen.[14] Van Leeuwen excoriates many modern English translations, including the NLT, the NIV, the NRSV, the REB, and the TEV, and the functional equivalence that ostensibly lies beneath them.[15] Yet almost all the issues he raises have been discussed at length by defenders of functional equivalence, sometimes to make the same points. Moreover, it is not long before Van Leeuwen himself makes telling admissions: "Yet translation is a difficult and, in some ways, impossible task. Translations always compromise and interpret.... A translator's first and most important job is to bridge the language gap. She seeks the best way of saying in English *what was said* first in Hebrew or Greek. But even this is not simple. No English word fully matches a Greek or Hebrew word."[16] How true. But if these points had been borne in mind in the earlier part of the essay, it would have been difficult for Van Leeuwen to maintain his stance on the translation of various expressions with such unflinching firmness.

To come to examples:

> FE [functional-equivalence] translations (again, most Bibles today) often change the language, images, and metaphors of Scripture to make understanding easier. But for serious study,

> readers need a translation that is more transparent to the "otherness" of Scripture. We need a translation that allows the Bible to say what it says, even if that seems strange and odd to readers at first glance. If God is "other" than we are, we should be willing to work at the "otherness" of the Bible, in order to understand what the Lord is saying through his Word. The purpose of the Bible is not to make Jesus like us, but to make us like Christ. The Bible is designed to change us, to make us different, heirs of Abraham according to the promise fulfilled in Christ (Acts 2).
>
> We need translations for people who are eager and willing to make the effort to overcome the difficulty of reading a book that is in fact foreign to us. Indeed, when we come to serious Bible study, whether in a church group, Sunday school, or college classroom, this type of translation becomes necessary, for we are trying to get as close as possible within the limits of our own language.... The danger of FE translations is that they shape the Bible too much to fit our world and our expectations. There is a danger that the Bible gets silenced because we have tamed and domesticated it.[17]

In the right context, much of this is well said. Indeed, I said similar things in my earlier essay on dynamic equivalence and shall say them again below. But I say them within the context of acknowledging converse dangers that Van Leeuwen does not recognize. For a start, Van Leeuwen confuses the "foreignness" of any text written in a "foreign" language with the "otherness" of God. This then becomes a tool to justify preserving more direct translations as a function of preserving foreignness and thus the otherness of God. But the question that must always be asked is whether the original text sounded "foreign" to the first readers and hearers. In other words, is the "otherness" of God and thus the "foreignness" of the Bible's message concretized in the foreignness of the language itself? In some cases, that may be so (e.g., some forms of apocalyptic); in some cases, the language may be syntactically smooth and contemporary to the first readers but of difficult vocabulary (e.g., a few parts of Paul); in still other cases, the text may be linguistically contemporary with the first readers but essentially alien and even offensive in its content. These variations cannot all be preserved by the mere expedient of opting for a more direct form of translation. In fact, the more direct form of translation may draw attention to the foreignness of the original language to the modern reader (though it was not foreign to the first readers) and thus actually distract the reader from the far more important "otherness" of God. In short, what sounds like high theological motivation becomes a blunt instrument that fails to recognize the subtleties of translation. One thinks, by analogy, of the brilliant recent translation of *Beowulf* by Seamus Heaney.[18] Within the constraints of terms and idioms that simply must be preserved, Heaney manages to bring to life an astonishingly "contemporary" translation that nevertheless pulsates with the life of ancient Scandinavian mythological heroes.

Moreover, Van Leeuwen does not at this point mention the opposing danger. Sometimes in the name of preserving more formally direct translation, linguistic conservatives are in fact merely preferring traditional expressions that sound natural to them—and are thus preferred because they are well-known to them. But that doesn't mean they are necessarily the best forms for new generations of readers who are both biblically illiterate and less attuned to more archaic forms of English expression. The appeal to preserve the "foreignness" of Scripture, though it *can* be related in some instances to preserving the Bible's distinctive outlook and God's "otherness," *may* be an appeal to preserve the inside-track traditional language that Christians love and to which they feel loyal. But none of this balancing challenge is introduced.

Translators have long talked about three criteria in translation: accuracy, naturalness, and clarity. These criteria bear on translation principles, linguistics, presuppositions, theology, communication theory, exegesis, and the like. But all of these criteria are tricky. In particular, "naturalness" is a desirable goal insofar as the original text is "natural" (linguistically?) to the first readers. Because the structures of two languages may be very different, however, a more direct translation, formally closely allied with the source language, may introduce an element of "unnaturalness" in the receptor language. One may better preserve naturalness, on occasion, by a less direct translation. On the other hand, where the original text is anything but "natural" to the original reader, owing perhaps to its message or to its vocabulary, then ideally the receptor language should convey the same degree of unnaturalness, and for similar reasons. That can be trickier than one might think. For instance, some of the parables of Jesus, though linguistically fairly simple, were doubtless stunningly shocking to the first hearers and readers. It is difficult to imagine that they could retain such shock value to regular Bible readers today, precisely because we are so familiar with them (at least at some superficial level).

It appears, then, that Van Leeuwen's appeal is ducking some complex questions in defense of a linguistically conservative platform. The issue becomes even more tricky when one considers a fourth translation criterion that has been discussed in recent years, namely, perceived authenticity.[19] This perceived authenticity is on the part of the intended audience, which may entertain a slightly different set of assumptions than the translators themselves. Moreover, initial readers may operate with a different set of assumptions from those of long-term, well-informed Bible readers. Inevitably good translation involves some compromise among the four basic criteria. Where one criterion takes over absolutely, however, other things are soon lost. It is perfectly acceptable to argue that one of the criteria has been shortchanged (e.g., accuracy), but informed comment will surely not wish to ignore equally sophisticated discussion of the other three. As one very sophisticated linguist wryly said after reading his way into this debate, perhaps one of the reasons that impel some people to lay more stress on accuracy (by which they usually mean a greater tilting to more direct translation, though in all fairness accuracy is a more complicated matter than that) is that what they really want is not so much a better translation as a "crib" on the original languages.

Under the banner of "other examples of FE translations' obscuring the text,"[20] Van Leeuwen writes, "Similarly, Paul often refers to the '*pistis* of Christ.' *Pistis* means 'faithfulness' or 'faith.' Was Paul saying here that we are saved by ***our*** 'faith in Christ' or that 'the faithfulness of Christ' in his life and death saves sinners? When translations decide questions like this for us, they may prevent us from a Spirit-led, fuller understanding of God's Word."[21] But this is positively cranky; it has nothing whatsoever to do with functional-equivalence theory or otherwise (as a perusal of more direct translations quickly discloses). English has no word that means both *faith* and *faithfulness.* The limitations of our language mean that we *must* choose, and with the choice of the word comes the choice of how to take the genitive of the person. We may, if we wish, include a footnote to provide the alternative. But translators have to make judgment calls on which passages are so doubtful that an alternative in a footnote is called for—and in this instance I know teams of translators on *both* sides of this issue who are convinced that the alternative is not worth including! In any case, this has nothing whatsoever to do with functional equivalence.

Consider another of Van Leeuwen's discussions:

> It is hard to know what the Bible *means* when we are uncertain about what it *says*. In class, teachers with Greek and Hebrew often find themselves retranslating a passage to show students more directly what the literal [*sic!*] Hebrew and Greek said.
>
> The problem with FE translations (i.e., most modern translations) is that they prevent the reader from inferring biblical *meaning* because they change what the Bible *said*.[22]

The example that Van Leeuwen deploys at this point is Colossians 3:9–10, which he quotes from the KJV: "Ye have put off the old man with his deeds; and have put on the new *man*."[23] "The KJV," he writes, "at this point offers a transparent or direct translation of the Greek." He then adds parenthetically, "I prefer not to call it 'literal' because translations always add, change, and subtract from the original. The only literal Bible is written in Hebrew and Greek."[24] I doubt if *literal* is the best word by which to refer to source languages, but I note that in the block quote above, Van Leeuwen says he is pursuing the *literal* Hebrew and Greek in the translation. Terminology aside, however, Van Leeuwen goes on to say that the paired expressions "the old man . . . the new *man*" "are simple and clear, like the Greek. What Paul *said* here is plain. What he *meant* is not, at least to most readers."[25] Van Leeuwen argues that this does not mean what the NIV says: "You have taken off *your old self* with its practices and have put on *the new self*." Such an expression may unwittingly lead the unwary away from what Paul meant (namely, "from Christ") to modern individualistic notions of the "self," which is surely "one of America's greatest idols."[26] Van Leeuwen points out, rightly, that the original is tied up with what Paul means by being "in Adam" and being "in Christ." Thus "the old man" doubtless refers to Adam, the first man, while "the new man" refers to Christ, the last Adam, the true "image of God" (cf. Col 1:15; Rom 5:12–21; 1 Cor 15:45–50; Eph 4:22–23). All of this, I think, is exegetically responsible. Then Van Leeuwen concludes, "Today it might be better to translate the phrases as 'the old Adam . . . the new Adam,' to show that Paul preaches Christ in Old Testament terms."[27]

I think this is an admirable suggestion. But it is not "direct" translation; it is, precisely, the fruit of functional-equivalence theory. Van Leeuwen's suggestion is most definitely not a matter of preserving what the Greek *says* so that the contemporary reader can properly infer what the Greek *means.* Rather, Van Leeuwen has interpreted the Greek every bit as much as the NIV translators have interpreted the Greek. In this case, I think his interpretation better reflects the *original meaning.* But "the old Adam . . . the new Adam" is *not* what the original text *says*, even if it nicely catches what the original text *means.* Van Leeuwen's own example, then, serves only to justify functional-equivalence theory, all his strictures and protestations notwithstanding.

Or consider two brief essays by Tony Payne, both written to promote the recent ESV over against the NIV, the former now being distributed in Australia by Matthias Media, with which Payne is affiliated.[28] The kinds of points he makes have often been made by those who defend functional equivalence (and

I will clarify some of them below). Unfortunately, however, not only is his selection lacking evenhandedness, but his argumentation sometimes betrays linguistic and even (in one particular) theological naïveté.

Payne criticizes the NIV in four areas, in each of which he finds the ESV superior:

1. *The NIV breaks up long Greek and Hebrew sentences into shorter, simpler sentences.* The price that is paid, Payne says, is the loss of a lot of connective words (such as "for," "but," "therefore," etc.), whose absence makes the flow much less clear. Similarly, the NIV often renders participial clauses as new sentences. The gain is found in punchier English; the price is in the loss of the logical cohesion, so that it actually becomes harder to follow the thought of the original. To lose the "for" at the beginning of Romans 1:18 is to lose the connection with verses 16–17.

There is truth in what Payne is saying. Nevertheless, the issue is somewhat more complicated. For a start, Greek often resorts to long sentences, Hebrew much less frequently: though he mentions both languages, Payne's strictures, insofar as they carry weight, apply only to the Greek. More important, stylish Greek loves not only long sentences but endless embedded subordination (i.e., hypotaxis); by contrast, contemporary English loves shorter sentences and parataxis.[29] The implication is that good translation, which tries to be as natural as is the source, must transform syntactical subordination into coordination—always assuming, of course, that one is not losing too much of something else of value. That is why translation always involves judgment calls and why focusing on only one criterion will always produce a poor translation.

Similarly, Greek loves to include a substantial array of particles (Attic Greek, of course, even more so than the Koiné); good English style tries to minimize them. Where English translations try to preserve most of these (in more direct translations), a very high percentage of sentences begin with "And"—as in the KJV. That is one of the reasons why the Book of Mormon, which apes the language style of the KJV, sounds so phony to many modern ears. The logical connections that are carried by such particles are often carried, in English, by the flow of thought or by other discourse markers.

Of course, in any particular instance, one may usefully argue that this or that translation does not have the balance quite right. On the whole, my own preference would be for the NIV to be a tad tighter here and there. But it is disingenuous to make too many sweeping statements, and this for at least two reasons. First, there is some variation regarding the force of such connectives in different New Testament writers, and often the meaning of a particle learned by a student (usually culled from a lexicon) is in many of its textual occurrences something far more subtle. One thinks, for instance of the fine recent work by Stephanie Black.[30] To argue in such cases that one must render Greek particles by English particles is hopelessly naive. Second, precisely because particles are subtle things, one can always find instances where any particular translation has it wrong. In my view, the NIV's "Yet" at the beginning of John 11:6 is indefensible. On the other hand, scarcely less defensible is the ESV's rendering of 1 Corinthians 1:30: "... Christ Jesus, whom God made our wisdom and our righteousness and sanctification and redemption"—as though Christ Jesus is "made" all four of these things in this context. The Greek's *Christō Iēsou hos egenēthē sophia hēmin apo theou, dikaiosunē te kai hagiasmos kai apolutrōsis* is better preserved in the NIV's "Christ Jesus, who has become for us wisdom from God—that is, our righteousness, holiness and redemption." The flow of the context favors this rendering as well.[31]

2. *Payne objects that, while the original text carried a number of possible meanings, the NIV removes the uncertainty by fastening on one of the possibilities.* The advantage is clarity, but this "places the responsibility for interpretation into the hands of the translator rather than the reader."[32] For instance, in Romans 1:17 the NIV uses the expression "righteousness from God," while the original, Payne asserts, is actually "righteousness *of* God," which could refer either to the righteousness that comes from God or to the righteousness that belongs to God (i.e., "God's righteousness").

Overspecification certainly is a problem in translation. This is probably the best of Payne's four points. His grounding of it, however, is untenable. As noted above, he thinks that this practice places the responsibility for interpretation in the hands of translator rather than reader. Surely we are not to return to the astonishing naïveté that thought that translation could be done without interpretation? Consider, for example, the many languages that use either an exclusive "we" or an inclusive "we"—with no other alternative. That means that every time the Greek Testament uses a Greek form of "we," which does not intrinsically specify whether or not the usage is inclusive or exclusive, translators into such languages *must* decide which way to render it—and of course this is unavoidable overspecifying.[33] Because of the differences between languages, translation always involves some instances of overspecifying and underspecifying. And once again, there is a judgment call to be made. In my judgment, NIV overspecifies a bit too often; RSV/ESV leaves things unnecessarily ambiguous a bit too often, with resulting loss of clarity. But Payne mentions only the former. And the notion that one can translate responsibly *without* interpretation is, quite frankly, shockingly ignorant of the most basic challenges facing translators. Moreover, even in the example Payne cites (Rom 1:17), the Greek does *not* have, literally, "righteousness *of* God"; rather, it has *dikaiosunē . . . theou,* i.e., the genitive of the word rendered "God." How to render this genitive is precisely the question. It *is* true to say that the English rendering "righteousness of God" preserves more ambiguity. But there are thousands of instances of the genitive in Scripture where Payne would agree that the context makes it abundantly clear that the genitive should *not* be rendered by an English "of . . ." phrase. Apparently the NIV translators thought this passage belonged to that set. One may criticize their judgment in this instance, of course, but not on the grounds Payne adduces.

3. *Payne criticizes the NIV for translating one Hebrew or Greek word by a number of different English words, depending on the context.* This, he says, is done to produce more stylish, flowing English, but one loses the connections that a reader of the original will be able to make. For instance, Paul says that Jesus was descended from David "according to the *flesh*"—and *flesh* is an important word in Romans that gets hidden in its first occurrence when it is rendered "human nature" in the NIV, and elsewhere in Romans "sinful nature." Payne comments, "Again, these translations are defensible in themselves, but they remove the connection between the ideas. They don't allow the reader to build up an idea of what Paul means by 'flesh'."[34]

There are two major misconceptions in these judgments, apart from the difficulty of rendering the Greek word *sarx.* The first is that for Payne's argument to work, the word in the receptor language must have exactly the same semantic range as the word in the source language—and as has repeatedly been shown, this is rarely the case. That is why *all* translations use a variety of words to render one source word, or one word in the receptor language to render several words in the source language.[35] One can argue about whether any translation has got the balance of things right: Has the pursuit of smooth idiom in the receptor language introduced a higher percentage of different words in the receptor language than is strictly necessary? What is "strictly necessary"? Different translators will judge this matter differently. But Payne's sweeping judgments on this point are linguistically indefensible. Second, they become even worse when he says that the translations he is condemning "don't allow the reader *to build up* [emphasis mine] an idea of what Paul means by 'flesh.'" This, of course, is to smuggle in "illegitimate totality transfer" through the back door, and that is inexcusable.[36] The *board* decided to *board* up the old boat with a piece of *board,* while the passengers climbed on *board.* Supposing those four uses were scattered through half a dozen pages of some writing or other, would it be useful or helpful to speak of "building up" an idea of what the author means by "board"?

I do not think that the NIV always renders *sarx* in the best way. But it is an extraordinarily difficult word. Here's another author who takes the NIV to task over the same word:

> Unfortunately, the translators of the NIV had a proclivity for settling exegetical questions in their translations, thereby becoming interpreters rather than translators. Among their most serious blunders resulting from this practice was the decision to translate the Greek word *sarx* ("flesh") by the theological prejudicial phrase "sinful nature." This is unfortunate, I say, because this obvious interpretive bias is *wrong*. The specialized use of the word flesh refers neither to man's sinful *nature* nor to the sinful *self* that he developed, but to the sinful *body* (as Paul calls it in Romans 6:6). When Paul speaks of the body as sinful, he does not conceive of the body as originally created by God as sinful . . . , but rather the body plunged into sinful practices and habits as the result of Adam's fall.[37]

Here again the NIV translators are being condemned for being interpreters rather than translators (!), but the "obvious" meaning they missed is one that Jay Adams thinks is correct but almost no one else does.[38] The kindest thing that can be said is that the language condemning the translators of a great breach of principle, instead of a *different* understanding of the text from that of the critic, is intemperate. But certain expressions are widely recognized as highly disputed and difficult (see the essay by Douglas J. Moo on "flesh" in this collection), and should breed a gracious humility rather than a condemnation of translators.

One more example may help to clarify things. In Ephesians 2:11 Paul speaks of (literally) "Gentiles in the flesh." The NIV renders this "Gentiles by birth." On any meaning, "Gentiles in the flesh" is not an English locution; moreover, I doubt that many would be bold enough to argue that this means "Gentiles in the body" or "Gentiles in the old nature" or "Gentiles in the old era," or any of the other specialized meanings that *sarx* is alleged to have in other contexts. The NIV has the meaning of *the entire expression* right, even though it loses the word "flesh," and even though Greek *sarx* never means "birth." The RSV/ESV preserves "Gentiles in the flesh," but even though this is a more "direct" translation, I doubt that it preserves greater accuracy than the NIV. It certainly does not contribute to a Pauline total notion of *sarx* (illegitimate totality transfer). And it loses the naturalness of the NIV rendering.

4. *Payne accuses the NIV of replacing concrete biblical expressions or metaphors with more abstract equivalents.* The example he provides is this: The Bible often

tells us to "walk in love" or "walk as children of light," or not to "walk in darkness" or the like, and the NIV frequently renders such expressions by the more abstract "live a life of love" or "live as children of light" or the like. "'Walk' is not a hard English word to understand," writes Payne, "nor is the metaphor a difficult one to grasp. Yet in changing it, the NIV removes some of the power of the word's imagery."[39]

In this particular case, I'm inclined to agree with Payne—though I confess I'm not quite certain whether or not my ease over this idiomatic use of the verb "to walk" is a reflection of my own familiarity with scriptural language rather than a fair reading of common usage in the contemporary culture. And I am not sure that the more direct rendering of "walk" is *always* the most helpful—e.g., ESV "let us also walk by the Spirit" (Gal 5:25), since "to walk by something/someone" in contemporary English has a rather different meaning than what Paul had in mind! The NIV's "let us keep in step with the Spirit" preserves the metaphor, though it does not use the word "walk," and is certainly more contemporary and less liable to be misunderstood than the RSV/ESV rendering. And these are merely two or three caveats in an instance where I am sympathetic to Payne's criticism of the NIV's rendering of a particular idiom! Yet somehow Payne has elevated an observation—probably a correct observation, though possibly stretched too far—into a generic criticism without evaluating a host of other metaphors where the NIV's approach might earn it high marks.

In short, Payne thinks the NIV philosophy of translation is this: "Better to have something simple, the NIV seems to think, even if it is not what the original text actually says."[40] Wait a minute: this form of argument is deceptive and manipulative, for anyone with a high view of Scripture will always want to side with "what the original text actually says." But the original text does not actually *say* "flesh" and "walk" and the like; it says *sarx* and *peripateō* and the like, and the issue is how best to render such expressions. Payne's assumption seems to be that the more direct translation is "what the original text actually says." In fact, what the original text actually says is in Aramaic and Hebrew and Greek, and the dispute is over when the more direct translation is the better translation and when a functional equivalent is the better translation. To write "Better to have something simple, the NIV seems to think, even if it is not what the original text actually says" is to displace reasoned discussion about translation principles by manipulative rhetoric.

It gets worse, and this is where the theological naïveté is introduced. After the sentence just quoted, Payne writes the following:

> This betrays something of a lack of trust, in my view, in what has traditionally been called the "perspicuity of Scripture"—

> that God's word *is* clear and understandable for the person who reads it with a regenerate heart. Who are we, after all, to tinker with God's words, just because we think we are doing God a favour in making them "easier"?[41]

Quite apart from the fact (once again!) that "God's words" were in Aramaic, Hebrew, and Greek and that Payne presupposes that his preferred practice of more "direct" translation involves less tinkering with God's words than any other approach—a claim sometimes true and sometimes patently false—this is a rather bad abuse of *claritas Scripturae,* the doctrine of the perspicuity of Scripture. That doctrine has an interesting and complex history.[42] At the time of the Reformation, for instance, the issue turned on whether Scripture boasts an esoteric element that could only be unraveled by the inside knowledge or insight of the Magisterium. The Reformers insisted that it does not—that there is a clarity, a perspicuity, to Scripture itself, so that the special mediation of the Magisterium is by no means a criterion for understanding. All of this tied in very well with the Reformation insistence on the priesthood of all believers. But never, to my knowledge, was the doctrine used by responsible theologians to deny that some parts of Scripture are difficult to understand (see 2 Pet 3:16); still less has *claritas Scripturae* been used to defend a particular translation theory.

Moreover, the way Payne has cast his argument it is difficult to see why we still need teachers in the church. Transparently, however, the New Testament documents insist on the role of teachers. This is not because they have some sort of inside track, some key to understanding, some special enduement of the Spirit unavailable to other believers. But they do have understanding, and some are more knowledgeable and insightful than others (otherwise, how shall we understand Galatians 2:11–14?). All things being equal (and they never are), those with a good grasp of Hebrew and Greek will grasp what Scripture says better than those without a good grasp of those languages. At no point does *claritas Scripturae* vitiate such distinctions. And at no point is it fair to accuse those who translate Scriptures, using a slightly different balance of translation theory, of jettisoning *claritas Scripture*. Such rhetoric is both uninformed and misdirected.

The purpose of these observations is not to bad-mouth the ESV or to defend the NIV or TNIV against all comers. Translations have various strengths and weaknesses; further, they serve various constituencies. Clearly there are "better" and "worse" translations according to a particular set of criteria. Some translations may be fine for private reading but somehow seem less appropriate as pew Bibles. I shall return to this observation one more time after the next section. For the purpose of this essay, however, my point is that before talking about the limits of functional equivalence, it has become necessary to warn against the reactionary wing that demonizes functional equivalence with occasionally insightful rhetoric, but is more often linguistically uninformed, is rarely balanced, and is sometimes shrill.

THE DEBATE OVER GENDER-INCLUSIVE LANGUAGE

The third change in the climate springs from debates on gender-related issues in Bible translation. The debates have become overheated and highly politicized, primarily, I think, not because many on the linguistically conservative side insist that those who disagree with them are wrong (after all, that is what debaters do, and each side thinks the other is wrong), but for two other reasons: (1) Many on this side insist that their opponents are not only wrong in their linguistic judgments but that they are compromising the truthfulness of Scripture, and inevitably that gets a lot more attention; and (2) the same people are organizing politically, inviting many high-profile evangelical leaders, whether or not they know anything at all about Greek, translation theory, or any language other than English, to sign on to the agenda. Entire denominations have been torn asunder in debate. In quieter moments, one wonders if any conceivable damage that could be done by the NIV or TNIV could be any worse than the division, bitterness, and strife stirred up by those who have made this a dividing issue.

The history of the debate is now so well-known that it need not be repeated here. Moreover, some contributions from all sides have been thoughtful and informed and have advanced the discussion. From the linguistically conservative side, the volume by Vern S. Poythress and Wayne A. Grudem patiently explains its authors' position and deserves careful reading[43]—as do some of the most thoughtful reviews.[44] On the other hand, those who are, theologically speaking, complementarians (such as Grudem and Poythress), but who are convinced on linguistic grounds that some revisions of contemporary English translations are mandated by changes in contemporary English, are well represented by Mark Strauss.[45]

This is not the place to rehash all the issues that have been raised. My purpose here is to mention a selection of translation issues that the gender-issue debate has put on the table. This is only a small sampling. I include them because they have in some measure changed public perceptions as to the legitimacy of functional equivalence, and so some of them should be aired again before turning, finally, to a review of the limitations of functional equivalence.

Various Approaches to Translation

One of the themes of the book by Poythress and Grudem (to which reference has already been made) is that linguistics teaches us that texts carry not only large-scale meanings but countless fine "nuances" (one of their favorite words). In particular, of course, they are interested in the "nuances of meaning" that are lost, they aver, in inclusive translation. They speak of four different levels on which people approach translation:[46]

- *The naive approach,* adopted by the general public (at least the monolingual general public), which assumes that translation is nothing more than a matter of replacing words in one language with words in another language, *ad seriatim.* It assumes that the structures of language are identical and that the semantic ranges of both the source word and the receptor word are identical. Poythress and Grudem rightly assert that such a view of translation is simply wrong.
- *The theoretically informed approach,* which displays a basic understanding of linguistics with respect to form and function. People working at this level will recognize, for instance, that one Hebrew word in Ezekiel 37 must variously be rendered "breath," "wind," and "Spirit" (37:5, 9, 14 respectively). And it is at this level, Poythress and Grudem assert, that their opponents in the gender-inclusive language debate are operating.
- *The discerning approach,* which uses native speakers' intuitive sense of the subtleties. Here, the native speaker would recognize the three different meanings of the Hebrew word in Ezekiel 37 but would also recognize the subtle interplays between them that a reader of a translation will miss.
- *The reflective approach,* the fourth and highest level, which analyzes and makes explicit all the subtleties and complexities that the native speaker might well intuit.

Much of this, of course, is correct. But the question is whether an ordinary translation normally *can* get much beyond the second level. If the *meaning* of the one Hebrew word in the different verses is variously wind, breath, and Spirit (in English!), those are the words the translation will have to use (second level). A translation could, doubtless, preserve one English word for the one Hebrew word (say, "wind"), but the preservation of formal equivalence would entail an indefensible semantic loss. Footnotes can of course draw attention to the presence of one Hebrew word behind the three English words (drawing attention to the third level), but most translations will not resort to such niceties except in cases where the meaning is totally lost unless the wordplay is grasped. As for analyzing and explaining the subtle connections and complexities (fourth level), that is what commentaries and preachers do.

Of course, it is possible to construct a Bible with various layers of footnotes, which in effect lift the translation pretty close to level 3, with occasional insight at level 4. That is now being done in the rather remarkable NET Bible.[47] But observe that it is not the translation per se that is being lifted to a higher level. Rather, it is the complex system of notes that lifts the discussion. In other words, the NET Bible is not simply a translation, but a translation-cum-explanation-cum-commentary. It is, in effect, a fine crib for those who don't know their Hebrew and Greek very well. But so far as the actual translation goes, although the notes explain a little more of what goes into the decisions, one is still left with level 2, occasionally rising to level 3.

In other words, Poythress and Grudem rightly explain some rudiments in linguistic theory and then abuse their own theory by not admitting that basic translations really cannot frequently rise much beyond level 2. While the goal is certainly to preserve as much meaning as possible, translation is an inexact discipline, and something is invariably lost in any basic translation. One is constantly forced to make decisions—which is one of the fundamental reasons why there are commentaries and preachers. But somewhere along the line, Poythress and Grudem start referring to any loss of any meaning at any level as a "distortion" and an "inaccuracy," finally challenging the integrity of those who admit such things. But *all* translators, including Poythress and Grudem, are inevitably bound up with making choices about the "nuances" they get across. In that sense, *all* translations are driven by choices, and all presuppose interpretation and an assumed grid of what is most importantly preserved.

New Testament scholar Daniel Wallace provides an interesting example of the complexity of competing principles, of the difficulty of making decisions.[48] While working on the NET Bible, he and his co-translators struggled with the sentence, "I will make you fishers of men" (KJV, RSV, NIV, and many others). The Greek phrase rendered "fishers of men" is *halieis anthrōpōn,* and, unwilling to give the impression—to some contemporary readers—that the disciples were to be fishers of adult males only, they were unsatisfied with "men." Further, although "fishers of men" is a common expression among many churchgoers, in fact the word "fishers" is archaic. It is no longer used except in that expression. The NRSV resolves these two problems by rendering the clause, "I will make you fish for people." But Wallace rightly points out that this sounds as though Jesus will *force* his disciples to "fish for people," which is scarcely what is meant. Moreover, the shift from noun to verb ("fishers" to "fish") might be thought to signal a shift from a new occupation to merely a new activity. The NLT and the TEV avoid the first problem but not the second, with, respectively, "I will show you how to fish for people" and "I will teach you to catch people." But both "show you" and "teach you" introduce nuances that are not quite faithful, either—and still we are left with verbs. Some have suggested, "I will make you fishermen of people," which solves several problems and removes the archaism, though most would acknowledge that the expression sounds thoroughly awkward and cumbersome. Still, it is better than "I will make you fishers of mankind" or "I will make you fishers of humankind," since these renderings give the impression that the mission includes Gentiles, which is certainly not what the disciples would have understood at that point in redemptive history—and probably not quite what Jesus himself meant at that point in redemptive history, either. As Wallace comments, "This text illustrates the clash of translational objectives of accuracy, readability, and elegance. At bottom, we believe that the great value of the NET Bible is its extensive notes that wrestle with such issues, for the footnotes become a way for us to have our cake and eat it too."[49] The NET scholars finally opted for "I will turn you into fishers of people," thus choosing to stick with the archaism because the alternatives struck them as worse.

The point of this discussion is not to commend or condemn the NET decision. It is to point out that the NET scholars implicitly agree with Poythress and Grudem when they acknowledge that translation is an inexact discipline that involves compromise—give and take—and that there are subtleties in the source text that demand the most careful evaluation about how best to preserve them without introducing too many extraneous notions. The difference, of course, is that the NET scholars, recognizing these tensions, work them out the best they can and by their system of notes provide some indication of their wrestlings and reasonings. By contrast, Poythress and Grudem articulate reasonably sound theory, but every time a decision goes against their favored "nuance," they accuse their opponents of distorting Scripture and introducing inaccuracies. At some point, one begins to suspect that it is *their* argument that is ideologically driven.

Issues of Changes in English Usage

Part of the debate turns on whether there has been sufficient change in English usage in the West, especially in America, to warrant more sensitivity in our translations to gender-inclusive issues. Valerie Becker Makkai, an associate professor in linguistics at the University of Illinois (Chicago), wrote the foreword to the book by Poythress and Grudem. There she devotes no small part of her space to arguing that the large-scale empirical studies have not been done to provide the hard evidence that would answer such questions. Doubtless she is correct. Large-scale empirical studies have not yet been done. But that does not mean that large-scale changes have not taken place; it simply means that the large-scale empirical studies have not yet been done to prove with hard numbers that such changes have (or have not) taken place. Rather more scathingly, in their sixth appendix Poythress and Grudem argue for the continuing usability of generic "he." Certainly it's easy enough to find sectors of society where inclusive language has made relatively little impression. For various reasons I move in quite different sectors, and, although I'm relying on what I personally observe rather than on large-scale empirical studies, I cannot help noting that generic "he" is more acceptable in culturally conservative sectors of the country than in culturally liberal sectors. But I have been doing university missions for thirty years, and in such quarters inclusive language dominates. Not to use it is offensive.

Implicitly, of course, Poythress and Grudem recognize that English usage *is* changing, since even the Colorado Springs Guidelines, to which they subscribe, allow for some accommodation in this regard. In fact, a recent essay by Mark Strauss documents how many inclusive-language changes the ESV has introduced to the RSV.[50] Some are changes from "men" to "people" (e.g., Matt 5:15). Sometimes, however, the ESV changes "men" to "others" (e.g., Matt 5:11–12 RSV: "Blessed are you when *men* revile you ... for so *men* persecuted the prophets who were before you"; ESV: "Blessed are you when *others* revile you ... for so *they* persecuted the prophets who were before you"). To change "men" to "others" is entirely acceptable to me; it is a bit strange to find it in a translation prepared by those who argue that translation should rise to what they call the third and fourth level. There is certainly some change in nuance from "men" to "others"—not least in contemporary culture where the word "others" is increasingly taking on an overtone, a nuance, of outsider that is not found in "men" (unless, I suppose, written by some "women"!). This change is far from rare (e.g., Matt 5:16 RSV: "Let your light so shine before men"; ESV: "let your light so shine before others"). Other changes include

- Matthew 7:9 RSV: "what *man* of you"; ESV: "which *one* of you";
- Matthew 16:24 RSV: "If *any man* will come after me"; ESV: "If *anyone* will come after me";
- Matthew 19:11 RSV: "Not *all men* can receive this saying"; ESV: "Not *everyone* can receive this saying";
- Matthew 22:16 RSV: "care for no *man*"; ESV: "you do not care about *anyone's opinion*."

I am not arguing that any of these translated phrases are wrong, still less that they're wicked. Some are better than others. But I am certainly saying that there are changes of "nuance" in such pairs as men/you, any man/anyone, men/others, and so forth—and the presence of such changes in the ESV, where Grudem has had such a strong hand, show that there is an implicit recognition of a change of English usage in the land. And I am saying that in countless passages they themselves implicitly recognize that translators *ought* to be aware of contemporary usage and that in basic translations (i.e., translations without cumbersome footnotes), it is difficult to operate beyond the second level, with occasional forays into the third. They are making such changes—I would not call them distortions or inaccuracies—all the time, and the changes certainly carry slight differences of nuance. But when others make similar changes with respect to the pronoun "he," Poythress and Grudem condemn them for distorting the Word of God.

In a rather heated review, Vern Poythress insists that both Mark Strauss and I are not sensitive enough to the fact that "feminists pay attention to generic 'he' and load it with connotations because [feminists] can thereby use it as a means of detecting ideological resistance. Once offenders are located, [these offenders] are persuaded to conform, or else labeled insensitive or chauvinistic." He adds the following:

> They [Carson and Strauss] could not frankly discuss the ideological connotation of generic "he" because it represents a land mine capable of exploding the illusion that the issue is merely clear communication. The central issue is ideology. It is a modern ideology that makes generic "he" unacceptable even though it is intelligible. Ideological influence heats up the whole issue. Messrs. Carson and Strauss want people on all sides to cool down. The desire for peace and sanity is admirable. But the ideological conflict will not go away. And God's Word does not change in order to appease modern feminists' ideas about language.[51]

Reviewers should be careful about what authors could or "could not frankly discuss," because they are extending a challenge that constitutes an invitation. I am more than happy to discuss it. Such a discussion could easily take up a chapter, but I shall restrict myself to the following points:

1. I acknowledge that much of the demand for reform of the English language on this point is from active feminists. Much of the push for change is ideologically driven. I don't think all of it is, but certainly much of it is.
2. Would Poythress want to say that *everything* that feminists and their forebears have introduced is bad? Would he like to disavow, say, universal suffrage? Granted that a fair bit of feminist rhetoric is overheated and mean-spirited, is it not fair to say that there have been countless abuses of women and that anything Christians can do to rectify injustice is a good thing, so long as we adhere to biblical perspectives on what justice is? I think that Dr. Poythress would agree. The implication, surely, is that it is important, in the face of feminist demands, not to tar the entire movement with one broad brush. One must try to assess where,

in the light of Scripture, feminist agendas make telling points, where their demands make little difference (from a biblical point of view), and where they seem to fly in the face of Scripture. That is why I, and Dr. Strauss, too, for that matter, are complementarians and not egalitarians. But this is a far cry from saying that there is nothing to be learned from feminist cries and from feminist writings. It is never wise to build a fence around Torah and try to become more righteous than Torah; it is always wise to discern where one should draw a line and where one should not draw it. By contrast, linguistic conservatism in the name of warning people against the "slippery slope"[52] discourages Christians from thinking through where the real issues are.

3. Although (as we have seen) the matter is disputed, my best guess is that, regardless of the motivations driving at least a good part of the push for reform of English usage, increasingly that push will prove successful. If so, increasing numbers of people who themselves will not be driven by an active feminist agenda will take on the English usage that was in substantial measure fomented by feminists. In other words, regardless of the reasons for change in the language, the language is changing. Implicitly, even the ESV acknowledges the point by allowing some changes that accommodate inclusive-language concerns.[53]
4. It is true that "the ideological conflict will not go away," as Poythress puts it. But that is merely another way of saying that the confrontation must take place at the right points. There is, for example, a growing and admirable literature that gives many good reasons why it is inappropriate to change the language of Scripture so as to address God as "our heavenly Mother" or the like. Meanwhile, I know not a few complementarians who are becoming unwilling to stand up for their beliefs, not because they are intimidated by feminists, but because they do not want to be associated with the increasingly shrill polemic that so roundly condemns fellow complementarians for not drawing linguistic lines where Poythress and Grudem draw them![54]
5. I entirely agree with Poythress's last sentence, namely, that "God's Word does not change in order to appease modern feminists' ideas about language." God's Word, after all, was given in Aramaic, Hebrew, and Greek, and it does not change. But the *translations* change as the receptor languages change, *regardless of the motivations that some entertain for those changes*. The proof, as we have seen, is the ESV itself. Where the line must be drawn is where a translation is domesticating God's Word such that the truth of Scripture is distorted. Translators may sometimes

differ as to when that is happening; certainly we need one another, so as to foster honesty and integrity in debate. But the countless minor accommodations and choices that *every* translator has to make in just about *every* sentence, demanded by the fact that the source language and the receptor language are different, should not be confused with such matters of substance.[55]

Issues of Varied Gender Systems around the World

In my book on inclusive-language translation, I devoted quite a bit of space to outlining the gender systems of various languages, showing how different they are in many instances from the conventions used both in the biblical languages and in English for that matter. Poythress and Grudem dismiss the argument:

> The underlying assumption in this objection is that *only what can easily be conveyed into all languages is worth conveying in English.* When we draw this assumption out into the open, it refutes itself.... Of course, we agree that some languages in the world may not have all the capabilities for expression that English does, and in those cases translators will have to do the best they can with those languages.... But all of those considerations are simply changing the subject, which is how to translate the Bible into English today.[56]

But here Poythress and Grudem are ascribing to me views I have never held and are not listening fairly to what I actually wrote. I have never held the view that "only what can easily be conveyed into all languages is worth conveying in English." Nor did that notion form any part of my assumptions. Rather, my discussion was responding to constantly repeated arguments to the effect that where we have the masculine pronoun in Hebrew, the English must have a masculine pronoun or else we are betraying the Word of God. By showing how varied are gender systems around the world, I demonstrated that in some receptor languages, preservation of a masculine pronoun may not even be an option, and that even in the move from Hebrew (or Greek) to English there are differences in their respective gender systems that make this sort of appeal to formal equivalence not only impossible (in some contexts), but nonsense. I provided many examples. Poythress and Grudem tackle none of them. This is not to say that preservation of formal equivalence is *always* a bad thing, of course; it is to say, rather, that appeal to loyalty and faithfulness toward the Word of God as the ground for preserving formal equivalence is both ignorant and manipulative, precisely because the significance and range of use of a masculine pronoun in Hebrew are demonstrably not the same as the significance and range of use of a masculine pronoun in English. A great deal depends on the gender systems of the respective languages and then on the individual contexts. Poythress and Grudem appear on occasion to have taken the argument on board, and then when someone disagrees with them over the exact force of a particular context, very quickly they resort to an appeal to Scripture's truthfulness and authority, as though the other party were abandoning it. Popular journalists have merely followed their lead, sometimes with even more inflated rhetoric. This stance, more than anything else, is what has heated up this debate.

Issues of Distinctions between Singular and Plural Forms

Although the ESV (which Poythress and Grudem favor) introduces, as we have seen, hundreds of changes (such as the change from "men" to "others") to accommodate the concerns of inclusive language in our changing culture, Poythress and Grudem are especially resistant to certain *kinds* of changes. They do not seem troubled by changes in nuance or the failure to meet "fourth level" translation theory when it comes to *their* approved changes, but their wrath knows few bounds when the TNIV deploys a plural instead of a singular. For instance, in Revelation 3:20 the NIV reads, "I stand at the door and knock. If anyone hears my voice and opens the door, I will come in and eat with him, and he with me." The TNIV reads, "I stand at the door and knock. If anyone hears my voice and opens the door, I will come in and eat with them, and they with me." In one circulated e-mail message, Grudem comments, "The TNIV mistranslates the masculine singular pronoun *autos,* substituting plural pronouns, thus losing the teaching that Jesus has fellowship with the individual believer. This type of change was made frequently (e.g., Luke 9:23; John 14:23; Romans 14:7)."

What shall we make of this reasoning? Certainly in some passages, the distinction between the singular and the plural *is* crucial and should be preserved. That is why generic solutions to translation problems must be assessed on a case-by-case basis. But the significance of the plural, in many contexts, must not be overstated or the comprehensiveness of the Greek generic *autos* overlooked. That is one of the reasons why they can sometimes be put in parallel: e.g., "You have heard [plural] that it was said, 'Love [singular] your neighbor and hate [singular] your enemy [singular].' But I tell you: Love [plural] your enemies [plural] and pray [plural] for those who persecute you" (Matt 5:43–44). Jesus' quotation takes over the singular form used in the LXX, but precisely because that singular form is recognized from the context to have generic force, we recognize that the OT command was not restricted to an individual but extended to everyone to whom the command applied. Even the singular "enemy" does not mean that believers only have one enemy. The utterance has a proverbial ring, with the force "your enemy, whoever that enemy may be." Jesus' commands, in the plural, certainly do not mean that he is removing the responsibility of the individual, mandating only corporate love without regard for the obligation of the individual disciple to love.

In other words, a plural command or a plural prohibition *may* signal a group activity, but it may not—the context must decide.[57] A prohibition against lust, written in the plural, certainly does not mean that the only thing that is prohibited is group lust (whatever that is). It means, rather, that all within the group addressed face the same prohibition. If the prohibition had been in the singular, but written in a context of moral constraints for a general audience and not to a named individual, then the singular form nevertheless applies to all who fall within the general audience. Yes, there is a small shift in nuance, but the application in the two cases is exactly the same.

As in the case with "I will make you [?] fishers [?] of men [?]," decisions have to be taken as to how best to get things across. Grudem prefers "If anyone hears my voice and opens the door, I will come in and eat with *him,* and *he* with me"; TNIV offers "If anyone hears my voice and opens the door, I will come in and eat with *them,* and *they* with me." But with the best will in the world, it is difficult to see how this change loses "the teaching that Jesus has fellowship with the individual believer," precisely because the preceding "anyone" is preserved in both instances.[58] And meanwhile, if for the envisaged readership of TNIV the pronouns "him" and "he" have the effect, whatever the ideology that has produced such changes in linguistic associations, of excluding approximately half of humanity, one could responsibly argue that the TNIV is, for such a readership, a *more accurate, more faithful* translation than the NIV or the ESV. As Craig Blomberg puts it in his review in *Denver Journal* of *The Gender-Neutral Bible Controversy,* "It is doubtful if most modern American listeners will interpret 'blessed are those who ...' (whether in the Proverbs or the Beatitudes) as a corporate reference that excludes individual application, but on more than one occasion I have add [sic] well-educated adults in churches that use the NIV ask me why the Proverbs were only addressed to men or sons and not applicable to women or daughters."[59]

Issues from Chapter 2 of Hebrews

Other theological errors have been ascribed to the TNIV. For convenience, it may be useful to focus on two verses from the Epistle to the Hebrews—Hebrews 2:6 and Hebrews 2:17.

Hebrews 2:6

> What is *man* that you are mindful of *him,*
> the *son of man* that you care for *him*?"
>
> HEBREWS 2:6 NIV, italics added

> What are *mere mortals* that you are mindful of *them,*
> *human beings* that you care for *them*?"
>
> HEBREWS 2:6 TNIV, italics added

The charge is made that the TNIV obscures the quotation from Psalm 8:4, mistranslates three words by turning them into plurals, and loses the messianic application of "son of man" to Jesus Christ. I have probably said enough about the use of the plural. Whether the TNIV obscures the connection with Psalm 8:4 will depend a bit on how it translates Psalm 8:4, which has not yet been published. The serious charge, in my view, is that this loses the messianic application to Jesus Christ. Yet here, too, the charge is less than fair. The expression "son of man" in the Old Testament *can* have powerful messianic overtones, of course (see Daniel 7:13–14), but it is far from being invariable: about eighty times it is used as a form of address to the prophet Ezekiel, without any messianic overtone whatsoever. So whether the expression has messianic content or not must be *argued,* not merely asserted. In Psalm 8, the overwhelming majority of commentators see the expression as a gentilic, parallel to the Hebrew for "man" in the preceding line. (Incidentally, gentilic nouns in Hebrew are often singular in form but plural in referent—which may also address the indignation over the shift to the plural.) In the context of the application of Psalm 8:4 to Jesus in Hebrews 2, one should at least recognize that the *nature* of the application to Jesus is disputed. Scanning my commentaries on Hebrews (I have about forty of them), over three-quarters of them do not think that "son of man" here functions as a messianic title but simply as a gentilic, as in Psalm 8. If this exegesis is correct (and I shall argue elsewhere and at length that it is), Jesus is said to be "son of man," not in function of the messianic force of that title in Daniel 7:13–14, but in function of his *becoming a human being*—which all sides recognize is one of the major themes of Hebrews 2. If one wishes to take the opposite tack—that "son of man" here is a messianic title—there are competent interpreters who have taken that line. But it is *not* a matter of theological orthodoxy, since understanding the text one way does not mean that the translator (or the commentator) is *denying* the complementary truth but is merely asserting that the complementary truth is not in view here.

One could even imagine a more subtle argument, one with which I would have some sympathy: It is possible to see in "son of man" in Psalm 8:4 a gentilic, rightly preserved in Hebrews 2, and then wonder if, owing to the frequency of "son of man" as a messianic title in the Synoptic Gospels, early Christian ears might have picked up an additional overtone, without reading a messianic interpretation into the entire passage. This is possible, though hard to prove. The possibility could be accommodated by a footnote cue after "human beings" in the TNIV, the footnote itself reading "Or, *son of man.*" But at the level of actual translation, it is difficult to find legitimate reasons for condemning the TNIV rendering in such absolutist terms.

Hebrews 2:17

> For this reason he had to be made like his *brothers* in every way, in order that he might become a merciful and faithful high priest in service to God, and that he might make atonement for the sins of the people.
>
> HEBREWS 2:17 NIV, italics added

> For this reason he had to be made like his *brothers and sisters* in every way, in order that he might become a merciful and faithful high priest in service to God, and that he might make atonement for the sins of the people.
>
> HEBREWS 2:17 TNIV, italics added

This, it is said, is doubly bad: In this context, the Greek word cannot mean "brothers and sisters," since Jewish high priests were exclusively male, and of course Jesus himself is male; and worse, the notion that Jesus was "made like his ... sisters in every way" is unthinkable, or conjures up the specter of androgyny, which the text certainly does not support. Once again, however, the charges are easy to make, yet not quite fair.

First, even the NIV's translation, "brothers in every way," must be read in its context. This does not mean that Jesus must be like each "brother" in every conceivable way—as short as all of them, as tall as all of them, as old or young as all of them, as married or unmarried as all of them, as heterosexual or homosexual as all of them, and so forth. The context imposes a couple of strong foci. Already verse 14 states, "Since the children [mentioned in the previous verse] have flesh and blood, he too shared in their humanity so that by his death he might destroy him who holds the power of death." In other words, Jesus must become thoroughly human; he must take on "flesh and blood" and in that sense be "like his brothers in every way." But if the focus is on *being human,* then for Jesus to become "like his brothers and sisters in every way" is not contextually misleading. The second constraint is found in verse 16. There we are told that "it is not angels he helps, but Abraham's descendants." It is surely a cause for wonder and praise that there has arisen a Redeemer for fallen human beings, though not for fallen angels. But now the human focus becomes narrowed by the historical context of Jesus' incarnation: he did not become a generic human being, but a descendant of Abraham. The purpose of his coming was that "he might become a merciful and faithful high priest in service to God, and that he might make atonement for the sins of the people" (2:17)—which surely shows that his identification is with "the people," and not only with males (unless we are prepared to argue that only the males had atonement made for them?).

Second, all sides recognize now, I think, that sometimes Greek *adelphoi* can refer to a crowd of both men and women, making the rendering "brothers and sisters" *in some contexts* admissible, especially if being read by some who think that "brothers" automatically excludes women. But despite the connections with all of humanity, and then with all of the Jewish race (and not males only) that the context affords, it remains true that Jewish high priests were invariably men. The TNIV expression does not deny that point, of course, but it does not clarify it either. Jesus is not like a Jewish high priest in *every* respect, anyway—this epistle will go on to show many parallels between Jesus and Jewish high priests (e.g., 8:3) but also quite a few differences. The point here is not that Jesus is like a Jewish high priest "in every way" but that he is like those he comes to redeem "in every way." Still, the TNIV is vaguely awkward—though whether that awkwardness is worse than the awkwardness felt by those for whom "brothers" is a restrictive expression may be debated.

Third, in any case the charge that the TNIV text says Jesus is "made like his . . . sisters in every way," opening up the possibility of androgyny, is inept. The dots of the ellipsis are important, because the expression "brothers and sisters" is a unified pair that must be taken together, like "flesh and blood." Verse 14 should not be rendered, "Since the children have . . . blood, he too shared in their humanity"—for it is the *paired* expression "flesh and blood" that indicates humanness.

Other passages have been highlighted by Poythress and Grudem and by journalists who have followed them, but they are, quite frankly, no more convincing than these. I am not always persuaded that the TNIV has taken the best option. But that is rather different from saying that the TNIV is theologically compromised.[60]

There is an array of other matters that could be raised. Most of them have little to do with translation theory in general or functional equivalence in particular, so I must not pause long to explore them here. Still, I am uncertain why such animus has been raised against the NIV/TNIV, and not against, say, the

TEV, NLT, and a host of other Bible versions. *World* magazine has invested a lot of polemic in critical comments about the money that is involved in the NIV and TNIV—but this is true, of course, of all Bible publishers, and even of the publishers of *World,* who doubtless sell more copies when a debate heats up.[61] Would it not be good to recognize that there are people of good will on both sides of this debate? Both sides are trying to be true to Scripture, and to make their understandings known; and both make money in the process.[62]

Since I wrote my little essay on the limits of dynamic equivalence a couple of decades ago, these, then, are the three changes that have taken place in the climate of discussion—the continuing development and maturation of translation theory,[63] the linguistically conservative stances being adopted in some quarters, and the rising tide of agenda-driven responses to even the most confessionally faithful inclusive-language translations.

The first of these three developments means that some of my early articulation of the limitations of functional equivalence is now less urgent, since the best-informed translators have matured in various ways. The second and third developments adopt stances that are so critical of functional equivalence that their adherents will think that what I have written in the past is, if anything, too mild. But that is why I have thought it necessary to review some of the limitations on more direct translation in the first part of this essay. Too many of the linguistic conservatives can detect problems with functional equivalence (both real and imagined) but cannot detect problems with more direct translation. The changed climate means that such limitations have to be spelled out so that the strengths of functional equivalence are understood, at least in measure, before some of the limitations of the theory are reviewed. But now it is high time to turn to the latter.

The Limits of Functional Equivalence in Bible Translation

For the vast majority of people actually engaged in Bible translation, the importance of functional equivalence is a given—and rightly so. Its victory is hailed by numerous pieces of evidence. There is widespread recognition of the inadequacy of merely formal equivalence in translation, buttressed by thousands and thousands of examples. Undergirding such recognition is the awareness that expressions such as "literal translation" and "paraphrase" are steeped in ambiguity and, in any case, belong, not in mutually exclusive categories, but on the same spectrum:[64] A "too literal" translation can be as bad as a "too paraphrastic" translation, if for different reasons. Few translators of any competence would today deny such fundamental priorities as the following:

1. Contextual consistency has priority over verbal consistency (or word-for-word concordance).
2. Dynamic equivalence has priority over formal correspondence.
3. The aural (heard) form of language has priority over the written form.
4. Forms that are used by and acceptable to the audience for which a translation is intended have priority over forms that may be traditionally more prestigious.[65]

Functional equivalence displays its triumph in the publishing houses—in the continuing parade of helps,[66] front-rank research,[67] manuals of problems,[68] reflective textbooks,[69] assorted popularizations,[70]and sane assessments of recent translations.[71] Missiologists are now comfortable with classifications of languages based not on their roots (e.g., Indo-European, Semitic) but on their use (or nonuse) in literature and education (primary, secondary, tertiary, quaternary), and they have become sensitive to the differences between translating the Bible in an "overlap language" (one in which the colloquial and the literary forms of the language overlap significantly, e.g., English) and translating the Bible almost exclusively at a literary level (e.g., Arabic).[72] As they have been sensitized to the kinds of readers, so they sympathize with the very different linguistic needs of diverse readers within any particular language or dialect. There is a new appreciation for the work of the receptor-language stylist in the translation process;[73] and in the best seminaries, lecturers in Greek and Hebrew take extra pains to convey a literary feel for the biblical languages and to introduce the rudiments of discourse analysis and aspect theory, no less than the rudiments of the grammar produced in the rationalistic period. Even unreconstructed grammarians such as myself, thoroughly convinced that a profound and growing knowledge of the source languages is a great desideratum in Bible translation, are no less concerned to expose their students to the elements of modern linguistic theory and practice. At least in part, all of this has come about because functional equivalence, rightly understood, is essential for good translation. Only the linguistically incompetent would argue today that the translator needs facility in the languages with which he or she is working but not an understanding of the content of the text. At its best, functional equivalence, far from jeopardizing good translations, is essential for fidelity in translation—fidelity in conveying not only meaning but also tone, emotional impact, naturalness/awkwardness, and much more.[74]

Inevitably, some have abused "dynamic equivalence" and "functional equivalence" to justify poor translations, or even to justify entire theological agendas. I hasten to add that the most careful scholars in this field do not err in such ways. What is still one of the finest books in the area—*The Theory and Practice of Translation* by Eugene Nida and Charles Taber—abounds in wise and sensitive caveats. For example, translators are carefully warned against trying to get behind the biblical writers, or ahead of them,[75] and are cautioned not to confuse linguistic translation with "cultural translation," transforming the Pharisees and Sadducees, for instance, into present-day religious parties.[76] In other words, the historical particularity of the text must be respected.

Sadly, though, similar care is not shown by all. The caveats and restrictions that protect a responsible use of functional equivalence and make it such a useful way of thinking about translation are sometimes overlooked or abandoned. This route has become easier to follow, as professional missiologists have come to think of contextualization in highly diverse ways[77] and as the theoretical developments that have fed into postmodern epistemology generate their own pressures on translators and their art. Such developments are so complex I dare not broach them here, except tangentially. But it may be useful to offer a number of reflections on functional equivalence and related matters, reflections that may help translators avoid the pitfalls inherent in some of these developments.

Limits on the Equivalence of Response

The most common descriptions of functional equivalence, and certainly all the early descriptions of dynamic equivalence, as insightful as they are, laid so much stress on the equivalence of response that they invited abuse. For example, in the classic treatment, Eugene Nida describes dynamic equivalence translation as the "closest natural equivalent to the source-language message" and insists it is "directed primarily toward equivalence of response rather than equivalence of form."[78] Elsewhere he writes the following:

> Dynamic equivalence is therefore to be defined in terms of the degree to which the receptors of the message in the receptor language respond to it in substantially the same manner as the receptors in the source language. This response can never be identical, for the cultural and historical settings are too different, but there should be a high degree of equivalence of response, or the translation will have failed to accomplish its purpose.[79]

Or as Norm Mundhenk remarks, "In the final analysis, a translation is good or bad, right or wrong, in terms of how the reader understands and reacts."[80]

I have no quarrel with these quotations, all three of which stress equivalence of response, *as long as they are referring to linguistic priorities alone.* Clearly, a translation is poor if by preserving formal equivalence in word order or syntactical construction or the like it obscures the meaning of the original text or transmutes it into something quite different or remains completely opaque to those whose tongue is the receptor language. Moreover, selecting appropriate linguistic priorities requires a sensitive knowledge of the receptor culture, since there may be cultural associations between linguistic constructions and cultural values such that an entirely false impression is conveyed by a more direct translation—false, that is to say, as measured by what was originally conveyed. "Blessed is the man who does not ... stand in the way of sinners" (Ps 1:1 NIV) is a shockingly poor rendering of the Hebrew, because to stand in someone's way in English means "to hinder someone," whereas the thought in Hebrew is "to walk in someone's footsteps," "to walk in someone's moccasins," or, less metaphorically, "to adopt someone else's lifestyle and values and habits." There are far more difficult cases discussed in the standard texts; and, as pursued by those with genuine expertise, functional equivalence in such cases is surely an eminently worthwhile goal that no one competent in two or more languages would wish to gainsay.

Nevertheless, the emphasis on equivalence of reception is open to abuse. If translators begin to think that what is referred to lies at the level of the receptor's epistemology, then of course it is impossible to measure. Moreover, the passion to communicate well may begin to overlook *what* is being communicated, for we have already seen that there are several goals the translator must bear in mind, including both accuracy and comprehensibility. To focus all one's attention on the former (understood in the fashion of the most "direct" translation theories) at the expense of the latter is no virtue; to focus all one's attention on the latter at the expense of the former is betrayal.[81]

There are several other ways in which the emphasis on equivalence of response is open to abuse. Perhaps it is best to provide illustrations of several kinds of abuse. To focus discussion, I shall draw them from the writings of well-known linguist, anthropologist, and missiologist Charles Kraft.

Kraft argues that the "response" element of functional equivalence may usefully be extended somewhat further to take into account the peculiar social location of the receptor culture. At the extreme, the resulting "versions" may be called "transculturations" (to use the language of Kraft).[82] He writes, "In a translation it is inappropriate to give the impression that Jesus walked the streets of

Berkeley or London or Nairobi. But a transculturation, in order to reach its target audience more effectively, may do exactly that."[83] These transculturations "dare to be *specific to their audiences and free to be true to God's imperative to communicate rather than simply to impress.* In this they demonstrate the deep concern of their authors for the total communicational situation, not simply for one or another aspect of it."[84] Kraft then goes on to suggest (as he does elsewhere) that those who disagree with his diagnosis and who react negatively against "proper transculturation" are the modern equivalents of the "orthodox" retainers of the old cultural forms against whom Jesus "waged a running battle for culturally relevant transculturation," or of the "orthodox" Judaizers of Acts 15.[85]

These assessments raise a host of issues. A glimpse of them may be afforded by a series of questions:

- Did Jesus primarily or even marginally set himself against the Jewish religious leaders of his day out of concern for the transculturation of an *agreed* message, or out of a fundamental break with his opponents' understanding of Scripture? How much of his disagreement stemmed from their failure to perceive the new developments on the salvation-historical plane—his claims to fulfill Old Testament expectations concerning the coming of the Messiah?
- How valid is the constant disjunction Kraft raises between his own approach to "dynamic-equivalence transculturation" and a kind of incompetent fixation on mere content devoid of desire and/or ability to communicate? Is the disjunction essentially fair, or does it approach caricature?
- To what extent do the questions that Kraft insists on putting to the biblical text—and making the biblical text answer in his terms—domesticate the text so that the message of the text is essentially lost? To what extent must interpreters allow the text, progressively, to raise the right sort of questions—questions it is prepared to answer in its own terms?

More broadly: When we say that we aim to generate the same response in the readers of the receptor language as in the readers of the source language, what do we mean? Suppose the readers of the original New Testament documents were largely alienated by the truth of what, say, Paul, wrote. Should we aim to reproduce similar alienation today in order to preserve "equivalence of response"? What does "equivalence of response" mean when we compare the response of urban, secularized, twenty-first-century readers of Leviticus or Romans and the response of their respective first readers or hearers? Is it not better, if we are going to define functional equivalence in terms of equivalent response, to understand equivalence in linguistic categories, i.e., in terms of the removal of as many as possible of the false linguistic barriers (along with the associations each linguistic category carries) that actually impede the communication of the content of the text?

Each of these questions could easily generate its own paper, and one or two of them will reemerge in subsequent points. It is clear, however, that the hidden fallacy against which many of these questions are directed is the unwitting assumption that "response" is the *ultimate* category in translation. Strictly speaking, this is not true; theologically speaking, it is unwise; evangelistically speaking, it is uncontrolled, not to say dangerous. Of course, the concerns Kraft is feeling are real ones that constantly need addressing. Nevertheless my criticism is fundamental: his solution, the elevation of response above truth, fails precisely in the areas where it claims to be strong, for the response is *not* rendered equivalent by such means as he advances. The aim of a good translation is to convey the total content, or as much of it as possible in roughly equivalent compass—informational, emotional, connotational, etc.—of the original message to the reader (or hearer, where the translation is publicly read) in the receptor language.

In the same ways, to speak of "dynamic-equivalence theologizing"[86] and "dynamic-equivalence churches"[87] is misleading and even dangerous, because the categories are not linguistic. Once again, the concerns behind these labels are real. For example, biblically faulty and/or culturally myopic ecclesiastical structures may be imposed on a mission church as though the entire blueprint were handed down from heaven, complete with robes for the choir and Roberts' Rules of Order.

Nevertheless, all such evils are better addressed without talking of "dynamic-equivalence churches" for at least a couple of reasons: First, as the expression is used by its inventor, social custom becomes so controlling that the Scriptures are not permitted to reform society. Kraft appeals to the Kru of Liberia who state, "You cannot trust a man with only one wife,"[88] concluding that Kru church leadership need not be monogamous, despite the strictures of Paul (and Jesus!) on this point. Kraft thinks that eventually polygamy would likely die out among the Kru, "just as, through God's interaction with the Hebrews, polygamy died out in Hebrew culture—over the course of a few thousand years."[89] Until then, polygamy should be tolerated. There seem to be, from Kraft's treatment, few things the Bible clearly demands of church structure—or even of morals—that could not be jettisoned in favor of "dynamic-equivalence churches." Second, and more important, the extension of the expression "dynamic equivalence" (or the more recent "functional equivalence") to areas far removed not only from linguistic priorities but also from translation itself reflects back on problems of translation and muddies otherwise clear distinctions. In Kraft's hands, all the emphasis is on "dynamic"; the "equivalence" has pretty well dissolved. Applied to translation, almost any distance from the source text could be justified.

Limits on the Dichotomy between Meaning and Message

Whereas dynamic equivalence and functional equivalence started out belonging to the realm of translation and were set in opposition to various kinds of linguistic formalism, the extension of their use to far broader issues has been facilitated on the one hand by a variety of faddish theoretical constructs that do not stand up to rigorous scholarship but are cited with ill-deserved authority as though the subjects with which they deal were closed—e.g., the Sapir-Whorf hypothesis,[90] the new hermeneutic,[91] and some communication theory—and on the other hand by the epistemological relativism endemic to postmodernism. The Sapir-Whorf hypothesis, in its crudest form, makes human beings the determined captives of their language, and their language becomes a guide to their "social reality."[92] In its extreme form, the new hermeneutic calls into question the possibility of objective knowledge as text and interpreter progressively "interpret" one another, round and round without *terminus,* lost in profound relativity. Some forms of communication theory, conjoined with structuralism, insist that there is a rigid dichotomy between meaning and message. And the various strands that have fed into postmodern epistemology conspire to convince many contemporaries that knowledge of objective truth is not possible for finite human beings, and this opens the door to individually determined or communally determined "meaning" whose distance from a theoretical "objective" content of a text is as impossible to calculate as the "objective" content is to know.[93]

All four of these notions lie not far from the surface of the following quotation (whether or not the author intended to make the connections):

> Contemporary understandings contend that a major difference between messages and meanings lies in the fact that messages can be transmitted in linguistic form while meanings exist only in the hearts and minds of people. Contemporary communiologists [sic] see communicators with meanings in their minds that they would like to transmit to receptors. Communicators take these meanings and formulate them, usually in linguistic form, into messages which they then transmit to receptors. Receptors then, listen to the messages and construct within their minds sets of meanings that may or may not correspond with the meanings intended by the communicator.

> Meanings, therefore, do not pass from me to you, only messages. The meanings exist only within me or within you.... The messages, then, serve as stimulators rather than as containers. Receptors, in response to the stimulus of messages, construct meanings that may or may not correspond to what the communicator intended.[94]

There is considerable insight here, of course. No finite knower ever understands anything substantial *exactly* as some other finite knower understands it, and the point needs reiterating from time to time. Each person is finite in understanding, and the potential for misunderstanding increases when the message is translated. Communicators do not always say exactly what they mean, and the best communicators will try to encourage the feedback necessary to discover whether their meaning has been absorbed by the receptors, at least to some substantial degree.

Nevertheless, the above quotation puts the case far too disjunctively. Doubtless *some* contemporary understandings contend that there is "a major difference between messages and meanings," but others, while recognizing that any individual communication may be imperfectly grasped, insist that the message/meaning disjunction, taken absolutely, is one form of the intentional fallacy; that human beings cannot entertain in their own minds complex meanings without propositions, and that therefore meaning and message, though not identical, cannot be divided absolutely; that the commonality of our creaturehood in the image of God makes verbal communication less problematic than some think; that even participant knowledge can be verbalized among those who share common participant experience (whether sex or knowing God); that individuals can in measure "distantiate" themselves from their own "horizon of understanding" and "fuse" their horizon with that of the communicator in order to assure *true* understanding of the message, even though it may not be *exhaustive* understanding; that meanings can and do pass from one person to the other (as judged by the ways many authors are upset when they think that reviewers have not understood what they have said and have misrepresented it); that messages are neither mere stimulators nor mere communicators, but the very stuff of the meaning, insofar as the two individuals share semantic ranges and the like and insofar as the communicators say what they mean.

As virtually always in the arguments of postmoderns, the passage presupposes that *either* one person can understand the meaning of another person exhaustively, omnisciently as it were, *or* one is forced to the sorts of disjunctions introduced here between meaning and message. If this antithesis is accepted, the postmodernist invariably wins, since it can always be shown that no finite human being can ever know the thoughts or meanings of another finite human being perfectly, exhaustively, omnisciently. But the antithesis is, of course, a false one. One may know something *truly* without knowing it *exhaustively;* I may understand a great deal of the meanings of, say, Paul, without knowing Paul's thought—even his recorded thought—exhaustively or perfectly. In other words, the *absolute* disjunction between meaning and message has in fact bought into an epistemological framework that thoughtful Christians will avoid. To seek to justify "dynamic-equivalence theologizing" on such doubtful epistemological premises is unsafe. In any case, such discussions, as important as they are, have removed dynamic equivalence and functional equivalence so far from the linguistic domain that more confusion than clarity has been added.

Limits on the Equivalence between Biblical History and Contemporary History

Functional equivalence must not be permitted to override the historical particularity of the Bible. There is a sense in which any text is historically conditioned, of course, in that it was written in a certain language at a certain time by a certain individual (whether or not that individual's identity is known). But the accurate understanding (and therefore accurate translation) of some literary forms depends rather more acutely on recognizing their historical particularity than is the case for some other literary forms.

Even in the case of proverbs and aphorisms, which are among the most timeless of literary genres, some will prove more easily translatable than others. "Do you see a man wise in his own eyes? There is more hope for a fool than for him" (Prov 26:12) is likely to be coherent in most languages; "better to live on a corner of the roof than share a house with a quarrelsome wife" (Prov 25:24) presupposes flat roofs frequented by humans, not snow-shedding sloped roofs never visited except to replace a gutter or a satellite dish. Still, it does not take a huge amount of explanation to render coherent the flat roof, whether to a mud-hut dweller in an equatorial jungle or to a high-rise apartment dweller in an urban jungle, and the preservation of the form, though not in this instance theologically urgent, has the advantage of reminding the reader that all of these things took place in a foreign land, a specific culture, and an historical time and place.

The challenges become more difficult when we leave aphorism for narrative. The problems of equivalence can be grouped under the headings (1) ecology, (2) material culture, (3) social culture, (4) religious culture, and (5) linguistic culture.[95] The problems are highly diverse, and there is no simple way to categorize the possible solutions. An Eskimo tribe reads a Bible that speaks of desert and lions; a Mexican tribe in Yucatan has never experienced the four seasons typical of temperate zones (cf. Mark 13:28). If we follow TEV's "police" or NEB's "constable" in Matthew 5:25, are we not unwittingly fostering, for many Westerners, images of a gun-toting officer in a squad car or of an English bobby? Perhaps these cases do not matter; perhaps "police" is acceptable. But many cases have stings in the tail. If, for instance, we replace "recline at food" or "recline at table" with "sit down to eat," we are going to have a tough job imagining how John managed to get his head on Jesus' breast—Leonardo da Vinci notwithstanding. Preservation of descriptions of what is to us an alien custom, reclining at tables, makes it possible to understand a later action, in this case John placing his head on Jesus' breast.

I am not now dealing with such obvious and domesticating distortions as "this is the essence of all true religion" (Matt 7:12 PHILLIPS) for "this sums up the Law and the Prophets" (NIV), or "then a diabolical plan came into the mind of Judas" (Luke 22:3 PHILLIPS) for "Then Satan entered Judas" (NIV). Rather, what is of interest at this juncture is that God has revealed himself to people in time-space history—to particular men and women, spatially and temporally and linguistically located. If we are not very cautious about the way we treat the historical particulars, we may introduce such substantive anachronisms that the story becomes intrinsically unbelievable—the more so as the receptor people grow in understanding and historical awareness. And certainly we lose the enormous theological implications of the truth that, according to Scripture, the personal-transcendent God has disclosed himself in real history.

There are ways of overcoming the obscurity intrinsic in references to customs and experiences unknown on receptor soil. Footnotes may be part of the answer (see discussion below); teachers are certainly part of it. But always we must at least ask how much we are losing when we remove too many indicators of historical and cultural "distance." How such problems are resolved may depend to some extent on the literary stage of development of the receptor group, but even if the group is coming across the printed page for the first time and enjoys virtually no comprehension of cultures other than their own, it must be remembered that this receptor group will likely use this new translation of the Bible for decades to come, maybe for a century or two. During all of that time, an increasing number of this receptor people will be exposed to new cultures and education. How well will the Bible translation serve them then? Christianity is a religion whose roots are deeply embedded in the particularities of history, and our translations must not obscure that fact.

LIMITS ON THE DISTORTION (WITTING OR UNWITTING) OF SALVATION HISTORY

An extension of the third point brings us to a fresh observation. Functional equivalence must not be permitted to mask the development of and internal relations within salvation history. Suppose, for instance, that a tribe has a long tradition of sacrificing pigs but has never so much as heard of sheep. Is it in that case justifiable to render John 1:29, "Look, the swine of God, who takes away the sin of the world!"? I would argue strongly for the negative, not only because of the importance of historical particularity, the importance of which was defended in the previous point, but because of the plethora of rich allusions preserved in Scripture across the sweep of salvation history.

In what sense could it be said that Jesus "fulfills" the Old Testament sacrificial system if that system typically sacrificed lambs at Passover, all the while proclaiming that pigs are ceremonially unclean, whereas Jesus is portrayed in John 1:29 as a swine? How then will John 1:29 relate to Isaiah 52:13–53:12, the fourth servant song, or to images of the warrior lamb in the Apocalypse (e.g., Rev 5:6)? Shall we change *all* such references to pigs ("We all, like swine, have gone astray . . .")? And if so, do we then make the biblical "pig references" clean, and designate some other animal unclean? No; it is surely simpler and more faithful to preserve "lamb" in the first instance. If this involves inventing a new word in a receptor language whose users have never heard of "sheep," so be it. A brief note could explain that the word refers to an animal frequently sacrificed by the people of the Bible, along with a succinct description of its relevant characteristics.

There is a second way in which appeal to functional equivalence must not be permitted to mask the development and internal relations of salvation history. We have witnessed a negative example in Charles Kraft's appeal to polygamy under the old covenant. What Kraft never struggles with is the nature of the continuity/discontinuity pattern when moving from the old covenant to the new. One can no more make legitimate appeal to the Old Testament to support polygamy among Christian leaders in Africa than one can appeal to the Old Testament to defend continued Christian maintenance of all dietary laws. The fact that Christians disagree over certain elements of the continuity/discontinuity pattern is no justification for the failure to wrestle with the issue when dealing with something as sensitive in parts of Africa as is polygamy. In any case, my point is more general: One cannot hide behind "functional equivalence" to justify the obliteration of salvation-historical distinctions that are fundamental to the most elementary understanding of the Bible as a cohesive document.

Limits on the Pursuit of Comprehensibility

One of the entirely salutary emphases of functional equivalence is its passion to make the Bible as comprehensible in translation as possible. But sometimes that entirely worthy goal can lose sight of the fact that some passages in the Bible *are* obscure. One recalls the shrewd remark of Bishop Stephen Neill: "I remember once exploding angrily in the Tamil Bible translation committee, when we had so smoothed out the complex passage Galatians 2:1–10 as to conceal completely the tensions and confusions which underlie the apostle's twisted grammar. This we had no right to do."[96]

In other words, faithfulness to the text should compel us to try to avoid making the translation a great deal easier to understand (in the receptor language) than the original is to readers of the source language.

Limits on the Authority of Stylists and Other Receptor-Language Specialists

In the light of the argument so far, I am inclined, somewhat hesitantly, to call into question the judgment of Eugene Nida and others, who argue that good exegetes and grammarians make poor translators.[97] Increasingly, they argue that translation projects should begin with stylists who enjoy some marginal knowledge of Greek and Hebrew but who are thoroughly competent in the receptor language, and then permit the specialists their say only at the cleaning-up stage.

Quite clearly, the gifts and training of the stylists, or, more broadly, of the receptor-language specialists, are vital. But I wonder if grammarians and exegetes are dismissed too rapidly. Most field translators for such organizations as Wycliffe Bible Translators (or SIL) and the American Bible Society have one theological degree, perhaps two—i.e., two or three years (i.e., four to six semester courses) of Greek and perhaps half that of Hebrew (or no Hebrew at all). Their problem, it may be, is not that they have too much Greek to be good translators, but too little. I would go further and suggest that even many teachers of Greek and Hebrew in colleges, seminaries, and universities do not enjoy much facility in the language they are teaching. These are precisely the kinds of people who are least likely to be sensitive to the demands of functional equivalence. How often, for example, have I taken second-year Greek students aside and explained at length how rarely a Greek participle should be rendered by an English participle, how many of the Greek connectives must find no formal equivalent in a specific English word but survive in the flow of the English sentence, and so forth. And I have learned that it is my *best* students in advanced exegesis and advanced grammar courses who learn such flexibility most thoroughly. To be good translators, they would benefit from further study in linguistics, sociolinguistics, and literary style; but at a guess, advanced competence in the source languages will not prove a hindrance but a strength in most cases, *provided the teacher is aware* of the linguistic complexities and subtleties that surround translation. It is the student of Greek and Hebrew who has a mechanical view of language who will have most difficulty grasping these elementary points and who in the name of fidelity will defend more "direct" translations, even when the result is largely incomprehensible to the target readers and hearers.

One of the reasons I have suggested this alternative—that front-rank Bible translators need a good deal *more* training in Greek and Hebrew, not less—is to combat the drift in many academic circles toward less training in the source languages and toward so great a flexibility in translation that, as we have seen, "communication" becomes an ideal abstracted from the message to be communicated. New voices loudly insist there is an impregnable wedge between the meaning of the source and the meaning of the receptor. To provide at least some safeguards, we must encourage translators to pursue studies not only in linguistics and style but also in the languages, history, culture, symbolism, genre, and theology of the biblical documents. Only then is it possible to "fuse horizons" with high reliability and counteract the growing tide of relativism and arbitrariness.

Limits on Our Expectations of What the Bible by Itself Will Usually Achieve

This way of making the point must not be misunderstood. It is certainly not a demand that limits be placed on the Bible's truthfulness, authority, and so forth. We have all heard stories of people who have simply read the Bible and been wonderfully converted. I know of one fascinating conversion brought about when the person in question, a Muslim student studying in the West, stole a Gideon Bible from a hotel nightstand, read it through, and was converted. In the hands of God, the Bible is a powerful book.

Yet sometimes translators give the impression that doing their job right is all that is needed. Although functional equivalence is an important—indeed, essential—component of good translation, we should tone down our claims for what it can achieve. Precisely because functional equivalence is so often described in terms of equivalent response, we are in danger of giving the impression that, provided we get our translations right, we can practically guarantee a massive turning to Christ, revisiting Acts 2, perhaps (even if no one is so gauche as to put it that way). But this means we have no place for an Ethiopian eunuch who needed an explanation of a grammatically clear text (Acts 8:26–40), no place for the hardness of the human heart (1 Cor 2:14), no place for the work of the Holy Spirit, no reflection on the diversity of worldviews that various readers bring to the text and therefore the diversity of faithful responses needed to confront these worldviews (compare the sermons of Acts 13 and Acts 17).[98] The Scriptures themselves encourage us to multiply the number of evangelists, pastor/teachers, and other workers, thereby discouraging the notion that the *entire* task depends exclusively on the quality of the Bible translation used. This is not to justify obscure translations on the basis of, say, total depravity: If people do not understand the Word of God, it is said, it is not because we retain the Elizabethan English of the KJV, but because their hearts are hard. The element of truth in the claim is that, even with the most contemporary and most readable translations, conversion is finally a function of the work of the Spirit. Nevertheless, the Spirit uses means, and appeal to the work of the Spirit does not justify our preference for traditional formulae and archaic language if we claim to be witnesses to *this* generation and the *next* generation. But having again established these checks and balances, in our defense of functional equivalence we should, especially at the popular level, curb our exuberance, lest we jeopardize our credibility by the extravagance of our claims. The proper use of functional-equivalence translations decreases the likelihood of misunderstanding arising from poor translation, but it is not a universal spiritual panacea.

Limits on the Use of Study Notes

At several points in this essay I have suggested that it is better in many cases to preserve the historical distance of the original text and provide an explanatory note than to make the "translation" so contemporary that the historical particularity is lost. This raises the question of the place of study notes and study Bibles. For there are converse dangers. It is possible to deploy so many "direct" translations that a great number of notes are required to make the text understandable to those with a good working knowledge of the receptor language but with no knowledge whatsoever of the source language. Eugene Nida and Charles Taber offer several wise observations in this regard, the best of which, perhaps, is their judgment that "it is best at least to make sense in the text and put the scholarly caution in the margin, rather than to make nonsense in the text and offer the excuse in the margin."[99]

But my purpose here is to offer a further caution. Because I do not think that, by and large, functional equivalence should override the distancing that stems both from historical particularism and from the history of redemption (however much it may demand transformed linguistic structures), I favor a fairly liberal use of notes explaining cultural, religious, ecological, and linguistic points, especially in Bibles designed for groups made up largely of first readers who thus have very little knowledge of the biblical world. But great pains should be taken to make such notes as theologically neutral and objective as possible. Theological notes, hortatory comments, notes explaining the theological flow, homiletical hints—in my view all such things should be relegated to separate books.

I recognize that I am out of step with current publishing practices when I write this. The impetus for the judgment is both theoretical and experiential. At the theoretical level, surely it is desirable to avoid giving the impression that the authority of the notes has the authority of Scripture itself—a confusion easy to fall into when both are printed on the same page. Experientially, I learned some lessons from my boyhood in Quebec. At the time, if Roman Catholics read the Bible at all, they had to read a Bible approved by the Roman Catholic Church, one with approved notes (such as the Léger version of the New Testament). I witnessed firsthand how such notes could reinforce the theological biases of people such that it was hard for readers to listen to what the text was actually saying. Even when theoretical allowance is made for the distinction between text and note, the constant rereading of both on the same page blurs this distinction and shapes the theological convictions of many readers.

What applies to the Léger version applies, *mutatis mutandis,* to the New Scofield Reference Bible, the Ryrie Study Bible, and a dozen others.[100] A few years ago I was asked to assume a major role in producing a new study Bible. Consistency demanded that I decline. It is better, I think, to reserve such study helps and comments (which are, in fact, sorely needed) to separate publications.

It would be good to avoid transmitting our mistakes in this area to places where Bibles are appearing in new languages for the first time. Equally, it would be salutary to remember that the God of the Bible ordained that there be evangelists and teachers in the church. Translation of the Scriptures is not the only thing needed for adequate communication of the gospel. God has equally mandated the training and deployment of evangelists and pastor/teachers. Failure to account for this aspect of our task may unwittingly encourage a "translation" that is to some degree a perceived *replacement* of human agents or, worse, a mere crib for those with little more than a smattering of the original languages.

Having said this, however, a fairly liberal use of notes that are as theologically neutral as possible—notes that focus on historical, linguistic, and cultural matters—may not only prove to be a good thing but may also remove some of the pressure to de-historicize biblical texts.

In short, there are limits to be imposed on any Pollyannaish enthusiasm for unconstrained functional equivalence—just as there are limits to be imposed on the dour warnings of linguistic conservatives.

Notes

1. D. A. Carson, "The Limits of Dynamic Equivalence in Bible Translation," *Evangelical Review of Theology* 9 (1985): 200–213.

2. See, for example, *Notes on Translation* 121 (October 1987): 1–15.

3. Some further refinements along the same line found their place in my essay celebrating the 175th anniversary of the American Bible Society: "New Bible Translations: An Assessment and Prospect," in *The Bible in the Twenty-First Century,* ed. Howard Clark Kee (New York: American Bible Society, 1993), 37–67.

4. Eugene A. Nida and Charles R. Taber, *The Theory and Practice of Translation* (Leiden: Brill, 1974).

5. Jan de Waard and Eugene A. Nida, *From One Language to Another: Functional Equivalence in Bible Translating* (Nashville: Nelson, 1986).

6. See, for example, Peter Trudgill, *Sociolinguistics: An Introduction to Language and Society,* 2d ed. (London: Penguin, 1983); Johannes P. Louw, ed., *Sociolinguistics and Communication,* UBS Monograph Series 1 (London: United Bible Societies, 1986). For easy access to the subject, see M. Paul Lewis, "Of Sociolinguistics, Bible Translation, and Dancing," *Notes on Translation* 15, no. 2 (2001): 55–61.

7. See especially Ernst-August Gutt, *Translation and Relevance: Cognition and Context* (Oxford: Basil Blackwell, 1991).

8. See, among other things, Robert-Alain de Beaugrande and Wolfgang Dressler, *Introduction to Text Linguistics* (Longman Linguistics Library; New York: Longman, 1981); E. A. Nida, J. P. Louw, A. H. Snyman, and J. v. W. Cronje, eds., *Style and Discourse: With Special Reference to the Text of the Greek New Testament* (Cape Town: Bible Society, 1983); and, worked out in a study of a concrete biblical text, see George H. Guthrie, *The Structure of Hebrews: A Text-Linguistic Analysis* (Leiden: Brill, 1994).

9. One thinks of the considerable advances, for instance, in semantics, phonemics, aspect theory, functional syntax, lexicography, and the like.

10. Well illustrated, though overdone, by John A. Beck, *Translators as Storytellers: A Study in Septuagint Translation Technique* (New York: Peter Lang, 2000).

11. Extraordinarily helpful is the reference work of Mona Baker, ed., assisted by Kirsten Malmkjær, *Routledge Encyclopedia of Translation Studies* (London and New York: Routledge, 1998). One of the best places to find up-to-date bibliography is in *T-I-C Talk,* the newsletter of the United Bible Societies Translation Information Clearinghouse, available both in hard copy and on the Web at http://www.ubs-translations.org.

12. See, for example, the important work by Eugene A. Nida and William D. Reyburn, *Meaning Across Cultures* (Maryknoll, N.Y.: Orbis, 1981).

13. As a fine example, see the book by Robert L. Thomas, *How to Choose a Bible Translation: Making Sense of the Proliferation of Bible Translations* (Fearn, Scotland: Mentor, 2000).

14. Raymond C. Van Leeuwen, "We Really *Do* Need Another Bible Translation," *Christianity Today* 45, no. 13 (22 October 2001): 28–35.

15. I say "ostensibly" because, gender questions aside, the NRSV tends to belong to the more "direct" end of the translation spectrum.

16. Van Leeuwen, "We Really *Do* Need," 33.

17. Ibid., 30.

18. Seamus Heaney, trans., *Beowulf: A New Verse Translation* (New York: Farrar, Straus and Giroux, 2000).

19. Cf. T. David Anderson, "Perceived Authenticity: The Fourth Criterion of Good Translation," *Notes on Translation* 12, no. 3 (1998): 1–13. Iver Larsen, "The Fourth Criterion of a Good Translation," *Notes on Translation* 15, no. 1 (2001): 40–53, prefers the term "acceptability," but on the whole I prefer the older expression.

20. Van Leeuwen, "We Really *Do* Need," 32.

21. Ibid., 32–33.

22. Ibid., 30.

23. Quite correctly, Van Leeuwen points out that the word *man* in its second occurrence in this quotation is merely presupposed in the original by the context. The KJV italicized all such words—a practice rightly dropped by modern translations.

24. Van Leeuwen, "We Really *Do* Need," 30.

25. Ibid., 31.

26. Ibid.

27. Ibid.

28. Tony Payne, "Is this the English Bible we've been waiting for?" *The Briefing* 278 (November 2001): 13–15; idem, "FAQs on the ESV," *The Briefing* 283 (April 2002): 23–24.

29. This is why teachers of beginning Greek often give their students the Gospel of John to read. Like English, it deploys much more parataxis and fewer long sentences than the more stylistic Greek of Paul (let alone the Greek of Hebrews and Luke-Acts!).

30. Stephanie L. Black, *Sentence Conjunctions in the Gospel of Matthew: kai, de, tote, gar, oun and Asyndeton in Narrative Discourse,* JSNTSup 216 (Sheffield: Sheffield Academic Press, 2002). Her careful compilations are worth the price of the book; her analysis is superb. Not least important is her demonstration that in Matthew the sentence conjunctions function as "multiple-purpose tools with low semantic content" (p. 332; she is quoting the words of S. C. Dik, *Coordination: Its Implications for the Theory of General Linguistics* [Amsterdam: North-Holland Publishing Company, 1972], 269). There follows a summary of the contribution made by each conjunction.

31. There is also an interesting textual variant here that serves to draw attention to the rare (for Paul) *te*. I am indebted to Peter T. O'Brien for drawing my attention to this passage.

32. Payne, "Is this," 14.

33. On these and related problems, see chapter 3 of my book *The Inclusive-Language Debate: A Plea for Realism* (Grand Rapids: Baker, 1998).

34. Payne, "Is this," 15.

35. Any student who has spent a few minutes with the old Englishman's bilingual concordances has some idea of the challenges, even in the KJV.

36. The subject has been extensively discussed. See, for instance, my *Exegetical Fallacies,* 2d ed. (Grand Rapids: Baker, 1996), 53, 60–61.

37. Jay E. Adams, *More Than Redemption* (Phillipsburg, Pa.: Presbyterian and Reformed, 1979), 110.

38. Interestingly, some modern proponents of nouthetic counseling—or "biblical counseling," as it is more widely called today—are, rightly and wisely, distancing themselves from Adams on this point: see Edward Welch, "How Theology Shapes Ministry: Jay Adams's View of the Flesh and an Alternative," *Journal of Biblical Counseling* 20, no. 3 (Spring 2002): 16–25.

39. Payne, "FAQs on the ESV," 24.

40. Ibid., 23.

41. Ibid.

42. See my brief discussion, "Is the Doctrine of *Claritas Scripturae* Still Relevant Today?" in *Dein Wort ist die Wahrheit,* eds. Eberhard Hahn, Rolf Hille, and Heinz-Werner Neudorfer (Wuppertal: R. Brockhaus Verlag, 1997), 97–111. The doctrine is in need of recasting to face some of the pressures from postmodern epistemology. In this regard it is linked with the sufficiency of Scripture, on which see especially Tim Ward, "Word and Supplement: Reconstructing the Doctrine of the Sufficiency of Scripture" (Ph.D. diss. Edinburgh University, 1999).

43. Vern S. Poythress and Wayne A. Grudem, *The Gender-Neutral Bible Controversy: Muting the Masculinity of God's Words* (Nashville: Broadman and Holman, 2000).

44. See especially the insightful review by Heinrich von Siebenthal, *Trinity Journal* 23 (2002): 111–118; and the review by Craig L. Blomberg in *Denver Journal,* available on the Web at http://www.gospelcom.net/densem/dj/articles01/0200/0204.html.

45. I am thinking not only of Strauss's earlier book *Distorting Scripture? The Challenge of Bible Translation and Gender Accuracy* (Downers Grove, Ill.: InterVarsity Press, 1998) but also his article in this volume ("Current Issues in the Gender-Language Debate") and several recent papers, such as "The Gender-Neutral Language of the *English Standard Version* (ESV) and "Examples of Improvement in Accuracy of the TNIV over the NIV When Following the Colorado Springs Guidelines."

46. Poythress and Grudem, *The Gender-Neutral Bible Controversy,* the excursus on 82–90.

47. The New English Translation (NET) is available online at www.netbible.org.

48. Daniel B. Wallace, "An Open Letter Regarding the Net Bible, New Testament," *Notes on Translation* 14, no. 3 (2000): 1–8, esp. 2–3.

49. Ibid., 2–3.

50. See Strauss, "The Gender-Neutral Language of the *English Standard Version* (ESV)."

51. Vern Poythress, "Searching Instead for an Agenda-Neutral Bible," *World* (21 November 1998): 24–25.

52. So Poythress and Grudem, *The Gender-Neutral Bible Controversy,* 186–87.

53. I cannot help remarking, rather wryly, that in the light of the ESV the argument of Poythress and Grudem sounds a bit like this: "The language is not changing, so we do not need to respond to the demands of inclusive language. But if it is changing, the changes are driven by a feminist agenda, so they are wrong and must be countered if we are to be faithful to Scripture. Because of the changes, we will make some minor accommodations in our translations, but if others make any other changes, they are compro-

misers who introduce distortions and inaccuracies and should be condemned, because changes aren't necessary anyway!"

54. I am tempted to say that I have not seen Poythress and Grudem address this point, but I would never be tempted to assert that they "could not frankly discuss" the matter. I'm quite sure they could—and probably will.

55. The FBA (Forum of Bible Agencies), whose members account for 90 percent of all Bible translation, initially responded to this controversy by issuing a statement about the TNIV: "It is the consensus of the FBA that the TNIV falls within the Forum's translation principles and procedures." (This, the Forum has been quick to insist, does *not* constitute an endorsement of the TNIV, not least because the Forum does not endorse any translation.)

Ellis Deibler, a leading Bible translator and linguist who worked with Wycliffe Bible Translators, offers a penetrating review of the Colorado Springs Guidelines (on the Web at http://www.tniv.info/resources/evaluation.php). Among other things, he writes, "The Council on Biblical Manhood and Womanhood (CBMW) has issued a paper entitled 'Translation Inaccuracies in the TNIV: A Categorized List of 904 Examples.' I should like to make a few comments on its contents. First of all, the word *inaccuracies* is totally misleading. Every one of the examples cited is a case of *differences in opinion on how a certain term ought to be translated in English,* but none of the examples is an inaccuracy. Calling them *inaccuracies* is a gross distortion of the truth."

56. Poythress and Grudem, *The Gender-Neutral Bible Controversy,* 202.

57. The tendency to read too much into a plural is not restricted to linguistically conservative translators. It is fairly common and is often theologically driven. For example, many commentators insist that Philippians 1:6 ("he who began a good work in you will carry it on to completion until the day of Christ Jesus") says nothing about the security of the individual believer, since the "you" in the quotation is plural: The one who began a good work in them will continue it in the group *as a whole,* without saying anything about the individual Christian (similarly in 2:13).

58. English purists may object to the move from the singular "anyone" to the plural pronouns. Those of us who love the cadences and structures of older English entertain an innate sympathy for that perspective—in precisely the same way that we still prefer "It is I," preserving the nominative pronoun, even though popular usage has driven the experts to concede that "It's me" is now grammatically acceptable. On the long haul, usage shapes grammar, no matter what the purists say. And in the present case, current usage is increasingly sanctioning the usage of the TNIV in this regard. The examples are legion, but not to be missed is the example provided by Scott Munger in his letter to the editor of *Christianity Today* 46, no. 6 (12 May 2002): 8: "Shaking a baby can cause brain damage that will affect them the rest of their lives"—an example drawn from James Dobson, who, presumably, did not phrase himself this way because he was succumbing to feminist ideology, but because he is in touch with current English usage. Munger's original letter, though not the *CT*-edited form of it, provided the reference—"Child Welfare and Parental Rights," CT284/24848, © Focus on the Family, July 18, 2000. As Craig Blomberg points out in his review, "[Poythress and Grudem] say nothing about the fact that in spoken English only a tiny handful of people ever still complete a sentence like 'No one brought _____ book to class' with any pronoun other than 'their,' and

that the Modern Language Association has since the late 1980s authorized such usage for standard printed materials" (see note 44).

59. See note 44.

60. Perhaps I should mention one more criticism of the TNIV. I relegate it to this footnote, because it has nothing directly to do with the inclusive-language debate, which is the subject of this section, though it illustrates the kind of criticism that is at issue. In a circulated e-mail message, Grudem criticizes the TNIV for its rendering of John 19:12, which reads in the NIV (italics added), "Pilate tried to set Jesus free, but *the Jews* kept shouting, 'If you let this man go, you are no friend of Caesar.'" and in the TNIV (italics added), "Pilate tried to set Jesus free, but *the Jewish leaders* kept shouting, 'If you let this man go, you are no friend of Caesar.'" The charge is that by inserting the word "leaders" the TNIV arbitrarily absolves other Jews from the responsibility for Jesus' death (with a lot of references then provided). But it has long been shown that in John's gospel, the word *Ioudaioi* can variously refer to Jews generically, to Judeans (i.e., to Jews living in Judea), and to Jewish leaders. A great deal depends on context. That is not how *we* use the word "Jews," but it was how the first-century word was used, at least at the hands of some authors. Again, then, Poythress is appealing to formal equivalence. But in this case, no less than in the debate over inclusive language, there is a cultural component that has arisen during the past century. We live this side of the Holocaust, and a great deal of sensitivity has arisen regarding anti-Semitism. Some of the literature goes over the top, trying to make out that *no* Jew had *any* responsibility for the death of Jesus, that it was all the plot of nasty Romans (who aren't around to defend themselves). But thoughtful Christians will admit, with shame, that more than a few Christians *have* been guilty of anti-Semitism (in the same way that, even when feminist literature goes over the top, thoughtful Christians will admit that more than a few Christians *have* been guilty of abusing women). Most emphatically this does *not* give us the right to change what the Bible actually says, as though the agendas of contemporary culture could ever have the right to domesticate Scripture. But this *ought* to make us eager to avoid miscommunication, to appear to be saying things to some readers and hearers that we do not intend to say, and which the text is certainly not saying (whether misogyny or anti-Semitism, or anything else). Some of the clarifications will be in the hands of the preacher and teacher, of course. Nevertheless, I would argue robustly that precisely *because* I am committed to accurate translation, to render *Ioudaioi* invariably by "Jews" is to translate poorly, both because there is a great deal of evidence that the referent is often more restricted than that and also because the failure to make some of those restrictions clear (as they were, implicitly, to the first readers) is to invite charges of anti-Semitism that are as unfair as they are unnecessary.

61. It is possible that some of the ire directed against the publishers of the NIV and the TNIV stems from two related facts: (1) The NIV is the closest thing to a "standard" English Bible for Evangelicals, so any modifications have the potential for upsetting a huge number of people. (2) Some journalists are claiming that by publishing the TNIV the publishers are going back on the promise *not* to change the NIV. Without being privy to private discussions, I would make three observations. First, since its initial publication the NIV has undergone many minor changes. An ongoing committee assesses criticisms, changes in contemporary linguistic usage, and allegations of mistakes. An

updated NT appeared in 1978 (when the OT was added to the 1973 NT) and a revised edition of the whole Bible was released in 1984. Earlier editions were no longer printed. That is one of the reasons why the NIV has retained a contemporary feel. Second, it was the anticipation that the next round of changes would include more sensitivity to inclusive-language issues that propelled the eruption a few years ago. The Bible of forty million people was being "changed," and it was easy to rally indignation. Realistically (in retrospect!), doubtless the changes being contemplated were more numerous and more substantive than earlier changes, so the outrage, though largely misinformed, was understandable. Third, as far as I am aware, the publishers, under pressure, eventually promised to make no more changes to the NIV, including changes of an inclusive-language sort. What this means, of course, is that the NIV will eventually become dated. But nowhere did the publishers promise, so far as I am aware, never to produce *any* translation that would be sensitive to issues of gender in contemporary usage. I do not see how they could make that promise. But I thought at the time, when I read the published reports, that the careful wording of the publishers, which left them plenty of room to publish inclusive-language versions under some rubric other than the NIV, was going to raise hackles when they did so, as well as many charges of deceit. And that, of course, is exactly what has happened—see, for instance, the article "Hypocritical Oath," in *World* 17, no. 9 (9 March 2002), and related essays in *World* 17, no. 7 (23 February 2002).

62. Because my views have been repeatedly dismissed on the grounds (it is said) that I was a translator for the NIV and therefore benefit financially from my arguments, I suppose I had better set the record straight. I did a bit of *pro bono* consultation for the NIV, making comments on the translation of one New Testament book about thirty years ago at the request of Dr. Edwin Palmer. I was not paid a cent. I have worked on a couple of other (non-NIV-related) translations. Why this should invalidate my arguments any more than the fact that Dr. Grudem worked on the ESV should invalidate his, I have no idea.

63. On this point, I have neglected to mention, as well, the increasingly sophisticated analyses of the translations of others. In particular, current analyses of the LXX as a translation are far more sophisticated than similar works two or three decades ago and typically reflect on a far greater number of variables. For one recent example (of which there are many), see Robert J. V. Hiebert, "Translation Technique in the Septuagint and Its Implications for the NETS Version," *Bulletin of the International Organization for Septuagint and Cognate Studies* 33 (Fall 2000): 76–93.

64. On the spectrum of translations, see, for instance, John Beekman and John Callow, *Translating the Word of God* (Grand Rapids: Zondervan, 1974), 19–32; and Eugene H. Glassman, *The Translation Debate: What Makes a Bible Translation Good?* (Downers Grove, Ill.: InterVarsity Press, 1981), 23–34.

65. Nida and Taber, *The Theory and Practice of Translation,* 14.

66. We may think, for instance, of the growing list of handbooks and commentaries for translators published by United Bible Societies (UBS).

67. It is risky to single out individual items for special praise. In addition to several items already mentioned, however, and representing quite different achievements, one may think of recent developments in the arena of discourse analysis, such as George H. Guthrie, *The Structure of Hebrews: A Text-Linguistic Analysis,* NovTSup 73 (Leiden: Brill,

1994); of sophisticated and creative individual essays such as that of Kenneth L. Pike, "Agreement Types Dispersed into a Nine-Cell Spectrum," along with other contributions to *On Language, Culture, and Religion,* eds. Matthew Black and William A. Smalley (The Hague: Mouton, 1974), 275–86; of continual developments in computer software that provide lexical, grammatical, and functional searches; and much more.

68. See, for example, Mildred Larson, *A Manual of Problem Solving in Bible Translation* (Grand Rapids: Zondervan, 1975).

69. In addition to the works cited at the beginning of this essay, see Nida and Taber, *The Theory and Practice of Translation;* William L. Wonderly, *Bible Translations for Popular Use* (London: UBS, 1968); and many others.

70. The list is so long that it cannot usefully be included here. Many articles in *The Bible Translator* fit into this category; those in *Notes on Translation* are generally semi-popular.

71. Once again, the list is becoming lengthy. The current round of books was perhaps kicked off by Sakae Kubo and Walter Specht, *So Many Versions? Twentieth-Century English Versions of the Bible* (Grand Rapids: Zondervan, 1975); Jack P. Lewis, *The English Bible from KJV to NIV: A History and Evaluation* (Grand Rapids: Baker, 1981). Useful is the recent essay by Steven Sheeley, "Re(:) Englishing the Bible," *Review and Expositor* 97 (2000): 467–84. Because of their relevance to one section of this essay, one should perhaps also consult some of the lengthier reviews of the NRSV: in particular, Sakae Kubo, "Review Article: The New Revised Standard Version," *Andrews University Seminary Studies* 29 (1991): 61–69; and D. A. Carson, "A Review of the New Revised Standard Version," *Reformed Theological Review* 50 (1991): 1–11.

72. See the popular summary by Eugene A. Nida, "Bible Translations for the Eighties," *International Review of Mission* 70 (1981): 132–33.

73. Nida, ibid., 136–37, goes so far as to recommend that Bible translation teams consider adopting the procedure of United Nations and European Union translation departments, whose first drafts are produced by stylists of the receptor language, the specialists then checking their work as a second step (instead of the inverse order).

74. Cf. Beekman and Callow, *Translating the Word of God,* 33–44.

75. Nida and Taber, *The Theory and Practice of Translation,* 8.

76. Ibid., 12–13.

77. See, among other things, D. A. Carson, "Church and Mission: Reflections on Contextualization and the Third Horizon," in *The Church in the Bible and the World,* ed. D. A. Carson (Carlisle: Paternoster, 1987), 213–57, 342–7; Paul G. Hiebert, *Anthropological Reflections on Missiological Issues* (Grand Rapids: Baker, 1994); Daniel Carro and Richard F. Wilson, eds., *Contemporary Gospel Accents: Doing Theology in Africa, Asia, Southeast Asia, and Latin America* (Macon, Ga.: Mercer Univ. Press, 1996).

78. Eugene A. Nida, *Toward a Science of Translating* (Leiden: Brill, 1964), 166.

79. Nida and Taber, *The Theory and Practice of Translation,* 24.

80. Norm Mundhenk, "The Subjectivity of Anachronism," in *On Language, Culture, and Religion,* 260.

81. This is one of the points raised by Anthony Howard Nichols, "Translating the Bible" (Ph.D. diss., University of Sheffield, 1997), passim. I have questions about some of his work, but his trenchant criticism of the way in which many non-Western versions are being created today less from the original Hebrew and Aramaic and Greek texts and

rather more—indeed, almost entirely—from English versions, especially the GNB, is well deserved. (One of the problems of Nichols's work, I think, is that his critique of dynamic-equivalence theory is primarily leveled against the GNB. But the GNB is an example, I would argue, for a rather more extreme deployment of dynamic-equivalence theory than is, say, either the NIV or the TNIV—in exactly the same way that the NASB is a more extreme deployment of direct-translation theory than is, say, the KJV. The critique that one may usefully offer of a method or an approach is somewhat limited if one focuses on only one result of that method.)

82. Charles H. Kraft, *Christianity in Culture: A Study in Dynamic Biblical Theologizing in Cross-Cultural Perspective* (Maryknoll, N.Y.: Orbis, 1979), 276–90. Note that Kraft titles this chapter "Dynamic-Equivalence Transculturation of the Message."

83. Ibid., 284.

84. Ibid., 286 (emphasis is Kraft's).

85. Ibid., 287.

86. This is the title of chapter 15 of Kraft, *Christianity in Culture*.

87. Cf. Charles E. Kraft, "Dynamic-Equivalence Churches," *Missiology* 1 (1979): 39–57.

88. Ibid., 54.

89. Ibid. One marvels at Kraft's biblical chronology.

90. A useful place to begin is Harry Hoijer, "The Sapir-Whorf Hypothesis," in *Intercultural Communication: A Reader*, eds. Larry A. Samovar and Richard E. Porter (Belmont, Calif.: Wadsworth, 1972), 114–23.

91. In some ways discussion of the new hermeneutic has been eclipsed, at least in the Anglo-Saxon world, by discussion of postmodern epistemology. On the new hermeneutic, the most sophisticated place to begin, perhaps, is A. C. Thiselton, *The Two Horizons: New Testament Hermeneutics and Philosophical Description* (Grand Rapids: Eerdmans, 1980).

92. Those informed by postmodernism cannot help but compare Michel Foucault's "totalization."

93. I have tried to wrestle with some of these questions in *The Gagging of God: Christianity Confronts Pluralism* (Grand Rapids: Zondervan, 1996) and in several subsequent essays.

94. Charles H. Kraft, "Communicating the Gospel God's Way," *Ashland Theological Bulletin* 12 (1979): 34–35.

95. See Eugene Nida, "Linguistics and Ethnology in Translation: Problems," *Word* 1 (1945): 196.

96. Stephen Neill, "Translating the Word of God," *Churchman* 90 (1976): 287.

97. See especially Eugene Nida, "Bible Translation for the Eighties," *International Review of Mission* 70 (1981): 136–37.

98. See William D. Reyburn, "Secular Culture, Missions, and Spiritual Values," in *On Language, Culture, and Religion,* 287–99.

99. Nida and Taber, *The Theory and Practice of Translation,* 30.

100. I view with unmitigated horror the multiplication of Bibles with notes designed for narrower and narrower groups. It will not surprise me if we soon have Bibles designed for left-handed athletes from Nebraska. These trends merely serve the idolatrous notion that God and his Word exist primarily to serve us in all our self-focused individuality.

4

CURRENT ISSUES IN THE GENDER-LANGUAGE DEBATE: A RESPONSE TO VERN POYTHRESS AND WAYNE GRUDEM[1]

Mark L. Strauss

In recent years the evangelical community in the United States has been rocked by a sometimes divisive debate over gender-related language in Bible translation.[2] Though discussed in academic circles for some time, the issue erupted onto the evangelical landscape in 1997 with the public outcry associated with the publication in Great Britain of an inclusive-language edition (NIVI) of the popular New International Version (NIV).[3] The debate has come to center stage again with the publication of the New Testament of Today's New International Version (TNIV), a revision of the NIV that utilizes gender-inclusive language for masculine generic terms in Greek. While all recent Bible translations utilize gender-inclusive language to some degree,[4] the popularity of the NIV among evangelicals has made the TNIV a lightning rod of controversy.

Three monographs were published in the wake of the NIVI controversy: my own *Distorting Scripture? The Challenge of Bible Translation and Gender Accuracy,* D. A. Carson's *The Inclusive Language Debate: A Plea for Realism,* and most recently, Vern Poythress and Wayne Grudem's *The Gender-Neutral Bible Controversy: Muting the Masculinity of God's Words.* Carson's work and mine take a similar perspective, generally defending the use of gender-inclusive language in Bible translation; Poythress and Grudem take the other side, generally rejecting the use of such language.

This essay is an attempt to summarize and briefly assess the present state of the debate. On the one hand, there are many more agreements than differences on several basic issues. I will therefore begin with a lengthy list of agreements. On the other hand, there remain critical philosophical and methodological differences. In the second part of the essay, I will examine and critique Poythress and Grudem (henceforth, P&G) in key areas where we differ.

Important Areas of Agreement

When I first began writing on this issue, it seemed to me the opponents of inclusive language were especially vulnerable to criticism, since they were making what appeared to be very naive linguistic errors.[5] They would certainly disagree with this assessment, claiming either that I was misreading them or that they only sounded this way because they were writing to a naive and uninformed Christian public.[6] In any case, the linguistic naïveté that (it seems to me) characterized the early stages of the debate has undergone significant correction, resulting in a great deal of agreement on the fundamentals of Bible translation and on the validity of using certain kinds of gender-inclusive language in Bible translation. The advance in the discussion suggests the benefit of serious dialogue, and it is in this spirit that I offer this essay.

Agreements Related to the Nature of the Bible

1. All parties[7] agree on the inspiration and authority of the Bible. This debate is not one of "liberals versus conservatives" since all involved in this discussion are theological conservatives with a very high view of Scripture.[8]

2. All parties agree that inerrancy relates only to the autographs as written in their original languages. Diversity of manuscripts means that textual criticism must be used to reconstruct as accurately as possible the original text. Furthermore, no translation is inerrant, since all are produced by fallible human interpreters (for elaboration, see point 5 in the next section).

Agreements Related to the Nature of Bible Translation

1. All parties agree that the goal of translation is to transfer the *meaning* of a text from the source (or donor) language to the receptor (or target) language. The goal is to reproduce *as much of the meaning as possible.*[9]

2. All agree that no two languages are the same with reference to word meanings, grammar, or idiom, and so a strict literal or "formal equivalent" translation is impossible. The translation of *meaning* must always take precedence over the reproduction of *form.*[10]

3. All agree that since languages differ in these ways, no translation captures precisely all of the meaning of the original.[11] Some nuances of meaning are

inevitably lost in the translation process. Nevertheless, essential faithfulness in translation *is* possible because of the flexibility and adaptability of language forms. It must be reiterated, however, that this is never *absolute* faithfulness.

4. All agree that languages are constantly changing, so that it is necessary to periodically examine and update Bible translations to accurately reflect contemporary usage.[12] All also agree that masculine generics like "man" or "men" have declined in use in recent years, with a corresponding increase in inclusive terms.[13]

5. All agree that translation is an inexact science practiced by fallible human beings.[14] All translations contain errors, imprecise language, and ambiguities. (Indeed, all communication contains *some* imprecision and ambiguity.) This does not mean that translation cannot be done accurately and reliably, but only that it cannot be done perfectly. Translation must therefore be a give-and-take process involving measured compromise and balance. It is an art as well as a science.

6. With reference to lexical semantics, all agree that words (or, more precisely, *lexemes*) do not generally carry a single all-encompassing or so-called "literal" meaning but rather have a range of potential senses (a semantic range).[15] The sense intended by the author must be determined by the context in which the word is used. An accurate translation is one that determines the correct sense of a word or phrase in the source language in each particular context and chooses an appropriate word or phrase in the receptor language to capture that sense. Consistent word-for-word replacement is an unreliable method of translation.

7. Related to this, all agree that the various senses of a Hebrew, Aramaic, or Greek lexeme (its semantic range) do not overlap exactly with the various senses of an English lexeme.[16] In other words, there is never absolute synonymy between lexemes (either within a language or across languages). For this reason, an English word or expression must be chosen that most accurately represents the meaning of the Hebrew, Aramaic, or Greek *in each particular context.*

8. All agree that words carry connotative as well as denotative meaning and that both kinds of meaning are important for accurate communication in translation.[17]

Agreements Related to Gender Language

1. All agree that gender-accurate (gender-inclusive, gender-neutral) translation is *a good thing,* when the use of such language *accurately represents the meaning of the original text.* In many cases the use of an inclusive term improves the accuracy of the translation.[18] An example of this is the translation "person" in contexts where Greek *anthrōpos* is used generically to refer to either a man or a woman. Romans 3:28 (TNIV, italics added) accurately reads, "For we maintain that *a person* is justified by faith apart from observing the law."

2. All agree that care should be taken *not* to use inclusive language when the original author intended a gender-specific sense.[19] The (biological) gender distinctions of the original text should be respected.

3. All agree that translations should seek not to obscure cultural features, including patriarchal ones, that were part of the original meaning of the text.[20]

4. All agree that gender-specific terms should be used with reference to historical persons when males or females are specified in illustrative material, and in parables where characters are male or female.[21]

5. As a possible qualifier to the previous point, all agree that words should be translated according to their *sense* in context, not according to extraneous features associated with their referents.[22] For example, an author may use *anthrōpos* in the sense of "human being," even though the person referred to happens to be a male. James 5:17 is accurately translated "Elijah was a human being *[anthrōpos]* just like we are," because *anthrōpos* in this context means "human being," not "male human being" (the "we" is surely inclusive). Though Elijah was a male, this characteristic is extraneous to the sense of *anthrōpos* in context (cf. Acts 10:26; John 10:33; 1 Tim 2:5).

6. All agree that there is nothing inherently immoral or evil in masculine generic terms. The goal of translation should not be to abolish male references but to determine which English words and phrases most accurately and clearly reproduce the meaning of the original text.[23]

7. All agree that grammatical gender is different than natural or biological gender (sex).[24] It is therefore incorrect to demand the reproduction of grammatical gender across languages with different gender systems.

8. All agree that Greek *anthrōpos* is accurately translated "person" or "human being" when the author intended to refer to either a man or a woman.[25]

9. All agree that Greek *anthrōpoi* is accurately translated with inclusive terms like "people" or "human beings" when the author intended to include both men and women.[26]

10. All agree that Hebrew *ʾîsh* sometimes has an inclusive sense, and in these cases it is accurately translated with expressions such as "each one" or "each person."[27]

11. All agree that *adelphoi* is accurately translated "brothers and sisters" when the referents include both males and females.[28]

12. All agree that Hebrew *bānîm* is accurately translated "children" when the referents include both males and females.[29] While most would say the same about Greek *huioi,* P&G affirm this only reluctantly and with qualifications.[30]

13. All agree that Greek *pateres* may be translated "parents" instead of "fathers" when the referents include both males and females.[31]

14. Do Greek *pateres* and Hebrew *ʾābôt* ever mean "ancestors"? Most commentators would say yes.[32] P&G seem to agree with this in principle, but they reject this translation in practice and do not discuss passages where both males and females are in view (e.g., 1 Sam 12:6; Heb 3:9).[33]

15. All agree that the translation "man" for the human race is one of the most difficult issues in gender-related translation and that there are no easy answers. Neither English "man" nor terms like "humanity" or "humankind" can capture all of the wordplays present in the Hebrew *ādām.*[34] Whichever translation is used, footnotes are appropriate to explain the wordplays of the original text.

16. Similarly, all agree that the translation "son of man" for Hebrew *ben ādām* and Greek *huios tou anthrōpou* is another difficult issue without easy answers. While these phrases usually mean "human being," this translation may obscure messianic references in some contexts.[35] Again, explanatory footnotes are sometimes necessary.

A number of other agreements could be added to this list, but these are sufficient to demonstrate common presuppositions and philosophical perspectives.

Critical Areas of Disagreement

If all parties agree that gender-accurate (gender-inclusive, gender-neutral) translation is a good thing in principle, why do P&G so vehemently oppose it in practice?

A Question of Definition: What Is Gender-Inclusive Language?

One way P&G avoid this apparent contradiction is by introducing a unique definition of inclusive language. I have elsewhere defined inclusive language as the use of inclusive terms when the author was referring to members of both sexes.[36] An example I have provided is the translation "human being" or "person" for the masculine generic use of *anthrōpos.* P&G are unhappy with this definition and this example. They write the following:

> Unfortunately, Mark Strauss's book *Distorting Scripture? The Challenge of Bible Translation and Gender Accuracy,* uses loose terminology at this point. It says that such a translation of *anthrōpos* uses "inclusive language" (p. 37). It thereby uses the label broadly, to speak about usages that are not in dispute. But the same label, "inclusive language," has a narrow use to designate usages that *are* in dispute.[37]

P&G here wish to define inclusive language with reference to "disputed" examples. This is a very subjective definition. Who decides, after all, which examples are disputed and which are not? Take, for example, the translation "brothers and sisters" for the masculine generic *adelphoi.* Wayne Grudem once wrote that this was an inaccurate translation since the term meant "brothers."[38] In other words, this was a disputed case (and hence an example of inclusive language?). Now, however, he recognizes that this is an acceptable translation of *adelphoi* in many contexts.[39] It is no longer disputed. Would this mean that it is no longer an example of inclusive language? This, of course, is invalid. Identifying gender-inclusive language only with reference to so-called "disputed" examples is imprecise and highly subjective. Remarkably, P&G accuse me of using "loose terminology" when I define inclusive language (objectively) as translating masculine generics with inclusive terms.[40]

By defining inclusive language with reference only to "disputed" examples, P&G are attempting to isolate and downplay the many examples of inclusive language that actually enhance or provide more accuracy to a translation. This is a very effective (if not a very fair) way to win an argument. You choose the examples you wish to discuss while ruling out your opponents' examples. This purpose comes out when P&G make this argument:

> By using the label "inclusive language" in a broad way as well as the narrower way, Strauss bundles the uncontroversial usages into the same collection with the controversial ones—it is all "inclusive language." One thereby gets the false impression that since the old (undisputed) practices of the KJV and the NIV were all right, so are the new disputed usages.[41]

But these *are,* in fact, all examples of inclusive language. And the earlier so-called undisputed examples in the NIV and the KJV *do* confirm that there is nothing inherently inaccurate or wrong with using inclusive language for masculine generic terms in Hebrew and Greek. As P&G themselves acknowledge in many examples, the use of inclusive or neutral terms is helpful and effective *when the author intended to include both men and women.*

To be fair to P&G, this attempt to redefine terms represents a relatively small part of their argument (though it surfaces again on pages 115–16 and 159–60 of their book). They focus more on the loss of nuances of meaning—a loss they claim characterizes gender-inclusive translation. To this point we now turn.

The Loss of Subtle Nuances of Meaning

From the large number of agreements noted above, one might gain the impression that the two sides are not very far apart. Unfortunately, this is not the case. Why? Because P&G consider most "permissible" inclusive language to be *unusual exceptions* to the general need to retain masculine generics in Bible translation. These masculine terms, they argue, contain subtle and important *nuances* of meaning that are lost in inclusive translation. (Phrases like "subtle nuance," "slightly different, and "not identical" appear throughout their book.)

The basis for this approach is developed in an excursus, where P&G attempt to analyze linguistic complexity by identifying various levels at which people approach translation.[42] Their stated goal here is to move beyond the form-versus-meaning dichotomy that has characterized much of the discussion on this topic. Their first level, "the naive approach" often taken by the general public, assumes that languages are all the same and that translation can be done with simple word-for-word replacement. P&G admit that this is simply wrong. The second level, "the theoretically informed approach," moves beyond naïveté to a basic understanding of linguistics with reference to form and function. For example, in Ezekiel 37 the same Hebrew word *rûaḥ* (one form) is used with three different senses—breath (37:5), wind (37:9), and Spirit (37:14). It is primarily at this theoretical level, they suggest, that the gender-inclusive language debate has taken place and at which their opponents are operating. The third level they call "the discerning approach: using native speakers' intuitive sense of subtleties." At this level people recognize that the basic theoretical formulations at level 2 are only summaries, and that "the phenomena of language and human communication vastly surpass it in complexity."[43] For example, a native speaker, while recognizing the different senses of *rûaḥ* in Ezekiel 37, may also intuitively perceive certain interplays of meaning between these senses. At the fourth and highest level, "the reflective approach," translators attempt to analyze and make explicit the subtleties and complexities that may be sensed by native speakers at the third level. Here an interpreter might seek to show how Ezekiel 37 can achieve its effect by playing on more than one sense of the same word *rûaḥ*.[44]

Some of the points made in this section are helpful. Meaning expressed through language is indeed extraordinarily complex and intuitively perceived, and the whole is greater than the sum of the parts. But what P&G fail to make clear is that, for the most part, their so-called levels 3 and 4 are impossible to attain in a basic translation. Because every language is different, when you gain one thing with a particular translation, you lose something else. For example, by consistently translating a particular Hebrew word (such as *rûaḥ*) with a single English word (say, "spirit"), you would retain the verbal parallels in the Hebrew, but you would miss the best sense of the word in each particular context. Or, with reference to the present debate, by seeking to retain a masculine nuance you might lose (or suppress) an inclusive one.

The great anomaly of P&G's work is that they first set out a basically sound linguistic theory and then spend much of the rest of the book contradicting it in practice.[45] They affirm that translation is an inexact science and art involving give-and-take and compromise. While the goal is to preserve as much of the meaning as possible, all translation inevitably loses something. Meaning functions on many levels and in many dimensions simultaneously. The rest of P&G's book then involves often hairsplitting criticism of the subtle and nuanced loss of meaning in gender-inclusive translation, mostly ignoring the fact that this is inherent in *all translation.* Somewhere along the way, P&G begin referring to these subtle and slight changes as "distortions" of God's Word, even challenging the scholarly integrity of the translators who produce them.[46]

Please do not misunderstand me. I am in no way advocating a cavalier approach to Bible translation. No one serious about careful translation is interested in reproducing only the "main idea" or the "basic meaning" with little regard for details. (Yet this is the charge P&G repeatedly make against their opponents.[47]) But the simple fact is that it is *impossible* to capture all of the nuances of meaning. Translators must constantly make hard decisions and compromises. The questions in each case are, *What nuances are present? Which should be retained and how do we retain them? Which must be sacrificed because of the inexactitude of the language?* The goals, of course, are accuracy and balance, seeking to retain enough of one nuance without unduly or excessively compromising others. It is also necessary to give priority to the more important nuances.

The impression one gets while reading P&G is that it is the *male-oriented* nuances that must be preserved at all cost. But what about the subtle loss of inclusive meaning created by using "he" or "man"? This, it seems, is of little importance.

Examples illustrating this can be found throughout their book. In a section on generic "he," they compare Proverbs 16:9 in the RSV and in four versions that use inclusive language in order to show (and to poke fun at) the variety of ways generic "he" is avoided:

- RSV: A man's mind plans *his* way, but the LORD directs *his* steps.
- NCV: *People* may make plans in *their* minds, but the LORD decides what *they* will do.
- NIVI: In *your* heart *you* may plan *your* course, but the LORD determines *your* steps.
- NLT: *We* can make *our* plans, but the LORD determines *our* steps.
- NRSV: The human mind plans *the* way, but the LORD directs *the* steps.

P&G criticize the four versions that use inclusive language because "all of the changes involve *some* change in meaning."[48] This is certainly true. But it is also true that *every translation* involves "*some* change in meaning," since every word is changed from the source language to the receptor language, and since no two languages are the same with reference to word meanings or idiom. For the next few pages P&G go on to show in detail how subtle nuances of meaning are lost in these other versions. There is no mention, however, of the subtle loss of meaning in the RSV, which they identify as the "literal" (and presumably the accurate) translation. But we must remember that the so-called "literal" RSV is also an interpretation of the Hebrew. Hebrew *ādām* has been interpreted and translated as "man" (it could have been translated "person" or in various other ways); Hebrew *lēḇ* has been interpreted and translated as "mind" (it could have been accurately translated "heart" or in various other ways); Hebrew *yāḵîn* has been interpreted and translated as "directs" (it could have been translated "determines" or in various other ways). We could go on and on. It becomes even more complicated and difficult as we move from words to phrases and clauses. There is, in fact, no such thing as a "literal translation" (i.e., single, uniform, corresponding exactly with the Hebrew), since every Hebrew word or phrase in this verse (and in virtually any verse) could be translated in a variety of ways. Every translation constantly involves interpretive decisions, all of which change the words (from Hebrew or Greek to English) and all of which inevitably change subtle nuances of meaning. By translating Hebrew *ādām* as "man" instead of "person" and by using the masculine pronoun "his," the RSV certainly loses *something* with reference to the inclusive sense of the original Hebrew. Yet P&G do not point out the meaning deficiencies and ambiguities of the RSV or other traditional versions, but only those of these more inclusive versions.[49]

P&G also spend a great deal of space trying to show that generic "he" is understandable even to those who consider it exclusive-sounding. It is "serviceable," they say.[50] Chapter 11 is titled "Ordinary People Can Understand Generic 'He'." While this may be true, it sounds suspiciously like the "only the main idea but miss the nuances" argument they level against their critics. Should we not seek the most accurate expression rather than settling for one that, while understandable, gives the perception of exclusion for many readers?

Ironically, P&G inadvertently demonstrate the potential confusion of using masculine terms when *they themselves* misunderstand masculine generic "man" to be gender-specific (i.e., male). In their discussion of Greek *anēr,* they argue that the Greek lexicons do not recognize the sense "human being." To prove this they cite various lexicons, including the Liddell-Scott *Greek-English Lexicon.* The first two entries for *anēr* in Liddell-Scott are (1) *man,* opposed to *woman,* and (2) *man,* opposed to *god.* P&G use this data to deny that the term ever loses its distinctively male sense.[51] But what is the sense of "*man,* opposed to *god*"? The first sense, "*man,* opposed to *woman,*" is clearly "male human being," but the second is clearly "human being." P&G have read the generic use of "man" in this second entry, and have misunderstood it to be gender-specific (i.e., male). In this way they illustrate the potential for contemporary English readers to misunderstand "man"!

Now of course I am not saying that *avoiding* masculine generic "he" or "man" is the perfect solution either or that these other, more inclusive versions necessarily get it right in the example from Proverbs 16:9. The avoidance of masculine generic "he" can create problems as well as solve them.[52] The point is that *all translation* involves subtle loss of meaning. I could take any verse in the RSV or any other version and point out the subtle loss of meaning produced in almost every word because of the move from Hebrew or Greek to English.[53] Those translations that avoid masculine generic "he" are trying to compensate in one direction; those that use it are compensating in another. There is no perfect solution because some meaning will be lost either way. Balance and discernment are therefore needed. Translators must make hard choices on a case-by-case basis, examining a wide range of factors arising from both the source language and the receptor language, and the original author and the contemporary readers.

In light of the complexity of translation and the necessity for careful discernment and balance, it is remarkable that in their practical application section (chapter 14), P&G warn readers only to use "reliable" versions in their Bible study and reading. Among these they list the NKJV, NASB, RSV, and NIV.[54] The unreliable ones would be all the inclusive versions (NRSV, NLT, NCV, GW, NIVI, CEV, TNIV, NET, etc.). But what about the unreliability of the Greek text behind the NKJV (which follows the Textus Receptus throughout)? Should not readers be warned about that? Or what about the so-called "liberal bias" claimed by many evangelicals concerning the RSV? Should not readers be warned about this? Or what about the obscurity and consequent distortion of meaning that so often result from the wooden literalness and linguistic naïveté of the NASB and the NKJV?

This same question of reliability arises with reference to gender language. What about the hundreds of times that these traditional versions do not use the so-called "permissible" inclusive language that P&G admit *improves the accuracy* of the translation?[55] Are not these versions "unreliable" since they certainly miss many nuances of inclusive meaning? For example, the four so-called reliable versions all translate *anthrōpos* in Romans 3:28 and elsewhere as "man": "For we maintain that a man is justified by faith" (NASB, NIV; cf. NKJV, RSV). P&G strongly affirm that *anthrōpos* here means "person." In fact, they call this an "undisputed" passage and even criticize me for using it as an example of "inclusive language" (claiming it is so obvious nobody would dispute it).[56] Yet the NKJV, NASB, RSV, and NIV all missed this "obvious" meaning and translated "man." Where is the criticism of this loss of meaning? Another example is the translation *adelphoi* as "brothers" even when it means "brothers and sisters"—a significant loss of meaning. P&G go so far as to admit that the whole book of Romans may be better translated in the NIVI than the NIV.[57] Yet they still consider the NIV to be reliable and the NIVI to be unreliable. It seems the meaning losses in these four traditional versions do not matter so much, since they lose *inclusive nuances* instead of masculine ones. Is a social agenda at work here?

The Christian public deserves more than such simplistic categories as "reliable" and "unreliable," especially with reference to the major scholarly achievements of the NRSV, TNIV, NLT, TEV, NIVI, NCV, GW, CEV, NET, NJB, and others. Believers should be encouraged to use and study a variety of Bible versions and should be educated as to their various strengths and weaknesses. They should be taught that language always involves a measure of ambiguity and imprecision and that every Bible version makes difficult interpretive decisions. They should be taught that there is no perfect translation, but that the multiplicity of English versions available means that different nuances of meaning and different interpretations of individual passages can be examined carefully and then explored in greater detail through the many excellent commentaries. They should be taught that the more functional-equivalent[58] versions tend to capture the sense or meaning of the original text more accurately, while the more formal-equivalent versions can reveal structural features, verbal allusions, and wordplays often lost in functional equivalence. Most of all, they should be taught that, despite the inevitable ambiguities and uncertainties, God's Word can be accurately understood and appropriately applied to our lives. This is not a condescension to some "only the basic meaning but miss the nuances" fallacy, as P&G claim, but a fundamental fact about the nature of language and translation.

While formal-equivalent versions are helpful tools to allow students of the Word to explore verbal connections and structural features of the original languages, this is by no means the same as retaining the (so-called) levels 3 and 4 meaning. To begin to attain this kind of precision in meaning-transfer, one would need much more than a simple translation. One would need a full explanatory commentary, exploring in-depth questions of genre, style, lexical semantic ranges, cultural connotations, implication, wordplays, register, sentence structure, paragraph structure, discourse structure, social relationships, and many more factors. All of these features and more were part of the intended meaning of the author. This kind of meaning-retention simply cannot be attained in a translation—whether that translation seeks formal or functional equivalence.[59]

The implication running through P&G's book is that formal equivalence, and more particularly the retention of masculine terms, capture these nuances more precisely than functional equivalence. But there is little evidence to support this. In fact, a *freer* translation has the potential of capturing more of the meaning, since it has the freedom to add explanatory words or phrases. Take a passage like Matthew 9:10, where Jesus calls Matthew and then attends a banquet at his home:

- "as he was reclining in the house" (closest formal equivalent)
- "as He was reclining *at the table* in the house" (NASB)
- "as Jesus sat at the table in the house" (NKJV)
- "While Jesus was having a meal in Matthew's house" (TEV)
- "While Jesus was having dinner at Matthew's house" (NIV)
- "That night Matthew invited Jesus and his disciples to be his dinner guests" (NLT)

Which translation is most accurate? The closest formal equivalent—"reclining in the house"—leaves out much of the meaning. It does not explain that Jesus was reclining around a low table or that this posture indicates a more formal banquet or dinner party. Nor does it express the nature of first-century meals as rituals of social status. Someone might argue that these ideas are better left to a commentary, but they are, in fact, all critical parts of the *original meaning* that the author intended and that a first-century reader would have immediately recognized. None of them would be evident to today's English reader. Here the translation goal of transferring "as much of the meaning as possible" runs directly counter to the goal of producing a word-for-word or even a phrase-for-phrase translation.

All of these translations must therefore make compromises and trade-offs. The NASB tries to capture the cultural posture by describing Jesus as "reclining at the table" but does not mention the meal. The NKJV introduces the modern idea of *sitting* at a table and fails to identify the nature of the meal. The TEV identifies this as a meal, and the NIV speaks more formally of a "dinner," but neither mention the reclining position. The NLT suggests a formal dinner with invitations and guests but again fails to mention the posture of the guests. All of these translations lose important nuances of meaning.

The simple fact is that the many differences in word meanings, idioms, and cultural background make the attainment of so-called levels 3 and 4 equivalence impossible in a standard translation. Yet we should not despair. Even with its imprecision, human language is a marvelous means of communication. Although translation is never an exact science, English speakers are blessed (some would say spoiled) with dozens of excellent Bible versions that *together* provide greater insight into the meaning of the text. Furthermore, we are doubly blessed by the many excellent reference tools and commentaries that shed even greater light on the meaning of the text in its literary and historical context.

Considering the complexity of meaning and translation, it would be prudent not to use such generalizing labels as "reliable" and "unreliable" in this debate.

When Is a Generic Not a Generic? The Issue of Male Representation

Central to the claim of loss of meaning for P&G are passages that use the resumptive masculine pronoun "he" (e.g., "God will give to each person according to what *he* has done," [Rom 2:6, italics added]).[60] P&G mount a two-pronged attack against the use of inclusive language in these passages. First, as noted above, they claim that the methods used (such as using plurals for singulars, second person for third, passive constructions, singular "they," etc.) all result in subtle loss of meaning. I have already responded to this claim, pointing out that all translation inevitably loses something and that the use of masculine terms in English is just as likely to alter the meaning of the original as changes in person or number.[61] Second, P&G claim that these passages are not in fact true generics but rather portray a male representative as an example for a generic application.

We must therefore distinguish two kinds of expressions: (1) *true generics,* which refers to people in general (e.g., "a person is justified by faith"), and (2) *male representative generics,* which uses a male as an illustration for a general principle. P&G claim that masculine pronouns like Greek *autos* are not true generics but rather indicate male representation, where a male figure stands for both men and women.[62] They write, "'He' includes both men and women, but does so using a male example as a pictorial starting point."[63] Masculine terms should therefore be retained to transfer as much of the meaning as possible.

There are serious linguistic problems with this conclusion. For one thing, in the vast majority of cases it is impossible to determine whether an author intended a passage to be a true generic or a male representative. P&G give no guidelines in this regard, yet strongly criticize versions that assume a true generic over a male representative.

Without such guidelines, P&G are inconsistent in their translation of masculine terms. For example, they affirm that the Greek masculine pronoun *autos* should be translated "he" because it indicates a male representative. Yet they concede that terms like *anthrōpos* and *ādām* (also masculine terms) are often true generics, meaning not "a man" but "a person." But what happens in the multitude of cases where *anthrōpos* or other masculine generics are followed by a resumptive masculine pronoun? For example, the English Standard Version (ESV) appropriately translates 1 Corinthians 2:14, "The natural person (*anthrōpos*) does not accept the things of the Spirit of God." *Anthrōpos* is understood here to be a true generic, meaning "person." But the sentence continues, "for they are folly to *him (autos)*." Do the (supposed) male nuances associated with *autos* now turn the whole passage into one of male representation? If so, we should go back and translate *anthrōpos* as "a man" whenever it is followed by a masculine pronoun but may keep it as "person" when there is no resumptive pronoun. This is obviously absurd. Grammatically, pronouns *follow* their antecedents; they do not govern them. If *anthrōpos* is a true generic, meaning "person," then the resumptive pronouns that follow are also true generics (meaning "him or her"). P&G have the tail (the pronoun) wagging the dog (the antecedent). In beginning Greek we teach our students that a pronoun replaces a noun (its antecedent) and gets its meaning from that noun—not vice versa!

One problem seems to be that P&G are imposing English meanings onto Greek words. They are assuming *autos* means "he," and since "he" sounds so male-oriented to English ears, it should be translated with masculine terms. But the Greek text does not say "he"; it says *autos,* which is a different lexeme in a different language with a different semantic range. Its gender functions grammatically, not biologically. We should not impose the male connotations of "he" onto *autos* unless we are sure they are there. And in most generic contexts, there is no evidence that they are there. Indeed, when *autos* is preceded by a true generic term, we must assume it, too, is a true generic. It does not mean "he"; it means "that person to whom I just referred." Again, pronouns follow their antecedents; they do not govern them.

This imposition of English meanings onto Greek words is evident elsewhere in P&G's discussion. For example, they find it perfectly acceptable to translate pronouns like *oudeis* ("no one"), substantival adjectives like *pas* ("everyone"), and substantival participles like *ho pisteuōn* ("the one who believes") with inclusive terms.[64] But in fact these are all *masculine* generics, just like *autos.* If the masculine gender of *autos* indicates a male nuance or male representation, why not these others? Should not *ho pisteuōn* be translated "the man who believes"? But, as P&G admit, these terms are functioning as true generics and so may be translated with inclusive terms. Does it not follow that in similar contexts *autos* may also be translated with inclusive terms?

In an earlier article, Wayne Grudem defends this idea of male representation. He writes that when the original audience of Revelation 3:20 read "If anyone hears my voice and opens the door, I will come in and eat with him *[autos],*" they would have envisioned a male representative standing for the whole group. He explains it this way:

> They surely did not envision a group, for the Greek expressions are all singular. Nor did they envision a sexless gender-neutral person, for all human beings that they knew were either male or female, not gender-neutral. Nor is it true that they were so used to grammatical gender in all nouns and pronouns that they would have envisioned a sexless person, for pronouns applied to (adult) persons were either masculine or feminine, and these pronouns did specify the sex of the person referred to. They would almost certainly have envisioned an individual male representative for the group of people who open the door for Jesus.[65]

This argument is dubious. Grudem assumes that because the grammatical gender of *autos* is masculine, the reader must necessarily "envision" a male representative. But this again confuses biological and grammatical gender. Grudem is here applying an English (biological) gender system to Greek grammatical gender. If *autos* is a true generic, then it *does not carry* biological gender distinction. In Spanish the term for "person"—*la persona*—is feminine. If my Spanish-speaking colleague said about me that *La persona que enseña griego está aquí* ("the person who teaches Greek is here"), Spanish-speaking persons would *not* by necessity "envision" a female person. They would recognize the feminine gender as a purely grammatical category.

Grudem's claim that no one envisions a "sexless" person is also dubious. The word "person" itself is "sexless" (= non-gender-specific). Does this mean that this term has no semantic value? Readers need not "envision" a gender-specific individual for the term to carry semantic value. If what Grudem says were true, no true generics would exist in any language.

Nor can it be said that *pronouns* always evoke a certain sexual identity. *Autos* can refer to a person without specifying the sex of that person. It is significant that Grudem qualifies "adult" persons in his statement, since he knows that Greek *tekna* ("children") is neuter and that it may be followed by neuter pronouns. Ephesians 6:4 reads, "Fathers, do not exasperate your children [*tekna;* neuter plural]; instead, bring them [*auta;* neuter plural] up in the training and instruction of the Lord." Does the neuter gender of *auta* mean that children (and even adults, who are often called *tekna* in the New Testament) were viewed as neutered or sexless? Of course not. No Greek reader would impose biological gender on the basis of a word's grammatical gender. Again, English categories related to sex are being artificially imposed onto a very different Greek gender system. Grudem cannot imagine a Greek speaker using *autos* without envisioning a male. But this is because Grudem is thinking in English rather than in Greek.

The assumption that masculine terms by necessity carry some sexual connotations also has the potential for great abuse, of course. The Hebrew term for "spirit" is feminine *(rûaḥ)*; the Greek term is neuter *(pneuma)* and is often followed by neuter pronouns. Would the original readers have envisioned the Spirit as a "she" in the Old Testament and as an impersonal "it" in the New Testament? Of course not. Hebrew and Greek pronouns follow their antecedent's gender without any necessary sexual connotations.[66]

This is not the case in English, since most nouns do not carry grammatical gender. The masculine pronoun "he" almost always carries *some* male nuances because it is used almost exclusively of persons. This renders it an imprecise and somewhat ambiguous pronoun for true generic contexts. Does this make it wrong? Not wrong, but imprecise—a shortcoming in the English language, which produces a measure of ambiguity in translation. But to argue, as P&G do, that "he" is the *correct* translation while other renderings (such as plurals for singulars, second person for third, singular "they" for singular "he," or passive constructions) are distortions of the text is simplistic and naive.

What some English speakers have trouble comprehending is that, because Greek pronouns such as *autos* were used for *all* masculine nouns—whether animate or inanimate—in many contexts this pronoun sounded exactly like "it" sounds to English ears. Matthew 5:15 reads, "Neither do people light a lamp *[lychnos]* and put it *[autos]* under a bowl." The Greek noun *lychnos* is masculine, so it is followed by the masculine pronoun *autos*. Matthew 16:25 reads, "For whoever wants to save his life *[psychē]* will lose it *(autē)*." *Psychē* is feminine and so is followed by the feminine pronoun *autē*. No one would argue that *autos* should be translated "him" and *autē* "her." In such contexts the gender of *autos* is purely grammatical, with no sexual connotations whatsoever.

Similarly, it would be perfectly natural for a Greek speaker to hear *autos* as fully inclusive when following an inclusive noun like *anthrōpos*, referring to a person. In this case it does not mean "he" but rather "that person just mentioned."

But what about the suggestion that these examples are, in fact, "male representative" passages? Even if we assume for the sake of argument that this category is present in the Bible, it is still nearly impossible to determine whether the original author had a male representative or a true generic in mind. How should we translate in such cases? Which meaning gets the benefit of the doubt? Some would say that, because the biblical revelation is for all people, doubtful passages should be translated inclusively. If it is *representative,* then who is represented? Only males, or all people? In most cases, it is the latter, so an inclusive rendering would be more accurate.

P&G, on the contrary, would argue that masculine terms should be used to preserve "male nuances." This is because they believe that God intentionally designed masculine generics in Greek and Hebrew to reflect the God-ordained priority of the male. It is to this questionable premise that we now turn.

Were Masculine Generics Ordained by God to Affirm Male Priority?

At certain points in their discussion, P&G come very close to the *divine language fallacy,* which claims that Hebrew and Greek are perfect and precise languages created especially for divine communication. In answering the argument that masculine generic terms were simply part of the grammatical structure of the biblical languages, they claim that *all* of the connotations and associations of the language are divinely established and controlled:

> In a broader sense these passages are all the more meaningful because of the fact that God in his sovereign control of history *did* choose that just these resources would be available to biblical writers. What is not a "choice" from the standpoint of a human author [i.e., the presence of masculine generic terms]... is still a choice from the standpoint of the divine author *who controls language,* culture, and history and uses it as he wills.[67] [bracketed text and second italics are mine]

In other words, P&G are arguing that God intentionally established and ordained masculine generic terms in Hebrew and Greek in order to affirm the priority of males. They continue on to declare, "Everything the Bible says, and even the manner in which it says it, involves subtle moral implications, because the Bible is, among other things, a definitive example of morally pure speech."[68]

I am not sure what P&G mean by "morally pure speech," but I suspect they are avoiding unqualified phrases like "pure speech" or "perfect language," since all language contains ambiguity and imprecision. But the assertion that God sovereignly "controls language" sounds very close to the fallacy that God created Greek and Hebrew as perfect languages for revelation. While it remains a divine mystery how an imperfect vehicle (language) can communicate inerrant truth, this mystery cannot be resolved by naively assuming that Hebrew and Greek are precise and perfect vehicles for divine communication. As all linguists and translators would agree, no language can bear such a burden. (Nor does God require it—as the appearance of grammatical infelicities in Scripture shows.[69])

Nor will it do to argue that, because God is absolutely sovereign, he controls the development of all languages. Whether this is true or not is irrelevant to the discussion, since all languages remain imperfect instruments of communication. Gender systems around the world differ dramatically, making it impossible to reproduce the formal gender distinctions of Hebrew and Greek.[70] Recently I was speaking with a Bible translator who informed me that personal pronouns do not have any gender distinctions in the language of the Isan people of Northeast Thailand. Think of the loss of masculine nuances there!

If we suppose that the formal characteristics of the biblical languages are God-ordained, we open an impossible Pandora's box for translators. Greek, for example, does not have a present progressive form. Does this mean we should never introduce a present progressive in English translation so as to accurately reflect God's revelation? Of course not. The ultimate goal of translation is to *reproduce meaning,* not form.

This brings us back to some fundamental issues of linguistics and Bible translation philosophy. I have discussed these issues at greater length in earlier works and will not repeat all of my arguments here.[71] Instead I will summarize some basic linguistic errors that (it seems to me) characterize P&G's work.

Other Linguistic Errors

Illegitimate Totality Transfer

One linguistic fallacy that permeates P&G's discussion is "illegitimate totality transfer," or the all-encompassing meaning fallacy.[72] This fallacy assumes that the various senses of a particular lexeme necessarily impose their meaning on each other. While words may have various senses depending on the context and their various collocations, they do not carry all of these senses into any one context. For example, when I speak of a *fresh* water lake, there is no sense of "clean" or "brisk"; nor is there any sense of "non-saline" in *fresh* air. Two different senses of a lexeme do not necessarily force their meanings on each other. This does not mean that there cannot be interplay between various senses, but only that this interplay is not universal or necessary. The claim that *autos* always or necessarily carries male connotations when it refers to persons is an example of this fallacy. *Autos* can function as a masculine personal pronoun (with a male antecedent) or as a generic pronoun (with a generic antecedent). But it is an example of illegitimate totality transfer to claim that *autos* necessarily carries male connotations into its generic contexts.

Form and Meaning Confusion

P&G repeatedly insist that they are not confusing form and meaning and that their opponents are misrepresenting them in this area.[73] Yet this fallacy persists, as they frequently assume that the retention of form is somehow *necessary* for the retention of meaning. We have already noted examples of this: (1) the assumption that so-called "level 3" meaning may be attained through the reproduction of grammatical forms;[74] (2) the claim that the masculine grammatical gender of *autos* (a formal characteristic) necessarily carries male connotations (a semantic feature); (3) the continued insistence that the retention of formal characteristics such as person and number necessarily results in closer equivalence of meaning; and (4) the frequent assumption that semantic distinctions in Greek mirror those in English. For example, they argue that in passages like Romans 8:14–22, *tekna* should be translated as "children" and *huioi* as "sons," since the Greek uses two different terms that have two different meanings.[75] While it may be true that *huioi* and *tekna* have different nuances of meaning in Romans 8 (there is seldom, if ever, exact synonymy between lexemes), it does not necessarily follow that *huioi* means "sons." In this context, both *tekna* and *huioi* are probably closer in meaning to the English gloss "children" than to "sons." The fact that we have two words in English and two words in Greek does not mean that the semantic values are parallel.

How should we then translate in this case? As usual, there is no perfect solution. If we do detect a significant male component in *huioi,* then alternating between "sons" (for *huioi*) and "children" (for *tekna*) is probably best. If the meaning of *huioi* is closer to "children," however, then either using "children" for both or alternating between another term like "offspring" is probably best. But when P&G claim that "children" for *huioi* is inaccurate because it "is not identical to the original" and because "a nuance has changed,"[76] they are setting an impossible standard. No translation is identical to the original, and nuances *always* change. As often is true in New Testament contexts, the nearest English equivalent to *huioi* in Romans 8 is probably "children," regardless of what *tekna* means (cf. Matt 5:44–45; Luke 6:35; Rom 9:26; Gal 3:26; Heb 2:10; 12:7–8).[77]

Literal (or Root) Meaning Fallacy

While P&G affirm that words have a range of potential senses rather than a single all-encompassing meaning, at times they fall into the "literal meaning fallacy," which assumes that one sense of a lexeme is the base or core sense that controls all others. While one may appropriately speak of a *primary* sense of a word, this is very different from a *literal* meaning. A primary sense refers to the most common meaning and may serve a pragmatic function in translation: *Try this first to see if it works.* To call a primary sense the literal meaning, however, assumes the lexical fallacy that one sense of a lexeme governs or controls all others. For example, to say that "flesh" is the literal meaning of the Greek term *sarx* is to assume that this sense somehow imposes its meaning on other senses of *sarx* ("life," "human being," "sinful nature," etc.). This is a fallacy. It is context alone that determines which sense of a lexeme is intended within its semantic range.

P&G subtly fall into this fallacy at various points in their book. While discussing the Greek term *adelphoi,* for example, they write, "To be exact, the masculine plural form *adelphoi* does not literally mean "brothers and sisters," but something like "brothers, and maybe sisters as well [look at the context to see]."[78]

While correctly noting that context determines the sense of *adelphoi,* the fallacy persists that *adelphoi* literally means "brothers, and maybe sisters." This gives the false impression that "brothers" is the controlling or literal meaning—and sisters may sometimes be tacked on. But in fact, context alone determines whether *adelphoi* means "physical brothers," "physical brothers and sisters," "figurative brothers," or "figurative brothers and sisters."[79] None of these four are the literal meaning (unless you mean by literal "nonfigurative," in which case the first two are both literal). All of them are potential senses within the semantic range of *adelphoi.*[80]

While it is legitimate to speak of a primary (most common) sense of *adelphoi,* this meaning must always give way to the sense of the word in each context. (Ironically, "brothers and sisters" [figurative] is the primary sense of *adelphoi* in the New Testament Epistles.)

This distinction between literal and primary may seem like a small thing, but it has far-reaching implications, since the literal fallacy gives the false impression that the grammatical gender of such words as *adelphoi* in some sense controls their meaning. This inappropriately opens the door for talking about supposed nuances of male meaning that must always be preserved in translation.

The Example of Singular Adelphos

Several of the fallacies discussed above appear together in P&G's discussion of the singular *adelphos.* While acknowledging that the plural *adelphoi* can mean "brothers and sisters," they reject the translation "brother or sister" for the singular. They write, "The plural is used to cover mixed groups, but the singular always covers only one person. That one can be either male or female. If the one is male, *adelphos* is the appropriate term. If the one is female, *adelphē.*[81]

The statement "the singular always covers only one person" is a confusion of form and meaning, since generic uses of a word do not refer to only one person but to people or classes of people (e.g., "man shall not live on bread alone" [Matt 4:4]). It is also a "literal meaning fallacy," since it fails to recognize that *adelphos* can function either with an individual referent (e.g., "he is my brother") or as a generic term ("a brother should not hurt a brother"). Just as the English generic "a person" can mean "a man or a woman" and the Greek *anthrōpos* (masculine!) can mean "a man or a woman," so *adelphos* can mean "a brother or a sister."

P&G recognize that *adelphos* can be used in generic contexts, but they still reject the translation "brother or sister." Why? Because they claim these are male representative passages.

> But what happens when one uses *adelphos* in an example like Matthew 5:22, which is intended to express a general truth? The effect is somewhat like what we have seen with generic "he." The masculine form of *adelphos* leads the listener to picture in his mind a male example. But the male example illustrates a general truth.[82]

The assumption that these are male representative passages again confuses form and meaning—that a grammatically masculine form necessarily carries male connotations. P&G also repeat the fallacy that a masculine term requires the reader to envision a man. This would mean, as we have seen, that the Spanish *la persona* would force the hearer to envision a woman. This is linguistic nonsense.

Furthermore, there is little evidence in these contexts that *adelphos* is a male representative rather than a true generic. Consider these examples from 1 John:

> Anyone who claims to be in the light but hates his *adelphos* is still in the darkness. Whoever loves his *adelphos* lives in the light, and there is nothing in him to make him stumble. But whoever hates his *adelphos* is in the darkness and walks around in the darkness; he does not know where he is going, because the darkness has blinded him.
>
> 1 JOHN 2:9–11 (cf. 1 John 3:10, 15)

This passage is clearly about hating or loving a fellow believer, whether male or female. Nothing in the passage suggests a male standing as a representative for a group. If the Greek term here were *anthrōpos,* P&G would surely not object to the translation "Anyone who hates *a person*" instead of "Anyone who hates a *man,*" since they admit that *anthrōpos* is fully generic in similar contexts. But there is little, if any, difference between the masculine generic function of *anthrōpos* and the masculine generic function of *adelphos.* Just as *anthrōpos* can mean "a person" (= "a man or a woman"), so *adelphos* can mean "a sibling" (= "a brother or a sister").

We could add to these linguistic arguments the lexical evidence. Contrary to the claims of P&G,[83] the Greek lexicons affirm this sense of *adelphos.* Louw and Nida identify one meaning of *adelphos* as "a fellow believer," noting that the masculine form "may include both men and women."[84] Bauer says that *adelphos* is used of "everyone who is devoted to [Jesus]" and of "Christians in their relations w. each other."[85] Liddell and Scott note one sense of *adelphos* as "a fellow Christian."[86]

Political Correctness and the Gender-Language Debate

In conclusion, a word should be said about the political and social motivations present in this debate. Throughout their book P&G repeatedly warn of the politically correct agenda of radical feminism that is driving gender-language changes. These are legitimate concerns. I, too, am a conservative evangelical who has concerns about feminist agendas. But we must not let our theological agendas cloud our judgment concerning sound hermeneutical and linguistic principles. We must instead set out clearly the goals, methods, and philosophy of Bible translation and then draw conclusions based on these, rather than on our abhorrence for certain cultural tendencies.

We must also be cautious, because the claim of political correctness can cut both ways. To be politically correct in most conservative evangelical contexts is to strongly oppose any hint of feminism. Many conservative and evangelical leaders are antifeminist, and have come out strongly against any inclusive-language changes. I know of professors at conservative institutions who would endorse the TNIV if it weren't for the fear of losing their teaching positions.

The first response among many evangelicals upon hearing of a "gender-neutral Bible" is indignation and disgust. Witness, for example, the near hysteria against the NIVI provoked by a series of articles in *World* magazine several years ago.[87] P&G suggest that this reaction was in fact a response based on level 3 linguistics—the intuitive reflexes of native speakers of the language.[88] But nothing I read in *World* magazine and other popular sources reflected anything but level 1 naïveté: major confusion of form and meaning provoked by a ideologically motivated suspicion of feminism. In fact, the strongest reactions occurred *before* people had even seen or read the NIVI or the TNIV. How could they intuitively perceive that these changes were wrong before they even knew their nature? Witness also the fact that many people had been happily reading a dozen or so inclusive-language versions (NLT, NCV, CEV, TEV, NRSV, etc.[89]) without any negative reaction—until they were informed that these were "gender-neutral" versions![90] Only then did the "Bible rage" begin.[91]

In short, let us all watch our agendas. The great challenge we face as biblical scholars and translators is to reproduce the meaning of God's Word in the most accurate and reliable way we can. The decision to use or not use inclusive language in each case should be based on this goal alone.

Notes

1. With gratitude and joy I offer this article in honor of Dr. Ron Youngblood on the occasion of his retirement. Ron has been a wonderful mentor, friend, and colleague during my years at Bethel Seminary San Diego. I am grateful to New Testament scholars Darrell Bock, Dan Wallace, Roy Ciampa, and Craig Blomberg, linguists and Bible translators Wayne Leman, Peter Kirk, and Mike Sangrey, as well as Ben Irwin, associate editor at Zondervan—all of whom read early drafts of this work and offered many helpful suggestions. I come away from this experience convinced that all research in New Testament should be examined and critiqued by linguists and Bible translators, and all research in Bible translation should be examined and critiqued by biblical scholars. As iron sharpens iron, so these disciplines need each other.

2. No universally accepted terminology has been established in this debate. The terms *gender-inclusive, gender-accurate,* and *gender-neutral* have all been used. While each of these may carry different nuances, depending on the context, all three refer to translations that replace masculine generic terms with inclusive (non-gender-specific) ones. I will discuss this definition later in this essay.

3. The debate is chronicled in my book *Distorting Scripture? The Challenge of Bible Translation and Gender Accuracy* (Downers Grove, Ill.: InterVarsity Press, 1998), 20–22; and in greater detail in D. A. Carson, *The Inclusive-Language Debate. A Plea for Realism* (Grand Rapids: Baker, 1998), 28–38; and in Vern S. Poythress and Wayne A. Grudem, *The Gender-Neutral Bible Controversy: Muting the Masculinity of God's Words* (Nashville: Broadman & Holman, 2000), 13–29.

4. In addition to the NIVI and the TNIV, translations or major revisions that intentionally use inclusive language—to varying degrees—include the New Jerusalem Bible (NJB; 1985), the New Century Version (NCV; 1987), the New American Bible (NAB; NT and Psalms revised; 1988, 1990), the Revised English Bible (REB; 1989), the New Revised Standard Version (NRSV; 1990), the Good News Bible (GNB; revised 1992 [also called Today's English Version, TEV]), *The Message* (1993), the Contemporary English Version (CEV; 1995), God's Word (GW; 1995), the New Living Translation (NLT; 1996), the New English Translation (NET; 1996–2001), the International Standard Version (ISV; 1998), the Holman Christian Standard Bible (HCSB; 2000), and the English Standard Version (ESV; 2001). Among these, the last two arose in the context of opposition to the NIVI and so are more reserved than the others in their use of inclusive language.

5. See my article "Linguistic and Hermeneutical Fallacies in the Guidelines Established at the 'Conference on Gender-Related Language in Scripture,'" *JETS* 41, no. 2 (June 1998): 239–62; on the Web at http://biblepacesetter.org/bibletranslation/files/list.htm. This is a revised version of a paper originally presented at the forty-ninth annual meeting of the Evangelical Theological Society (20–22 November 1997).

6. The latter reason is given by Poythress and Grudem, *The Gender-Neutral Bible Controversy,* 88; the former on page 89 of their book. I will leave it to those who wish to consult the early writings on this debate to judge for themselves whether this was a real or only a perceived naïveté.

7. When I say "all parties" here and in the following discussion, I am referring to Carson, Poythress, Grudem, and myself, though in most cases I believe it would include others who have written on this topic (including Grant Osborne, John Kohlenberger, Andreas Köstenberger, Darrell Bock, Craig Blomberg, Jon Weatherly, and others).

8. In light of this agreement, it is somewhat odd that P&G devote an entire chapter (in a very long book) to a defense of the authority of Scripture.

9. Strauss, *Distorting Scripture?* 77, 84; Carson, *The Inclusive-Language Debate,* 70; Poythress and Grudem, *The Gender-Neutral Bible Controversy,* 70–71.

10. Strauss, 77–86; Carson, chapter 3, esp. p. 72; Poythress and Grudem, 58–61.

11. Strauss, 28, 78–82, 134, 153; Carson, chapters 3–4, passim, esp. pp. 58–60; Poythress and Grudem, 67, 70–71, 189, 342. This point is particularly well developed by Carson.

12. Strauss, 99–100, 145; Carson, 17–18, 72–74, 90, chapter 9; Poythress and Grudem, 89.

13. Strauss, 140–46; Carson, 183–92; Poythress and Grudem, 96, 224.

14. Strauss, 28; Carson, chapter 3; Poythress and Grudem, 70–71.

15. Strauss, 94–102; Carson, 52–53, 61–62; Poythress and Grudem, 58–59.

16. Strauss, 94–98; Carson, 48; Poythress and Grudem, 58–59.

17. Strauss, 100–102; Carson, 64; Poythress and Grudem, 169–72.

18. Strauss, chapters 5–6, esp. pp. 133–36; Carson, passim, esp. chapters 5–8; Poythress and Grudem, chapter 5 ("Permissible Changes in Translating Gender-Related Terms"), where they point out examples of inclusive language that "improve the accuracy of translation" (p. 91). See also pp. 167, 180 note 23, 295.

19. Strauss, 127–29; Carson, 16–17; Poythress and Grudem, passim.

20. Strauss, 130–32; Carson, 103–105; Poythress and Grudem, passim.

21. Strauss, 129, 130, 157; Poythress and Grudem, 101–7.

22. Strauss, 134–35; Carson, 75–76, 121; Poythress and Grudem, 267–68.

23. Strauss, 16; Carson, 16–17; Poythress and Grudem, 182.

24. Strauss, 86–88; Carson, chapter 4; Poythress and Grudem, 85, 201, 202, 336.

25. Strauss, 104–12; Carson, 120–28; Poythress and Grudem, 95–96.

26. Strauss, 104–12; Carson, 120–28; Poythress and Grudem, 93–95.

27. Strauss, 104–12; Carson, 120–28; Poythress and Grudem, 247.

28. Strauss, 147–51; Carson, 130–31; Poythress and Grudem, 160, 263–68 (with some qualifications).

29. Strauss, 155–62; Carson, 131–33; Poythress and Grudem, 255.

30. See especially their discussion on pages 261–63, esp. 262 note 37.

31. Strauss, 151–55; Carson, 133; Poythress and Grudem, 107–8.

32. Strauss, 151–55; Carson, 133.

33. They write, "Both the Greek and Hebrew terms can refer to more distant ancestors as well," but clarify that "it turns out that instances of this kind usually refer to grandfathers, great-grandfathers, and other *male* ancestors" (250–51). Their use of "usually" seems to allow that "ancestors" may at times be an acceptable translation (251 note 252).

34. Strauss, 188–90; Carson, 166–70; Poythress and Grudem, 234–38.

35. Strauss, 162–63, 188–91; Carson, 170–75; Poythress and Grudem, 242–45.

36. Strauss, *Distorting Scripture?* 14–15.

37. Poythress and Grudem, *The Gender-Neutral Bible Controversy,* 94.

38. Wayne Grudem, "NIV Controversy: Participants Sign Landmark Agreement," *CBMW News* 2, no. 3 (June 1997): 5.

39. See Wayne Grudem, "What's Wrong with 'Gender Neutral' Bible Translations?" (Council on Biblical Manhood and Womanhood, 1997), 17; Poythress and Grudem, *The Gender-Neutral Bible Controversy,* 263–68.

40. At this point P&G are confusing the category of what may be labeled "gender-inclusive Bible versions" (versions that intentionally and systematically utilize inclusive terms for masculine generic ones) with "gender-inclusive language" (the use of inclusive terms for masculine generics). When discussing particular examples of translation (as in their quote above), we are obviously dealing with the latter. P&G are objecting to the wholesale and uncritical use of inclusive language that results in significant loss of meaning. But everyone would agree on this. Both D. A. Carson and I (not to mention many other conservative evangelicals) have always argued for a careful case-by-case exegesis to determine when inclusive language is and is not acceptable.

41. Poythress and Grudem, *The Gender-Neutral Bible Controversy,* 94.

42. Ibid., 82–90.

43. Ibid., 83.

44. Ibid., 87.

45. Craig Blomberg expresses a similar perspective in a review of P&G's *The Gender-Neutral Bible Controversy:* "Unfortunately, this book is such a complex combination of important observations, misleading half-truths, and linguistic naivete that it will only stir up emotions once again, further clouding what is really at stake (and what is not) in this debate" (Craig Blomberg, "Review of *The Gender-Neutral Bible Controversy: Muting the Masculinity of God's Words,*" *Denver Journal,* vol. 4, 2001; available online at http://www.gospelcom.net/densem/dj/articles01/0200/0204.html).

46. Poythress and Grudem, *The Gender-Neutral Bible Controversy,* 117, 127–28.

47. Ibid., 65, 70, 73, 189–91, 193, 340, etc.

48. Ibid., 126.

49. P&G seem to be functioning from the perspective that masculine generic "he" retains *all* of the meaning, while other generic expressions change subtle nuances (though elsewhere they admit there is no absolute identity between languages). With reference to various inclusive translations they write, "The differences due to starting point may be subtle, but they are there—differences in nuance in the total meaning-impact, not merely differences in phrasing with *no* meaning difference" (114). Again: "two radically different wordings are typically *not completely identical in meaning*" (67). Again: "Speech and writing operate in too many dimensions for a rough paraphrase to get everything right" (78). But this goal of complete identity of meaning or getting "everything right" is never attained by *any* translation—and certainly not by retaining the formally equivalent "he." See more on this below.

50. Poythress and Grudem, *The Gender-Neutral Bible Controversy,* 215.

51. Ibid., 325.

52. Examples of this may be found in the NRSV, which I believe went overboard in its attempt to capture all of the inclusive nuances. I have elsewhere criticized the NRSV and other versions in this regard (see Strauss, *Distorting Scripture?* 153–54, 214, etc.).

53. Indeed, P&G sound almost like philosophical deconstructionists (Jacques Derrida, etc.) as they page after page seek to show the loss of meaning in translations which use inclusive language. What they (and the deconstructionists) do not acknowledge is that while any sentence can be "deconstructed" to show ambiguities and imprecision, the essential meaning can be preserved and communicated.

54. Poythress and Grudem, *The Gender-Neutral Bible Controversy,* 295.

55. For examples of the hundreds of times the TNIV improves the gender language of the NIV, even when following the Colorado Springs Guidelines, see my article, "Examples of Improvement in Accuracy of the TNIV over the NIV When Following the Colorado Springs Guidelines," available on the Web at http://biblepacesetter.org/bibletranslation/files/list.htm. For other examples of improvements in accuracy in the TNIV over the NIV, see the TNIV Website at www.tniv.info.

56. Poythress and Grudem, *The Gender-Neutral Bible Controversy,* 94–96.

57. Ibid., 180 note 23.

58. "Functional equivalence," previously called "dynamic equivalence," refers to the meaning-based translation theories developed by Eugene Nida and others.

59. The English translation that comes closest to this goal is the NET Bible, which uses extensive footnotes to explore alternate interpretations and various nuances of meaning (see it at www.bible.org/netbible/index.htm).

60. Poythress and Grudem point out in their chapter on generic "he" that "from now on we are talking only about backward-referring generic 'he'" (111).

61. For a discussion of these alternatives to masculine generic "he," see Strauss, *Distorting Scripture?* 117–27.

62. Poythress and Grudem, *The Gender-Neutral Bible Controversy,* chapters 7–11, pp. 111–232, 277–78; esp. 142ff.

63. Ibid., 143.

64. Ibid., 92, 98.

65. Wayne Grudem, "A Response to Mark Strauss' Evaluation of the Colorado Springs Translation Guidelines," *JETS* 41, no. 2 (June 1998): 274. See the same basic argument in Poythress and Grudem, *The Gender-Neutral Bible Controversy,* 142ff.

66. Of course the Spirit is not a "he" either but rather a person. Ideally, English would have a singular pronoun that did not indicate sexual identity, but only personhood. Better yet (like some languages around the world), English would have pronouns reserved only for deity. Like all languages, English again falls short of perfection, and so for now, linguistically, "we see through a glass darkly" (1 Cor 13:12 KJV).

67. Poythress and Grudem, *The Gender-Neutral Bible Controversy,* 192–93.

68. Ibid., 193.

69. I am grateful to Darrell Bock for this insight.

70. See especially Carson, *The Inclusive-Language Debate,* chapter 4. P&G celebrate that English still has the ability to express supposedly God-ordained masculine generics. But what about those languages that do not use masculine generics or whose pronouns have no gender distinctions? Will they have to muddle along with inferior and

unreliable translations, incapable of communicating the male nuances that God built into Hebrew and Greek? Should we engineer masculine generics for these language so they can more accurately express God's Word? Of course not. The beauty of God's Word is that its meaning can be translated with accuracy into any language in the world, whatever the gender system may be.

71. See my article "Linguistic and Hermeneutical Fallacies" (see note 5), and *Distorting Scripture?* passim, esp. chapter 4.

72. I am grateful to Ben Irwin, associate editor at Zondervan, for making this point. For discussion of this fallacy, see James Barr, *The Semantics of Biblical Language* (Oxford: Oxford Univ. Press, 1961), 218; Moisés Silva, *Biblical Words and Their Meaning* (Grand Rapids: Zondervan, 1983), 25–27; D. A. Carson, *Exegetical Fallacies,* 2d ed. (Grand Rapids: Baker, 1996), 60–61.

73. See Poythress and Grudem, *The Gender-Neutral Bible Controversy,* 190–91.

74. Ibid., 191 note 3.

75. Ibid., 257–58. This distinction should be maintained, they argue, since "It is God's business to decide what meaning components are important to include in the Bible, not ours!" But it is we, of course, with the help of the Spirit, who must determine which meaning God intended.

76. Poythress and Grudem, *The Gender-Neutral Bible Controversy,* 257.

77. For more on these terms see Strauss, *Distorting Scripture?* 155–66.

78. Poythress and Grudem, *The Gender-Neutral Bible Controversy,* 264.

79. We should remind the reader that, technically speaking, these English phrases are not the actual *senses* of the Greek term but rather English *glosses* meant to represent, as closely as possible, its various senses.

80. The fact that *adelphoi* is not used for sisters alone does not change this fundamental lexical point. While it is true that "only sisters" is not within the semantic range of *adelphoi,* this does not push its meaning closer to the idea of "brothers" in any particular context, since context alone determines which sense within the semantic range is intended.

81. Poythress and Grudem, *The Gender-Neutral Bible Controversy,* 269.

82. Ibid.

83. Ibid., 269 note 47; 276 note 52.

84. J. P. Louw and E. A. Nida, *Greek-English Lexicon of the New Testament Based on Semantic Domains,* 2d ed. (New York: United Bible Societies), 1:125; 2:4.

85. W. Bauer, *A Greek-English Lexicon of the New Testament and Other Early Christian Literature,* 2d ed., eds. W. F. Arndt, F. W. Gingrich, F. W. Danker (Chicago and London: University of Chicago Press, 1979), 16.

86. H. J. Liddell and R. Scott, *Greek-English Lexicon with a Revised Supplement,* 9th rev. ed., eds. S. Liddell and P. G. Glare (Oxford: Clarendon, 1996).

87. See Susan Olasky, "The Stealth Bible: The popular New International Version is quietly going 'gender-neutral,'" *World,* 29 March 1997: 12–15; *idem,* "The Battle for the Bible," *World*, 19 April 1997: 14–18.

88. Poythress and Grudem, *The Gender-Neutral Bible Controversy,* 88.

89. See note 4.

90. See Strauss, *Distorting Scripture?* 22.

91. For this designation see Carson, *The Inclusive-Language Debate,* 15–16.

5

TRANSLATION AS A COMMUNAL TASK

Herbert M. Wolf[1]

In the latter half of the twentieth century, most of the translations of the Bible were group projects rather than the work of a single individual. Committees and consultants worked together to produce renditions that were striving to be, at one and the same time, accurate and readable. Trying to get committees to succeed is a formidable challenge. We all know that too many cooks can spoil the broth, and each biblical scholar and theologian approaches Scripture a little differently. In a way, a committee translation could be compared to hiring fifteen interior decorators to work on the same house. One good decorator could do the job, while fifteen highly skilled individuals have too many ideas and differing tastes. How could you possibly get them to agree, and what would the house look like when it was finished? Although a Bible translation produced by a group or groups of individuals could encounter the same problems, happily there are other factors that neutralize the potential weaknesses of a committee. Rather than ruining the creative ability of the individual, a committee—if functioning smoothly—can capitalize on the strengths of each person and at the same time prevent the idiosyncrasies of any single contributor from affecting the translation adversely. The committee becomes a team that can produce a better translation than any one person.

Interpretive Communities

Recent books on biblical interpretation have wrestled with the role of interpretive communities as we seek to understand Scripture. Some scholars suggest that the biblical text can never be understood apart from the way the practices and procedures of a particular interpretive community impose a meaning on the text.[2] The interpretation determines the meaning rather than discovers the meaning. Such a subjective approach—which could also be called an internal realistic one—emphasizes that a community's engagement with the text plays a large role in assigning any meaning that the text may have. The interests of the interpreting community really govern interpretation, and the reader benefits from knowing the discipline of being part of God's people.[3] Kevin Vanhoozer rightly protests that, with the Reformers, we should "not assign final authority to the opinion of the interpreting community, or even to the encounter of that community with the text. No, final authority belongs to Scripture alone,"[4] and our approach to understanding Scripture should be one of hermeneutical realism.

Yet Anthony Thiselton warns us that every individual reads the Bible "in the light of horizons of expectation which have been derived from, and shaped by, the communities to which the individual reader belongs."[5] We are shaped by our families, our local churches, our schools, and the traditions that are part of this context. Moisés Silva has observed that all Bible interpreters are indebted to theologians who down through the centuries have made great strides in explaining the Scriptures and in formulating the creeds. As we approach the text of the Bible, our understanding depends on those who have preceded us and shaped our knowledge of Scripture and theology.[6] Even the Reformers retained a strong connection with the Christian church, and they did not interpret Scripture isolated from earlier roots. John Calvin himself consulted commentaries and theologians and was deeply indebted to them. And we are indebted to Calvin and Martin Luther and all the theologians who have worked within their interpretive circles to explain the Scriptures.

Missiologists point to the role of the community in formulating theology and in establishing categories of knowledge. "Theology must be done in the community" rather than by the individual.[7] In an effort to communicate the gospel, missionaries are keenly aware of the importance of studying cultural contexts. The Bible must be translated into forms and meanings understood by a particular culture.[8] In spite of our Judeo-Christian heritage, even translations into English must contextualize to some extent. If we want to express the ancient Hebrew and Greek concepts, we must do so by using Western thought-forms and nuances, with a thorough understanding of the ancient cultural context as well as our own. The best translation will come from those who are immersed in the modern context and are as conversant as possible with the life and times of the biblical world. Contextualization completes the hermeneutical circle as it transfers the meaning of Scripture into the present situation.[9]

When the NIV was launched, it drew on a large number of interpretive communities in order to give the translation balance and a sense of history. Over the years the Committee on Bible Translation (CBT) has had members from the United States, Canada, England, and New Zealand representing many denominations, such as Anglican, Baptist, Brethren, Christian Reformed, Evangelical Free, Lutheran, Mennonite, Methodist, Nazarene, and Presbyterian. Such widespread representation was designed to minimize any bias in the translation and to incorporate the insights of as many different groups as possible. Particular denominations prefer different commentaries, so the translators brought with them a wealth of information about biblical exegesis and theology. This ensured that the committee was conversant with all the major schools of interpretation and could draw on the best in biblical scholarship.

In spite of their diversity, the translators shared many of the same commitments. All were convinced of the inspiration and authority of Scripture and of the unity of the Bible. All were in agreement that Scripture interprets Scripture and that proper exegetical technique paved the way for accurate translation. And although they held divergent theological viewpoints on some issues, each translator respected the views of the others. They went forward on their knees convinced that the Lord would prosper the work.

The Translation Process

Kevin Vanhoozer has described the "interpretive virtues" that readers need to cultivate as they approach the Bible. These qualities of openness, honesty, humility, attention, and thoughtfulness are also of great help in the translation process.[10] When the Committee on Bible Translation began its work, probably few realized the intensity and thoroughness of the project. The level of openness and honesty was at the same time refreshing and disturbing. As different interpretations and translation proposals were discussed, the pros and cons of each view were considered exhaustively. Any weakness was quickly pointed out, and the translators kept pressing for still a better translation. Each individual was highly critical of any suggestion, and it developed into a good illustration of the proverb that "iron sharpens iron" (Prov 27:17). For the person making a proposal, the close scrutiny involved a certain degree of humbling to which it was not easy to adjust. After all, we were teachers who were used to criticizing student papers and exams and who were not used to being criticized ourselves. This persistence meant that gradually the quality of the proposals improved as the quest for excellence continued. And all had to admit that, although the Bible in the original autographs is perfect, our own understanding of it is not infallible.[11]

If suggestions were rejected, sometimes new proposals were modifications of an earlier suggestion, with several people contributing to a formulation. At times a rejected proposal was later offered by a second individual, thinking it was his own suggestion. If adopted, the original proposer would wisely not object, because it is amazing how much can be accomplished if you don't care who gets the credit!

In arriving at the final translation of a verse, the committee would vote between the best alternatives. By this time the options would be narrowed down, and both alternatives would be viable ones. Before the final vote, the proposals were studied by English-language stylists, who sought to help Hebrew and Greek specialists whose English wasn't always the smoothest. The stylists did not have a vote on the actual translation, but their suggestions were often very helpful in determining the final outcome. The quality of the NIV depended on the judgment of the translators, who were able to evaluate all the evidence presented and then make good decisions.

Like any good committee, the NIV translators were able to utilize the strengths of each individual. Some translators were experts on particular Bible books or on archaeological matters. Others had superb knowledge of grammar and syntax and helped us understand the exegesis of a passage. Several members of the committee were highly skilled at English expression—competent to put into smooth idiomatic English whatever the original Hebrew or Greek required.

Because of the commitment of the committee to an accurate translation, the time spent on exegetical considerations was substantial. No stone was left unturned in an effort to find out the meaning of the text before we turned to the challenge of how to say it in English. Careful attention was given to genre and context and to understanding the argument of a given passage. Meanings of words and phrases were studied meticulously, and any parallel passages were closely examined. During the review of the NIV ongoing since 1990, special attention is being given to difficult passages. Each book is examined by a reviewer and a respondent, and their suggestions are then taken up by the full committee.

The communal nature of the translation process is illustrated in this review process. English-speaking scholars from all over the world are chosen to review a book in which they have expertise. In this way the CBT is able to benefit from the work of scholars who otherwise may not have contributed to the NIV. British scholars who have been involved in this review have noted that the translation of "saints" in the Pauline epistles is growing more problematic in Great Britain, because people assume that the term refers only to those individuals officially venerated by the church. Since "saints" is sometimes misunderstood in America also, the CBT recently voted to retain "saints" only in the salutations of Paul's epistles. Elsewhere we will use "believers" or "God's people" to render the Greek *hagioi*. Similarly, in verses 18 and 21 of Daniel 7, "saints" will be changed to "holy people," which currently is used in the NIV in Daniel 8:24.

Since 1978 many individuals have written the committee to offer suggestions for improvement. One of the most successful was a short article on Hebrews 11:11, submitted by J. Harold Greenlee.[12] By careful argumentation and an especially cogent explanation of *eis katabolēn spermatos,* Dr. Greenlee convinced the CBT to adopt its footnote as the correct text: "And by faith even Sarah, who was past age, was enabled to bear children." This has the decided advantage of putting the emphasis (on being "past age") where Genesis 18:13 puts it—on Sarah rather than on Abraham.

THE INFLUENCE OF TRADITION: THE KING JAMES VERSION

There is no question that the NIV translators were heavily indebted to the Authorized Version and to the power of its renderings. The CBT had no wish to change the theological terms or thought-forms of the KJV, and so it kept these wherever possible. Words such as *justification, redemption, sanctification, predestination,* and *grace* were retained as part of a rich heritage of theological terms. In the words of R. Laird Harris—who up until 1999 remained active in NIV work—the NIV was designed to do for our day what the King James translation did for its time. To the extent that we have succeeded, we are profoundly grateful. Because of the familiarity and beauty of many well-loved expressions and verses, we left such verses largely untouched. For example, Colossians 1:18 contains a magnificent description of Jesus Christ as "the head of the body, the church; he is the beginning and firstborn from among the dead, so that in everything he might have the supremacy." The verse employs a wordplay on Christ as the "firstborn" so that he might have "first place." Since the KJV used "preeminence" for this term, the NIV was reluctant to reflect the wordplay and chose instead "supremacy."

I remember the impassioned plea of Dr. Frank Gaebelein to retain the KJV "apple of the eye" in Deuteronomy 32:10 rather than changing it to the more accurate—and prosaic—"pupil of the eye." The Hebrew literally has "'little man of his eye," referring to the pupil—because one can see his or her image in another person's pupil. Dr. Gaebelein argued that "apple of the eye" has become such a well-known expression that we must not change it. His view prevailed, and the NIV retained the colorful term also in Psalm 17:8 and Proverbs 7:2.

Psalm 23 is another passage where the influence of the KJV is strongly felt. The NIV originally changed "The LORD is my shepherd, I shall not want" to "The LORD is my shepherd, I shall lack nothing," and this was harshly criticized by literature professors as having no poetic merit. Actually on this point the Committee on Bible Translation was caught in the cross fire between literature professors and Christian Education teachers who had been worn out trying to explain "I shall not want" in Sunday school classes. (They should have been thankful they didn't have to use the New English Bible with its rendering "I shall want nothing"!) Duly chastened, the NIV retreated to the current "I shall not be in want."

The NIV made only slight changes in Isaiah 7:14 and left "virgin" rather than changing it to "maiden" or "young woman." Although the interpretation of the verse in the context of Isaiah 7 and 8 ("Immanuel" appears again in 8:8 and 8:10) remains difficult, a good case can be made for leaving *ʿalmâ* as virgin.[13] A double meaning may well be attended, and the strongly Christological material in Isaiah 9 and 11 warns us not to ignore the prophetic aspect of 7:14.

The frequently memorized Romans 1:16 currently reads in the NIV "I am not ashamed of the gospel, because it is the power of God for the salvation of everyone who believes." To make the verse a little clearer, the TNIV has "because it is the power of God that brings salvation to everyone who believes." In the review process we have tended to make relationships between phrases more explicit.

In 1 Corinthians 13:3 a textual criticism decision brings about in the TNIV a rather drastic change from both the NIV and the KJV. Rather than the graphic "and surrender my body to the flames" ("and give my body to be burned" [KJV]), the TNIV reads "and give over my body [to hardship] that I may boast." The one letter difference between *kauchēsomai* and *kauthēsomai* is indeed an easy scribal error, and the New Testament professors on the CBT were convinced that the more dramatic "surrender my body to the flames" was a later change.

In a few places the NIV felt it necessary to change time-honored theological terms, as in Romans 3:25, where we abandoned the word "propitiation" and opted for "a sacrifice of atonement." The Greek *hilastērion* was the usual Septuagint translation for *kappōret,* the cover of the ark of the covenant where blood was sprinkled once a year on the Day of Atonement.[14] And since the NIV regularly used "atonement cover" to translate the Hebrew term (see Lev 16:2, 14, 15), it made sense to use a similar rendering in Romans 3:25 (also cf. Heb 9:5). The simpler "sacrifice of atonement" is more understandable to the average reader.[15]

Another famous verse modified by the NIV is 2 Timothy 3:16, well-known from the KJV's "All Scripture is given by inspiration of God." The NIV has "All Scripture is God-breathed," a rendering of *theopneustos* that is probably more accurate and powerful than "inspired" in the way it "affirms God's active involvement in the writing of Scripture."[16] Because the Greek *theopneustos* literally means "God-breathed," this translation enables theologians to articulate the doctrine of inspiration even more precisely.

The Influence of Literary Studies

Biblical studies have long benefited from the contributions from related fields such as archaeology, anthropology, sociology, and linguistics, and advances in these subjects have illustrated the communal nature of the translation process. Insights from these studies have improved our understanding of the Bible and have helped clarify difficult passages. In recent decades the field of narrative art or rhetorical criticism has perhaps made the greatest impact on biblical studies, and the NIV made good use of such progress. The recognition of literary artistry has assisted the translators in both narrative and poetic passages. The TNIV will give further evidence of this influence.

Rhetorical devices such as inclusio, chiasm, symmetry, repetition, and refrains have been identified and utilized with good effect. As early as Genesis 1:1–2:3 the NIV set off 1:1–2 and 2:1 in separate paragraphs to indicate the summary nature of these verses and the inclusio that is produced. In his important book *The Art of Biblical Narrative,* Robert Alter refers to the "tightly symmetrical envelope structure" in Genesis 2:2–3 and to the inclusio with 1:1 in the repetition of "God created."[17] Throughout Genesis 1 the account of each day's creative activity is introduced by an offset "And God said" and concluded with a dash and the number of the day: "—the first day" in verse 5 through "—the sixth day" in verse 31. The indentation of the remaining lines in each day clearly marks the paragraph and produces a seven-stanza effect.[18]

The account of the tower of Babel in Genesis 11:1–9 contains a highly developed inverted or hourglass structure that goes beyond inclusio. Verses 1–2 and 8–9 are narrative "enclosures" that begin and end the account. Genesis 11:3–4 corresponds to 11:6–7, as both are made up of direct discourse and contain the phrase "Come, let us" (vv. 3, 7). Verse 5 is the narrow opening of the hourglass that provides the transition from one unit to the next, joining the activity of men in verses 1–4 to the response of God in verses 6–9. The account is thus perfectly symmetrical.[19]

Scholars have long recognized the literary significance of the Hebrew term *tôledôt*—"generations" or "account"—translated as *geneseōs* (i.e., "genesis") by the Septuagint. This term is found in ten headings that divide the book of Genesis into its main sections. Except for Genesis 2:4, where we have the sentence "This is the account of the heavens and the earth," *tôledôt* precedes the name of key individuals whose family history follows the heading. Sections one through five constitute primeval history, ending with "the account of Shem" in 11:10, while the last five divisions—starting with "the account of Terah" father of Abraham in 11:27 and ending with "the account of Jacob" in 37:2—comprise patriarchal history.[20] In the NIV there is a space before and after each heading to draw attention to its important function.

As we might expect, the book of Psalms contains more examples of rhetorical flourishes than any other part of Scripture. In the *NIV Study Bible* notes, John Stek—in a superb analysis—draws attention to numerous instances of poetic artistry. For instance, the well-known Psalm 110 is divided into two balanced parts (vv. 1–3 and 4–7), each beginning with an oracle (vv. 1, 4) and followed by thematically similar material. Psalm 107 has an introduction (vv. 1–3) and conclusion (v. 43) that frame six stanzas, four of which contain two refrains—one repeated in verses 6, 13, 19, 28 and the other in verses 8, 15, 21, 31. Its recitational style is closely linked with Psalms 104–106. Similarly, Psalm 139 is divided into four six-verse stanzas, and the opening verse ("O LORD, you have searched me and you know me") forms an inclusio with verse 23 ("Search me, O God, and know my heart").

The symmetry exhibited by Psalm 132 is truly remarkable. Each half of the psalm has an opening petition (vv. 1, 10), followed by an oath taken by David (v. 2) and by the Lord (v. 11). Each oath is followed by a quotation consisting of three couplets (vv. 3–5 and 11b–12). A second quotation in each half has to do with a resting place. In verse 8 the reference is to a resting place for the ark, while in verse 14 God affirms that he has chosen Zion as "my resting place for ever and ever." The prayer that the "priests be clothed with righteousness" and the "saints sing for joy" (v. 9) is answered by the Lord's assurance that he "will clothe her priests with salvation" and "her saints will ever sing for joy." The spaces in the NIV text after verses 1, 5, and 9 in the first half of the psalm and after verses 10, 12, and 16 in the second half highlight the beautiful balance of this song.[21]

A somewhat different sort of symmetry can be found in the book of Esther, a narrative many consider to be a literary masterpiece. Repetition and irony are highly developed as the story unfolds, and one of the most striking reversals in the book is a comparison of 3:1–4:3 with 8:1–17. In chapter 3 Haman was given the king's signet ring so that he could send the decree that ordered the murder of the Jews (3:10, 12). The royal secretaries were summoned and wrote out Haman's orders "in the script of each province and in the language of each people" and sent them to the satraps, governors, and nobles in the many provinces (3:12). In chapter 8 Mordecai the Jew was given the same signet ring to seal a counterdecree that would allow the Jews to destroy their enemies (8:2, 8, 11). The royal secretaries were once again summoned to write in the various scripts and distribute the new decree to the same recipients (8:9). "A copy of the text of the edict was to be issued as law in every province" (3:14). This entire verse is repeated in 8:13 with the important addition that "the Jews would be ready on that day to avenge themselves on their enemies." In both 3:15 and 8:14 there is a description of the sending out of the couriers, "spurred on by the king's command." The concluding paragraphs of this comparison (4:1–3 and 8:15–17) present a stark contrast between the wailing and weeping of Mordecai and the Jews and their feasting and celebrating. In 4:1 Mordecai put on sackcloth and ashes, while in 8:15 he is "wearing royal garments of blue and white ... and a purple robe of fine linen." Clearly, narrative art is highly developed in these chapters.

A New Testament example of inclusio is found in the book of Romans by closely comparing 1:5 and 16:26. Both verses refer to the Gentiles *(ethnē)* and contain the same phrase *eis hypakoēn pisteōs* ("to the obedience of faith"). In the NIV the two expressions are handled differently. Romans 1:5 translates *ethnē* as "Gentiles" while 16:26 uses "nations," and the prepositional phrase is rendered "to the obedience that comes from faith" in 1:5 and is turned into two verbs in 16:26—"so that all nations might believe and obey him." To correct this inconsistency and to make the inclusio clearer, the TNIV translates 1:5 "to call all the Gentiles to faith and obedience" and 16:26 "so that all the Gentiles might come to faith and obedience."

One small change in Revelation 1:4 illustrates the interplay between theology and literary usage. In our review of Revelation for the TNIV there was considerable discussion about the translation of "the seven spirits" before God's throne and the possibility that the current footnote ("the sevenfold Spirit") would be the more accurate rendering. The committee felt that there was a clear allusion to the sevenfold Spirit of Isaiah 11:2 and was ready to insert the footnote into the text. Then we realized that the mention of "the seven spirits" in 3:1 is linked with "the seven stars," and in 4:5 and 5:6 with "seven lamps" and with "seven horns" and "seven eyes." Although "the seven spirits" probably does refer to the "sevenfold Spirit," John's use of the "seven spirits" imagery does not permit a change in the translation. In the NIV the footnote reads "Or *the sevenfold Spirit*"; in the TNIV the footnote now reads "That is, the sevenfold Spirit." Hopefully the careful reader will be able to make the connection.

The Placing of Headings in the Text

The study of rhetorical criticism has shown the importance of identifying literary units. The use of chapter divisions, paragraphs, and spacing all contributes to this goal, and some translations use headings to help the reader identify the main subjects of a chapter or other literary unit. The NIV uses section headings in most books, but these were not part of the original translation process. During the course of our work on the TNIV, however, a number of headings have been changed, and the involvement of the whole committee in these decisions once again shows the superiority of collective wisdom over individual choice. As the CBT has considered suggested changes, the new headings have in some cases enabled the reader to understand the flow of a book much more clearly. Generally the headings have been made more descriptive, and new ones have been added. Occasionally they have been moved to different places, in the hope that it represents the structure of a passage more accurately.

In the TNIV a new heading has been added at Matthew 17:22 ("Jesus Predicts His Death a Second Time") and the heading at 20:17 reads "Jesus Predicts His Death a Third Time" (cf. 16:21). When the disciples asked Jesus, "Who is the greatest in the kingdom of heaven?" he placed a little child in front of them and gave his answer (Matt 18:1–9). The TNIV put the paragraph break at verse 6 (the NIV has it at verse 5) and added a new heading ("Causing to Stumble"). "The Triumphal Entry" has been modified to the more accurate "Jesus Comes to Jerusalem as King" in Matthew 21:1 (and the parallel passages in Mark, Luke, and John). There are a number of differences between the NIV and the TNIV in Romans 8 and 9. In the TNIV a new paragraph now begins with 8:14: "For those who are led by the Spirit of God are the children of God." Verse 18 is introduced with the revised heading "Present Suffering and Future Glory" rather than the NIV's "Future Glory." The heading "More Than Conquerors" has been moved from verse 28 to verse 31. In the TNIV chapter 9 begins with "Paul's Anguish Over Israel," while "God's Sovereign Choice" stands in front of verse 6 rather than verse 1.

About half of the headings in 1 Corinthians have been changed and several new ones have been added. For example, the TNIV's heading before 1:10 is "A Church Divided Over Leaders," and 2:6–16 is titled "God's Wisdom Revealed by the Spirit." The NIV has "On Divisions in the Church" before 3:1; the TNIV has "The Church and Its Leaders." Paul's lengthy chapter about marriage in 1 Corinthians 7 has been divided into three sections: "Concerning Married Life" (v. 1), "Concerning Change of Status" (v. 17), and "Concerning the Unmarried" (v. 25). This represents a better analysis than the NIV's lone heading ("Marriage") at the beginning of the chapter. In the TNIV the famous chapter on love is introduced by "Love Is Indispensable" (12:31b–13:13); the NIV has "Love." And a major shift occurs at the beginning of 1 Corinthians 14 (TNIV "Intelligibility in Worship"; NIV "Gifts of Prophecy and Tongues").

The placing of the heading in Ephesians 5 has been controversial because of the way verse 21 is connected to both the preceding and following contexts. But since there is no Greek verb for "submit" in verse 22, it is clear that the verb is understood from verse 21, and the two verses are linked quite closely. The TNIV solution is to use the heading found in Colossians 3:18—"Instructions for Christian Households"—before Ephesians 5:21. Verse 21 is rendered (as in the NIV) as a separate paragraph, so that the words of this verse ("Submit to one another out of reverence for Christ") could apply to the whole section from 5:22–6:9. The heading at Ephesians 4:17 in the TNIV reads "Instructions for Christian Living" ("Living as Children of Light" in the NIV)—a title that nicely complements "Instructions for Christian Households" in 5:21.

A series of changes in TNIV headings found in Hebrews 10–12 affects interpretation issues in these chapters rather significantly. The heading before Hebrews 10:19 is lengthened to "A Call to Persevere in Faith," while the title for chapter 11 reads "Faith in Action" (a more graphic rendering than the NIV's "By Faith"). The first three verses of chapter 12 are linked in the TNIV to chapter 11, as the heading no longer appears at the beginning of verse 1 (as in the NIV) but just before verse 4. The closer connection of these verses to chapter 11 allows us to see more clearly the example of Christ in the midst of the "great cloud of witnesses" to inspire us to persevere in the faith.

How Theology Affects the Translation Process

The determination of literary units plays an important role in our understanding of Scripture, but an equally important issue is the way our translation of theological terms affects interpretation. Exodus 33–34 provides an interesting example of how both the placing of a heading and the translation of theological terms affect the overall interpretation of the passage. In Exodus 33:12–23 Moses pleads with the Lord and prays that the Lord will go with his people as they journey to the promised land. God had threatened to keep his distance from the people after they had engaged in the worship of the golden calf (Exod 32). Yet God assured Moses that he had found favor in his eyes and that he was pleased with him. In response, Moses boldly asked the Lord to show him his glory, and God agreed to let him see his back as he passed by and proclaimed his name, the LORD, in Moses' presence. The Lord said, "I will have mercy on whom I will have mercy, and I will have compassion on whom I will have compassion" (Exod 33:19).

At this point chapter 34 begins with a new heading ("The New Stone Tablets"), which makes us prone to miss the fact that the first nine verses of chapter 34 continue the narrative of 33:12–23. Moses does chisel out two new stone tablets, but the next morning the glory of the Lord passes in front of Moses on Mount Sinai as the Lord proclaims his name, "The LORD, the LORD, the compassionate and gracious God, slow to anger, abounding in love and faithfulness"

(34:6). Bowing to the ground, Moses acknowledged the Lord's favor and gratefully responded, "then let the Lord go with us" (34:8–9).

The way verses 6 and 7 of Exodus 34 stand out with their theological description of who God is—a description repeated many times in the Old Testament—obscures their connection with the surrounding context and particularly with the last half of chapter 33. Our English translations also hide the fact that the Hebrew word for "favor" *(ḥēn)*, the verb "have mercy" *(ḥānan)* [33:19], and the adjective "gracious" *(ḥannûn)* [34:6] all come from the same root. The idiom "to find favor" in one's eyes occurs in 33:12, 13 (twice), 16, 17, and 34:9. In 33:13, 16, and 17 the NIV translates it "you are pleased with me" (33:13, 16) and "I am pleased with you" (33:17), renderings chosen for stylistic reasons. The King James Version translates all of these as "find grace" in one's sight and also renders the first verb in 33:19 "[I] will be gracious to whom I will be gracious." The consistency of the KJV gives the reader an opportunity to see the connections between "grace" and "gracious," but the expression "to find grace" in one's eyes is not part of current English usage. And when we hear the word "grace" today, we are so conditioned by Paul's use of grace in the New Testament that we fail to hear the broader nuance of "favor." Grace has become a technical word almost limited to "salvation by grace"—skewing the broader dimension of "grace" as "favor."[22] When theologians talk about grace, it likewise takes on its more specialized New Testament meaning amid a soteriological setting.

The NIV could have used the KJV's "be gracious" in 33:19, but when this verse is quoted in Romans 9:15 the KJV switches to "I will have mercy on whom I will have mercy." Since "mercy" is more appropriate to the New Testament context and since the Septuagint of Exodus 33:19 is identical to Romans, it made good sense to use the same translation in both passages. Besides, the KJV regularly translates *ḥānan* "to have mercy" in the book of Psalms (e.g., 51:1; 123:2–3), and the NIV normally follows suit. The translation "have mercy" provides the third way—along with God's showing "favor" and being "pleased with" Moses—to explain the different facets of God's grace. Through this variety of renderings the reader can capture the dimensions of this rich and important concept.

Yet the chapter break (and the new heading) at 34:1 disrupts the continuity of this passage and obscures the emphasis on the presence of God. When Moses pleads for God's presence to go with his people as a sign of his favor, Yahweh (the LORD), "the compassionate and gracious God" (34:6), is favorably disposed to this request and agrees to go with them (v. 9).[23] Moses is thus assured that he has found favor in God's eyes. To tie 34:1–9 more closely to chapter 33, translators must remove the heading at the start of chapter 34. In his commentary on Exodus, John Durham employs the title "Moses' Request and Yahweh's

Response" for 33:18–34:9.[24] This decision clearly affects the interpretation of the passage and enables the reader to tie the two chapters together. A new heading (such as "The Covenant Renewed," as in the NRSV) could be placed before 34:10.[25] Perhaps the layperson's knowledge of "grace" as God's "unmerited favor" will link the several occurrences of "finding favor" with the "gracious God" who not only brought Israel out of Egypt, the land of slavery, but also forgave them for the worship of the golden calf.

The TNIV translators faced a similar problem with the word "grace" in Proverbs 3:34: "He mocks proud mockers, but gives grace to the humble." We changed "gives grace" to "shows favor" in order to avoid an overly theological interpretation of "grace." "Favor" already appears in Proverbs 3:4 in a context of winning "favor and a good name in the sight of God and people." The same change to "shows favor" was made in the TNIV in James 4:6 and 1 Peter 5:5, where Proverbs 3:34 is quoted. Since James 4:6 begins with the statement, "But he gives us more grace," readers will again see "grace" and "favor" in close proximity and will observe that "favor" is sometimes the more appropriate Old Testament translation.

Without question the theological implications of the word "grace" affect the way translators can handle this word in a particular context. The New Testament understanding of grace, as well as the definitions of grace formulated by theologians down through the centuries, color the meaning of the word today. Translators have to take into account the perceptions of the readers, whose concepts of grace and other theological terms have been formed in the context of these developments, especially if they've been regularly exposed to biblical preaching or Christian literature. The translation committee must act as an interpretive community aware of how pastors, commentators, and theologians understand Scripture, and translation decisions must factor all of this in. The committee's choice of words and its organization of sentences into paragraphs and literary units make a big difference in how clearly Scripture is heard. Although translators do not determine meaning, unless they understand the roles of community, culture, and theology, the translation will not communicate clearly and accurately.

Notes

1. Editors' Note: Shortly after completing this essay, Herbert Martin Wolf, professor of Old Testament at Wheaton College and Graduate School, died at his home on 18 October 2002 after a battle with cancer. He was born 15 July 1938 in Springfield, Massachusetts, and studied at Wheaton College, Dallas Theological Seminary, and Brandeis

University (Ph.D.). Subsequently, he returned to Wheaton and served there as a beloved and respected educator for thirty-five years. Among his publications are *Haggai and Malachi* (1976), *Interpreting Isaiah: The Suffering and Glory of the Messiah* (1985), and *An Introduction to the Old Testament Pentateuch* (1991). He was also for many years a member of the Committee on Bible Translation for the New International Version. Herb's scholarly gifts and gracious spirit will be greatly missed.

2. See Stanley Fish, *Is There a Text in This Class? The Authority of Interpretive Communities* (Cambridge, Mass.: Harvard Univ. Press, 1980), 338, 346.

3. See Stanley Hauerwas, *Unleashing the Scripture: Freeing the Bible from Captivity to America* (Nashville: Abingdon, 1993), 9.

4. Kevin Vanhoozer, "'But That's Your Interpretation:' Realism, Reading, and Reformation," *Modern Reformation* (July/August 1999): 27. Vanhoozer contrasts hermeneutical realism with the nonrealist and internal realist approaches on pages 25–28.

5. Anthony Thiselton, *New Horizons in Hermeneutics* (Grand Rapids: Zondervan, 1992), 65.

6. See Moisés Silva, "Has the Church Misread the Bible?" in *Foundations of Contemporary Interpretation*, ed. Moisés Silva (Grand Rapids: Zondervan, 1996), 29.

7. C. Norman Kraus, *The Authentic Witness: Credibility and Authority* (Grand Rapids: Eerdmans, 1979), 71. Cf. Paul G. Hiebert, *Anthropological Reflections on Missiological Issues* (Grand Rapids: Baker, 1994), 27.

8. See Hiebert, *Anthropological Reflections,* 47, 49.

9. See Richard A. Muller, "The Study of Theology," in *Foundations of Contemporary Interpretation*, 659. Also cf. Silva, "Has the Church Misread the Bible?" 30, and Vern S. Poythress, "Science and Hermeneutics," in *Foundations of Contemporary Interpretation,* 525.

10. See Vanhoozer, "But That's Your Interpretation," 28. Cf. Vanhoozer, *Is There a Meaning in This Text?* (Grand Rapids: Zondervan, 1998), 376–78.

11. See Poythress, "Science and Hermeneutics," 504.

12. J. Harold Greenlee, "Hebrews 11:11: By Faith Sarah Received Ability," *Asbury Theological Journal* 54 (Spring 1999): 67–72.

13. See Herbert M. Wolf, "A Solution to the Immanuel Prophecy in Isaiah 7:14–8:22," *Journal of Biblical Literature* 91(1972): 449–56, and idem, *Interpreting Isaiah* (Grand Rapids: Zondervan, 1985), 90–93, 257–59.

14. See Douglas Moo, *Romans 1–8,* Wycliffe Exegetical Commentary (Chicago: Moody Press, 1991), 231–37.

15. See Kenneth Barker, *The Accuracy of the NIV* (Grand Rapids: Baker, 1996), 85.

16. Study note on 2 Timothy 3:16, *NIV Study Bible,* rev. ed. (Grand Rapids: Zondervan, 2002), 1885.

17. Robert Alter, *The Art of Biblical Narrative* (New York: Basic Books, 1981), 143.

18. Cf. the discussion of the nature of Genesis 1:1–2:3 in Herbert Wolf, *An Introduction to the Old Testament Pentateuch* (Chicago: Moody Press, 1991), 82–84.

19. See Ronald Youngblood, *How It All Began* (Ventura, Calif.: Regal, 1980), 148–49. Cf. I. M. Kikawada, "The Shape of Genesis 1–11," in *Rhetorical Criticism: Essays in Honor of James Muilenberg,* eds. J. J. Jackson and M. Kessler (Pittsburgh, Pa.: Pickwick Press, 1974), 18–32.

20. See "Literary Features" in the Introduction to Genesis, *NIV Study Bible,* 2–3.

21. See John Stek, "When the Spirit Was Poetic," in *The NIV: The Making of a Contemporary Translation,* ed. Kenneth L. Barker (Grand Rapids: Zondervan, 1986), 81.

22. Cf. Moisés Silva's discussion of the change in *euanggelion* from "good news" to "gospel" in the New Testament *(Biblical Words and Their Meanings* [Grand Rapids: Zondervan, 1983], 77).

23. John I. Durham, *Exodus,* Word Biblical Commentary, vol. 3 (Waco, Tex.: Word, 1987), 455.

24. Ibid., 449.

25. But note that the NRSV also retains a heading ("Moses Makes New Tablets") at the start of the chapter.

6

ENGLISH BIBLE TRANSLATION IN POSTMODERN PERSPECTIVE: REFLECTIONS ON A CRITICAL THEORY OF HOLISTIC TRANSLATION

Charles H. Cosgrove

It was still the modern age (at least for me) when I studied Hebrew with Ronald Youngblood at Bethel Seminary some twenty-five years ago. Now we are all in a "postmodern" world. In honor of Ron and his important contributions to the NIV, and in gratefulness for the keys to the Old Testament he imparted to me and my classmates (always with just the right combination of exacting precision and wry humor), I want to reflect on the implications of postmodernity for English Bible translation.

First a comment about terminology. By "postmodern" I do not mean *anti*-modern but rather the late-modern ascendance, recovery, and development of certain minority trajectories of modernity (and premodernity) to correct certain other more dominant tendencies of the modern age. In my conception, postmodernity marks a momentous self-critical shift *within* modernity, not a rejection or surpassing of modernity. My purpose, however, is not to draw neat distinctions between modernity and postmodernity but rather to sketch something of the present postmodern scene of English Bible translation in all its variety and fresh questioning. I propose to do so in a provocative way. Much of what I assert and describe is too new for any of us to have settled opinions about. I know I don't.

I have organized this essay conceptually under the rubric of "holistic translation": translating the Bible *as a whole* (as a canonical integrity), translating the *whole communicative effect* of Scripture (language, genre, and medium), and translation as an activity of the *whole people* of God (the democratization of translation).

The Bible as a Whole: Canon and Translation

In traditional historical-critical hermeneutics, what counts as the true meaning of the biblical text is its "original" meaning. The perception that all (or almost all) the "books" of the Bible have a tradition history of some kind or other makes "original" a problematic criterion. For some scholars, "original" means the earliest stage of the tradition, for others the final form of the text as it came from its ancient author(s) or editor(s). The development of canonical criticism, particularly in the tradition of Brevard Childs, further complicates what counts as original. Childs and others have stressed that a given biblical writing (say, Ruth or Matthew) has a canonical identity that is positively related to *but not the same* as its historical identity as an ancient text viewed apart from its incorporation into the Christian Bible. A canonical process extending to the formation of the Bible as a whole and theological conceptions of what it means for a text to be "Scripture" shape the identity (for the church) of the individual biblical books and the Bible as a whole.

"Canonical interpretation" attends to the canonical shape of the biblical writings. At the same time it introduces questions about which text is canonical and about what counts as canonical. For most of the twentieth century, biblical scholars took for granted that the text-critical approximations of the original Hebrew (and Aramaic) text of the Old Testament, as reconstructed by text critics (such as those at work on the *Biblia Hebraica*), and Greek text of the New Testament were what counted as the canonical text to be translated or interpreted. Canonical interpretation, however, harbors implicit challenges to these assumptions. If what is to be translated is a canonical text, and if canon (or canonization or canonical process) is itself a substantive feature of this text and not simply a "later" perception or pronouncement of the church not substantially affecting the meaning of the text, then *text criticism itself* and *translation* (which depends on text criticism) have to deal with canon as a substantive (meaning-making) aspect of the Bible.

Neither the science of text criticism nor canonical criticism has yet really come to terms with this issue, which puts translators at a disadvantage when they try to determine the implications of canonical interpretation (or the concept of "canon") for translation. But let me suggest one area of inquiry,[1] the role of canonical context in translation decisions.

Old Testament scholar Gerald Sheppard has pointed out a number of examples of how canonical context impinges on translation. One is the way in which choice of meaning for a term can be redirected by a new context.[2] The verb *qāpʾû* in Exodus 15:8 probably meant "churned" in the original prebiblical song: the deeps churned and the Egyptians fell off their barges into the sea. In the context of Exodus 15, however, where the song sits in a prose narrative that speaks of a parting of the waters, it makes sense to translate *qāpʾû* in a way that fits this different description of the exodus deliverance. Thus, the NIV has "the deep waters *congealed*" and the NJPS reads "the deeps *froze.*" Sheppard comments that those who reconstruct the sense of the original (prebiblical) ancient song and those who read the song in its present context "are not translating precisely the same text."[3] The Song of the Sea, in exactly the same Hebrew words, warrants a different translation as biblical rather than as prebiblical text.

A second example of canonical considerations in translation concerns how different parts of the canon impinge on each other—for instance, how the fourfold Gospel shapes our perception of each individual Gospel, how the New Testament shapes our reading (and translating) of the Old Testament, and how the Old Testament shapes our reading of the New. The purely historical-critical approach, when practiced on the assumption that meaning resides exclusively in the discrete text considered apart from its identity and place in the canon, disallows considerations of canonical context for interpretation, including translation. By contrast, canonical interpretation demands consideration of canonical place and function. In another place, I have used the term "codetermination"[4] to describe how different parts of the canon influence each other (i.e., properly shape our perceptions of them). Sheppard provides a nice example from Psalm 2. Contemporary translations tend to render *mᵉšîḥô* in Psalm 2:2 "his anointed." Some premodern interpreters, such as Henry Ainsworth, treated Psalm 2 as a messianic psalm, based on its use in the New Testament, and translated *mᵉšîḥô* accordingly as "his Christ."[5] Today, considerations of global canonical context and inner-biblical codetermination reopen translation questions closed off by an older style of historical criticism and call for a new appreciation of the canonical sensitivities of premodern translators such as Ainsworth.

A third example of the role of canon in translation concerns the preservation and even production of canonical resonance within the Christian Bible. Sheppard describes Ainsworth's efforts to facilitate, by his translation of the Psalms, the premodern hermeneutic of the *analogia scripturae* (using Scripture to interpret Scripture, which Ainsworth called "conferencing" Scripture with Scripture): "[Ainsworth's] translation is attentive to a Christian, literal-sense mode of using Scripture to interpret Scripture. For that reason he seeks to translate some Hebrew words concordantly, but not others, by rendering the Hebrew consistently with the same English word."[6] Considerations of local (e.g., Pentateuch, Psalms, Gospels) and global (whole Bible) canonical contexts can be arguments for various kinds and degrees of concordant translation aimed at promoting inner-biblical resonance. For example, Ainsworth uses the word "meditate" for verbs built on the Hebrew root *h-g-h* in Psalm 1:2 and Psalm 2:1 to associate by contrast what we ought to do ("meditate day and night" on God's law) with what the nations do ("meditate vanity").[7] Ainsworth translates Psalm 2:1b on the assumption that Psalms 1 and 2 are part of the same book: the Psalms as a canonically shaped book of the Bible.

Global canonical concordance confronts special problems when it means assimilation through translation of Hebrew and Greek words (such as translating *bᵉrît* and *diathēkē* consistently as "covenant"). Even more troublesome is the question whether translation of the Old Testament should be guided at all by New Testament quotations of Old Testament texts on the grounds that an English Bible ought to make it possible for its readers to hear (experience) the verbal identities between New Testament quotation and Old Testament source that the New Testament authors and at least some of their audience heard between these same scriptural quotations and the Septuagint. This is an old concern of Bible translators on which canonical interpretation sheds fresh light.

The Whole Communicative Effect: Translation of Language, Rhetorical Form (Genre), and Medium

Thanks largely to the work of Eugene Nida (and the appeal of his work to practicing translators), functional-equivalence (formerly "dynamic") translation has become a major competitor with what Nida and company define as its opposite—formal-correspondence translation. The aim of functional-equivalence translation is to produce the same semantic effect (for the readers/hearers) that the text had in its original language, time, and place. This often requires wording in the target language that departs significantly from literal translation (formal correspondence). Preserving the message requires changing the form.[8]

Moving from one language to another is by definition a change in language form, no matter how "literal" the translation. Hence, the distinction between formal correspondence and functional equivalence must involve some other, more specific, notion of dispensable form than that of language form (language system) per se. The distinction must have something to do with transferable patterns in the source language that can obscure the meaning when they are taken over (or imitated by close analogues) in translation. My own impression is that these patterns (as form) are primarily word choice and syntax. Formal correspondence seeks to match the word choice and syntax of the original; functional equivalence seeks to match the sense in the idioms of the target language. Thus, in Amos 2:4, the KJV's "For three transgressions and for four" is formal correspondence, while the NEB's "For crime after crime" is an effort at functional equivalence.

"Form" in the concept of formal equivalence could also mean literary or oral form and genre (the subject matter of form criticism). But this sense of form is evidently not the kind that most advocates of functional-equivalence translation have in mind as dispensable. Contemporary translations regarded as exhibiting a good measure of functional-equivalence translation, such as the NRSV and NIV, do not substitute one literary form for another. They translate Hebrew poetry as poetry, Hebrew prose as prose. By contrast, the New Living Translation, which is robustly committed to dynamic translation, does not set up prophetic oracles as poetry. Is this because the translators reject the view that the oracles constitute a form of Hebrew verse? Or is it because they think that elevated English prose is functionally closer in rhetorical effect in our time to the rhetorical impact of poetic Hebrew oracles in ancient Israel?

The question of "setting up" a text as prose or poetry assumes that we have to do with a *printed text.* The ancient scribes did not set up poetry the way our modern English Bibles do. In terms of an expanded notion of functional-equivalence theory, we could say that our practice of *printing as verse* the psalms, prophetic oracles, and other literature judged to exhibit the marks of poetry amounts to an effort at functional equivalence at the level of *medium* (through "transmediatization"—more on this concept below). The print medium of the modern Bible is a manifestly different form (different semiotic system) than the chirographic medium of the ancient biblical manuscripts. Only an expanded version of functional-equivalence theory can justify our modern print Bibles with their special systems of communication. More specifically, to justify modern print translations we must hold that chirographic form is incidental to communication or that print media in the modern age function in ways equivalent to chirographs in the ancient world. Notice that the second alternative accepts the proposition that medium counts, that the medium produces something essential in the original message and therefore must be preserved or translated into the corresponding medium of the receiver culture.[9]

The preceding discussion suggests that translation ought to attend to questions of rhetorical form (genre) and media, along with traditional questions about transfer of "message" as "content" or "thought." One trend of postmodern theology is to challenge traditional distinctions between form and content and the hierarchy that subordinates one to the other. The movements dubbed "narrative theology" and "narrative preaching" reflect the view that the medium is an essential part of the message. This also entails that so-called "propositional theology" is only one type of theological discourse, not necessarily superior to others and, in the judgment of some, inferior to story and poetry. I will not dwell on the modern antecedents to this postmodern trend. My purpose is only to suggest that a confluence of contemporary currents argues for attending in Bible translation to language, genre, and medium (in their interrelation) and asking what it means to translate all three, whether "concordantly" or "functionally."

In what follows, I briefly examine these three dimensions under the headings *translingualization, transgenrelization,* and *transmediatization.*

TRANSLINGUALIZATION

A radical postmodern verdict on translingualization—moving from one language to another—is that it is "impossible." At best, translation is paraphrase.[10] At worst, every translator is a traitor.[11] This is an old worry made more acute in our time by certain traditions of contemporary cultural anthropology, notably, the view of radical "emicism" that cultures are incommensurable, each culture a closed (incommunicable) system.

Yet we all know that translation in ordinary practical ways is possible (and commonplace) across language systems and that people do make sense of cross-cultural encounters (as opposed to always being simply baffled by them). In "Found in Translation," a provocative essay that uses "translation" as a metaphor for cross-cultural interpretation, Clifford Geertz considers the mystery that "other people's creations can be so utterly their own and so deeply part of us."[12] In the same essay Geertz quotes the following lines from a poem by James Merrill titled "Lost in Translation":

> Lost, is it, buried? One more missing piece?
> But nothing's lost. Or else: all is translation
> And every bit of us is lost in it
> (Or found . . .).[13]

Whatever Merrill's meaning, I take Geertz to be saying that we are "found" in our translations of other people's creations, despite—or better, mysteriously "in"—the loss that all translation entails.

Literary theorist Frank Kermode has described a similar power of "the classic." Kermode analyzes the paradoxical capacity of the classic—whether in translation (e.g., Virgil's *Aeneid* translated into English) or not (e.g., *Wuthering Heights* for the English-speaking reader)—to change while retaining its identity and to do so in ways that permit the classic to speak powerfully to generations of readers who can no longer recover the past epistemes in which the classic originally made sense.[14] Kermode describes this power as a "surplus of the signifier."[15]

Viewed from the vantage of postmodern hermeneutics, translation is simply one more form of what happens to any linguistic event through "distantiation" (Paul Ricouer's term), that is, through removal of the utterance from its original (dialogical) rhetorical setting. In this perspective, functional-equivalence translation looks like an effort to produce a remainderless translation of a source that harbors surpluses productive of fresh "remainders" as the text, translated or not, moves through time and place.[16] But so, also, does literal translation or no translation at all. Repetition (recital) without translation, concordant (formal-equivalence) translation, and functional-equivalence translation are all, in effect, productive and not simply preservative of meaning.[17]

If there is any validity to the postmodern perspective I've described, it compels us to ask not (or not only) which method of translation is best at *preserving fully without exceeding* the original meaning but which method engenders *productions of meaning that we can approve.*[18]

TRANSGENRELIZATION

Transgenrelization is a tricky matter with many subtleties. It is difficult to define ancient genres, especially when one considers genre in terms of rhetorical function. Formal-equivalence theory appears to take for granted that genre translates automatically when translators render words and syntactical relations more or less literally. This assumes that genre as form is in the words and syntax as form. But genre is as much a "system of expectations" (E. D. Hirsch[19]) or "probability systems" (Kermode[20]) resident in readers as it is specific linguistic forms. Better, the rhetorical forms are cues in the discourse triggering cognitive and affective experiences in readers based on social conventions about what is funny, tragic, frightening, enobling, comic, ironic, and so forth.[21] Is Jonah a satire making a serious point through humorous cardboard-character role reversals? If so, what might a functionally equivalent transgenrelization of Jonah look like for, say, contemporary Americans who have grown up with *Saturday Night Live* or *The Simpsons*?

Poetry

Ancient Hebrew-speaking Israelites distinguished various parts of the Bible as songs but had no word to differentiate poetry from prose. Are the psalms *poetry,* or are they a kind of Hebrew prose suited to singing? Of course, even this way of putting the question assumes our modern poetry/prose distinction. A scholarly tradition inaugurated early in this century identified various examples of early Christian poetry ("hymns") in the New Testament (such as the Song of Mary and the Christ Hymn of Philippians 2). One difficulty with this view is that all ancient Greek poetry and song were metrical; none of the New Testament hymns are. Perhaps they are prose hymns, for which we also have examples in wider Greek literature. Or perhaps they are instances of elevated prose rather than quotations of traditional hymns. Our uncertain knowledge about how ancient speakers performed Hebrew "poetry" or elevated Greek prose makes it difficult to know what a contemporary functional equivalent might be.

Music

The question of how to translate the psalms and hymns of the Bible in genre-sensitive ways raises the larger question of whether music should figure in translation. A widely accepted scholarly tradition holds that the psalms were sung not only in the temple but also in the synagogue, that Scripture readings were cantillated in both temple and synagogue, and that the early church took over these worship practices of psalm singing and Scripture cantillation. If the psalms were sung and Scripture was cantillated in the early church, does this call for translations designed for singing? Should a contemporary psalmbook include modern musical notation as an aspect of translation? If so, using what tunes? Dubious reconstructions (or imitations) of ancient Hebrew melodies or contemporary musical styles? Presumably, functional equivalence would call for contemporary melodies; yet, without the ability to reconstruct the original Hebrew melodies, we lack all means of testing functional equivalence. The same goes for cantillation. Thomas Boomershine laments that "the musical codes which were an essential element of the original medium of the texts have been wholly eliminated from our texts."[22] But we cannot read these old codes, assuming that they are in fact *musical* signs.[23]

One way to avoid these questions is to follow a more recent competing reconstruction of early Jewish and early Christian worship, according to which both psalm singing and cantillation of Scripture arose in synagogue and church liturgies well after the first century.[24] If Jesus, Paul, and the earliest churches as a whole did not sing the psalms or cantillate Scripture, then perhaps this relieves the translator of the burden of doing justice to musical aspects of Scripture. However, even if cantillation did not arise until the fourth or fifth century, one might still argue that the final stage in the history of the canonical process by which the Christian Bible came into being included the church's perception that Scripture should be intoned. In that case, cantillation is arguably one of the final "shapings" of Scripture and as such a proper element of what is to be "translated." I am speaking theoretically. It is hard to imagine that communions in which cantillation is practiced (Greek Orthodox, Roman Catholic, Anglican/Episcopal, some Lutheran churches, etc.) would leave to biblical scholars questions of whether and how to intone Scripture. But the thesis that representing genre—including musical form—is part of the translation calls for consultation among biblical scholars, historians of ancient church music, and the guardians of the various traditions of singing Scripture.

Narrative

We immediately recognize biblical stories in translation as stories. But are biblical stories in translation really the same kinds of stories with the same or similar rhetorical functions they had in antiquity?

I have already mentioned the problem of how to do justice to the genre of Jonah. Another example is the biblical book of Acts. Richard Pervo has argued that Acts stands within the novelistic style of ancient history-writing.[25] But Acts does not "read" like a novel in most modern English translations, including those that use a dynamic-translation approach to sentence units. The rhetorical effect of Acts is probably better achieved by the contemporary novelistic approach of Walter Wangerin's "retelling" of the Bible (which includes some of the story of the early church in Acts).[26] Wangerin's "Bible" is not only highly periphrastic, it is also inventive. Where biblical stories are highly economical by our standards, Wangerin's treatment abounds in description of the sort that makes for a more contemporary novelistic reading experience. Does this count as "translation"? It depends on what we mean by translation. Josephus claimed that his retellings of Israel's story in his *Antiquities* were *translations* of the Jewish Scriptures (*Ant*. 1.5). In fact, Josephus's translations are also rather free transgenrelizations. In addition to incorporating many extrabiblical traditions, Josephus retells the biblical stories in popular Greek historiographic style, including the invention of speeches for characters as well as inventive novelistic description of their thoughts, feelings, and actions. In effect, Josephus updates and rhetorically refashions the biblical history for a Greco-Roman audience.

Wangerin's retelling of the biblical story is not suitable for Bible study. It sacrifices too much content to the demands of functional equivalence in genre. Its value for Bible translation is the way in which it illustrates what transgenrelization might involve, at least for certain types of biblical narrative. The price Wangerin pays in fidelity to content in order to be novelistic also suggests that good functional-equivalence transgenrelization is likely to compete with good translingualization. In that case, translating the Bible holistically requires using multiple "partial" translations—traditional ones for translingualization, more experimental ones for transgenrelization and transmediatization.

TRANSMEDIATIZATION

An emergent area of work in Bible translation is the presentation of the Bible in electronic formats[27]—a work Thomas Boomershine refers to as "transmediatization."[28] The biblical world was a predominantly oral culture in which what little reading that did take place was done out loud, usually in group settings. The original medium of the Old and New Testaments is the manuscript—a chirograph—produced as a scroll and later a codex. Modern Bibles are printed books. Print culture begins with a momentous act of transmediatization—the printing of the Bible on Gutenberg's press.

Print culture eventually brings silent reading, which means individual private reading. The reading experience is interiorized, which corresponds with specifically modern forms of consciousness. In the spiritual life, this means the sense that the true self is *within* and that the encounter with God takes place there—in this inner place where Scripture is heard silently (which is also the inner sanctum of silent prayer and silent individual meditation).

Postmodernity brings with it the electronic or digital age. Books compete with audiovisual media such as film, television, video game, computer. The electronic era offers new media for Bible translation. We confront here a genuine *translation* question, not simply a question of how to make movies and multimedia presentations "based on" the Bible. To imagine that the Bible could never "be" a movie or multimedia presentation is to make the mistake of assuming that the Bible *is* the printed book. But the printed book is a transmediatization of the original chirographic form. Unless we are ready to say that our familiar modern printed Bible is not the Bible but is only a modern media presentation "based on" the Bible, we should be willing to consider that other contemporary media (including film) can also "be" the Bible. More precisely, other media can be translations of the Bible, just as a printed book can be a translation (transmediatization) of the Bible.[29]

A caution to the preceding logic is the plausible argument that print is analogous to chirograph, while audiovisual communication (television, video, film, etc.) is not.[30] Perhaps. But we should not underestimate how profound the shift to print was for how people came to experience Scripture. Moreover, we should not overlook certain similarities between audiovisual communication in an electronic age and the rhetorical enactment of texts in antiquity. The ancient chirograph was to be read aloud by a skilled reader (not read silently). Skilled readers dramatized with their voices and gestures when they read. This "theatrical" aspect of ancient reading of Scripture distances ancient oral performance of Scripture from silent reading in a print culture, as well as from the typical grave reading of Scripture from behind the lectern in most churches today. Ancient reading performance has greater affinities with the art of oral interpretation today. Moreover, ancient oral reading also has certain affinities with audiovisual communication, since the ancient reader combined aural and visual effects in rendering the text.[31]

These affinities between ancient reading and contemporary audiovisual media probably explain why some students of biblical media are especially concerned not only to explore new media for presenting/translating the Bible but also to recover ancient oral forms of Scripture presentation. This dual concern is especially evident in Thomas Boomershine's work. Boomershine describes silent reading of the Bible as anachronistic, a kind of "media eisegesis."[32] He reasons, "If the medium does significantly influence the meaning of a biblical tradition,... historical interpretation requires an effort to experience the tradition in its intended medium." [33] Boomershine's founding of and ongoing leadership in the Biblical Storytellers Network reflects his interest in fostering experiences of Scripture in something approximating their original oral medium. Fidelity to the original medium requires translations that do justice to the orality of Scripture, with sensitivity to contemporary oral expression.

At the same time Boomershine has been an advocate of the use of new media. Evidently, he does not regard multimedia translation as "media eisegesis." Perhaps this is because he sees audiovisual electronic media as analogous to oral performance. In any case, he makes his argument for transmediatization into electronic media on the basis of a "relevance theory" that resembles the functional-equivalence model of translation. Depending on the cultural setting, the very medium of the communication can raise expectations that the communication contains something valuable, perhaps even life-saving, Boomershine says. The medium of oral reading carried a promise of relevance in antiquity; in modernity the book has carried a similar aura of relevance.[34] Books no longer have this aura in postmodern America; electronic media do. Hence, Boomershine argues, to match the promise of relevance inherent to the ancient medium of oral reading, postmodern translation must turn to electronic media.

But do the forms of experience (and the kind of consciousness and self-understanding) fostered by the electronic media make possible a recovery of the experience of the oral word as early Christians or Jews knew it? The modern silent print book creates a different kind of experience of Scripture from that of the chirograph; electronic media create their own kinds of experience in ways very different from ancient oral reading or modern silent reading. Perhaps attention to media in translation shows that strict originalism in translation is not possible. We can capture something of the original experience of Scripture, but we will also inevitably experience Scripture differently than its first readers did.

Holistic Translation and the Whole People of God: The Democratization of Translation

I conclude with some thoughts about "who gets to do the translating." Professional, scholarly English Bible translation is alive and well. At the same time, English Bible translation by other than biblical scholars is on the increase in privately and commercially published forms, as well as by means of electronic formats (on the Internet). Then there are the unpublished occasional translations that ministers and teachers make. Some of these are acts of direct translation from the original languages, aided by sophisticated computer software.[35] Others take their cues from comparing published translations. Many English-speaking Christians can afford to own a number of printed and electronic Bibles. The democratizing or "flattening" *cultural effect* of postmodernity, epitomized by the Internet, creates a climate in which those so inclined are emboldened to do their own translating. Scholars in this environment are not authorities in the modern sense; they are retailers of presumably reliable goods. The client assumes authority for how to use those goods, which may involve transforming them. The age of officially and unofficially authorized translations is over, despite continued pleas by some that churches or whole denominations should officially adopt a single translation for everything. A critical theory of holistic translation reveals that no single translation is sufficient. Seen in this light, the democratization of translation is a good thing—if it means informed use of many translations to reformulate Scripture for a particular place and time or to teach Scripture in ways that reveal the dimensions of cognitive and affective content through rhetorical effects of genre and medium.

Conclusion

A holistic translation would be a faithful translingualization, transgenrelization, and transmediatization of the Bible. It would do justice to the integrity of the biblical writings as a scriptural (or canonical) whole. It would be translation for particular times and places as the work of the people of God in their own time and place. Obviously, holistic translation in this sense is an ideal concept, not a practical project. As a concept it can inspire and guide multiple strategies for rendering ancient Scripture in contemporary forms of communication—strategies that can be coordinated but not united in a single product. A critical theory of postmodern translation is interested not only in individual translation products but also in how various acts of translation interact in contemporary experience, use, and understanding of Scripture.

NOTES

1. Other areas for exploration include, for example, (1) the status of the earliest church's Scripture—the Septuagint—in contemporary judgments about what counts as the canonical text and (2) orthodox "corruptions" of Scripture as forms of canonical editing. On the latter subject, see Kent D. Clarke, "Original Text or Canonical Text? Questioning the Shape of the New Testament Text We Translate," in *Translating the Bible: Problems and Prospects,* eds. Stanley E. Porter and Richard S. Hess (Sheffield: Sheffield Academic Press, 1999), 281–322.

2. See Gerald T. Sheppard, "Issues in Contemporary Translation: Late Modern Vantages and Lessons from Past Epochs," in *On the Way to Nineveh: Studies in Honor of George M. Landes,* eds. Stephen L. Cook and S. C. Winter (Atlanta: Scholars Press, 1999), 260.

3. Ibid.

4. Charles Cosgrove, *Elusive Israel: The Puzzle of Election in Romans* (Louisville, Ky.: Westminster John Knox Press, 1997).

5. Henry Ainsworth in his *The Book of Psalmes: Englished Both in Prose and Metre* (1612), as cited by Sheppard, "Issues in Contemporary Translation," 277.

6. Sheppard, "Issues in Contemporary Translation," 281.

7. Ibid., 282.

8. Eugene A. Nida and Charles R. Taber, *The Theory and Practice of Translation* (Leiden: Brill, 1969), 5, 173, 202.

9. A third alternative would be to hold that the modern print form can be adapted to achieve functional equivalence in the contemporary media environment. Digital communication uses modified print (hypertext) formats.

10. That translation is always in some sense paraphrase has long been recognized. See "Introduction to the New Testament" in *The New English Bible* (n.p.: Oxford Univ. Press and Cambridge Univ. Press, 1970), vii.

11. Paul R. Raabe, "Translating for Sound," *Practical Papers for the Bible Translator* 51, no. 2 (April 2000): 201 (quoting the Italian proverb *Traduttore traditore*).

12. Clifford Geertz, "Found in Translation: On the Social History of the Moral Imagination," in *Local Knowledge: Further Essays in Interpretive Anthropology* (New York: Basic Books, 1983), 54.

13. Ibid., 50, quoting James I. Merrill, "Lost in Translation," *Divine Comedies* (New York: Atheneum, 1976), 10.

14. See Frank Kermode, *The Classic: Literary Images of Permanence and Change* (New York: Viking, 1975), 135–41.

15. Ibid., 135, 140.

16. See Brook W. R. Pearson, "Remainderless Translations? Implications of the Tradition Concerning the Translation of the LXX for Modern Translational Theory," in *Translating the Bible,* 82–84.

17. Repetition (recital) in the same language is productive of meaning, as Jorge Luis Borges entertainingly shows in "Pierre Menard, Author of the Quixote," in *Borges, A Reader: A Selection from the Writings of Jorge Luis Borges,* eds. E. Rodriguez Monegal and A. Reid (New York: Dutton, 1981), 96–103.

18. In this connection, treated from a semiotic perspective, see Ubaldo Stecconi, "Pierce's Semiotics for Translation," in Robert Hodgson and Paul A. Soukup, S.J., eds., *Fidelity in Translation: Communicating the Bible in the New Media* (New York: Sheed & Ward, 1999), 249–61.

19. E. D. Hirsch, *Validity in Interpretation* (New Haven, Conn.: Yale Univ. Press, 1967), 80–81.

20. Kermode, *The Classic,* 140.

21. On genre as a sociocultural formation, see William A. Foley, *Anthropological Linguistics: An Introduction* (Oxford: Blackwell, 1997).

22. Thomas E. Boomershine, "A Transmediatization Theory of Biblical Translation," *Bulletin—United Bible Societies* 170/171 (1994): 53. Boomershine treats music as medium. Without disputing that music can be thought of as medium, I have ordered music under genre. The variety of musical genres can be communicated in a variety of media.

23. One thinks first of all of what may be musical directions in the Psalms (in some of the superscriptions and in the occasional use of *slh*). E. J. Revell has argued that evidence of Second Temple *punctuation* of the Torah reflects chanting (or elevated reading), but his arguments only prove that punctuation aided perception of division into sense units, and was thus interpretive but not necessarily an aid to cantillation. See E. J. Revell, "Biblical Punctuation and Chant in the Second Temple Period," *Journal for the Study of Judaism* 7 (1976): 181–98. It is possible that marks for chant/cantillation were included in Second Temple scrolls (our knowledge of which is nil except for those found at Qumran), marks that were precursors of the later Tiberian system of *te'amim*. In this vein, Rochelle Altmann claims to be able to see cantillation marks in some of the psalm texts from Qumran. I am doubtful, but if she is correct, this suggests that the non-hymnic texts (including the Torah) were *not* intoned, since they do not display such marks. See Reply-To: orion@mscc.huji.ac.il., found on the Web at http://orion.mscc.huji.ac.il/orion/archives/1999b/msg00477.html.

24. See, for example, James McKinnon, "On the Question of Psalmody in the Ancient Synagogue," *Early Music History* 6 (1986): 159–91. According to my own careful reading of the entire corpus of Second Temple Jewish literature (Philo, Josephus, the so-called Old Testament pseudepigrapha, the Qumran writings, Jewish epigraphical evidence, and the New Testament writings), there are no references to singing or any other kind of music in the synagogue during the Second Temple period—unless one counts the worship at Qumran or that of the monastic Therapeutae as "synagogue" worship.

25. Richard I. Pervo, *Profit with Delight: The Literary Genre of the Acts of the Apostles* (Philadelphia: Fortress, 1987).

26. Walter Wangerin Jr., *The Book of God: The Bible as a Novel* (Grand Rapids: Zondervan, 1996).

27. See, for example, the contributions to Robert Hodgson and Paul A. Soukup, eds., *From One Medium to Another: Communicating the Bible through Multimedia* (Kansas City, Mo.: Sheed & Ward, 1997) and idem, eds., *Fidelity and Translation*. For a brief report on the American Bible Society's work in new media translation, see Scott S. Elliott, "'The Word' in Text, Sound, and Image: The American Bible Society's New Media Bible and the Research Center for Scripture and Media," *Council of Societies for the Study of Religion Bulletin* 30 (2001): 65–67.

28. Boomershine, "A Transmediatization Theory of Bible Translation," 50. Others use the term with a slightly different spelling—"transmediazation." See Elliott, "'The Word' in Text, Sound, and Image."

29. Bernard Brandon Scott makes a similar point, stressing that "full fidelity" in translation requires that we translate the theatrical oral medium of Scripture into the new media of the electronic age rather than treating the Bible as a modern book and translating only what we take that book to mean (the "signified"), apart from attention to the "signifier" (the ancient medium of communication, which was oral performance). See Bernard Brandon Scott, "A New Voice in the Amphitheater: Full Fidelity in Translating," in *Fidelity and Translation,* 101–18.

30. J. Ritter Werner suggests that translating the Bible into contemporary audiovisual media is best thought of as a form of midrash, a thesis that involves both the recognition that new media translation is necessarily creative and also the argument that the ancient norms governing Jewish midrash should guide new media translation. See J. Ritter Werner, "Midrash: A Model for Fidelity in New Media Translation," in *Fidelity and Translation,* 173–97. Joy Sisley maintains that it is inherent to new media translation that it displaces the text and produces something new that is not functionally equivalent. See Joy Sisley, "Power and Interpretive Authority in Multimedia Translation," in *Fidelity and Translation,* 203–17.

31. In reconstructing the oral performative nature of ancient Christian enactment of Scripture, we probably have much to learn from the practices of the rhapsode in the Greco-Roman world, from study of ancient storytelling, from what the rhetoricians and other ancient writers say about the use of voice and gesture in reading, and from any hints in ancient Jewish and Christian literature about performance practice. Those who regard the formation of the Christian Bible as a substantive shaping of Scripture (of both text and performance of text) will want to consider the performance of Scripture within the dramatic shaping of the Christian liturgy that makes its appearance in the fourth century C.E.

For a foundational article on the rhapsode, see Donald E. Hargis, "The Rhapsode," *Quarterly Journal of Speech* 56 (1970): 388–97. For an introduction to ancient storytelling, see Alex Scobie, "Storytellers, Storytelling, and the Novel in Graeco-Roman Antiquity," *Rheinisches Museum für Philologie* 122 (1979): 229–59. On the dramatic shaping of Christian liturgy, beginning in the fourth century, see Christine Catharina Schnusenberg, *The Relationship between the Church and the Theatre: Exemplified by Selected Writings of the Church Fathers and by Liturgical Texts until Amalarius of Metz, 775–852 A.D.* (Lanham, N.Y.: University Press of America, 1988) and the relevant literature cited there. On clues in the biblical text for oral performance, see Scott, "A New Voice in the Amphitheater,"110–18.

32. Thomas E. Boomershine, "Peter's Denial as Polemic or Confession: The Implications of Media Criticism for Biblical Hermeneutics," in *Orality, Aurality, and Biblical Narrative,* Semeia 39 (Decatur, Ga.: Scholars Press, 1987), 48, 65.

33. Ibid., 50.

34. Boomershine, "A Transmediatization Theory," 54–55.

35. Notable Bible Study software packages are *GRAMCORD, Accordance, Bible Windows, Bible Works for Windows,* and *Logos.*

PART TWO

THE HISTORY OF BIBLE TRANSLATION

7

THE BIBLE IN ENGLISH: AN OVERVIEW[1]

Dick France

Bible Translation before Translation into English

Translations of the Hebrew Scriptures became necessary by the third century B.C., when many Jews no longer understood Hebrew. Translation into Greek (the lingua franca of the Eastern Mediterranean) was focused in the large Jewish community of Alexandria. At first there were various individual translations, but by the end of the second century B.C. a standard collection known as the Septuagint was widely accepted. The Septuagint was in effect the Bible of the first Christians and is copiously quoted in the NT. It is not the product of a single translation project, and the styles adopted for the various books differ considerably—some of them departing quite freely from the Hebrew text as we know it. Different manuscripts of the Septuagint witness also to considerable variations in the accepted Greek text. Later Greek versions of the Hebrew Bible were essentially revisions of the Septuagint—some (notably that of Aquila) much more literal.

In Palestine and farther east, Aramaic was the prevalent language among Jews, and a variety of Aramaic versions of the Hebrew Bible (known as Targums) were produced around the same period, though it was many centuries before any sort of standard Aramaic text was established. Targums are typically much freer and even more expansive than the Septuagint and sometimes contain quite substantial interpolations. They are the witness to a developing and quite creative interpretive tradition within Jewish worship and preaching.

Translation of both OT and NT into Latin began very early in the Christian era, and again many independent versions were soon in use. Toward the end of the fourth century, however, Jerome was commissioned by Pope Damasus to revise existing translations so as to produce a standard Latin version of the whole Bible—the Vulgate—which became the accepted text of the Latin church, so that relatively few manuscripts of the "Old Latin" versions survive.

Translation into Syriac followed a similar course, with the early fifth-century Peshitta version supplanting earlier Syriac translations, some of which had been in existence since the second century.

The other major versions translated directly from the Greek are the Coptic versions deriving from the third and fourth centuries. Subsequent translations into Gothic, Armenian, Ethiopic, and Georgian are known as "secondary versions," since they were made not from the original language but from one of the earlier translations.

The character of these various early translations varied considerably. While some were the work of scholars such as Jerome, who possessed a formidable knowledge of relevant languages, most are not associated with any named translator. The motive of the translators was generally more religious than literary, namely, to make the sacred texts accessible to worshipers who did not know the original languages. The written Aramaic Targums, for instance, were a development from the practice in the synagogue of giving an oral, and in most cases probably extempore, Aramaic interpretation after the Hebrew text had been read.

Such versions are not likely to be marked by verbatim accuracy, and the character of many of the surviving versions from the Septuagint onward indicates that this was not always the primary concern of the anonymous translators. This was to be a significant factor when the Bible began to be translated into English, since it was Latin rather than Greek that dominated Western Europe, while Hebrew was little known among European Christians of the late Middle Ages.

The Problem of Textual Transmission

To return to "the original text" is, however, no easy matter when we are dealing with ancient texts passed on in manuscript form before the days of printing. In Bible translation the issue of *textual criticism* is particularly important and complex.

Until the middle of the twentieth century the earliest surviving manuscripts of the Hebrew Bible dated from the ninth century A.D., i.e., over a thousand years later than even the latest books of the Hebrew Bible were written. But the discovery of the Dead Sea Scrolls, together with a number of other recent discoveries, have now made available to us manuscripts of the Hebrew text written a thousand years and more earlier. The result has been, in general, to confirm the care with which the text had been preserved, even though a number of differences have emerged.

In addition to Hebrew manuscripts, there are full manuscripts of the Septuagint and other versions from the fourth century A.D. onwards, and partial texts that are even earlier. These often offer a significantly different reading from the Hebrew text tradition, but this is often to be explained by the freedom exercised by the Greek translator rather than as evidence of a variant Hebrew text to which he had access.

In the case of the NT, the time scale is less extended. There are complete Greek texts of the NT from the fourth century, and many earlier papyri of parts of it have survived, some from as early as the middle of the second century. In all, we have over 5,000 Greek manuscripts of the NT, though the majority of these are later and of lesser value. There is also a wide variety of manuscript evidence for the early versions in Latin, Syriac, and Coptic, as well as numerous citations from the NT books by early Christian writers whose works are preserved. The NT is thus vastly better attested than any other ancient literature. The works of Tacitus, by contrast, survive in only two incomplete manuscripts written many centuries after his time, between them covering only about half of what he is known to have written.

But a large quantity of manuscripts means a large range of variants, since no two manuscripts are exactly alike. Most of the variants are of minor importance—matters of spelling or grammar or of stylistic variation. Where there are differences of substance, in most cases experts are in little doubt as to which represents the original. But there remains a significant number of variants where translators must make a choice regarding the words to be rendered, or whether or not to include a disputed portion of text, which may be as little as one word but may be a whole verse or two. There is room here for sincere disagreement, even among those who are well versed in the discipline of textual criticism, and English versions of the Bible may and do differ accordingly.

Many of the most important biblical manuscripts have been discovered relatively recently, and the science of textual criticism has become far more sophisticated and, one hopes, more responsible. Translations of the Bible made before the present century are likely therefore to be based on less reliable texts. The need for constant retranslation arises not only from the development of the English language but also from the growing availability of evidence for the original texts themselves.

Translation of the Bible into English

Early English Translations

In medieval England, Latin was the language of literate people. Direct access to the Bible was restricted in practice to the clergy and monastic orders, and their Bible was the Latin Vulgate.

Perhaps the earliest renderings of biblical texts into English are in the Old English poems of Caedmon (seventh century). These are sometimes based on the Bible and amount virtually to free metrical versions of parts of the biblical text. Translations of parts of the Bible into Old English are said to have been produced in the early eighth century by Bishop Aldhelm of Sherborne (Psalms) and by Bede (John's gospel), but these have not survived. Probably the earliest actual translations preserved are those inserted between the lines of the Latin text of medieval manuscripts, notably the Northumbrian version inserted by Aldred into the Lindisfarne Gospels in the tenth century.

The first extant independent Old English version of the gospels, known as the Wessex Gospels, comes from the tenth century, as does Aelfric's translation of Genesis through Judges. But with the Norman conquest, translations into English virtually ceased, as Norman French became the language of the literate.

In the fourteenth century Richard Rolle produced a prose version of the book of Psalms in his south Yorkshire dialect, together with a verse-by-verse commentary, and copies of this work were made in other dialects. An anonymous Middle English version of parts of the NT for use in monasteries is also preserved from the fourteenth century.

But it was John Wycliffe (c. 1330–1384) and his associates who first attempted to put an English Bible into the hands of laypeople. Wycliffe, master of Balliol College, Oxford, was a "Reformer before the Reformation." His attacks both on the privileges of the church and on such Catholic doctrines as transubstantiation earned him the Pope's condemnation for heresy. His guiding principle was the supreme authority of the Bible. The "Wycliffe" translation is probably mostly not by Wycliffe himself, but the project was at the heart of his aim to restore the Bible's authority in the life of church and nation. It was based not on the original languages (which were not available then in England) but on the Latin Vulgate, which it translates so literally as to be sometimes almost unintelligible to those who do not know Latin. A revised version, produced after Wycliffe's death, probably by his secretary John Purvey, shows more respect for English idiom; the reviser's prologue states a remarkably modern-sounding aim: "to translate after the sentence and not only after the words ...; and if the letter may not be followed in the translating, let the sentence ever be whole and open [plain]."

The Lollard movement, which arose from Wycliffe's work, provoked fierce opposition from the church establishment. A provincial synod convened by the archbishop of Canterbury in 1408 issued the "Constitutions of Oxford," which forbade the production or use of vernacular Bibles without a bishop's approval. But Purvey's revised translation (rather than the earlier Wycliffe version) continued nonetheless to be widely read and circulated. It was, in effect, *the* English Bible throughout the fifteenth and early sixteenth centuries.

The Sixteenth Century

Two major factors separate later English translations from those of the fourteenth century. The first was the rediscovery in European scholarship of the Hebrew and Greek languages and the growing availability of biblical texts in the originals. The second was the invention of printing.

The first printed Hebrew Bible appeared in 1488, and the first printed Greek NT in 1516. The materials were therefore available for a translation from the originals to be printed in English, and William Tyndale (1494–1536) was the first to take up the opportunity. As one of the foremost champions of the Reformation in England, Tyndale was constantly engaged in controversy and spent his last twelve years in exile on the continent, where he was eventually burned as a heretic. His English NT was printed in 1526—not in England, where there was still strong official hostility to a vernacular Bible (particularly one suspected of "Lutheran" connections), but at Worms, from where it was smuggled into England and met with an enthusiastic black market.

The German connection is significant, since only four years earlier Martin Luther had printed the first German NT. Much of the cross reference and comment that accompanies Tyndale's translation is clearly based on Luther's. But the translation is Tyndale's own, based on Erasmus's 1522 Greek NT and using a vigorous, idiomatic English style that would be the basis of all subsequent English translations until the twentieth century.

Tyndale is by far the most significant figure in the story of the translation of the Bible into English. In addition to his NT, he also began the translation of the OT. He published the Pentateuch in English in 1530 and prepared translations of some other books subsequently incorporated into "Matthew's Bible" (see below). But he devoted more time to revising his NT; the extensively revised 1534 edition became the definitive text on which subsequent translators drew.

The first complete English Bible to be printed (in 1535) was the work of Tyndale's friend and associate Miles Coverdale (1488–1569). Its title page describes it as "translated out of Douche and Latyn into Englishe," as Coverdale made no claim to be an expert in Hebrew and Greek. But his NT was essentially Tyndale's, revised in the light of German versions, while his OT incorporated elements of Tyndale's and Luther's work based on the originals. It was his version of the book of Psalms, subsequently incorporated in the Great Bible of 1539, which became the Psalter of the English Book of Common Prayer.

"Matthew's Bible" (1537) was compiled by Tyndale's associate John Rogers, writing under a pseudonym. It is in fact the work of Tyndale, as far as he had reached (including the unpublished parts of the OT), the rest being drawn from Coverdale. It is notable as the first English translation to be published "with the king's most gracious license." Bible translation had at last received official approval.

The stage was thus set for an "authorized version," which was to be placed in every church in the land, so that "your parishioners may most commodiously resort to the same and read it." Coverdale was entrusted with the task of revising the "Matthew" Bible for this purpose, and the resultant version, issued with a preface by Thomas Cranmer, is known as the Great Bible (1539). This remained the officially recognized Bible until the reign of Elizabeth I. It was in all essentials the work of two men—Tyndale and Coverdale.

But it had one significant weakness. Apart from those Hebrew books Tyndale had translated, the rest of the OT (Coverdale's work) was not based on the Hebrew text. This was one of the motives for an extensive revision eventually published as the Geneva Bible of 1560 (so called because it was first printed in Geneva and was the work of men closely associated with the Reformation movement on the continent). This translation was not, as hitherto, the work of one man but of a group of scholars—the first English "committee translation." Its popular title, "the 'Breeches' Bible," derives from its translation of Genesis 3:7, where Adam and Eve sewed fig leaves together to make themselves "breeches."

The Geneva Bible was an immediate success and quickly supplanted the Great Bible, not only in private use, but in church use as well. This was the Bible of the Elizabethan church and of Shakespeare. An official revision of the Great Bible—the "Bishops' Bible" of 1568—never seriously competed with the Geneva Bible in general usage.

King James's Bible

James the First did not share the general enthusiasm for the Geneva Bible, largely on account of the notes published along with the text, which were felt to be partisan. So at the Hampton Court Conference summoned in the year after his accession, it was agreed to produce a new version, without commentary, "to be read in the whole Church, and none other." The work was entrusted to a large group (forty-seven in all) of the best scholars available, who represented a range of theological opinion and so could not be stigmatized as producing a partisan text.

The King James Bible of 1611 (generally known in Britain as the "Authorized Version") claims to be "newly translated out of the original tongues," but the translators did not start from scratch. The clause in the title adds, "with the former translations diligently compared and revised." The translators were, in fact, instructed to take the Bishops' Bible of 1568 as the basis of their work. The phrases of Tyndale's NT can often be heard, though the committee tended generally to revise in a more literal direction. But their preface ("The Translators to the Reader," unfortunately not included in most modern editions) makes it clear that they did much more than merely revise the Bishops' Bible (which, after all, was not based directly on the Hebrew text in many OT books), working in detail from the original texts.

The translators, well aware of the range of possibilities both in the reading of the original text and in the understanding of its words, added marginal notes, not of the "commentary" type the king disliked, but to indicate reasonable alternative renderings. In answer to the criticism that such notes undermined the reader's confidence in the text, they sensibly replied that "they that are wise had rather have their judgments at liberty in differences of readings, than to be captivated to one, when it might be the other."

They chose to avoid "concordance" translation, whereby the same English word is always used for the same word in the original. Indeed, they seem to have set store by variety in style, so that at times they vary the English renderings of a given word where the same word would have conveyed the sense perfectly well.

In these and other ways the KJV marked a significant advance on earlier versions, so that even without royal backing it would probably have supplanted even the Geneva Bible in both public and private use. Given the king's strong endorsement as well, it was assured of success. The term "Authorized Version" is not quite accurate, since it was never (like the Book of Common Prayer) imposed by Act of Parliament, but the clause "appointed to be read in churches" on its title page indicates its quasi-official status. For English-speaking Protestants from the mid-seventeenth century until 1881 there was, in effect, only one English Bible.

There is, however, one major weakness the 1611 version shares with all its predecessors—one that is no fault of its translators. The Hebrew and Greek texts available in the sixteenth and early seventeenth century were much inferior to what is available today, and at many points the words rendered by the King James' translators are not what is now agreed to be the original text. This problem is particularly serious in the NT, for which they were dependent on the Greek text issued by Stephanus in 1550. This text, misleadingly known as the "Received Text" (Textus Receptus), was based on the few Greek manuscripts then available, which were late in date and represented the Byzantine type of text that most scholars now believe to be a revision (and in some places expansion) of the original. In a few places no Greek text at all was available, and Stephanus's text was taken from the Vulgate, translated back into Greek. The most notorious example is the Trinitarian text in 1 John 5:7 that occurs in no Greek manuscript before the fifteenth century, where it is clearly derived from the Latin. The discovery of earlier texts and the advances in textual criticism mean that there are now serious textual questions to be set against the undoubted literary qualities of the KJV.

The above discussion may have suggested that Bible translation into English was an exclusively Protestant enterprise. Certainly Protestants took the lead, but a Catholic response began with the publication of the Rheims NT in 1582, followed by the OT published at Douai in 1610. This "Douai Bible" was deliberately based not on the Hebrew and Greek but on the Vulgate, the version prescribed by the Council of Trent. Its style was so much based on the Latin as to be quite obscure, and a major revision was undertaken by Bishop Challoner in the eighteenth century. A further revision of the Douai-Challoner NT, known as the Confraternity Version, was published in America in 1941.

Translations in the Nineteenth and Early Twentieth Centuries

The KJV had no significant rival for 270 years. There were of course a number of individual efforts at Bible translation, some of them worthy attempts to update the KJV (including one by John Wesley in 1768), others quite eccentric. But none made much lasting impression.

But the KJV, for all its good qualities, inevitably became dated in two respects: on the one hand there was the increase of knowledge about the Hebrew and Greek texts noted above, but there was also the fact that no language stands still, and the "biblical language" of 1611 became increasingly remote from ordinary speech. And, of course, the KJV itself was not faultless—even in its own time. So a Revised Version (hereafter RV) was produced in 1881 (NT) and 1885 (OT) by a committee set up by the Convocation of Canterbury, drawing on the best biblical scholarship of the time.

A parallel revision process was carried out in America, and the two committees kept in touch with each other's work. But the American revisers were not prepared to follow such strictly conservative guidelines as the British had. The resultant *American Standard Version* (hereafter ASV) of 1901 is thus of recognizably similar character to the RV but not identical (notably in its use of "Jehovah" instead of "the LORD" to represent the divine name).

The RV was deliberately a "revision," not a new translation. Its compilers aimed to keep as close as possible to the familiar wording, even retaining "all archaisms, whether of language or construction, which though not in familiar use cause a reader no embarrassment and lead to no misunderstanding." Where errors needed to be corrected or the language was now misleading, they aimed still to follow the style and diction of the KJV as closely as possible. On one point, however, they clearly felt differently from the 1611 translators in that they aimed, wherever the context allowed, to use the same English rendering for the same original word.

One feature of the new version that seems commonplace to us but was a major contribution to intelligent understanding was the layout of the printed text. Instead of each verse being printed as a paragraph in itself, with no indication of where a new section began, the RV printed the text in sense-paragraphs (though retaining verse numbers for reference). In the poetical books and in some other poetical material (though surprisingly not in the prophetic books), the text was set out in verse-lines rather than printed like prose.

In the reconstruction of the text to be translated, the RV represents a huge leap forward and was welcomed as such by most biblical scholars of the time (though with lively exceptions, such as the redoubtable Dean Burgon, whose fury at the loss of such familiar texts as the Trinitarian formula in 1 John 5:7 knew no limits). The RV was widely accepted as the "proper" text to use in schools and colleges. But the pedantic and archaic style of translation resulting from the revisers' principles was not calculated to excite the reading public, and it seems never to have caught the public imagination. The KJV remained most people's Bible.

But the principle of retranslation was now recognized, and during the first half of the twentieth century many new versions began to appear. Most of them were the work of individuals and could claim no official status. The following list of versions published before 1950 may give some idea of the gradual opening of the floodgates: The Twentieth Century New Testament (1902); R. F. Weymouth, New Testament in Modern Speech (1903); F. Fenton, The Holy Bible in Modern English (1903); J. Moffatt, The New Testament: A New Translation (1913; complete Bible 1928); Jewish Publication Society version (1917); E. J. Goodspeed, The New Testament: An American Translation (1923; complete Bible 1927); G. W. Wade, The Documents of the New Testament (1934); C. B. Williams, The New Testament in the Language of the People (1937); The New Testament in Basic English (1941); R. A. Knox (1945; complete Bible 1949); The New World Translation (of Jehovah's Witnesses [1950; complete Bible 1953]).

Two of these versions may be singled out for special mention. Moffatt's vigorous version (which sometimes reflects Scottish rather than English idiom) made a decisive break from "Bible English" and introduced many for the first time to a Bible in which the characters spoke like real people. Like all individual translations, it is at the mercy of the translator's preferences and ideas. It may be questioned whether it helps many ordinary readers to find at the beginning of the Gospel of John, "The Logos existed in the very beginning, the Logos was with God, the Logos was divine," while the introduction of Enoch into the text of 1 Peter 3:19 is a rather wild scholarly guess.

Moffatt's version remained a solo effort, with no authority but his own. R. A. Knox's version, on the other hand, received the official endorsement of the Catholic hierarchy and so stood alongside the Douai Bible as an official version. Like the Douai, it is a translation of the Vulgate, though with careful attention throughout to the original languages. Knox explained his principles in an important book titled *On Englishing the Bible* (1949). Prominent among them is the desire, while writing natural English, to avoid being merely contemporary. Rather, he aimed to produce such good, timeless English that it would not seem dated, even in two hundred years' time. Time will tell, but unfortunately for Knox's version it was only another twenty years before a much more widely read Catholic translation—the Jerusalem Bible—appeared.

But while this trove of individual Bible translations was being produced, the inadequacy of the more "official" RV (and its American counterpart) was increasingly felt, and a movement began toward a more extensive revision in the KJV tradition. The result was the Revised Standard Version (hereafter RSV) of 1946 (NT; whole Bible 1952), a revision by an American committee of the ASV.

The committee's aim was a thorough revision that nonetheless retained the "qualities which have given to the King James Version a supreme place in English literature." The RV and ASV had retained the archaic verb endings ("-est," "-eth") and the use of "thou" instead of the singular "you"; the new version abandoned these archaisms, except for retaining "thou" where God is addressed. The ASV's use of "Jehovah" was dropped again in favor of "the LORD." Clearly obsolete forms of expression were replaced, and the language has an altogether more modern feel, though it is far from colloquial.

Poetic material was set out more consistently in lines, and in other ways the typography was brought into the twentieth century, as illustrated by the use of quotation marks for direct speech.

The careful attention to developments in textual criticism that marked the RV was carried further in its successor. One interesting feature is the appearance (thirteen times) in Isaiah of notes that attribute the reading adopted to "one ancient ms." This is the great Isaiah scroll from Qumran, discovered in 1947 and published just in time for the committee to take it into account. Since this scroll dates more than a thousand years earlier than the Masoretic manuscripts on which previous translators depended, it marks a significant move forward in translating the Hebrew Bible, comparable with the influence of the great fourth-century codices on the RV of the NT.

Updated readings of the Hebrew and Greek texts and (relatively unadventurous) attempts to introduce more modern idiom inevitably attracted conservative criticism and vilification for the new version, including the widespread assertion that its translators were determined to undermine the divinity of Jesus. Looking back now it is hard to see what the fuss was all about, since the RSV is far more conservative and reassuringly familiar in its language than most more recent versions (each of which in its turn has received the same treatment). But the long dominance of the KJV had encouraged a resistance to change that the archaic style of the RV had not seriously threatened but that now awoke with vigor.

From the New English Bible to the Present Day

The RSV was still essentially in the tradition of Bible translation going back to Tyndale. It was a revision, not a new translation. We have noted above some more radically new translations in the first half of the twentieth century, but these remained individual contributions. There was still no genuinely new translation, carried out by a representative body and commanding wide recognition.

The New English Bible (hereafter NEB: NT 1961; whole Bible 1970) was the pioneer. The committee that produced it was set up jointly by many of the Protestant churches in Britain and contained many of the most respected biblical scholars of the day. They were "free to employ a contemporary idiom rather than reproduce the traditional 'biblical' English" and were assisted by a panel of "trusted literary advisers." The resultant style is certainly "new," though many ordinary readers have found it too literary, even donnish. But its publication marked a new era in English Bible translation. Many others soon followed. There follows a list, in chronological order and with minimal descriptions, of the more important committee or "official" translations (of very varied character) up to the time of writing. Because of the proliferation of new versions in recent years, the list necessarily becomes much more selective toward the end. (In most cases the NT was published first; dates given are for the whole Bible.)

- The Jerusalem Bible (1966), a new Catholic translation based on the French *La Bible de Jérusalem,* is stylistically elegant and widely used by Protestant readers. A New Jerusalem Bible (1985), following a new edition of *La Bible de Jérusalem* in 1973, is the work of Henry Wansbrough, with an even more elegant and readable style than its predecessor. It also took significant steps toward inclusive language.

- The New American Bible (1970), produced by members of the Catholic Biblical Association for the Roman Catholic bishops of America, has a more formal style. The NT, rather hastily prepared, was replaced by a new translation in 1987.
- The New American Standard Bible (1970) was a conservative attempt to update the ASV of 1901. Its English style is sacrificed to literal translation. It is little used outside America.
- The Good News Bible (1976; also known as Today's English Version) was produced under the auspices of the United Bible Societies and designed to be especially helpful for those for whom English is a second language. It uses language that is "natural, clear, simple, and unambiguous," following the principle of dynamic equivalence (as advocated in the works of Eugene A. Nida). The result is a vigorous and uncluttered style particularly welcomed among younger people for whom "Bible English" is an unfamiliar language.
- The New International Version (1978) was translated by a committee representing the evangelical constituency primarily in North America. An Anglicized version was also produced. The NIV has a moderately contemporary style that reads well in public or in private. It is currently the best-selling version in English. An inclusive-language edition was published in Britain in 1996. The New Testament edition of Today's New International Version, a version based on the NIV and incorporating inclusive-language changes, has recently been published.
- The New King James Version (1982) preserves the textual features of the KJV, but with modernized language and spelling. It is a rather quixotic enterprise, inspired by the dominance of the KJV in America and a backlash against modern textual criticism.
- Tanakh: A New Translation of the Holy Scriptures According to the Traditional Hebrew Text (1985), replacing the Jewish Publication Society Bible of 1917, is a totally new translation, using an "idiom for idiom" rather than "word for word" principle.
- The New Century Version (1987), an evangelical translation intended for young people, deliberately simplifies difficult language, with a good degree of imagination and rhythmic feeling.
- The Revised English Bible (1989) is a major revision of the NEB, with a much improved style and fairly consistent use of inclusive language.
- The New Revised Standard Version (1989) is a very extensive revision of the RSV, with the last of the "thous" removed and with the most comprehensive attention to inclusive language yet attempted.

- The Contemporary English Version (1995) is an American Bible Society version taking further the aim of the Good News Bible, with a view especially to oral reading and to those who do not have English as a first language. It uses inclusive language and has a considerably more paraphrastic style than most recent versions.
- The New Living Translation (1996) is a major revision of the Living Bible (see below), now not by one person but by an evangelical committee. It self-consciously moves away from paraphrase to "thought for thought" translation and so is much more mainstream than its predecessor.

Following the lead of the NEB, most recent committee versions, while drawn up by biblical scholars, have profited from the help of literary consultants. This feature, together with the continuing advances in biblical scholarship and textual criticism, means that Bible translation has entered a quite new phase since 1960. No previous generation (not even that of Tyndale and of the KJV) has been so well served with versions that both communicate effectively and can be relied on to convey the original sense as nearly as it can be ascertained. (It should be noted, however, that not all translations aim to be idiomatic; mention will be made later of an approach that prefers a deliberately "foreign" idiom in order to retain the features of the original language.)

Alongside these committee or "official" versions, the spate of individual versions has gone on increasing. Even to list them would be impossible. I mention just three that have been influential:

- J. B. Phillips, recognizing that young people no longer understood "Bible English," produced his famous *Letters to Young Churches* (the Epistles) in 1947 and completed the NT in 1958 and *Four Prophets* in 1963. His style is lively paraphrase, sometimes colloquial to the point of inelegance, but vigorous and arresting. In the days before the Good News Bible, Phillips filled a significant gap, particularly for younger readers, and is still widely read today.
- A more idiosyncratic paraphrase is the Living Bible of Kenneth Taylor (1971), in very colloquial American idiom and giving clear expression to the author's conservative theology. ("The theological lodestar in this book has been a rigid evangelical position.") But as a result of aggressive marketing it was for a time probably more widely read than any other individual version. It is replaced by the New Living Translation (see above).
- Eugene Peterson's *The Message* (1993) is a recent move along similar lines to the Living Bible, using powerful contemporary American idiom and

perhaps better described as an interpretation than as a paraphrase. It aims to use "the same language in which we do our shopping, talk with our friends, worry about world affairs, and teach our children table manners."

All these versions are, or intend to be, in "standard English" (though trans-atlantic variations have made "Anglicized editions" of some primarily American versions necessary). But attempts have also been made to translate the Bible or parts of it into non-standard English; I possess, for instance, *The Gospels in Scouse* and *Chapters from the New Testament translated into the Wensleydale Tongue*.

Some such versions are relatively lighthearted, but a more serious and scholarly version is W. L. Lorimer's *The New Testament in Scots* (1983), based on a lifetime of study of the Scots language. Here is Matthew 5:14–15: "Ye ar the licht o the warld. A toun biggit on a hill-tap canna be hoddit; an again, whan fowk licht a lamp, they pit-it-na ablo a meal-bassie, but set it up on the dresser-heid, an syne it gies licht for aabodie i the houss."

Translations have also been made into various forms of Pidgin English. Here are the first four beatitudes from Matthew 5:3–6 in a West African pidgin, as translated by the Mill Hill Fathers in Cameroon:

> Bless he live for people whe them de poor for heart;—
> na country for Heaven he go be them own.
> Bless he live for people whe them get strong heart;—
> them go chop country.
> Bless for people whe them de cry;—
> them go cool them heart.
> Bless for them people whe them de hungry for be holy;—
> them heart he go full up.

Some Issues in Bible Translation

We have noted that some English versions were made from the Latin (notably Wycliffe, Coverdale, Douai, Knox), and even today many translations made into African, Asian, and Latin American languages are (regrettably but understandably) made from an English version by translators who do not know Hebrew and Greek. But modern English translations are themselves routinely based on the Hebrew and Greek. The question that remains, however, is which Hebrew and Greek texts should be used.

The Text to Be Translated

The dramatic increase in known manuscripts and advances in text-critical method mean that we are no longer in the position of the KJV translators who had to depend on only a few late manuscripts. The translator who is not an expert in textual criticism can with a great deal of confidence work from the currently published critical texts. But where manuscript evidence is divided, critics are sometimes not in agreement, and a translator must take sides over the omission or inclusion of a suspect verse or over which of two words is more likely to have been in the original text. At such times, at least a basic acquaintance with the highly specialized science of textual criticism is needed.

A helpful innovation introduced into the United Bible Societies' edition of the Greek New Testament is a rating of each disputed reading from A to D, where A indicates the editors' virtual certainty over the text they chose to print, while D indicates that they had great difficulty in making up their minds. This Greek NT was designed for use by translators, who are thus allowed to share the textual critics' dilemmas and to know where they may responsibly part company from them. A companion volume, Bruce M. Metzger, *A Textual Commentary on the Greek New Testament* (1971, 1994), explains in laypeople's terms the basis on which each decision was made and the reasons for disagreements among the editors. With such helps, the translator is on much firmer ground. Nothing comparable exists for the Hebrew text, where the issues and methods are quite different.

Literal versus Dynamic Translation

Any translator is faced with the competing demands of the desire, on the one hand, to be as faithful as possible to the original and, on the other, to produce a version that communicates well and is a pleasure to read. The more disparate the structures of the languages involved, the greater this tension becomes.

But for the Bible translator there is the additional feature that the very words of the text to be translated are regarded by some potential readers, and perhaps by the translators themselves, as the product of divine inspiration. The form, as well as the content, of the original may thus come to be regarded as sacrosanct, the only acceptable version thus being one that mirrors as closely as possible the grammatical structures and lexical range of the Hebrew or Greek text. Such an attitude resembles the Muslim insistence that there can never be a "translation" of the Quran, only interpretations, because it is the Arabic text itself that is the locus of divine inspiration.

A recent example of a translation that deliberately reproduces the features of Hebrew language rather than using natural English idiom is Everett Fox's *The Five Books of Moses* (1996). Fox follows the principles of Martin Buber (1878–1965), conveniently set out in a recent English translation of some of Buber's writings titled *Scripture and Translation*. Buber believed that the impact of a text, particularly of the biblical text, cannot be reduced merely to its "meaning" but that the form and sound of the words are equally important and must be retained in a translation. The result, as found in Fox's translation, is intentionally foreign to the English ear and aims to impress with its strangeness rather than to eliminate the cultural and linguistic distance between the original text and the modern reader. To translate merely "sense for sense" is to lose the power of the original.

A less literary concern probably underlies those translations, ancient and modern, generally characterized as excessively literal (such as Aquila's Greek OT, the first Wycliffe translation, the New American Standard Bible). Such versions intentionally subordinate natural idiom to the "faithful" reproduction of the sacred text. The alternative is "paraphrase," a label often used as a term of disapprobation—paraphrase allowing the translator's own ideas to intrude into the text, so that on this view the authority of the original is relativized.

Over against this literalistic tendency stands the philosophy of translation that has come to be known as "dynamic equivalence" (more recently, "functional equivalence"). This philosophy is especially associated with the work of Eugene A. Nida, having come to prominence particularly in the context of the continuing enterprise of translating the Bible into the thousands of languages that so far have no Bible version. On this view, what matters is not the form of the text but its content, and it is the translator's responsibility to render that sense into the target language in whatever way will best communicate to native speakers of that language, without regard to such matters as the grammatical structure, word order, vocabulary, or cultural features of the original. Translations produced under this philosophy are typically more free, readable, and elegant and can fit more comfortably into the cultural context of the intended readers—but they are often suspected of having adulterated the sacred text.

The Good News Bible, produced for the Bible Societies, was a self-conscious paradigm of dynamic equivalence. But in fact virtually all English versions of the last half century have accepted the principle of translating idiom for idiom rather than word for word, even though the degree of freedom exercised has varied. Thus, even the relatively conservative New International Version, regarded by some as veering toward literalism, while it lists as its first concern "the accuracy of the translation and its fidelity to the thought of the biblical writers" (notice "thought," not "words") also affirms that "faithful communication of the meaning of the writers of the Bible demands frequent modifications in sentence structure and constant regard for the contextual meanings of words." The resultant translation claims, with considerable justification, to be in "clear and natural English."

The Problem of Religious Conservatism

Conservatism—in the sense of resistance to change—seems to affect people in matters of religion more readily than in other areas. Thoroughly modern people with radical political views may nonetheless be staunch advocates of the KJV and the Book of Common Prayer. Saint Luke long ago summed up the typical reaction to change in matters of religion: "The old is good" (Luke 5:39 NRSV). This is a hurdle every Bible translator must face.

Shortly after *Good News for Modern Man* (the New Testament of the Good News Bible) was published, I attended an English-speaking service in a remote hill-station in Nigeria. After reading a passage from the new version (designed for precisely that sort of situation where English was, at best, a second language), the Nigerian leader of the service put the book down, saying, "Now we will hear it from the real Bible," and he proceeded to read the same passage from the KJV. This devotion to the KJV as "the real Bible" is still to be found in many English-speaking congregations, after decades of "better" translations being freely available. To talk of a corrupt text and of language that does not communicate to most people today cuts no ice: The Bible is expected to speak in Elizabethan English. The colloquial language employed by Tyndale so that the Scriptures would be accessible to the ploughboy has thus become, with the passing of time, the esoteric language of religion, and the more remote it becomes from ordinary speech the more special and holy it seems.

The task of Bible translation is much easier where there is no existing version to be supplanted. I met a translator who had been commissioned to produce a dynamic new translation for a tribe in Zaire who already had a Bible version translated from the KJV and thus quite remote from the current form of the language. He told me how he read out of his fresh, new, colloquial version with pride and how the hearers commented favorably on the ease of understanding but then pointed out that, of course, it wasn't the Bible! It almost seems that, by definition, the Bible must be remote and unintelligible.

But the Bible, or most of it, was not written in a special "holy" language. The Hebrew prophets spoke in vigorous contemporary idioms, and the New Testament writers used "market Greek." A translation that will do justice to the intention of the original writers must put intelligibility before the maintenance of traditional language that no longer communicates effectively.

Public and Private Reading

In our day when the reading of books is an overwhelmingly private activity, we need to remember that the biblical books were written in a period of widespread illiteracy and that many of them were most likely originally designed for public reading. And even today, while most books are translated for private reading, Bible translators have to reckon with the fact that their work is likely to be read aloud in church as part of an act of worship.

One implication is that a translator must beware of expressions that may be perfectly clear in print but ambiguous or worse when heard orally. There is no visible punctuation to guide the hearer, and one cannot be sure that the skill of every church reader is sufficient to avoid misconstruction of sentences where punctuation is the only way of differentiating two meanings. Some translation committees have therefore wisely made a point of having their proposed translations read aloud before agreeing on them.

The makeup of a typical congregation makes heavy demands on a translator's skill. There will be some who love the reassuring old words of the KJV and others whose concern is to hear language that communicates directly in lively, contemporary style. Some will set great store by the dignity of the language, others by its freshness and ability to challenge. To satisfy all tastes is an impossible task, and the translator who has a sensitivity to public reading will usually settle for a compromise.

The wide range of types of translation now available, while potentially confusing for a newcomer, does allow those responsible for public worship the opportunity to select a version suitable for each particular group or occasion. Some versions, however, are not designed for public reading. More literal versions that do not read like idiomatic English may nonetheless be helpful for close, analytical study of the text by those who are not able to work in the original languages. On the other hand, a colloquial paraphrase such as the Living Bible, which would often be unsuitable for public reading, may arrest the attention of a new Bible reader and suggest new ways of looking at the text.

Inclusive Language

By the end of the twentieth century, the traditional English use of "men" to mean "people" and "he" as a pronoun for an unspecified person of either sex became increasingly unacceptable, and Bible versions have been adapted accordingly. Thus, while the RSV, the JB, the NEB, and the NIV had used the "generic masculine," their revisions in the 1980s and 1990s have gone to great lengths to be inclusive (or, as some now prefer to say, "gender-accurate") wherever the original did not appear to be gender-specific.

Such accommodation to modern sensibilities is easily lampooned as trendy and politically correct, but it is, in fact, a matter of good translation. Thus the

Greek *anthrōpos* (human being), while masculine in form, is clearly differentiated from *anēr* (a male person), and to use the same English term "man" for both was always liable to distort the sense. It has taken modern sensitivity to exclusive language to alert us to the poverty of the English language in this respect and to send us in search of better ways to convey the sense of the original.

But, of course, Hebrew and Greek also use generic masculine pronouns and terms of address such as "brothers" when clearly the whole church community is in view. In the current climate of thought, many female readers feel excluded by such terms, and so if a translator continues to offer literal (masculine) renderings, the effect is actually to misrepresent the biblical writers, who did not have only males in mind.

On the other hand, there is sometimes room for debate over whether the original did intend to be inclusive. The patriarchal culture lying behind much of the masculine language of the Bible is itself also part of the data to be translated, and it is a fair question as to how far the translator may properly obscure it.

There are certain well-tried devices to avoid gender-specific language, such as turning singular generic statements into the plural (and thus substituting "they" for "he"), or using the first or second person in place of the third where the context allows the sense to be conveyed in this way. Words like "people," "humanity," and "mortals" can be used in place of "man," "mankind," and "men." But there is the danger that by reducing the range of vocabulary available, the translation may be made less elegant (e.g., by too many uses of "people" in a short space). And there are disputes as to how open English idiom is to accept terms such as "humans" and "humankind," or whether it allows a "whoever" to be followed by a "they." Usage is fluid, and judgments as to what is currently acceptable will vary. But the issue will not go away, and it is hard to imagine any new translation in the future perpetuating the generic masculines of the traditional versions.

There are further problems for the Bible translator in this area. "Fishers of men" (Mark 1:17) is a well-loved phrase that aptly echoes the preceding mention of "fishermen." It is hard to see how an inclusive version can retain the familiar phrase or match the elegance of the wordplay. Or what about Jesus' regular self-designation as "the Son of Man," a very masculine phrase that means literally "a human being"? If "the son of man" in Psalm 8:4 becomes "human beings," what are we to do with Hebrews 2:6, where on the basis of that verse the writer sees the psalm as pointing to Jesus? Even with the generous use of footnotes, such issues are not easily resolved, and the Bible translator does not have the luxury of writing a commentary on his or her text!

All this has to do with biblical ways of speaking about people. Feminist discomfort with masculine language about God (a masculine devil seems to have been found less offensive) has not yet been reflected in mainstream Bible translation. This theological movement is a different issue from the exclusion of half the human race by the use of generic masculine pronouns, and translators have rightly not seen it as their business to address it.

BIBLIOGRAPHY[2]

Ackroyd, P. R., et al., eds. *The Cambridge History of the Bible,* 3 vols. (Cambridge: Cambridge Univ. Press, 1963-1970), especially vol. 2, pp. 338–491 ("The Vernacular Scriptures"); vol. 3, pp. 141–74 ("English Versions of the Bible 1525-1611") and pp. 361–82 ("English Versions since 1611").

Bruce, F. F. *History of the Bible in English,* 3d ed. (Oxford: Oxford Univ. Press, 1978).

Buber, Martin and Franz Rosenzweig. *Scripture and Translation* (Bloomington, Ind.: Indiana Univ. Press, 1994).

Daniell, David, ed. *Tyndale's New Testament: A Modern-Spelling Edition of the 1534 Translation with an Introduction by David Daniell* (New Haven, Conn.: Yale Univ. Press, 1989).

Daniell, David, ed. *Tyndale's Old Testament: A Modern-Spelling Edition with an Introduction by David Daniell* (New Haven, Conn.: Yale Univ. Press, 1992).

Davie, Donald, ed. *The Psalms in English* (London: Penguin, 1996).

Duthie, Alan S. *Bible Translations and How to Choose Between Them* (Exeter: Paternoster, 1985).

Hargreaves, Cecil. *A Translator's Freedom: Modern English Bibles and Their Language* (Sheffield: Sheffield Academic Press, 1993).

Knox, R. A., *On Englishing the Bible* (London: Burns & Oates, 1949).

Lewis, Jack P., *The English Bible from KJV to NIV* (Grand Rapids: Baker, 1982).

Nida, Eugene A., *Toward a Science of Translating* (Leiden: Brill, 1964).

Nida, Eugene A. and Charles R. Taber. *The Theory and Practice of Translation,* 2d ed. (Leiden: Brill, 1982).

Norton, David. *A History of the Bible as Literature,* 2 vols. (Cambridge: Cambridge Univ. Press, 1993).

Strauss, Mark L. *Distorting Scripture? The Challenge of Bible Translation and Gender Accuracy* (Downers Grove, Ill.: InterVarsity Press, 1998).

"Versions" (various authors). *The Anchor Bible Dictionary,* vol. 6, pp. 787–851 (New York: Doubleday, 1992).

NOTES

1. This is an adapted version of an article ("The Bible in English") contributed to *The Oxford Guide to Literature in English Translation* (Oxford: Oxford Univ. Press, 2000, reprinted by permission). Originally designed for a nontheological audience, it covers

ground that theologically informed readers will take for granted. But I hope that its attempt to stand back for an overview of the nature of the translator's task and of the way the task has been undertaken over the years will prove of some interest, even to those who know it all already! I am delighted that the editors chose to include this article in a volume honoring Ron Youngblood, whom I have known in his capacity as a translator since 1990 when I joined the Committee on Bible Translation responsible for the NIV. Ron had already served on that committee for many years before I arrived, and I owe him much for the insights I gained from his long experience and exemplary care as a translator. His sense of fun and keen eye for the ridiculous have enlivened many a heavy session. I respectfully salute him with one of his favorite "biblical" expressions: "Ho, such a one!"

2. Translations of the Bible into English have been detailed in the text and are not listed again here.

8

A TRANSLATOR'S PERSPECTIVE ON ALISTER MCGRATH'S HISTORY OF THE KING JAMES VERSION[1]

Walter W. Wessel[2]

I was raised in a devout Christian family. A small Baptist church in downtown Los Angeles, California, was the center of my family's social and religious life. It was a German-speaking church, built by immigrants about the turn of the century. As a young boy (this was in the 1920s), my place on Sunday mornings was in church seated next to my father. The entire service was in German, including the reading of Scripture. As I grew older the children in the congregation were allowed to leave the sanctuary just before the sermon and retreat to Junior Church—which was in English, led by a graduate of Moody Bible Institute. I remember her as a gifted teacher whose basic mission was to inculcate in us the Word of God. She placed great emphasis on memorizing Scripture passages and used creative ways to get us to do it. The Bible we memorized was, of course, the King James Version (KJV).

In my late teens I came across Dawson Trotman and the Navigators organization and eagerly enrolled in their Scripture memorization program. I memorized hundreds of Bible verses, and again, they were from the King James Version. At the time I was hardly aware of any other Bible, or even that the Bible I had come to love was a *translation*.

Many years later, in 1967, I joined a group of scholars who were invited to participate in a translation of the Bible that ultimately became known as the New International Version (NIV). We were not far into this project before most of us, especially the older members of the group, became keenly aware of how much we had been influenced by the wording of the King James Version. It took considerable effort and much vigilance to purge our minds of its antiquated language.

This is only a small and personal example of the King James Version's powerful influence. Historical theologian Alister McGrath tells the full story in *In the Beginning,* and it is a fascinating one indeed. In his introduction he asks the question: How did this remarkable translation come to be written? His reply was as follows:

> The full answer to this question is as fascinating as it is complex, and involves the Byzantine politics of Tudor and Jacobean England, the hopes and fears of English monarchs and would-be bishops, and the surge of confidence and pride in England and its national language under "Good Queen Bess." To answer this question is to throw open the doors to a lost world that was being transformed by the new technology of printing, in much the same way that today's world has been changed by the Internet. (p. 3)

Considerable historical research on the King James Bible has been published.[3] Alister McGrath's recent book is a welcome and valuable addition to this larger body of work. In this article I intend to summarize McGrath's volume and evaluate its insights from the perspective of a contemporary Bible translator.

Most books on the KJV begin with the accession of King James I and a discussion of the religious and political situation of that day. McGrath, by contrast, begins with the invention of movable-type printing in the middle of the fifteenth century, almost two hundred years before the KJV appeared. Up until the early Middle Ages, literacy was almost exclusively limited to the clergy. This all changed during the Italian Renaissance of the fourteenth century. Because the ability to read became a socially desirable accomplishment, there was a greater demand for things to read. The traditional way to reproduce books was the laborious and time-consuming method of copying manuscripts by hand. But this, of course, could not begin to supply the demand.

There were attempts before the fifteenth century, mainly in Germany, to provide a better way, but it was Johannes Gutenberg of Mainz, Germany, who successfully solved the problem. He was first to invent movable metal type and a new type of ink from lamp black and varnish. The movable metal type enabled him to speed up the process, and the new ink allowed him to print on paper rather than on the more expensive vellum (parchment).

Although Gutenberg first printed some short books with his new movable type and ink, it was his great desire to print a Bible—for two reasons: It was (1) a large book and therefore a challenge, and (2) a popular book, and thus had the potential for profit. Gutenberg began the project in 1449 or 1450. It took him six years to complete it. About 185 copies were printed. Most of them were printed on paper, the rest on vellum. It took 170 calf hides for each two-volume Bible of the latter variety. The initial (in 1456) cost of such a Bible was, according to McGrath, equivalent to the cost of a large town house in Germany. By 1520, due largely to the fact that Gutenberg's invention was exploited by many printers, the price was drastically reduced so that a printed Bible became only an "affordable luxury" (p. 18).

Translations into the Vernacular

McGrath turns next, as part of the background of the KJV, to the vernacular translations of the Scripture into English. The Gutenberg Bible printed the Latin Vulgate text. This severely limited its use both in England and on the continent, since Latin was the language of the clergy, scholars, and diplomats, not the common people.

Vernacular translations began to appear in Germany as early as 1466, and by 1483 nine of them were in circulation. In England it was John Wycliffe (c. 1330–84) who spearheaded the translation of the Bible into the vernacular. Whether Wycliffe did any actual translation work himself is not clear, but the two Wycliffite translations (the first in 1384, and the second at the end of the same year) made the whole Bible accessible to English readers in their own language for the first time.

John Purvey, Wycliffe's secretary, was no doubt responsible for much of the translation. In the *General Prologue,* a tract commending the second Wycliffe Bible, Purvey set down some principles of Bible translation that remain valid and important to this day:

> First, it is to be known that the best translating out of Latin into English is to translate after the sentence [meaning] and not only after the words, so the sentence be as open [clear] or opener, in English as in Latin, and go not far from the letter; and if the letter may not be followed in the translating, let the sentence be ever whole and open, for the words ought to serve the intent and sentence, or else the words be superfluous or false.[4]

The late F. F. Bruce, a noted biblical scholar, commented on this principle as follows:

> In other words, the translation must be intelligible without reference to the original. And if it is to be intelligible, it must be idiomatic, sufficiently idiomatic to convey the sense without

> difficulty to the reader whose only language is English. Yet the translator must bear in mind that it is Holy Writ that he is translating; therefore, he will not depart from the letter of the original more than is necessary to convey the true and plain sense.[5]

It is not surprising that the second Wycliffe Bible, whose translator(s) followed Purvey's principles and thereby produced a far more readable Bible, had more success than the first one, which was a literal, wooden translation. One is reminded of the more recent fate of the Revised Version of 1881–85. The translators hoped it would replace the KJV. It ailed, in spite of its impeccable scholarship and the advantage of having available more ancient and reliable biblical manuscripts. The reason? It was too literal and wooden. As someone commented, "It reads like a schoolboy's crib."

McGrath then discusses the rise of English as a national language. During the fourteenth century Latin and French were the languages of choice among the ruling classes in England. In the late sixteenth century this began to change. England, during the reign of Elizabeth I, had become a powerful nation, and the literary men of the day propelled English into the front ranks of living European languages. It came to be recognized that the English language had the capacity to express the full range of human emotions and thoughts. To write in English, or to translate into English, became a "political act, affirming the intrinsic dignity of the language of a newly confident people and nation" (pp. 25–26). McGrath, however, points out that the use of Latin died a slow death. Oxford and Cambridge Universities continued to use Latin as the preferred language of academic life, even after the church had dropped it. He suggests two reasons: (1) pure arrogance and (2) a desire to keep a guarded line *(cordon sanitaire)* between classical literature and the masses. But more likely, or additionally, Latin was the universal language of scholars.

The Renaissance gave rise to individualism. People of faith wanted a more personal religion. Instead of being told by priests and ministers what the Bible said and meant, they wanted to find out for themselves. Erasmus's work *The Handbook of the Christian Soldier* (1503) stressed the need for reform, including the need for the laity to play a more important role in the church. His strongest statement is found in the preface to his Greek New Testament:

> I totally disagree with those who are unwilling that the Holy Scriptures, translated into the common tongue, should be read by the unlearned. Christ desires his mysteries to be published abroad as widely as possible. I could wish that even all women

> read the Gospel and St. Paul's Epistles, and I would that they were translated into all the languages of all Christian people, that they were read and known not merely by the Scots and Irish but even by the Turks and Saracens. I wish that the farm worker might sing parts of them at the plough, that the weaver might hum them at the shuttle, and that the traveler might beguile the weariness of the way by reciting them. (pp. 55–56)

Martin Luther's contribution to the Reformation is well-known. I shall not summarize McGrath's entire treatment of it but focus on the part most relevant to his overall purpose. Luther recognized early on the importance of getting theological writings, and especially the Bible, to the people in language they could understand. In 1520 he published three popular religious pamphlets. One of them, *The Appeal to the German Nobility,* was particularly important. In it he stated the desperate need for reform in the church and urged that if the church leaders refused to respond, the laity should take up the task. He also demanded that the laity have the right to read and interpret the Bible for themselves. Luther considered the need for a good vernacular translation of the Bible so important that he decided to do one himself. And what a translation it turned out to be! He started off with the New Testament. It took him all of eleven weeks to translate Erasmus's Greek New Testament. What an incredible feat, especially when one considers the quality of the translation! Published in 1522, it is estimated that it sold five thousand copies in the first two months alone. He then turned to the Old Testament. For this task Luther enlisted a small group of scholars to assist him, because he recognized his own deficiency in the Hebrew language.

An interesting and important detail about Luther's translation is that he wanted his Bible to be in *spoken* rather than in *bookish* or *written* German. Before any word or phrase could be put on paper, it had to pass the test of Luther's ear. It had to sound right. It is not surprising, as we will see, that the translators of the KJV had the same concern.

The English Reformation

McGrath acknowledges that the seeds of the KJV were planted in the 1520s in Germany. However, he notes, "If any event may be said to have prepared the ground for the translation of the Bible into English, it was the Reformation in England, which began under Henry VIII" (p. 61). After a brief description of what happened, McGrath summarizes the difference between the reformations in Germany and England:

> Luther's Reformation was conducted on the basis of a theological foundation and platform. The fundamental impetus was religious (in that it addressed the life of the church directly) and theological (in that proposals for reform rested on a set of theological propositions). In England, the Reformation was primarily political and practical. (p. 65)

This, of course, does not mean that there were no religious issues involved. Henry placed himself not only as head of the state but also as head of the English church. By displacing the pope, some thought he might be willing to support a new translation of the Bible, but it did not happen in Henry's time.

The next section of McGrath's book is a history of the printed English Bible from Tyndale (1494–1536) to the KJV (1611). Particular attention is paid, and rightly so, to Tyndale's translation (1526) and to the Geneva Bible (1560). Tyndale's great achievement was the translation of the New Testament into English from the Greek text. McGrath calls his translation the precursor of the King James Bible. It surely was a landmark in the history of the English Bible. As much as ninety percent of the KJV reads like Tyndale. Its two remarkable successes were (1) that it was a first-rate translation and (2) that it forced the hand of the English church and state to produce an officially sanctioned Bible.

Such a Bible did not appear quickly. Instead, both church and state suppressed it. Tyndale himself was forced to leave England. He finished his translation and had it published in Germany. The story of how copies were brought back into England is well-known. After producing a revision of his translation in 1534, Tyndale, who was living in the free city of Antwerp, was kidnapped, strangled, and burned at the stake in the Belgium town of Vilvalde in 1536.

After Tyndale a succession of English Bibles appeared between 1534 and 1611. The Geneva Bible (1560) is particularly important to an understanding of how and under what political and religious conditions the KJV came into being. McGrath devotes considerable space to this, and his treatment of it is one of the most important and enlightening parts of his book.

When Mary Tudor came to the throne in 1553, she was determined to reestablish Catholicism in England. Protestants who could financially afford to do so fled to the continent. Some of them settled in Geneva, Switzerland (John Calvin's city). These folks were particularly active in producing books and pamphlets, some in Latin for a broad readership and some in English for the Protestants who had remained in the home country. By far the most important of these publications was the Geneva Bible, a translation into English. The foremost feature of this Bible, as far as the subsequent history of the translation of the Bible into English is concerned, was its copious marginal notes, particularly those notes that called into question the divine right of kings.

The Geneva Bible quickly became known and used in England. When Mary Tudor died in 1558 and was succeeded by Elizabeth I, Protestants hoped for significant concessions. But Elizabeth was reluctant because she feared a fresh outbreak of the religious wars that had plagued England in the recent past. William Whittingham, the translator of the Geneva Bible, even included a dedicatory epistle to Elizabeth in the hope that his Bible would be accepted for reading in the churches. But the religious authorities wanted no part of it. The theological notes were offensive to them. Despite all the opposition, however, by 1600 the Geneva Bible had become the most popular Bible in England.

At this point McGrath describes the immediate circumstances out of which the KJV came into being. Queen Elizabeth I died in 1603. During her reign England had become a strong Protestant country. There had been great expansion economically and militarily; in addition, "a new confidence in the English language" had begun to emerge (p. 131). The new king was James I, formerly James VI of Scotland. Since James came from Presbyterian Scotland, the Puritans in England expected that he would champion their cause. But they were wrong. While serving as king of Scotland, James had had some conflicts with the Presbyterians, and he didn't particularly like the Geneva Bible. The main reason? The marginal notes, especially those that cast doubts on the divine right of kings.

James was aware of the religious conflicts that had existed for a long time—and were still present—in England, so early in his reign he called a conference "for the reformation of some things amiss in ecclesiastical matters." The Hampton Court Conference, as it was called, began on 12 January 1604. To it were invited nineteen representatives of the established church, but only four Puritans. Not a whole lot was accomplished at the conference, with one notable exception. John Reynolds, the leader of the Puritan delegation, proposed that a new translation of the Bible be made. Although Richard Bancroft, the wily bishop of London and soon to be archbishop of Canterbury, opposed it, King James approved it. He made this statement:

> I profess I could never yet see a Bible well translated in English; but I think that, of all, that of Geneva is the worst. I wish some special pains were taken for a uniform translation, by the best learned men of both Universities, then reviewed by the Bishops, presented to the Privy Council, lastly ratified by Royal Authority, to be read in the whole Church and none other.[6]

So it was resolved that "a translation be made of the whole Bible, as consonant as can be to the original Hebrew and Greek; and this to be set out and printed, without any marginal notes, and only to be used in all churches of England in time of divine services" (pp. 163–64).

Although the KJV is commonly called the Authorized Version, there is no record of it being formally authorized by any body—either church or state. However, as McGrath points out, a fire in Whitehall in January 1618 destroyed the records of the Order in Council, including its registers, for the period between 1600 and 1613. So the question of official authorization remains open.

Translation Procedures

The procedures for the translation were largely controlled by Bishop Bancroft. He not only wrote up the "Rules for Translation," but he also controlled the selection of the translators. The Bible was divided into six sections, and the same number of translators was assigned to each. Altogether there were six "companies" of translators. Two met at Oxford, two at Westminster, and two at Cambridge. Each was responsible for an explicit section of the Bible, including the Apocrypha. Among their number were many of the most distinguished biblical and linguistic scholars of the day. The translation process was slow and deliberate. It took the second Cambridge company four years to complete its work. Other companies took even longer.

Although the information about procedure is not clear, it appears that when the companies completed their work, all the translations were brought together at Stationers' Hall in London. Each company sent two representatives to this meeting. A particularly interesting detail is found in the *Table Talk* of John Selden. He wrote that "they met together and one read the translation, the rest holding in their hands some Bible, either of the learned tongues [Hebrew, Latin, and Greek] or French, Spanish, Italian, etc. If they found any fault, they spoke up; if not, he read on" (p. 187). It looks very much like the translators took a page from Martin Luther, who also, as we've seen, tested his translation by having it read out loud.

The next step was to have the translation checked by Miles Smith and Thomas Bilson. Whether they put the final touches on the entire translation or only on the specific changes made by the committee at Stationers' Hall is not clear. A surprising development was an unauthorized review made by Richard Bancroft (now archbishop of Canterbury). It was one of his final acts. He died 2 November 1610, a year before the KJV was published.

The "Epistle Dedicatory" to James I was probably penned by Thomas Bilson, and the statement from the "Translators to the Readers" by Miles Smith. The latter contains some important information. First, the translators did not consider their Bible a new translation. Their purpose was "to make a good one better, or out of many good ones, one principal good one." It should be added here, however, that Richard Bancroft had already laid down as his first rule that the Bishops' Bible of 1568 (an Elizabethan revision of the Great Bible) was to be followed and as little altered as the truth of the original would permit. Second, the new Bible was produced not because the Puritans were concerned about the accuracy of existing English versions but because the translations used in the prayer book were corrupted. Next, the importance of putting the Bible into the language of the people was emphasized. In addition, it included an honest admission that there are words in the original languages of the Bible (especially Hebrew) about which one can only guess their meaning. In such cases marginal text notes (the kind modern readers of the Bible are familiar with, since they occur in almost all currently published Bibles) were included. Finally, the translators refused to be bound to translate a Greek or Hebrew word by the same English word every time it occurred. This was a wise decision, because words only have meaning in context. Furthermore, variety enhances style and readability.

The KJV, once translated, had to be printed. It is quite remarkable that, in view of the active part James I played in promoting it, the KJV was a private enterprise throughout. The king promoted it but refused to finance it. The KJV was funded by venture capitalists!

McGrath includes some information about its printing that is interesting and otherwise largely unknown. The English book trade had been controlled for many years by the Stationers' Company, and until 1695 printing was allowed at only four centers—London, Oxford, Cambridge, and York. Since the time of Henry VIII, Bibles printed in England by official sanction were under a trade monopoly. The king granted to a printer a "privilege" (which amounted to a monopoly), and the printer in turn paid the crown a royalty.

Christopher Barker had become the Queen's Printer in 1577. In 1599 he was able to persuade Queen Elizabeth to extend his privilege, not only to his own death, but also to that of his son. Christopher died in 1599, and his son Robert, having assumed the office of his father upon the accession of James I, became the official printer of the KJV. McGrath makes it clear that Barker got the job, not because he was the best and most reliable printer available, but because of the politics of the day. It wasn't until the printing houses of Oxford and Cambridge became involved that the textual accuracy of the KJV was assured.

The first edition of the KJV included in its title page the statement: "Appointed to be read in churches." McGrath points out that this does not mean that the work had been authorized for that purpose but that it was laid out in a way suitable for public reading in churches. As noted before, there is no evidence that the KJV ever received final written authorization from the bishops, privy council, or the king.

It is not surprising that the KJV did not receive an immediately overwhelming reception. In fact, initially it was the object of violent attacks from both Protestant and Catholic activists. An example of the former was that of Dr. Hough Broughton, a distinguished scholar who nevertheless had not been invited to be one of the translators. When the new translation appeared, he had this colorful response:

> The late Bible ... was sent to me to censure: which bred in me a sadness that will grieve me while I breathe, it is so ill done. Tell His Majesty that I had rather be rent in pieces by wild horses, than any such translation by my consent should be urged upon poor churches.... The new edition crosseth me. I require it to be burnt.[7]

One is reminded of the negative reaction in this country when the Revised Standard Version first appeared. One preacher is reported to have attempted to burn a copy in his pulpit with a blowtorch, and, having difficulty, he remarked that it was like the devil, because it was so hard to burn! But in time the RSV, like the KJV, became one of the most popular and respected of the English versions.

Translation Issues

It was the influential British biblical scholar C. H. Dodd who said, "There is no such thing as exact equivalence of meaning between words in different languages." As a result every translation ends up "looking like the back side of a Turkish tapestry."[8] In other words, the translator practices an impossible art. Likewise, the translators of the KJV faced some tough issues. One particularly large question they faced, according to McGrath, was this: How can one combine faithfulness to the text with elegance of translation? By way of an answer to his own query, McGrath paraphrases the response of the great English metaphysical poet John Donne, who claimed that "elegance results from a faithful translation and does not require to be imposed on the text" (p. 218). Perhaps, but I respectfully doubt it. The Revised Version of 1881 and 1885 was an accurate and faithful translation—far more faithful to the text than the KJV—but it definitely lacked elegance of style. It was precisely this lack that accounted for its failure to be widely accepted. Good style in translation must be worked for as diligently and consciously as accuracy.

There were other important issues with which the translators of the KJV had to deal. They had to determine how to handle idioms (which ones to take literally and which not to)—always a problem for translators. In addition, what were they to do with rare words? Hebrew words presented the biggest challenge, since knowledge of Hebrew in the seventeenth century was not as advanced as the knowledge of Greek. So they guessed at the meanings of some of the words and inevitably made mistakes. There was also the question of which manuscript of the text should be translated. This question related primarily to the New Testament. The translators used what was then considered the best Greek text: a revision by Theodore Beza of Erasmus's 1516 edition, known as the Textus Receptus (Received Text). It was essentially a medieval text, defective in many ways, but it was the best they had. The translators had to decide how poetry was to be handled. Despite the fact that the poetic nature of some sections of the Bible had already been recognized, the translators decided to make no distinction between poetry and prose in the layout of the text. Each verse was formatted as a separate paragraph, as in the Geneva Bible.

Arching over these detailed considerations was this: What was the translators' overall approach going to be? McGrath's answer is that a careful study of the actual style of the KJV suggests that its translators had consciously committed themselves to "ensure that every word in the original was rendered by an English equivalent," to "make it clear when they added any words to make the sense clearer, or to lead to better English syntax," and to "follow the basic order of the words in the original wherever possible" (p. 250). The result, suggests McGrath, is "a literal and formal translation that happens to correspond with the consensus of today's Bible translators" (p. 252). It is not clear to me what McGrath means by "literal and formal," but I'm sure that many contemporary translators who have produced accurate Bible translations would be reluctant to use these terms to describe their work. Literal translations are not necessarily the most accurate ones.

McGrath deals with another important and interesting subject: What role did the KJV have in the shaping of modern English? His overall answer is that it was foundational, along with the works of William Shakespeare. In England, unlike some of the countries of Europe, no official body was given the responsibility to shape the language and establish its norms, and so printed works had to fill the gaps. One of the "unintended functions" of the KJV was to do just that. Even though initially its language might have seemed strange to some readers, with continued usage it became generally accepted and a part of standard English. Latin,

Greek, and Hebrew words and idioms were taken into the KJV and have become so common that modern English readers are completely unaware of their origin. For example, Hebrew idioms like licking the dust (Ps 72:9), falling flat on one's face (Num 22:31), sour grapes (Ezek 18:2), and the skin of one's teeth (Job 19:20) have been deeply established in popular English usage. All this has greatly enriched the English language.

But why did the KJV retain words that were already becoming archaic (e.g., "thou" and "ye" and the verbal ending "eth")? McGrath points to the first of the very specific instructions given to the translators: "The ordinary Bible read in the Church, called the Bishops' Bible, [is] to be followed, and as little altered as the Truth of the original will permit" (p. 173).

One final issue, which McGrath calls eloquence by accidence, warrants comment. His contention is that the translators of the KJV achieved literary distinction because they were not deliberately pursuing it. While aiming at truth, they also achieved beauty and eloquence. How he comes to this conclusion is not clear to me. Two observations seem to contradict it. First, the translators deliberately rejected a wooden, mechanical approach—evidenced by their refusal to translate every Greek and Hebrew word by the same English word, no matter what the context. Second, they tested the translation by having it read out loud before finalizing it. These two factors seem to indicate *conscious* concern for English style.

❖❖❖

I found Dr. McGrath's book a delight to read. It is interesting—even fascinating—and it is written in nontechnical language. There are no distracting footnotes, except to explain a few obscure or obsolete words found in the KJV. It contains a valuable bibliography—one of the most comprehensive I've seen on the KJV and related subjects—and an adequate index. Perhaps McGrath's greatest contribution is his thorough treatment of the economic, social, religious, and political factors that influenced the production of English language Bibles, especially the KJV. No question about it, the KJV was a monumental achievement in the history of the translation of the Bible. McGrath's statement that "we shall never see its equal—or even its likes—again" (p. 310) is probably true. Attempts to resurrect it in our time have only been moderately successful, even though there are still those who think that "it was good enough for St. Paul [or St. James!] and thus good enough for me." Like all Bible translations the KJV was for its time. To be sure, it lasted for a longer time than any other English translation, but language changes and the crucial need continues, so far as the kingdom of God is concerned, for fresh, accurate, and understandable translations of the Word of God.[9]

Notes

1. Alister McGrath, *In the Beginning: The Story of the King James Bible and How It Changed a Nation, a Language, and a Culture* (New York: Doubleday, 2001).

2. Editors' Note: Not long after completing this essay, Walter Wessel, professor emeritus of Bethel College and Seminary, died on 23 April 2002, after a lengthy illness. After years of service in the pastorate, with InterVarsity Christian Fellowship, and at Biola, Western Conservative Baptist Seminary, and North American Baptist Seminary, Walt Wessel came to Bethel College to teach New Testament from 1961–81 and at Bethel Seminary San Diego from 1981–92. He also served as a chaplain in the U. S. Army Reserves. A meticulous scholar and the author of several books and commentaries, he served as an editor for the NIV, the *NASB Study Bible,* and the *NIV Study Bible.* Shortly before his passing, he completed his work as editor of the study notes for the TNIV. His loss will be felt keenly by his family and friends, as well as by nearly two generations of grateful students. As his longtime friend and colleague Clifford Anderson has said, "Peace be to the memory of this good soldier of Christ."

3. The history of the King James Version is treated in such standard surveys as *The Cambridge History of the Bible* (1963–70) and in a long list of histories of the English Bible that includes B. F. Westcott & W. Wright, *A General View of the History of the English Bible,* 3d ed. (London & New York: Macmillan, 1905), and F. F. Bruce, *History of the Bible in English,* 3d ed. (New York: Oxford Univ. Press, 1978). Some studies that focus more narrowly, like McGrath's volume, on the KJV include Albert Cook, *The Authorized Version and Its Influence* (Folcroft, Pa.: Folcroft, 1976); Cleland B. McAfee, *The Greatest English Classic* (Folcroft, Pa.: Folcroft, 1977); Olga Opfell, *The King James Bible Translators* (Jefferson, N.C.: McFarland, 1982); and more recently, Benson Bobrick, *Wide as the Waters: The Story of the English Bible and the Revolution It Inspired* (New York: Simon & Schuster, 2001).

4. Cited in F. F. Bruce, *The English Bible: A History of Translations* (New York: Oxford Univ. Press, 1961), 19–20.

5. Ibid., 20.

6. Ibid., 96–97.

7. Ibid., 107.

8. C. H. Dodd, "The Translation of the Bible: Some Questions of Principle," *Times Literary Supplement,* 20 March 1959.

9. I salute, on the occasion of his retirement, one of the best at this craft, Dr. Ronald Youngblood, longtime friend and colleague, to whom this Festschrift is dedicated.

9

TRANSLATION WAS NOT ENOUGH: THE ECUMENICAL AND EDUCATIONAL EFFORTS OF JAMES "DIEGO" THOMSON AND THE BRITISH AND FOREIGN BIBLE SOCIETY

Kent A. Eaton

Translation as Incarnational Missiology

Bible translation is ultimately an activity of the church grounded in mission. In fact, the translation process only comes full circle when it is carried out with the intention of introducing God's word to a specific audience. As Andrew Walls points out, the theological foundation of Bible translation is found in the incarnation itself as "God chose translation as his mode of action for the salvation of humanity.... There is a history of translation of the Bible because there was translation of the Word into flesh."[1] Translation leads to an encounter with the living God and a call to reorient every aspect of life to this One who made himself known to us in our cultures and through our languages. As Lamin Sanneh writes, "Christian missionaries assumed that since all cultures and languages are lawful in God's eyes, the rendering of God's word into those languages and cultures is valid and necessary."[2] In this way, Bible translators affirm the plurality of cultures and different perspectives of the faith. Quoting Andrew Walls again,

> As the incarnation took place in the terms of a particular social context, so translation uses the terms and relations of a specific context. Bible translation aims at releasing the word about

> Christ so that it can reach all aspects of a specific linguistic and cultural context, so that Christ can live within that context, in the persons of his followers, as thoroughly at home as he once did in the culture of first-century Jewish Palestine.[3]

A related implication of understanding translation as an ongoing incarnational process is to be aware of the means through which God's word penetrates all receptive elements of a given society with its power to call, convict, and redeem humanity. The *logos/sarx* did not seclude itself in Bethlehem's manger but called out loudly and clearly to those who had ears to hear. It is not surprising, then, that in the missionary journeys of Paul we find him *translating* theological concepts from Hebrew to Greek in his efforts to help his listeners comprehend the significance of the gospel. Likewise, it is less than surprising that Syriac, Latin, Coptic, and other versions of the Bible appeared in the first centuries of the church. Neither is it amazing that Ulphilas (c. 311–83), the great missionary "Apostle of the Goths," thought it an essential labor of love to develop a written language for the Goths and then translate most of the Old and New Testament into their language. Transmission is implicit in translation. Translation makes sense only when it includes proclamation; translation is never an end unto itself.

The essential commonality of translation and mission with the proclamation and distribution of the Bible is well illustrated by the labor of William Cameron Townsend (1896–1982). Long before he had the vision to begin the Summer Institute of Linguistics, Wycliffe Bible Translators, and Jungle Aviation and Radio Service (JARS), he had begun his ministry in 1917 as a colporteur, or Bible salesman, in Central America under the auspices of the Bible House of Los Angeles. Also, the great missionary conventions convened at the close of the nineteenth century and the beginning of the twentieth joined the themes of translation, missionary work, and literature distribution. For example, the leader of the American Bible Society, Edward W. Gilman, made this observation in his address to the 1888 Centenary Conference on the Protestant Missions of the World:

> We maintain that the conversion of souls and the extension of the Redeemer's kingdom are ever to be sought by bringing men into contact with the Bible as one book, complete, entire, and unique; by putting them under the influence of the written Word, translated into their own familiar speech, reproduced by pen or type, circulated so freely that every man may see with his own eyes the words of the Law and the Gospels, and then if need be, expounded and applied; until they believe to the sav-

> ing of the soul.... And this involves the whole work of translating, printing, and circulating the Scriptures of the Old and New Testaments among all nations.[4]

The 1910 World Missionary Conference also underscored that the mission of the church must include transmission through distribution: "The distribution of Christian literature is a matter of no less importance than its production." Yet the conference also underscored that "distribution is indeed one of the difficulties in the path of progress [in world missions]."[5] Missionaries were either translators themselves or those who built on the labor of other translators. The publication and distribution of God's Word, together with education and hospitals, has always been central to the church's understanding of its mission.[6]

Sowers of the Seed

As Protestant denominational mission organizations and interdenominational voluntary associations for missions and Bible translation emerged in the eighteenth and the nineteenth centuries, the colporteur[7] became an important means of addressing the problems inherent in Bible distribution. As the gospel entered a new context, the colporteur and missionary were many times one and the same person. However, as indigenous people emerged who were willing to take on the challenge, the missionary typically allowed these workers to gain their livelihood as Bible vendors. As one nineteenth-century writer attested, their work was highly valued: "Colportage is the mainstay of the work of Bible distribution, and by far the greater part of the Scriptures sold on mission ground pass through the hands of these men who quietly and unobtrusively have done and are doing a work unsurpassed in importance by that of any class of laborers in the field of evangelism."[8] Not surprising, colportage was the first step of many national workers toward vocational ministry.

The concept of the missionary colporteur and the popularity of this role became accepted and lauded following the highly publicized antics of George Borrow (1803–81), who traveled from Great Britain to Russia, Portugal, and Spain to sell Bibles. Like Borrow, colporteurs were many times charismatic, as free as the wind, striking out while somewhat unsure of where their journey might take them. For example, the subject of this chapter, James Thomson (1788–1854), once wrote that his methodology was to be guided by "diverse circumstances and occasions" that God providentially put in his path.[9] His work was viewed as an adventure of faith with many unexpected turns along the way. Yet, the role of a colporteur evolved beyond merely "tinker of the Word" and became incredibly complex in practice. Moving beyond sales, these people often found their work transformed into that of evangelists, church founders, and interim or itinerant pastors not unlike the Methodist circuit riders. Many times the foundation laid by colporteurs became the groundwork on which missionaries subsequently built churches. After the emergence of an indigenous distribution force, another important role of the national colporteur was to mentor the newly arriving male missionaries, who would begin their exploration of the area under the tutelage of these seasoned nationals who served as cultural tutors. These trips were a rite of passage in which the freshman missionaries earned their stripes.

Facing harsh climates, political chaos, and religious opposition—placing oneself in life-threatening conditions—went along with the job description. Understandably then, the colporteur came to enjoy an almost mythical status in the Protestant missionary literature. An early twentieth-century British missionary put it this way:

> No one can estimate the importance of this pioneer work, or the fatigue and strain of the weary journeys, bad food, disturbed nights, and endless conflicts with fanatics, priests, and authorities. Hunted out of some places, prohibited in others, refused lodging in others, books confiscated or torn up, mobs rallied to shout at and oppose them, what patience and perseverance was theirs![10]

In regions of the world that enjoyed a relative degree of literacy, literature distribution was often the primary means of doing missions. The venerable Plymouth Brethren product of German Pietism, George Müller, no doubt voiced the missiological principle guiding many Victorian Evangelical missionaries when in 1853 he wrote the following:

> Here is the great secret of success, my christian [sic] reader, work with all your might, but trust not in the least in your work. Pray with all your might for the blessing of God, but work at the same time with all diligence, with all patience, with all perseverance. Pray then, and work, work and pray, and still again pray, and then work, and so on, all the days of your life. The result will surely be abundant blessing. Whether you *see* much or little fruit, *such kind* of service will be blessed. We should labour then for instance, with all earnestness, in seeking to circulate thousands of copies of the Holy Scripture and hundreds of thousands of tracts, as if everything depended upon the

> amount of copies of the Holy Scripture and tracts which we circulate; and yet in reality we should not in the least degree put our dependence upon the number of copies of the Scriptures, and upon the number of tracts, but entirely upon God for His blessing, without which all those efforts are entirely useless. This blessing, however, should be sought by us habitually and preservingly in prayer. It should also be fully expected.[11]

Müller's words illustrate just how evangelism, missions, and Bible/tract distribution were becoming synonymous terms. Missionary work took place when Bibles or tracts were distributed. Missiological reflection on the means of doing mission was unnecessary, for the mode was thought to be divinely inspired. Guided, and sometimes blinded, by the imagery of "sowing seed," a reference to Jesus' parable of the sower in Matthew 13, many understood their primary task as literally scattering religious literature on as massive a scale as was physically possible and over as large a geographic area as could be achieved in order to "break up the fallow ground" so that conversions and churches would spring forth from the distributed literature. Sadly, some reports suggested, however, that pages of the Bibles and tracts ended up as cigarette paper or as fuel to start fires. On at least a few occasions in Roman Catholic countries, monetary prizes were awarded to people who could collect the most literature from the colporteurs to be handed over to the church for a ceremonial bonfire.[12]

The Patriarchal Colporteur

Not all agents of Bible societies and other colporteurs were content with allowing the pages to fly where they may with little thought given to developing a comprehensive and effective strategy. In fact, shortly after the organization of the British and Foreign Bible Society (BFBS) in 1804, one of its agents, James "Diego" Thomson, brought not only the Bible but a revolution, albeit ephemeral, in public education to many parts of South America. This combination of emphases was due in part to the fact that Thomson also served as the field agent for the British and Foreign School Society. An additional amazing facet of Thomson's work is that in a century characterized by mounting animosity between Roman Catholics and Protestants, Thomson for a time successfully united these two groups around his cause while collaborating as well with civil authorities throughout much of South America. He became living proof that the concepts of "ecumenical" and "evangelical" do not have to be mutually exclusive; one can, in fact, be both.

James Thomson is considered the patriarch of Protestantism and public education in South America. William Owen Carver is typical of mission historians in saying that Protestant Christianity came to South America in 1820 when Thomson "preached what is said to have been the first Protestant sermon in Buenos Aires."[13] The subtitle of Juan Varetto's biography of Thomson united the themes of education and Protestantism: "Apostle of Public Education and Initiator of Evangelical Work in Latin America."[14] So all-encompassing was the impact of Thomson's example that even a century later, mission strategists focused on Latin America were still following his basic methodology. One early twentieth-century missiologist, after commenting on Thomson's work, went on to say that "the free distribution of evangelical literature, the education of the children, and the preaching of the Word are the three great factors by which South America must be redeemed from her spiritual and moral degradation."[15]

Thomson was born in the county of Kirkcudbright, Scotland, in 1788. His father was a schoolteacher, and from him James received a solid elementary education and a love for learning that would be evident in his work in South America. Donald R. Mitchell, author of the most comprehensive study of the South American stage of Thomson's life observes, "Thomson's love for learning comes through repeatedly in his letters, and his success in setting up normal schools in South America is evidence of exceptional pedagogical skills."[16] His work also evidenced remarkable linguistic skills. During his South American stay, he initiated significant progress on the translation of portions of the New Testament into Quechua and Aymara, both of which are Andean languages.[17] Further proof of his scholastic aptitude is evidenced in the fact that he graduated as a medical doctor from the School of Medicine of McGill University in Montreal at the age of fifty-four. Arnoldo Canclini accurately summarized both the extraordinary gifts Thomson possessed as well as the lack of information on his early life:

> What he studied in his youth, where and to what level [he achieved], no one has been able to find out until now. Without a doubt, he had another kind of formation, given that he demonstrated not only a remarkable level of culture but also specialized knowledge, for example, in questions of pedagogy, that went well beyond the results of natural intuition, of which he was well endowed.[18]

During Thomson's youth in Scotland an educational revolution was taking place that would largely explain his later success as a colporteur and educator. In fact, Thomson never would have become so successful in establishing schools in South America were it not for the pedagogical innovations of Joseph

Lancaster (1778–1838), "the founder of one of the best-known systems of monitorial or mutual instruction of which there is any record in history."[19] Lancaster's system utilized more advanced students as tutors for the younger ones and thereby allowed the teacher to reach a potentially larger number of students. The idea flourished from its inception. Soon he gained the interest and financial support of the British monarch, George II. With very meager supplies in a large rented room, Lancaster began the morning meeting with the monitors to whom Lancaster imparted their daily lessons, which they, in turn, conveyed to the younger, less advanced students later in the morning when these children arrived. The monitors, selected for their relative expertise in a given subject, alternated between the student groups at regular intervals. So successful and innovative was Lancaster's methodology that his first school had as many as a thousand students. Interested educators from North and South America studied the approach in order to replicate it in their own contexts. Thomson was among those who had studied the movement officially and then went on to become the principal promoter and architect of these schools in the emerging republics in South America.

However, Thomson never saw himself exclusively as an educator, and education was not an end in itself. As a missionary with strong evangelical convictions, he believed that God worked normally through the written pages of the Bible. For an evangelical revival to take place in Latin America—one that would both restore piety and put the continent on the road to modernity—the general populace had to possess, read, and study God's Word. He was confident also that God would call Latin Americans into ministry as they became aware of the gospel message.

Promoting primary education as a method for carrying out Christian mission was not something new with Thomson. In fact, as Max Warren pointed out, mission through education was crucial to most ventures:

> In almost every place illiteracy was the first problem to be tackled. Elementary education was, in practice, the foundation upon which the whole expansion of Christianity was built up. With this would often go technical education of a simple kind designed to raise the economic level of the people.[20]

As a young man nurtured in a baptistic system, Thomson knew from experience that a democratically organized church that practiced the Reformation principle of the priesthood of all believers was dependent on an educated laity. Primary schools were an absolute necessity for the establishment of Protestantism in South America.

Ecumenical Seeds Are Sown

Thomson's journey into the ministry came at an interesting moment in Scotland's history—a time when older, traditional models of the church were being called into question. In fact, any missionary work such as that performed by Thomson and other Bible society agents logically could only be founded on an extremely broad ecclesiology that emphasized the universal church over denominationalism. Thomson repeatedly sought to demonstrate in his South American ministry that there was room for Roman Catholicism within the universal, or catholic, church. The restorationist impulse in the early nineteenth century had encouraged some Scottish Christians to abandon their customary ecclesial forms in an attempt to recreate a more pristine expression of the faith consistent with their own particular reading of the New Testament. This early nineteenth-century impulse gave birth to the Haldane movement, of which Thomson was a part. Shortly thereafter, in the 1820s, this restorationist impetus also helped to create in Ireland and Great Britain the more numerically successful movement of the Plymouth Brethren under the early guidance of John Nelson Darby and others.

In 1797, following distinguished service in the British Navy, the Haldane brothers—James and Robert—began a ministry of lay preaching and evangelism throughout Scotland. Although both men were members of the Church of Scotland, a rift developed with the state church once their converts multiplied and organized themselves in small home groups. This renewal movement eventually gave birth to the Congregational Union of Scotland. Shortly thereafter, in 1808, the Haldanes "embraced Baptist views."[21] The first church of the movement, the Leith Walk Tabernacle, was constructed in Edinburgh with Haldane money, and soon thereafter similar congregations began to appear throughout the nation. The Haldanes also supported the formation of seminaries for the training of pastors for these new congregations. The fact that Thomson became co-pastor with James Haldane at Leith Walk strongly suggests that he graduated from one of these schools.

One core value of the Haldane revival was its desire to form a nonsectarian movement. Like other restorationists, they were not motivated to create a competing denomination—something they would have viewed, with disgust, as sectarianism. Instead, they desired to promulgate a broader pan-evangelical movement open to all those of a similar ecumenical persuasion. Being genuinely convinced that true Christians could be found throughout the denominational maze, the Haldane centers of worship sought to open their doors to all like-minded evangelicals. Prior evidence of the brothers' broad understanding of the church can be seen in their financial support of the nondenominational London Missionary Society, which had formed in 1795. As Donald Mitchell observed, this context in which an open ecclesiology was practiced had an obvious impact on the life of Thomson: "Such a nondenominational tendency helped fashion Thomson as a servant of the whole Christian church, one who showed no partiality for any particular denomination, and who carried to his work abroad a strong distaste for any form of sectarianism."[22]

While acknowledging this cooperative spirit of the Haldanes, one sharp difference between the brothers and Thomson must be underscored in order to explain Thomson's subsequent success. The Haldanes had no patience with the Roman Catholic hierarchy—from the parish priest to the pope; this "evil" system of popery, or Romanism, was believed to keep people in bondage and hinder them from embracing the gospel. In fact, Kenneth Hylson-Smith noted that one prominent trait of the Haldanes was that of having "little sympathy with Roman Catholicism."[23] One of the principal evidences of this fact was the brothers' sharp opposition to the BFBS's inclusion of the deuterocanonical books in some of its Bible editions headed for Catholic countries.

Thomson, on the other hand, consistently reached out to Catholics and built significant relationships through which the work of education and Bible distribution was enhanced. The need to circulate Bibles completely transcended confessional divisions. The more open ecclesiology of Thomson put distance between him and the Haldanes, so that Thomson eventually detached himself from the movement. As Donald Mitchell suggested, Thomson saw little point in such contentious debates as those waged by the Haldanes against the Bible Society.[24]

On this issue one must note that Thomson's early years in ministry somewhat predated what would prove to be a century-long escalation of animosity between Protestants and Roman Catholics. While the two never did peacefully coexist in early Victorian Britain, their relationship went from poor to terrible as the nineteenth century progressed. Thomson was able to build bridges in South America before each group eventually demonized the other.

What were some of these issues that contributed to a deepening rift between British Protestants and Roman Catholicism in general? The most important single event as far as the work of Bible societies was concerned occurred in 1824, when Pope Leo XII unequivocally condemned their work in his 1824 encyclical *Ubi Primum:*

> The wickedness of our enemies is progressing to such a degree that, besides the flood of pernicious books hostile in themselves

> to religion, they are endeavoring to turn to the harm of religion even the Sacred Literature given to us by divine Providence for the progress of religion itself. It is not unknown to you, Venerable Brethren, that a certain "Society," commonly called "Biblical," is boldly spreading through the whole world, which, spurning the traditions of the Holy Fathers, and against the well-known decree of the Council of Trent, is aiming with all its strength and means toward this: to translate—or rather mistranslate—the Sacred Books into the vulgar tongue of every nation.[25]

Another early factor contributing to the deterioration of this relationship was the uproar over the British parliamentary decision in 1845 to more than double the rate of state funding for Maynooth College, the leading Irish Roman Catholic Seminary in Ireland. In the minds of many Anglicans and Nonconformists, this amounted to governmental endowment of "superstition, idolatry, and subversion."[26] Additional distance was created by the formation of the Evangelical Alliance (1846), an organization characterized by anti-Catholic rhetoric. The relationship further deteriorated and suspicions escalated beginning in 1850, "when a papal bull restored Catholic hierarchy to England."[27] The theological declaration of Vatican I (1869–70) under the leadership of Pius IX regarding papal infallibility served to underscore the theological divide between Catholics and Protestants and was enough to poison all ecumenical wells.[28] In addition, the rapid growth of traditional monastic orders under Pius IX and the founding of many new missionary societies challenged and threatened Protestants.

The growing rift began to take on continental-drift proportions once northern European Protestant missionaries entered wholeheartedly into those countries normally considered to be Roman Catholic with a view to convert Catholics to Protestantism. Throughout the nineteenth century the relationship became more and more bitter. Thomson had been fortunate; until his last years of ministry in Spain (where he was unable to replicate his Latin American success), he had been able to carry out his work in a context where the relationships between Protestants and Catholics had not yet completely soured.

The limited ecumenical liberty afforded Thomson was inseparable from the rapidly changing political landscape in Latin America. The winds of revolution that had liberated colonists and toppled a monarchy in North America (1775–83) and in France (1789–99) made its presence felt in practically all of South America in the early nineteenth century. From 1810 to 1816, independence was achieved in the region of the Rio de la Plata viceroyalty (present-day Argentina, Paraguay, and Uruguay). From 1816 to 1825, the rest of the colonials liberated themselves from Spanish rule. When the United States promulgated the Monroe Doctrine in 1823, which insisted that European governments could no longer colonize the Americas or meddle in the affairs of the newly independent republics, further Spanish or other European intervention became even less likely.

Thomson's timing was perfect. The collapse of Spanish colonialism ushered into power several leaders who desired to make basic education a priority for all citizens. Webster Browning, an early twentieth-century educational historian, summarized the situation:

> San Martín, Bolívar, O'Higgins, Artigas, and a host of less-known leaders were heralds of the new democracy, and it was largely through their help and sympathy that the distressing conditions of the preceding century gave place to an era of progress and it became possible to undertake the education and social uplift of the youth of the hitherto submerged classes.[29]

There had always been a close connection between the Spanish crown and the Roman Catholic Church. As the political pendulum in Latin America swung toward independence from Spain, the relationship of the Roman Catholic Church with the newly emerging independent states became confused. Thomson's sojourn in South America paralleled very closely this period in which the Catholic Church found itself in an extremely precarious position. More often than not, Roman Catholicism was still identified with the colonial oppressors. With the passing of time, however, nations eventually moved toward the recognition of Catholicism as the state confession. Yet Thomson entered into this intervening time and was able to seize the day and capitalize on the many temporary freedoms that the period of transition afforded him. However, so transitory were the opportunities that Thomson's successful track record was already coming to an end by the time he returned to the United Kingdom in 1825.

Sidney Rooy, historian of the church in South America, suggests that there was another ecclesial factor that helped spawn an open attitude toward Thomson's work, namely, the presence of many liberal priests:

> All of the clergy did not support the papal pretensions of Rome. To the contrary, many of the Creole priests, just like the intellectuals of the period, had read the books, previously proscribed, of European erudition (Rousseau, Voltaire, and the English deists). They shared with the English Protestants of the time a conviction regarding the power of reading and of education as the ideal instruments with which to begin an improve-

> ment in the general well-being of people and the community so that they might know the teachings of the Christian religion. They desired to teach the privileged how to read and at the same time become familiar with the Bible, but [they] knew that this would bring hope and happiness to all people.[30]

Thomson Arrives in South America

Such was the context James Thomson encountered on October 6, 1818, when he arrived in Buenos Aires after a three-month trip from Liverpool and began to solicit support from the Argentine government for the establishment of Lancaster-style schools in the city. In his future travels throughout the continent, governments characteristically courted Thomson and solicited his services by promises of salary, school facilities, and other means of support. However, at the beginning, he had to convince the newly formed government to allow him to introduce the Lancaster system in Buenos Aires. An important pattern of success emerged in Thomson's life that would be sustained for as long as he remained in South America. He had an uncanny ability to gain audience with those in power in the government or in the church and win them over to his cause. To be sure, the context favored his message and program, but the winsome Thomson instilled personal trust in others. Without this unusual talent for winning the confidence of the people in power, his schools and Bible distribution plans would never have gotten off the ground. Noting Thomson's engaging ways, one biographer stated, "He was a Protestant in a Catholic country, but he was too broad and sympathetic to try to force his opinions on other people, and he had a genius for making friends."[31] These friends were also indispensable allies.

Shortly after his arrival in Buenos Aires, the Argentine government became so convinced of the merits of Thomson's educational revolution that the convent of San Pedro was expropriated for use as a central school facility, and the newly formed Lancasterian School Society was invited to superintend all existing schools in the city and entire country. Remarkably, Thomson was also successful from the very beginning in securing the support of the Roman Catholic Church—in spite of the convent eviction. This is evidenced by the fact that the first secretary of the newly formed society, Father Bartholomew Muñoz, was a priest. The level of general admiration for Thomson can be gauged by the fact that within three years the government declared him an honorary citizen of Argentina. By this time the educational society in Argentina was responsible for as many as one hundred boys and girls schools with over five thousand children on the rolls.

From this point forward Thomson traveled frequently from one country to another. On the one hand, it's easy to understand how his work as a colporteur necessitated that he be in constant motion. After all, the job of a Bible society agent was basically that of extending the Scriptures over the greatest geographic area possible—a task not to be completed by staying put. Particularly in a continent where printed Bibles were uncommon, the call to Thomson to continue his quest could not be overlooked. Yet there is also a sense in which Thomson was victimized by his own multiple interests—salesman, educator, Bible translator, administrator, and (later) medical doctor. He moved as freely between these tasks as he did between countries, many times to the detriment of the longevity of his efforts. He did not intend that the ministries that he had been instrumental in founding should suffer and flounder after he moved on, but his rapid transition between countries and ministries is one way of explaining the short-lived nature of the results he achieved. In his favor it has to be mentioned that the changing political and ecclesial conditions favoring conservative Roman Catholicism also worked together to snuff out the life of the ministries he had begun. However, we are left to wonder what the result might have been had Thomson chosen to stay in one location long enough to develop the right people and the adequate structures to build on his foundational work.

In 1821 Thomson arrived in Chile to establish the Lancasterian schools at the invitation of Bernardo O'Higgins (1778–1842), the Chilean general and politician who ruled the country after its successful revolt against the Spanish in 1817. Thomson's reputation had preceded him. One newspaper editor greeted the news of Thomson's upcoming arrival by stating the following:

> The happy day is now arrived when the infinitely valuable art of reading is to be extended to every individual in Chile. Our benevolent government has brought to this place Mr. James Thomson, who has established in Buenos Aires elementary schools upon that admirable system of Lancaster.... There is therefore no obstacle in the way for everyone in Chile to obtain education.[32]

Neither Thomson's nor the general public's high expectations were disappointed as the first schoolroom, which seated two hundred students, was immediately filled. This classroom was intended by Thomson to become a replicable model. Soon a second school was established, and four teachers were selected to be trained in the methodology. So supportive was President O'Higgins that he served as the first president of a school society founded by Thomson and later signed a decree (in 1822) honoring Thomson as an official citizen of Chile.

Believing he had established a firm foundation with the establishment of three schools in Santiago, one of which was to train future teachers to be sent throughout the country, Thomson did not extend his one-year contract but chose instead to journey on to Peru at the invitation of that country's leader and liberator from the Spanish—General José de San Martín (1778–1850).

In spite of the initial popular support for O'Higgins, political forces opposed to his financial, political, and social reforms united to depose and exile him to Peru in 1823, where he remained until his death. No doubt the Chilean president's short political tenure did nothing to favor the continuance of the Thomson schools; the two men had been too closely aligned.

In 1822 Thomson set out to duplicate the apparent successes of Argentina and Chile in Peru. The government was certainly as supportive in this country as it had been in the others; buildings were furnished, and Thomson's salary and the government promised to meet the expenses. Yet, unlike his previous experience, a rapid change of political circumstances came about soon after the beginning of the schools. The newly formed Peruvian congress met to debate the formation of a new constitution, and, much to the detriment of the ecumenical activities of Thomson, the document recognized the Roman Catholic Church as the exclusive religion of the state. However, before Thomson was able to digest the degree to which the situation would impede his work, war broke out with Spain, and Thomson eventually found himself on the road to Bogotá, Colombia.

Soon after his arrival in Colombia in 1825, Thomson achieved perhaps his greatest ecumenical feat yet in the founding of the Colombian Bible Society. The irony is that Thomson apparently never intended to spend much time in Colombia, a country that, prior to his coming, had established an early form of public education in 1821. He had simply run out of Bibles and financial resources and was prepared to wait for both to catch up before proceeding. Given his previous creative track record, Thomson wasted no time in meeting with numerous influential officials. Thomson's knowledge of how to turn on a dime at the Spirit's leading served him well once again. If a national Bible society could be formed to print and warehouse Bibles, he would not be so utterly dependent on shipments from Great Britain. The people who may well have been most interested in the missionary's message about the establishment of a national Bible society were James Henderson, the British consul, and Pedro Gual, minister of foreign affairs. Henderson provided the advice and contacts needed in order to gain momentum. For his part, Gual was soon to be elected as the first president of the newly formed Colombian Bible Society.

In addition to the support of these two men, several existing sociopolitical factors favored widespread acceptance of Thomson's idea. As noted by Donald Mitchell, these included "an insistence on freedom of the press; a favoring of religious toleration which would encourage the immigration of Europeans; the extension of elementary education; and the subordination of ecclesiastical authority to that of the Legislature."[33]

Only two months after his arrival in Colombia, two hundred church and governmental dignitaries met with Thomson at the university chapel to debate the formation of a voluntary society. The meeting ended not only with the first collection for the society but also with the election of an executive committee. In addition to the already mentioned Pedro Gual, it included the Colombian minister of finance, José María Castillo, who was the newly elected vice president. Senator José Sans de Santa María was the society's treasurer, and a leading university educator, Father Antonio Marcos Gutiérrez, was the secretary. In addition to this board of directors, another committee of twelve members was formed, which included six church officials labeled by Juan Varetto "all people of great social influence."[34] In only two months Thomson once again had achieved what many would have believed to be an impossible task—the formation of an ecumenical parachurch organization. The decision was made to circulate two versions of the Scriptures widely accepted in Spanish Roman Catholic circles—the Scío and Torres Amat translations. By not insisting on the Reina Valera version preferred by the Spanish Protestant minority and most widely circulated by Bible societies, Thomson once again proved to be a skillful negotiator who was willing to make concessions to build a consensus.

One of the most perplexing questions surrounding the work of James Thomson in Latin America is finding explanations for the short-lived existence of the Colombian Bible Society. None of the society's records have survived to recount the story of its demise, but external references to its activities appear to fade away by early 1827, less than two years after its beginning. Clearly, the initial euphoria over the prospects of a national Bible society could not have waned more quickly. Predictably, Thomson had no inclination to nurse the society along through its infancy. By 1826, well before its demise, he was already back in Great Britain. The other early pillar, Pedro Gual, had to vacate his role with the Bible society in 1826 after being called to serve his country as a diplomat in Panama. In addition to the leadership vacuum, one can cite growing opposition to the work of the society from a substantial percentage of clerics. However, the most reasonable explanation for the rapid death of the dream may be that it was ahead of its time in Colombia. Donald Mitchell gives this explanation:

> Its directors had overestimated the influence of liberal teachings and attitudes, just as they had underestimated the latent conservative strength which lay in the tendency of the mass of people to cling to familiar forms and to give unreflective obedience to priestly directives. They were to learn that the revolutionary changes of the 1820s had worked very little fundamental alteration in the religious viewpoint of the nation.[35]

During the next twenty years Thomson's work was much more typical of agents working under the auspices of Bible societies, as he sought ways to facilitate the distribution of Bibles. Now at home in the Spanish-speaking world, most of this stage of his life was spent in Mexico, the Caribbean, Central America, and Venezuela.

The one exception was the years spent in Canada (1838–42). In addition to establishing local Bible society auxiliaries there, Thomson was concerned with promoting the distribution and study of the Scriptures among French-Canadian Catholics and showed special interests in ministry among Canada's Native American population. As noted previously, during this stage of his life Thomson took time to successfully complete medical studies. According to his letters, the primary motivation for this study was to become better equipped to minister to the physical needs of South Americans. Apparently Thomson had previously found himself frustrated with his own inability to minister holistically to those with whom he came in contact during his travels.

Thomson in Spain

Back home in the British Isles, a number of political, economic, and religious factors were leading many evangelicals to focus their missionary interests and resources on Spain. As Spain repeatedly occupied the attention of the British news media, it was predictable that Thomson, the BFBS, and mission boards would carry out a concerted missionary effort in Spain. Wanting to build on the previous experience of George Borrow and attempt a more ecumenical approach, Thomson arrived in Madrid in 1847, where he would stay for a period of a year and a half and then return briefly in 1849. However, his ministry efforts at this time consisted largely of colportage as a Bible society agent. Having opened a book depository in Madrid for his Bibles and evangelistic literature, he made frequent trips throughout the country. He was, however, credited by University of Murcia professor Juan Vilar with establishing a kind of house church in Madrid where at least eleven people met together for the study of the Bible. Vilar also noted that he was effective in establishing relationships with progressive intellectuals and university professors, a feat not often accomplished by foreign missionaries in Spain or even by Spanish Protestants themselves.

Apparently, though, Thomson was unable to bridge the Catholic-Protestant divide in this context. Sociopolitical factors now did not favor his methodology, as they had in South America, in spite of the fact that the opportunity for education was beyond the reach of the vast majority of Spanish children. Notwithstanding, contemporary Spanish historians note his important contribution to the future of Spanish Protestantism. In 1994 Juan Vilar wrote, "Together with Borrow and Juan Calderón [an ex-Franciscan from Alcazar de San Juan, working primarily out of the United Kingdom], he should be considered the first and principal catalyst of Protestantism in Madrid before the Second Reformation."[36]

Upon returning to Scotland, Thomson established the Spanish Evangelization Society in Edinburgh, which specialized in the translating and distribution of Protestant literature throughout the Spanish-speaking world. Until his death in 1854, he also wrote extensively and worked tirelessly for the organization of a British missionary society focused on Latin America. Unfortunately, this progressive figure did not live to see his dream realized.

The Lasting Legacy of James Thomson

James Thomson would be surprised to find that in the century and a half following his death, Christendom has become even more divided than it was in his day. Yet he would, no doubt, be encouraged by signs that the ecumenical impetus that he so valued is not limited to mainline denominations. He would celebrate the fact that the long-standing wall separating western Evangelicalism and Roman Catholicism is being dismantled in multiple locations. For example, in the spring of 1994 a noteworthy group of Roman Catholics and Evangelical Protestants issued a statement titled "Evangelicals and Catholics Together: The Christian Mission in the Third Millennium." Many today see this as a sign of hope; perhaps no longer in North America does one have to abandon the label *Evangelical* in order to work closely with the ecumenical community. Can it be that the Evangelical movement has really progressed to the extent that it has become secure enough to begin building bridges rather than continuing to define itself based on its cultural and theological differences with the rest of the church? Is the movement beginning to see that unity in Jesus Christ can be achieved without embracing uniformity of belief and practice? According to the editors of *First Things,* this statement noted "a growing 'convergence and cooperation' between Evangelicals and Catholics in many public tasks, and affirmed agreement in basic articles of Christian faith while also underscoring the continuing existence of important differences. The signers promised to engage those differences in continuing conversations, and this has been done in meetings of noted theologians convened by Mr. Charles Colson and Father Richard John Neuhaus."[37] The follow-up statement issued after a meeting of Evangelical and Catholic leaders in New York City (6–7 October 1997) has given even more reason to hope for a church that embraces diversity and encourages dialogue rather than bitter name-calling. The prologue to this statement holds great promise:

> We give thanks to God that in recent years many Evangelicals and Catholics, ourselves among them, have been able to express a common faith in Christ and so to acknowledge one another as brothers and sisters in Christ. We confess together one God, the Father, the Son, and the Holy Spirit; we confess Jesus Christ the Incarnate Son of God; we affirm the binding authority of Holy Scripture, God's inspired Word; and we acknowledge the Apostles' and Nicene creeds as faithful witnesses to that Word.[38]

These watershed declarations probably do not so much prophetically point to the future as acknowledge the existing prevailing tides. Recent generations of Evangelicals have long since recognized the deficits of their spiritual theologies and have looked to liturgical worship, to contemplative meditation and retreats, embracing a wider range of spiritual disciplines than before, and to spiritual direction to supplement the deficiencies of their traditions largely built on negativism. Yet these declarations do not have to be prophetic in order to be significant, as the outcome is at least a more complete recognition of the unity of Christ's body. Regardless, James Thomson would be pleased and would remind us that we are not in uncharted territory or on "unfamiliar paths."[39] Yes, the sociopolitical forces that helped to generate an unparalleled openness toward Thomson and the Scriptures cannot be repeated. But at the same time, momentum created both by communication technology and by organizations such as the European Union and North American Free Trade Agreement (NAFTA) are providing their own unique circumstances in which global cooperation is being fostered as never before. Thomson would look for ways through which the church could harness this momentum—in spite of the multiple questions regarding the repercussions of globalization. Thomson would point to the United States government's openness to cooperation with faith-based initiatives as representing opportunities to step forward in faith rather than retreat out of fear of partnerships with Caesar. He would continue to remind us that any ministry endeavor must ultimately address the social, intellectual, physical, and spiritual needs of others and that such a holistic framework must be built on humility and on service to others. Thomson would tell us that to build bridges with different expressions of the church does not mean anyone has to forsake her or his own national or confessional identity. The process of Bible translation itself is enhanced to the extent that our translators represent an ever-widening expression of God's family. Lastly, Thomson's example reminds us that far more can be accomplished for Christ's kingdom when we work together ecumenically than we could ever do separately.

Notes

1. Andrew F. Walls, *The Missionary Movement in Christian History* (Maryknoll, N.Y.: Orbis, 1996), 26.

2. Lamin Sanneh, "Pluralism and Christian Commitment," *Theology Today* 45, no. 1 (April 1988): 27, quoted in *Classic Texts in Mission and World Christianity,* ed. Norman E. Thomas (Maryknoll, N.Y.: Orbis, 1995), 279.

3. Walls, *The Missionary Movement,* 29.

4. Edward W. Gilman, "Power of the Printed Bible," in *Report of the Centenary Conference on the Protestant Missions of the World Held in Exeter Hall, London, 1888,* ed. James Johnson (New York: Fleming Revell, 1888), 285–86.

5. *World Missionary Conference, 1910, Report of Commission III, Education in Relation to the Christianisation of National Life* (Edinburgh and London: Oliphant, Anderson & Ferrier, 1910), 337–38.

6. Émile G. Léonard defined the "three permanent missionary preoccupations" of Protestants: "The press in order to print, the school, and the hospital next to the Church are the characteristic marks of Protestant missions from its origins" (*Historie Générale du Protestantisme,* vol. 3 [Paris: Presses Universitaires de France, 1964], 509).

7. This French noun can be translated "peddler" but is used in English to refer to itinerant Bible distributors and salespeople. Female colporteurs were usually referred to in the Victorian era simply as "Bible women."

8. Edwin M. Bliss, ed., *The Encyclopaedia of Missions,* vol. 1 (New York: Funk & Wagnalls, 1891), 164.

9. Arnoldo Canclini, *Diego Thomson* (Buenos Aires: Asociación Sociedad Bíblica Argentina, 1987), 99.

10. H. S. Turrall, *Galicia, North-West Spain* (Bath, England: Echoes of Service, ca. 1920), 14.

11. George Müller, "Mr. Müller's Narrative relative to the Scripture Knowledge Institution," *The Missionary Reporter* (October 1853): 59.

12. "Crónica general," *La Revista Popular* (Madrid: 18 November 1871): 372; "Llamamiento a todos los católicos españoles para un certámen antiprotestante," *La Cruz,* vol. 2 (Madrid: 1870): 250.

13. William Owen Carver, *The Course of Christian Missions* (New York: Fleming H. Revell 1939), 269.

14. Juan C. Varetto, *Diego Thomson, Apostol de la Instrucción Pública e Iniciador de la Obra Evangélica en la América Latina* (Buenos Aires: Imprenta Evangélica, 1918).

15. Alfred DeWitt Mason, *Outlines of Missionary History* (New York: George H. Doran, 1916), 230.

16. Donald R. Mitchell, "The Evangelical Contribution of James Thomson to South American Life 1818–1825" (Ph.D. diss., Princeton Theological Seminary, 1972), 12.

17. Reported in William Mitchell, "James Thomson and Bible Translation in the Andean Languages," *Technical Papers for the Bible Translator* 41, no. 3 (July 1990): 341–45.

18. Canclini, *Diego Thomson,* 18.

19. Webster E. Browning, "Joseph Lancaster, James Thomson, and the Lancasterian System of Mutual Instruction, with Special Reference to Hispanic America," *Hispanic American Historical Review* 41, no. 1 (February 1921): 53. The Lancasterian ideals have received a good deal of attention recently. In fact, in the summer of 2001, a new Lancasterian Society submitted formal articles of incorporation in the state of Texas (Articles of Incorporation of the Lancasterian Society; they can be viewed on the Web at http://www.constitution.org/lanc/art_inc.htm).

20. Max Warren, *The Missionary Movement from Britain in Modern History* (London: SCM Press, 1965), 74.

21. Mitchell, "The Evangelical Contribution of James Thomson," 19.

22. Ibid., 20.

23. Kenneth Hylson-Smith, *Evangelicals in the Church of England* (Edinburgh: T. & T. Clark, 1988), 96.

24. Mitchell, "The Evangelical Contribution of James Thomson," 24.

25. Henry Denzinger, *The Sources of Catholic Dogma,* trans. Roy J. Deferrari (St. Louis, Mo.: B. Herder, 1957), 400–401.

26. Walter L. Arnstein, *Protestants versus Catholics in Mid-Victorian England* (Columbia: University of Missouri Press, 1982), 6–7.

27. Ibid., 7–8. Shortly thereafter, the church's hierarchy was reestablished in the Netherlands (1853). Many countries such as Russia (1847), Spain (1851), Austria (1855), and the Latin American republics among which Thomson labored established concordats with the Vatican from 1852 to 1862—signaling Rome's growing international political influence. Further deterioration took place from the 1850s onward, as British citizens were outraged by the refusal of Spanish Catholic priests to bury British Protestant soldiers and sailors on Spanish soil, even though they had died while protecting Spain's borders. The *London Times* reminded its readers often that this most Catholic of nation's insistence on not "profaning holy ground" was further evidence that the Inquisition was still alive and well.

28. This pronouncement followed on the heels of the pope's previous announcement of "the Immaculate Conception," which declared Mary—Jesus' mother—free from original sin.

29. Browning, "Joseph Lancaster," 52.

30. Sidney Rooy, *Mision y encuentro de culturas* (Buenos Aires: Kairos, 2001), 87.

31. Margarette Daniels, *Makers of South America* (New York: Missionary Education Movement of the U.S. and Canada, 1916), 85.

32. Cited in Daniels, *Makers of South America,* 86–87.

33. Mitchell, "The Evangelical Contribution of James Thomson," 281.

34. Varreto, *Diego Thomson,* 113.

35. Mitchell, "The Evangelical Contribution of James Thomson," 312–13.

36. Juan B. Vilar, *Intolerancia y libertad in la España contemporánea* (Madrid: Ediciones Istmo, 1994), 290. The term "Second Reformation" is used by some of the historians of Protestantism in Spain to refer to the nineteenth-century period in which the country briefly experimented with religious liberty. This period began with the 1869 constitution that ousted the Bourbons and concluded when they were reestablished on the Spanish throne under Alfonso XII in 1874.

37. The editors, "The Gift of Salvation," *First Things,* 79 (January 1998): 20.

38. Ibid.

39. In *Unfamiliar Paths: The Challenge of Recognizing the Work of Christ in Strange Clothing* (Pasadena, Calif.: William Carey Library Publishers, 1997), David E. Bjork, a veteran Evangelical missionary to France, recounts his experiences as he explored ways to work with Roman Catholic clergy in his area.

10

THE NEW INTERNATIONAL VERSION: HOW IT CAME TO BE

John H. Stek

"Who despises the day of small things?"

ZECHARIAH 4:10

The beginning of the New International Version (NIV) was truly a "day of small things."[1] The soul of one man grew so frustrated that it finally stirred him to action. He began to make noises that aroused others—eventually a host of others. And their efforts produced an English version of the Bible that for the first time in three centuries successfully challenged the dominance of the King James Version.

That lone soul was Howard Long. He was not a biblical scholar or a well-connected ecclesiastic. Although a man of many parts—inventor, pilot, engineer, college physics instructor, businessman, traveling representative for General Electric—he was first of all a devout Christian who seized every opportunity to point others to Jesus Christ. The Bible that had long nourished his faith was the King James Version. It felt comfortable in his hands, sounded familiar and sweet in his ears, and much of it was "written on his heart." But when he opened it to show others the Way, he met with incomprehension—or worse. The Bible he read to them and urged them to read was to them sometimes quite unintelligible, generally rather strange and quaint, and occasionally even hilarious.

With such a version in hand, anyone who wished to spread the gospel through one-on-one evangelization could only know frustration. And loneliness. Howard Long tried out the more recent English versions, but for various reasons found them unsatisfactory. He also tried translating the old English Bible into more modern idiom as he witnessed to others, but that failed to serve. However good his effort, it had no weight, no authority. His was only a lone voice against an old and greatly venerated text.[2]

But this lone soul was really not alone. Howard was a member of the Christian Reformed Church in Seattle, Washington, a congregation of a modest-sized denomination that had sprung up among Dutch immigrants in the 1850s. And Howard had a pastor—just the right pastor as it turned out. Pastor Peter De Jong was a man of firm convictions with a ready pen who did not hesitate to take on the establishment whenever he felt the cause warranted it.

The Role of the Christian Reformed Church

Howard turned to De Jong when he could no longer restrain his frustration. With that, the ball began to roll. The pastor brought the matter to the consistory (the governing body of his congregation) and convinced the elders and deacons to carry the matter to the classis (the denomination's regional judicatory). The consistory specifically proposed that the classis overture the general synod of the Christian Reformed Church (CRC) "that the Christian Reformed Church endeavor to join with other conservative churches in sponsoring or facilitating the early production of a faithful translation of the Scriptures in the common language of the American people."[3]

Their proposal failed to gain sufficient support in the classis. But that didn't stop De Jong and his consistory. Utilizing a right accorded them in the Church Order of the CRC, they brought their overture directly to the general synod of 1956. Whether or not a majority of the delegates to that synod were inclined to favor the overture is not recorded, but sufficient interest was present to assure that the synod did not reject it out of hand. It referred the matter "to the teaching staff of the Old and New Testament departments of our Seminary [Calvin Seminary in Grand Rapids, Michigan] for thorough consideration and report to the Synod of 1957."[4] And so it was that the future of one man's dream of a modern English version of the Bible that he could use effectively and without embarrassment came to be on the agenda of an American denomination.

The arena was expanding but not explosively; the CRC was still in large part an ethnically bounded communion that remained somewhat aloof from the larger ecclesiastical world around it. And the committee charged to study the matter was neither large nor particularly illustrious. It had but four members—Henry Schultze, Ralph Stob, Martin Wyngaarden, and Marten Woudstra. All were well regarded within their own communion, but none of them were widely known beyond it. They held advanced academic degrees from leading institutions, but they were churchmen, preachers, and educators rather than focused academicians.[5]

If any delegates to the Christian Reformed synod of 1956 thought that the Seattle consistory had confronted them with a wild, unrealistic dream, and that shunting the matter off to the small committee of these four men would be a good way to put it quietly to rest, they were in for a surprise. The report this committee submitted to the synod of 1957 made quite clear that the proposal "had legs" and that the committee itself was ready to press forward toward the fulfillment of Howard Long's dream. In the course of their studies and consultations, that lone soul's dream had become their own.[6]

It had taken little persuasion to convince the committee that the need was real. They had not been trained in linguistics, but they all had a well-developed sensitivity for language. The three older scholars had all been bilingual since childhood. Schultze, in fact, had grown up in a home where German, Dutch, and English had all been commonplace. Woudstra's early training in the schools of Holland had made him familiar with German, French, and English, in addition to his native Frisian and Dutch. So all four had picked up an early feel for the complexities and subtleties of language and the ways in which languages differ. Additional studies of Latin, Greek, Syriac, Hebrew, Aramaic, and other Semitic languages later sharpened their awareness and their insights. Subsequently, as educators, their extensive contact with post-World War II students reminded them daily of changes that had taken place in English just since their own early years.

But it was not enough that they were convinced. The synod had charged the committee to seek out also the views of others among American Evangelicals. Through extensive correspondence (with churches, Bible societies, biblical scholars, evangelistic agencies, and publishers of Christian periodicals and church education materials), the committee learned that there was widespread interest among the burgeoning Evangelical community in the production of a new version that spoke the language of twentieth-century English. Many shared their judgment that the King James Version had long since become antiquated, that the language of the American Standard Version (ASV) of 1901 was also too archaic and too obviously "translation English" to ever replace the old literary jewel, and that the Revised Standard Version (RSV) of 1952 stood little chance of gaining wide acceptance among Evangelicals.[7]

The committee was particularly encouraged by a communication from the secretary of the Evangelical Theological Society (ETS), informing them that a sizeable number of the society's members had endorsed the idea of an extensive revision of the ASV. Somewhat surprisingly, the committee's report made no mention of the soon-to-appear Berkeley Version in Modern English (1959), an effort on the part of some Evangelicals to fill the need so widely felt. Contributors to that version even included members of the CRC—Martin Wyngaarden himself, as well as Leonard Greenway and Gerard Van Groningen, with Peter De Jong serving as one of the consultants. Most likely the committee judged that both the process and the selection of translators for this project left much to be desired and held little prospect of producing a satisfactory version.

So the committee's advice to the synod in 1957 was that it endorse the Seattle overture and appoint a committee to carry out the overture's intent. In standard synodical procedure, all such reports are examined by an advisory committee appointed from the synod's own delegates; these overtures come to the table of the synod only as accompanied by that committee's advice. In this case, the synod's advisory committee was not persuaded. Its recommendation was that the synod not endorse the overture of the Seattle consistory, because the study committee had not demonstrated "an urgent necessity" for a new translation and had "not demonstrated that there are sufficient conservative churches interested in this project."[8]

As a delegate to that synod I, with others, expressed dismay that a project of such import for the English-speaking church and world would be dismissed with so little consideration. (Little did I realize that within a few years I would be among those charged with seeing the project through.) Happily our voices prevailed. The synod decided to defer action until the next year, because the judgments of other communions had been solicited and official answers hadn't yet been received.

Howard Long's dream was ebbing but still alive. At the synod of 1958 the study committee finally received the endorsement it desired.[9] Thereafter, the members of the Bible department of Calvin Seminary carried on, reporting their activities each year to the synods and receiving annual extensions of their mandate—though, it must be said, at times without much positive encouragement. It was a demanding task. During the 1958–59 academic year, the committee met almost weekly, as they reported:

> [We are working on] preparing an extensive document for circulation through the English-speaking Protestant evangelical world, both in the United States and in the British Commonwealth. In this document several of the major angles of the work of Bible translation are discussed. General directives are suggested for each of these areas. The document draws widely on published reports concerning the experience gained by experts in this field. This experience was carefully evaluated by

> the committee. It was adapted to the specific needs of the moment as understood by the committee.[10]

This document has nowhere been published,[11] but it served well to advance the committee's discussions with the representatives of the National Association of Evangelicals (NAE), who soon became part of this story. In 1960 the committee told the synod the following—in light of the translation projects recently completed (the RSV and the Berkeley Version) and those currently underway (New English Bible, New American Standard Bible, Jerusalem Bible, and New American Bible), as well as the magnitude and complexity of such an undertaking:

> [It is our judgment that it is] wise not to aim at an immediate production of a new version at this point. This would indeed be an impossibility. But on the other hand, no opportunity must be lost in exploring the entire field of Bible translation. The general requirements for such a translation must be considered and subjected to careful study. The value of what is available must be weighed. The interest in producing a translation of high caliber must be kept alive and strengthened. Contacts with promising prospects for future translation work must be made and renewed. Trial translations of selected portions of Holy Writ must be circulated for thorough scrutiny and improvement. A general desire to be satisfied with nothing but the best must be aroused.[12]

It is clear that the committee, while not having second thoughts about the urgent need for a new modern English version, was feeling its way very cautiously and growing in its awareness that a great deal of groundwork still needed to be done before it could send to the synod a prospectus for a well-designed translation project for that body to endorse.[13]

National Association of Evangelicals' Cooperation

Enter the National Association of Evangelicals. Organized in 1942 as an Evangelical response to the National Council of Churches, in the late 1950s it included more than thirty (mostly very small) denominations in its membership and hundreds of individual congregations from more than thirty other denominations (many of them mainline); affiliated with it were upwards of a hundred other organizations such as seminaries, Christian colleges, and parachurch evangelistic and Bible-distribution agencies. It was the major ecumenical organization through which American Evangelicals from across a broad spectrum of the fragmented Evangelical community could act jointly.

It is surely no mere coincidence that it was the year 1957 that saw the establishment of a Bible translation committee as a subcommittee of the NAE's educational commission. This took place at the very next annual gathering of the association following the letter of inquiry from the CRC committee concerning interest in the production of a new English version. Upon the urging of Earl Kalland of Denver's Conservative Baptist Theological Seminary, a committee of three was charged with assessing whether or not there was a need for such an undertaking and, if so, how it might best be implemented. Those appointed to serve were Stephen Paine, president of Houghton College, Burton Goddard, dean of Gordon Divinity School, and John Walvoord, president of Dallas Theological Seminary—with Dr. Paine designated as the chairperson.[14]

Stephen Paine bore the main burden of the NAE committee's work for the next few years, carrying on extensive correspondence and serving as the chief facilitator of the ongoing discussions. Not least among his correspondents was the CRC committee, since the interests of that committee and his converged. The two committees met in April 1961 when the NAE annual conference convened in Grand Rapids. Representing the NAE were chairperson Paine, Earl Kalland, and Wheaton College's Merrill Tenney, as well as—by special invitation—H. A. Hanke and Herbert Mekeel. Bastiaan Van Elderen, who had recently replaced the deceased Henry Schultze on the Calvin Seminary faculty, had succeeded Schultze on the CRC side.[15]

During the rather informal discussions between the two committees at that initial meeting, which lasted only three or four hours, it became apparent that the CRC committee was well ahead of its NAE counterpart in its reflections on the many issues involved in launching such a daunting venture. The CRC representatives were, however, in no hurry to rush ahead. They had become sufficiently aware of the extensive groundwork still to be laid and of the many potential pitfalls ahead. Their willingness to give time for the NAE representatives to catch up, as well as to explore more fully the mind of the NAE itself, opened the way for fruitful joint efforts. In fact, the two committees needed each other. The CRC committee needed the broader ecumenical base that the NAE could provide and facilitate, and the NAE committee recognized that it could build on the research and studies already undertaken by the CRC committee.

The most important outcome of the first conversation between representatives of the CRC and the NAE was a consensus that the next step to advance the related mandates of the two committees was to facilitate some kind of general meeting of interested organizations and denominations, reaching as far as possible beyond the limited confines of the CRC and the NAE. However, such a meeting, it was judged, should be called under the official sponsorship of neither the CRC nor the NAE, lest attendance be prejudiced in any way. When the NAE representatives proposed this procedure to the larger education commission of the NAE, it obtained the commission's approval. From that day forward, the NAE and CRC committees had a shared focus for their joint efforts.[16]

When next the two committees met (21 December 1962, at Calvin Seminary), the NAE was represented by Paine, Kalland, Tenney, and Goddard and the CRC by Stob, Woudstra, Van Elderen, and John Stek (the last named having replaced Martin Wyngaarden on the Calvin Seminary faculty). At this meeting the two committees constituted themselves as the Joint Committee on Bible Translation and established as their single agenda "to call a Bible Translation Conference for the purpose of exploring the need for a new English version or revision of the Bible." That done, subcommittees were appointed to do preparatory work for the conference in three areas: programming, personnel, and translation policy.[17]

On 29 December 1964 the joint committee met at Nyack Missionary College, Nyack, New York, to take up the reports of the three subcommittees and finalize the plans for the Bible translation conference. Present from the NAE committee were Goddard, Kalland, Paine, and Mekeel. The CRC committee was represented by Woudstra, Stek, and Andrew Bandstra (Bandstra had replaced Ralph Stob on the Calvin Seminary faculty). Although considerable follow-up work had to be left to designated subcommittees of the joint committee, a number of decisions were made to shape the future course of events:

1. A Bible translation conference would be scheduled to be held in the greater Chicago area sometime in August 1965.
2. Invitations to the conference would be sent to some fifty biblical scholars drawn from a list prepared by the personnel subcommittee.
3. Ten to fifteen individual cosponsors of the invitation would be sought.
4. A general concept of the program of the conference was developed and committed to a subcommittee to implement.
5. The basic content of a letter of invitation was approved; it included the statement that those extending the invitation "are inclined to suggest a prompt and persistent effort in the next decade or two toward a better translation of the Scriptures than the various existing translations, whose merits we do appreciate."
6. The joint committee formalized its understanding that in calling together a meeting of scholars, "we envision the possibility that from this meeting there will arise initiative and action which will take the project beyond the need for further guidance by this commission."[18]

As it turned out, the joint committee had no need to meet again. Shortly the baton would be passed, and a new, more broadly based committee would take the matter in hand.[19]

A Decisive Bible Translation Conference

As anticipated, the baton was passed the following summer at the Bible translation conference initiated by the joint committee. The committee's December 1964 decision set in motion a flurry of activity by its subcommittees and officers (especially chairperson Woudstra and secretary Goddard). Then, on 26 August 1965, thirty-two biblical scholars (from the fifty-some who had been invited) gathered near Chicago for a two-day conference on the campus of Trinity Christian College in Palos Heights, Illinois. The conference's specific purpose was to consider what, if anything, should be done by the broader Evangelical community to provide a modern English version of the Bible that would be acceptable throughout the English-speaking world for both personal and liturgical use and for evangelistic outreach in the late twentieth-century context. Invitations to the conference had been endorsed by a number of well-known Christian leaders,[20] and conferees came from twenty-eight different Bible institutes, colleges, and theological faculties—Assemblies of God, Baptist (Conservative, Southern, Northern, Canadian), Presbyterian (United, Reformed, Orthodox, "Covenanter"), Lutheran (Missouri-Synod), Wesleyan Methodist, Nazarene, Mennonite, and Christian Reformed. Seven members of the joint committee were present: Bandstra, Stek, Woudstra, and Wyngaarden (CRC), and Goddard, Kalland, and Paine (NAE).

The day was hot and humid, and that night "the windows of heaven were opened," intense lightning lit up the darkness of the night, heavy thunder shook the earth, and tornadic winds downed large oak trees on the campus. It was a reminder that mere humans should not presume to deal lightly with what had come through the sovereign word of the Lord. And the conferees approached the matter at hand soberly. Prepared papers assessed various areas of concern: Martin Wyngaarden the RSV, Stephen Paine and William Lane the New American Standard Bible (NASB) then in progress, John Stek the human resources available, Charles Pfeiffer certain developments in biblical and related studies that bore directly on Bible translation, and Marten Woudstra various problems faced by translators of the Bible. These papers stimulated wide-ranging discussions that prepared the way for decision time.

Of the several factors brought under consideration, beyond all doubt the most decisive was the conferees' assessment of the various modern English versions already available or sufficiently advanced to be responsibly evaluated. Although a few were unhappy that the Berkeley Version had not been given more attention, most agreed that the papers prepared on the RSV and the NASB had fixed the conference's attention on the two most likely versions to replace the KJV and the ASV (among those willing to allow the KJV to give way to a modern English version).

For most of those present, the NASB, which was currently being produced under the sponsorship of the Lockman Foundation, held the greater promise. A few of the conference attendees were contributing to its production. Many others were members of the Evangelical Theological Society, whose central statement of faith stressed the verbal inspiration and the inerrancy of Scripture (in the autographs). To these the main attraction of the NASB was its attempt to meticulously reproduce as fully as possible a word-for-word, clause-for-clause mirror reflection of the original-language texts, retaining their word order and reflecting their every grammatical nuance—to reproduce form as well as content in the service of "accuracy." But others were convinced that this supposed great strength of the version was in fact its major weakness. It was founded on unsound linguistic assumptions concerning how languages differ from each other in communicating meaning. And it resulted in an artificial English style that aggravated the very features that had rendered the ASV unattractive to most readers.

As for the RSV, the very makeup of the gathering was an expression of discontent with it, at least in its current form. This discontent was more strongly felt among the Old Testament scholars present than among those who worked mainly in the New Testament. That the RSV represented an advance on many fronts in Old Testament scholarship and was a significant updating of the English language were generally recognized. But many found too many evidences that the translators worked from the Charles Briggs tradition of biblical scholarship rather than the B. B. Warfield tradition.[21] The version reflected many higher-critical conclusions that Evangelical scholars did not share. At the same time it failed to reflect the canonical unity of the Scriptures to which Evangelicals held. Rather clearly, the translators of the RSV viewed it as their task to translate the sense intended by the several human authors—as these had been "discovered" by higher-critics. For many of the Evangelicals at the conference, the task of Bible translators was to translate the sense intended by the one transcendent Author, the inspiring Holy Spirit. For them, the lines drawn in the Liberalism-Fundamentalism conflict were still very much in place.

There were some present, however, for whom this contrast was too sharply drawn. Or, stated differently, while the one position was too historicist, the other was too supernaturalist. Yet, for them, too, the RSV was significantly flawed. It clearly was only a half step toward a modern English version. Of this the retention of the archaic "thee" and "thou" in all words addressed to God—most notably in the psalms—was a stark example. But there were other rather glaring weaknesses as well. For example, little attention had been paid to intertextuality within the canonical collection, either within the same book, the same Testament, or linking the New Testament with the Old.[22]

When on the afternoon of August 27 the assembled conferees considered all that had come on the table, they took two actions that launched the new translation project. They formally adopted the following consensus: "It is the sense of this assembly that the preparation of a contemporary English translation of the Bible should be undertaken as a collegiate endeavor of evangelical scholars." Then, to advance the project, they decided that to implement the work of the conference "a continuing committee of fifteen be established" by the following ten key persons: Goddard, Kalland, Mekeel, Paine, Tenney, Bandstra, Stek, Van Elderen, Woudstra, and Wyngaarden.

This was effectively the full membership of the joint committee, but the members of this temporary commission were deliberately named individually to mark beyond question that the joint committee was no longer the agent to carry the project forward. In fact, those named were themselves given only a single mandate: to put in place a committee of fifteen, including "at least five of the members of the appointment committee" (to ensure continuity), to which would be entrusted the implementation of the wishes of the conference.[23]

The Formation of the Committee on Bible Translation

And so the project was launched. It was not a venture sponsored by any single denomination or by any ecumenical association or council of churches, but by an ad hoc conference of biblical scholars from a wide spectrum of confessional traditions. They in turn entrusted it to an independent "committee of fifteen" (soon to take the name the Committee on Bible Translation), which was responsible before God to fulfill its commission in such a way as to keep faith with the conference that mandated it. While this committee of fifteen was also charged with exploring ways of establishing communication with the committee of the RSV with a view to making suggestions for revision in that version, the committee's main task was clear.

With a commission and mandate now in place, events began to unfold rapidly. Several major steps forward were taken in Nashville, Tennessee on 29 December 1965. The commission appointed in Palos Heights established the called-for committee of fifteen. That committee then went to work immediately. To advance its work, it appointed an interim editorial committee, chaired by R. Laird Harris, to begin formulating goals, procedures, and translation policies. And to broaden the base of interest and involvement in the project, it decided to call together a general conference on Bible translation in the summer of 1966.[24]

The momentum was building. Most important, a number of biblical scholars had committed themselves to making the production of a new modern English version of the Bible the central focus of the rest of their productive lives, and they were organized to go forward unitedly. To authorize their joint efforts they had the mandate of the Palos Heights conference; to sustain them they had the simple trust that the Lord would provide both the human and financial resources required.

March 25 and 26 saw the committee of fifteen together again, this time at Moody Bible Institute in Chicago, Illinois. At this meeting it decided many matters of consequence. It filled out the authorized complement of fifteen members, with the following scholars consenting to serve:

- E. Leslie Carlson, Southwestern Baptist Theological Seminary
- Edmund P. Clowney, Westminster Theological Seminary
- Ralph Earle, Nazarene Theological Seminary
- Burton L. Goddard, Gordon Divinity School
- R. Laird Harris, Covenant Theological Seminary
- Earl S. Kalland, Conservative Baptist Theological Seminary (Denver)
- Kenneth S. Kantzer, Trinity Evangelical Divinity School
- Robert Mounce, Bethel College (St. Paul)
- Stephen W. Paine, Houghton College
- Charles F. Pfeiffer, Central Michigan University
- Charles C. Ryrie, Dallas Theological Seminary
- Francis R. Steele, North Africa Mission
- John H. Stek, Calvin Theological Seminary
- John C. Wenger, Goshen Biblical Seminary
- Marten H. Woudstra, Calvin Theological Seminary

To have a public face that was more indicative of its specific purpose, the committee took as its name the Committee on Bible Translation (CBT). Groundwork was also laid for the planned general conference of Christian leaders, biblical scholars, and publishers of Christian literature. Sensing the need to present to the conference more than just the general idea of a new modern English version, the committee formulated a tentative statement concerning the goal it had in mind, the original-language texts to be employed, the style of English to be achieved, and the modus operandi of the translation process. Then, to further the same purpose for which the conference was being called, the committee decided to establish a broad advisory board made up of those who wished to publicly promote the work and to be consulted along the way for advice and counsel.

Two other matters were also addressed. First, with a view to the immediate task of engaging translators for the work, the committee decided that "everyone [engaged in the work of translation] is to subscribe to the following doctrinal statement (or to a similar statement expressing an equally high view of Scripture): 'The Bible alone, and the Bible in its entirety, is the Word of God written, and is therefore inerrant in the autographs.'"[25] Since this statement had the appearance of linking the project too closely to the Evangelical Theological Society (its key sentence echoes the doctrinal basis of that organization), it was revised at the CBT's next meeting (held 26–27 August 1966).[26] Accordingly, article 7, section 1 of the constitution of the CBT, which was adopted in July 1967, reads, "All those engaged by the Committee as translators or editors shall be required to affirm the following article of faith: 'The Bible alone, and the Bible in its entirety, is the Word of God written, and is therefore inerrant in the autographs'; or the statement on Scripture in the Westminster Confession, the Belgic Confession, the New Hampshire Confession, or the creedal basis of the National Association of Evangelicals; or some other comparable statement."

Second, in response to a communication from Eugene Nida of the American Bible Society, the committee put on record its intent that "in the event of the achievement of a successful translation and its being copyrighted we make some provision for its availability to the Bible societies and similar mission agencies apart from the normal channels of trade."[27]

At the meeting of the general conference on Bible translation held at Moody Memorial Church (August 26–27), everything was achieved that the CBT had hoped for—and more.[28] Some eighty interested persons attended. About fifty were spokespersons for or representatives of various Christian organizations involved in evangelism, Bible distribution, church education, and publication of Christian periodicals or other literature. Thirty were biblical scholars. Their prepared papers surveyed the events that had led to the convening of the conference, outlined the CBT's tentative plans for implementing its mandate, explored many of the challenges the venture posed, and proposed how the broader Evangelical community might be of assistance.

These presentations triggered spirited discussions. As could be expected, at this stage the choir was not yet in perfect harmony. But it did become abundantly evident that there was a widespread conviction among Evangelicals that a new modern English version of the Bible was very much needed and that those versions recently produced, as well as those in process, did not have much prospect of attaining such widespread acceptance as to take the place of the King James Version. There also emerged a general consensus that the undertaking outlined by the CBT held sufficient promise to warrant wide support. Many of those in attendance offered to serve on the proposed advisory board to support and help shape and promote the project.

And a relationship was born that would soon become a strategic partnership. Going into the conference the CBT had a treasurer but not a penny in the bank and no source of funds on the horizon. All those who attended did so at their own expense or of that of the agencies they represented. To these conferees the CBT's executive secretary suggested five possible ways the project might be financed but acknowledged that every one of them could well prove to be impractical. Then he added this simple appeal: "Perhaps some of you who are far more experienced than we are in financial matters can counsel us in the problem of financing."

In God's good providence the New York Bible Society (NYBS) was represented at the conference by two men of vision. Youngve R. Kindberg, its general secretary, and Morris M. Townsend, a member of its board of managers, had come to investigate firsthand the new venture in Bible translation they had heard about. For some time they had been looking—in their minds, unsuccessfully—for a new modern English version for use in the society's ministry. When they heard how the CBT's project had come to birth, what its specific goals were, and what its envisioned modus operandi was for the translation process, they were sufficiently impressed to approach the officers of the CBT with an offer to recommend to the board of managers of the NYBS that it underwrite the entire project.[29]

That prospects for full funding of the project should come to the CBT so quickly—and do so "out of the blue"—was seen by the committee as a gift from heaven. That the offer came not from a commercial publisher but from an agency devoted to the distribution of Bibles and the spread of the gospel made it all the more attractive—a true Godsend. Careful negotiations ensued throughout the rest of 1966 and all of 1967.[30] The CBT was concerned, first, that its efforts to achieve the best possible translation of the Scriptures not be compromised by interference from any outside institution or agency—not even by one that "held the purse." Second, it was insistent that the committee continue to have sole editorial control over the text of the translation and over all later revisions. Third, the CBT desired that no encumbering restrictions be placed on the availability of the version to evangelistic agencies and those devoted to Bible distribution.

For its part the Bible society had a number of major concerns of its own:

1. that the CBT remain true to its purpose, confessional basis, and policies as set forth in its own constitution and bylaws (finalized and adopted by the committee on 11 July 1967),
2. that the NYBS recover all the funds it invested in the project,
3. that the work be pushed forward as rapidly as possible without compromising quality, and
4. that the society hold the copyright.

At a plenary meeting held on 5 December 1967, the board of managers of the NYBS endorsed the recommendation of its executive committee that the society underwrite the entire translation project. It did not flinch at the estimated cost in current dollar value of $850,000. Accordingly, in the summer of 1968 a written agreement specifically addressing all the basic concerns of both parties was formalized.[31] This agreement, without amendment, continued to govern the relationship throughout the years of cooperative effort that followed. At the invitation of the CBT, and further to strengthen the bonds between the two bodies and to assure free communication between them, Youngve Kindberg became a member of the Committee on Bible Translation.[32]

The Task Proceeds

Meanwhile, the CBT was also busy with other matters. The conferees at the Palos Heights meeting had instructed the committee of fifteen to establish contact with both the committee in charge of revising the RSV and the Lockman Foundation (which was engaged in producing the NASB). The purpose was to explore the possibility that either one or both might be open to input from the committee of fifteen sufficient to make the major effort of a completely new translation unnecessary. At the August 26 meeting of the CBT, Burton Goddard reported that a two-hour conversation with Luther Weigle, then-chairman of the RSV committee, had brought to light that his committee was considering only very minor revisions (primarily only matters of punctuation and capitalization).[33] And a later communication from the Lockman Foundation made clear that, since its project was nearing completion, it was not open to any kind of cooperative effort.[34]

This left the CBT free to pursue its mandate with a single focus. There was much to be done, and the committee met during every break in the academic year—December 1966 at The King's College, New York; March 1967 at Moody Bible Institute; July 1967 at Calvin Theological Seminary; November 1967 at

Moody Bible Institute; and December 1967 at the headquarters of the NYBS. And all the while, members of the executive committee of the CBT, as well as special subcommittees, were hard at work. Before the end of 1967 the committee had, in addition to matters already noted, approved a position paper through which the CBT could inform all inquirers concerning its goals and policies; completed putting in place an advisory board made up of those who were willing to support the project with counsel, prayers, encouragement, and publicity; and begun the formulation of a translation manual for the guidance of translators. In addition, the CBT had prepared sample translations of chapters 1–9 and 15 of Exodus and chapters 1–10 of Acts as initial models for translators to follow. It had also designed the process through which the translation would be produced, appointed ten translation teams (five Old Testament teams and five New Testament teams), and assigned to each its initial area of responsibility. Finally, it had made provision for the appointment of intermediate and general editorial committees, formulated basic guidelines for their separate functions, and established a tentative schedule for their initial meetings in the summer of 1968.

Of these achievements, the preparation of sample translations and the designing of the translation process were the most decisive for the project. To detail all the matters taken up in the translation manual (both initially and later as the need for more and more policy decisions surfaced) would expand this account beyond its allotted space. In any event, what these were can be discerned from a careful reading of the final product. But no history of the NIV would be complete without an account of the process by which it came to be.

The basic texts adopted by the CBT were, for the Old Testament, the Leningrad Codex B19A as published in Kittel's *Biblia Hebraica* (later in *Biblia Hebraica Stuttgartensia*), and, for the New Testament, the critical edition published by United Bible Societies under the editorship of Kurt Aland, Matthew Black, Bruce Metzger, and Alan Wikgren (1966, 1968), together with the latest edition of Eberhard Nestle's *Novum Testamentum Graece*.[35] These texts were assigned, book by book, to translation teams made up of two translators, two translation consultants (trained biblical scholars), and a stylist consultant (when available)—each team to produce an initial translation in accordance with the translation manual. These initial translations were then carefully scrutinized and revised by intermediate editorial committees of five biblical scholars, drawn from the translation teams, to check them against the original-language texts and conform them to the policies and style called for in the manual. Each edited text was then submitted to close reading by a general editorial committee of eight to twelve members, including representatives of the intermediate editorial committees, other biblical specialists in both Old and New Testaments (initially two or three of them members of the CBT), at least one theologian (whose main responsibility was to represent the concerns of the various confessional traditions), and an English stylist.

Thereafter, the text as edited by the general editorial committee was distributed to selected outside critics and to all members of the CBT in preparation for a final review by the committee. In its editorial review, the CBT established the text to be published and took full responsibility for it. This final step itself had three stages:

1. The committee worked through the tentative translation of each book in plenary session, making final decisions on all translation problems still unresolved and revising the English to achieve a uniform style.
2. The committee read the Englished text orally to make sure that its rhythm flowed well, to eliminate monotonous repetition of sounds and the immediate juxtaposition of harsh consonants, and to remove obstacles to oral reading by nonprofessional readers.
3. The text as revised by the CBT was submitted to one or more English stylists for a final check, with their criticisms and proposals subsequently acted on by the CBT.[36]

Such, at least, was the process the committee designed. And for the most part it was honored in the execution, though adjustments and modifications were often required by the exigencies of particular circumstances.

An Executive Appointment

As the work began, it soon became evident that if a "machine" of this complexity was to work efficiently, a central office was required, with a full-time person in charge, who through training and experience could fully appreciate the task at hand and the process by which it was to be accomplished. In July 1967 the CBT began exploring the possibility of establishing the full-time paid position of executive secretary.[37] At its meeting on November 25 it drew up a list of those who would be approached to serve in this capacity.[38] When the committee met in April 1968, Edwin H. Palmer, the committee's first choice, was in attendance as the newly appointed executive secretary.[39]

Ed Palmer—ex-marine, occasional instructor in systematic theology at Westminster Theological Seminary, at the time of his engagement as executive secretary the pastor of a large Christian Reformed congregation in Grand Rapids, Michigan—soon proved himself to be a happy choice. Because of his quick mind, boundless energy, bold spirit, engaging personality, and intense enthusiasm for the project, he quickly became an indispensable adjunct to the committee. His was a daunting task. He carried on virtually all the correspondence between the CBT and the translators and editors. He kept the one hundred plus members of the advisory board informed of developments through periodic "inform-o-grams." He received, duplicated, and distributed the initial translations and all their subsequently edited forms as they moved up through the editing process. He set up the various meetings of the intermediate editorial and general editorial committees (preparing, duplicating, and distributing typescripts of the translation texts in the various stages of their evolution; establishing agendas and work schedules; arranging for times, places, and transportation). Finally, he prepared all the materials that made up the agenda for the CBT's final editing of the text.

This last task was no small one in itself. All the changes made by the general editorial committee had to be inserted into the emerging text. That text then had to be distributed to all members of the CBT and to a number of additional critics. All the revision proposals submitted by these persons had to be collected and collated and sent to each member of the CBT to vote on them in the privacy of his own study. These votes had to be recorded and collated, and a list of all the proposals—with the "mail vote" recorded—had to be prepared and sent to the members of the committee prior to its editing meetings. All this and more fell to Palmer to accomplish—without computer, fax machine, or modern copier. It was an impossible task, but he did it, always efficiently and on time—with the help of his wife "Peter," eager teenage sons, and a good secretary.

The year 1968 was the one in which everything began to come together. Palmer started his work as executive secretary on April 1. The Old Testament and New Testament intermediate editorial committees met July 1–10. The general editorial committee met July 15–26, and the CBT met for its editorial review July 29–August 8. All who were involved learned much that summer. Procedures were refined and significant progress was made toward fine-tuning the basic style of the final product. The intermediate and general editorial committees treated portions of several books from both the Old and New Testaments. They gave priority, however, to the Gospel of John, and the CBT devoted all its editorial work to that book in order to establish a model for the style of the version as a whole. Capitalizing on the experiences of the summer, the CBT finalized its basic translators' manual when it met in November.[40] Also in 1968 two changes of long-term significance occurred in the membership of the CBT: Robert Preus of Concordia Theological Seminary replaced Edmund Clowney, who had resigned due to heavy responsibilities at Westminster Seminary,[41] and

Larry Walker of Southwestern Baptist Seminary replaced Leslie Carlson, who had died the previous year.[42]

In 1969 the tempo of the work increased on all levels. By the end of the year, teams of translators, including scholars from Canada, Australia, and the United Kingdom, had been formed for almost all sixty-six books of the Bible. The members of the various editorial committees gained valuable experience in the art of editing by committee. And the CBT became aware that certain adjustments in procedures were necessary in order for the editorial process to function more efficiently and more effectively. The year also brought further changes in the membership of the CBT. Francis Steele and Kenneth Kantzer both resigned due to heavy responsibilities elsewhere. Richard Longenecker replaced Kantzer, while the Steele vacancy was left open to be filled at a later date.[43]

Selecting a Name

In its own editorial work that year the CBT concentrated on completing the Gospel of John. In this it was significantly aided by an experiment conducted by Burton Goddard in a public high school in Boxford, Massachusetts. Members of the freshman and sophomore classes (twenty-one from each class) were asked to read portions of the emerging text of John's gospel, indicating their level of comfort with its style and marking all words, phrases, and idioms they did not readily understand.[44] By summer's end the text of the Gospel of John was ready for submission to the New York Bible Society. And before the end of the year the NYBS published a paperback edition under the title *The Gospel According to John: A Contemporary Translation.*

This name was the result of extended discussions and consultations. The CBT had first taken up the matter of naming its version in December 1966,[45] and subsequently various names had been under consideration. In March 1967 the following were proposed:

- The Holy Bible: Common English Version
- The Holy Bible: A Contemporary English Translation
- The Holy Bible: International Translation
- The English Bible: An International Version
- The Holy Bible: A Translation by Evangelicals.[46]

At its July meeting the CBT decided to drop from consideration the last three suggestions and replace them with Twentieth Century English Bible.[47] In November 1967 still more names were put on the table:

- The Holy Bible in Contemporary English
- Plain English Bible
- An English World Bible
- The Holy Bible: A Translation for Today
- The Bible Translated by Evangelical Scholars
- Twentieth Century American Bible
- The Holy Bible: An English Version
- The Holy Bible: Twentieth Century Version
- The Holy Bible: Contemporary English Version
- The Holy Bible in Basic English
- The Holy Bible in Today's English
- The Holy Bible: Twentieth Century Authorized Version
- The Holy Bible: Twentieth Century Standard Translation
- The Holy Bible: God's Word for Today.[48]

After weighing all these possibilities, the committee at its 1968 summer meeting found a preference among its members for The Holy Bible: A Contemporary Translation (ACT).[49] Final action, however, was deferred until later. That came in August of 1969 when the CBT and the New York Bible Society agreed on tentatively adopting this name.[50] Consequently, the new version came to be popularly known initially as "The ACT Bible."

The early 1970s were years of intense effort. There were still some translation teams to be put in place and books to be assigned, and all existing translation teams were under pressure to complete their assignments as quickly as possible. The editorial committees, as well as the CBT, were also hard at work, meeting for extended periods during the spring, summer, and year-end academic breaks. To provide some sense of the pace of the work, between June 21 and July 8 the CBT spent over 118 hours editing Habakkuk, Amos, and the Gospel of Mark.[51] But highly favorable reviews of the Gospel of John encouraged all to press on. At its summer meeting, the CBT decided "to expedite the translation of the New Testament with a view to completing it as early as possible in the year 1972." Due to mounting indebtedness, the New York Bible Society was growing impatient for a marketable product.[52] With that in view, the executive committee of the CBT, in consultation with the society, decided that the CBT should devote the entire summer of 1972 to its final editing of the New Testament.

Besides the translating, editing, and policy making, other developments of consequence were under way. William J. Martin of Regent College, Vancouver, was invited to join the CBT to fill the Steele vacancy.[53] The NYBS had expanded its sphere of ministry and correspondingly added to its name the descriptive adjective *international*. It thereby became the New York Bible Society International (NYBSI), which in turn triggered a change in the name of the translation to The New International Bible: A Contemporary Translation.[54] Provisions were made for the production of a United Kingdom edition of the version.[55] Zondervan Publishing Company entered into formal agreement with the NYBSI to be the sole American licensee for commercial trade editions.[56]

Pressing toward Publication

June 1972 found the members of the CBT and their spouses housed in Pension Kuebler in the little village of Martinsmoos in the Black Forest of West Germany, southwest of Stuttgart. While the intermediate and general editorial committees were meeting at other venues in the United States, as had been the custom also for the CBT up to this point, the Committee on Bible Translation met at this quiet European site to be away from the distractions of institutional duties and to provide some vacation time in what would otherwise be an utterly exhausting summer. The daily schedule typically ran from 6:30 A.M. to 6:00 P.M. In addition, the committee's members usually devoted a few hours of every evening to individual preparation for the work of the next day. Occasionally the committee met again from 7:30–9:00 P.M. And this lasted with only a few short breaks for ten weeks.

In that time the CBT edited Hebrews, Galatians, First and Second Thessalonians, the Johannine epistles, First Corinthians, Colossians, Philippians, First and Second Timothy, Titus, Philemon, Jude, and Revelation, and it made a number of revisions in the Gospel of John. On 25 August 1972, at 8:30 A.M., the committee completed its work on the New Testament, gave thanks to God for his sustaining mercies, and rose to sing the doxology.

One more step remained, however. The results of the CBT's editorial work on the text still needed to be submitted to English stylists for a final review. When the CBT met again in December 1972, it considered all the proposals offered by the stylists, and on 1 January 1973 it completed its final editing and committed the text to the executive secretary to convey to the publishers.[57] Meanwhile, at the urging of the representatives of Zondervan Publishing House and the NYBSI, the CBT authorized a final change of name to The Holy Bible: New International Version.[58]

Throughout 1973, while the translation teams and lower editorial committees busied themselves with advancing the work on the Old Testament, the CBT dealt mainly with oversight of the production of the New Testament and other administrative responsibilities. Widespread distribution of prepublication page proofs among advisory board members and other gatekeepers brought a flood of very favorable reviews but also many proposals for revision, all of which the CBT had to assess. The big push for completion of the Old Testament came in 1974 and following.

But the well had run dry. Initially the overall cost was estimated to be somewhat in excess of $500,000—if, as proposed by the Bible society, translators and editors were to be remunerated at the modest rate of five dollars per hour.[59] Given the state of the economy at the time and the connections that members of the NYBSI's board of managers had with movers and shakers on Wall Street, this seemed within relatively easy reach when spread over the ten years estimated for completing the project. A more detailed calculation undertaken in mid–1967 put the estimated cost at $850,000.[60] But the pace at which translation teams and editorial committees could work had been overestimated.[61] At the same time, the combination of a bear market and double-digit inflation brought significant shrinkage to both the Bible society's reserves and the sources of its income. By the end of 1973 it was apparent that new sources needed to be tapped. At this point Executive Secretary Palmer took it upon himself to establish the 450 Club and set out to find 450 donors who would commit to contributing $250 each year for four years. These efforts met with moderate success, but it was not enough to avert the growing crisis. The NYBSI's financial statement relative to the project issued early in 1976 indicated that by the end of 1975 total expenses had amounted to $1,266,809, of which only about half had been covered through various sources of income. The rest had been covered by loans from several banks.

Late in 1975 the NYBSI put before the CBT the full depth of the financial crisis it faced. At a special meeting with the CBT held on November 8 in Kansas City, Missouri, it presented the committee with the distinct possibility that it would have to abandon the project. It had reduced its staff by more than half and had mortgaged its property to the limit, and it saw no way to raise the significant amounts of money needed to cover the estimated remaining costs. The CBT's response was to readjust procedures and schedules so that the project could be finished by the end of 1977 rather than the projected 1979. This gave the society sufficient relief to hang on for the time being. However, the crisis did not pass until a series of meetings held early in 1976 between the CBT, representatives of the NYBSI, representatives of Zondervan Publishing House, and a Florida businessman resulted in assurances that the needed funds would be forthcoming. Most significantly, Zondervan guaranteed the society that it would advance royalties for up to $250,000 through 1978.[62] With a great sense of relief and many prayers of thanksgiving, the committee could turn its attention without distraction to completing the project.

That it did get done—on schedule—was due to the readiness of many scholars to devote most of their summer breaks to the work. In 1974 twenty-six Old Testament scholars gathered at the University of St. Andrews in Scotland for ten weeks (June 19–August 22) of intense effort. In 1975 twenty-eight scholars worked for ten weeks (June 18–August 21) at the Metsovian Polytechnical Institute of Athens. The following summer saw thirty-five scholars gathered from June 25 to August 27 at the Colegio Mayor Montellano, a residential complex associated with the University of Salamanca in Spain. And finally, in 1977, sixteen scholars met from June 13 until August 18 at the Belgium Bible Institute in Heverlee, Belgium, just outside of Leuven. All of these individuals had contributed to the project earlier as members of translation teams or editorial committees (or both) and consequently had a vested interest in seeing it through to completion. The European venues were an added attraction. These venues were also attractive to the Bible society due to the economies realized.[63]

From year to year, the work of the editorial committees shifted as the editorial process progressed. Intermediate editorial committees were at work alongside the general editorial committees and the CBT through the summer of 1976. That summer two general editorial committees worked side by side to complete that level of editorial review. Meanwhile, because it had not been able to meet the necessary schedule of its work, the CBT invited four Old Testament scholars (Elmer Smick of Gordon-Conwell Seminary, Bruce Waltke of Dallas Theological Seminary, Herbert Wolf of Wheaton College Graduate School, and Ronald Youngblood of Bethel Theological Seminary)—all of whom had worked on translation teams, intermediate editorial committees, and the general editorial committee—to assist it in the final editorial review.

A precedent had been set for this as early as 1974, when Kenneth L. Barker of Dallas Seminary had been invited to sit with the CBT during its editing work.[64] Shortly thereafter he was appointed a full member of the CBT to replace the long-inactive Charles Pfeiffer.[65] For the 1977 summer session in Belgium, Gleason Archer (Trinity Evangelical Divinity School) and Roy Hayden (Oral Roberts University) were also invited to assist. This expansion of the CBT for editing purposes allowed the committee to divide into two sections and thus to double the pace of its work. To broaden the base of exegetical insight and to assure consistency of style, the decisions of each section were reviewed by the members of the other section before the text was finalized.

Even these accelerated procedures were not enough to enable the CBT to complete its work by the end of the session in Heverlee. Its chosen deadline—the end of 1977—had kept it under constant pressure but did not cause it to rush its work. The final editing of Isaiah, for example, took the committee virtually the whole ten weeks of the summer of 1975 (approximately three verses an hour). This was an extreme case, resulting from the fact that the text the CBT had received from the general editorial committee was more paraphrastic than the established policy allowed. Even so, the CBT continued to the end to work at a deliberate pace. In the months following the Heverlee meeting it met for approximately twenty-two weeks to finish all its editorial work.[66] This included assessing the criticisms and proposals for revision of the New Testament that various readers and scholars had submitted since its publication in 1973.

An Ongoing Task

And so the translation project set in motion by the Palos Heights conference in 1965 was completed. More than one hundred biblical scholars had contributed to the work, and they had been assisted by a number of English stylists at various levels.[67] Most notably among these were Margaret Nicholson and Frank Gaebelein. The former had read and criticized the edited text at every level of its development; the latter had sat for many years with the general editorial committees as they did their work. With the translation finished, the conversion of manuscript into book form was promptly and efficiently carried out by the publishers (New York Bible Society International, Zondervan Bible Publishers, and Hodder & Stoughton [for the U.K. edition]), so that before the end of 1978 the completed version was presented to the reading public.[68] And Howard Long's dream, which had started it all, was finally realized.

Yet that was still not the end of it—the task of translating the Bible is never finished. The CBT realized this from the beginning. Already in its agreement of cooperation with the NYBS it had provided for its continued oversight of the text. And in early 1977 it had tentatively set aside the third week of May 1979 to consider revisions of the complete Bible.[69] However, when it met on 28 May 1979, it decided to authorize no new revisions until 1983, the twentieth anniversary of the publication of the New Testament. That year, the CBT[70] met from June 23 until August 6 at the Spanish Bible Institute in Castelldefels, Spain, and worked through all the criticisms and proposals for revision that had accumulated through the years. In this revision, whatever changes were made had to be approved by at least a seventy percent majority of the CBT.[71] Even so, some scores of changes were adopted, giving rise to the addendum to the committee's Preface to the NIV (revised August 1983) and to the new copyright date of 1984.

This, then, is how the NIV (1973, 1978, 1984) came to be. It is, of course, not the whole story. It is, really, little more than the bare, dry bones of the story. How the translated text was formatted and produced in bound forms is a story untold here, as is the story of the Anglicization of the text. And the flesh-and-blood story of the translators at work—the agony and the ecstasy of translating the ancient sacred texts, the exhilarating challenge and humbling effect of doing it while sitting around a table with learned peers, the sacrifices made, the stress and strain of meeting endless deadlines, the utter fatigue that at times set in, and yet the deep satisfaction of laboring at the task as a community of fellow believers devoted to a work that lay close to the heart—this, too, is another story.[72] Space constraints prohibit telling the full story here. The whole story would, no doubt, require many volumes—or else the skills of a poet.

Notes

1. The story of the NIV has been told elsewhere: Carolyn J. Youngblood, "The New International Version Translation Project: Its Conception and Implementation," *JETS* 21 (September 1978): 239–49; Burton L. Goddard, *The NIV Story: The Inside Story of the New International Version* (New York: Vantage, 1989); Richard Kevin Barnard, *God's Word in Our Language: The Story of the New International Version* (Colorado Springs: International Bible Society, 1989). Youngblood's account is based on primary sources; Goddard's, largely on personal reminiscences and his private files; Barnard's, primarily on interviews with many of the principals in the project. For the early history (1956–66), see also Stephen W. Paine, "Background of This Bible Translation Project" (unpublished paper, Bible translation conference, Moody Memorial Church, Chicago, Illinois, 26–27 August 1966).

2. For a fuller account of Howard Long's frustration, see Barnard, *God's Word in Our Language,* 15–18.

3. *Acts of Synod 1956 of the Christian Reformed Church* (Grand Rapids: Christian Reformed Publishing House, 1956), Overture 27, 539–40.

4. *Acts of Synod 1956,* 61.

5. The first three named were all born in the 1890s, and of them only Wyngaarden lived to see the actual launching of the translation project; Woudstra was a post-World War II immigrant from the Netherlands, and thirty years their junior.

6. See "The Possibility of a New Translation of the Bible," *Acts of Synod 1957,* 348–56.

7. Why? Because it was produced by scholars who stood in the Charles Briggs higher-critical tradition of biblical scholarship rather than in the confessional tradition of Benjamin Warfield ("what Scripture says, God says"). These two men are mentioned here because they epitomized the Liberalism-Fundamentalism conflict that raged in the mainline churches in America during the first three decades of the twentieth century, a conflict that cast a long shadow throughout that century.

8. *Acts of Synod 1957,* 24.

9. *Acts of Synod 1958,* 102–3.

10. *Acts of Synod 1959,* 292–93.

11. It exists in mimeographed form (seven single-spaced pages, titled "The Committee on Bible Translation: Christian Reformed Church," addressed to "Dear

Reader(s),"and signed by Schultze, Stob, Woudstra, and Wyngaarden). The paper is undated, but since an attached note informs the reader that Schultze died "before the final draft was presented," it is to be dated in March/April 1959 (Schultze died 6 March 1959).

12. *Acts of Synod 1960,* 155.

13. The committee never had in view that the Christian Reformed Church, either alone or in concert with other churches, would be the *sponsoring* body for the production of a new English version of the Bible.

14. Goddard, *The NIV Story,* 8–9. Three of these four names will appear frequently in the narrative that follows.

15. Ibid., 9.

16. Ibid., 11–12; *Acts of Synod 1962,* 162.

17. Minutes of the Joint Committee on Bible Translation (21 December 1962); Goddard, *The NIV Story,* 13–14; *Acts of Synod 1963,* 196.

18. See "Minutes of the Second Meeting of the Joint Committee on Bible Translation" (29 December 1964).

19. For that reason the Christian Reformed committee made its final report to the synod in 1966—including a "Survey of the Bible Translation Project" dating back to 1956. See *Acts of Synod 1966,* 374–85.

20. Among them were John Bradbury, editor emeritus of the *Watchman Examiner;* Gordon W. Brown, dean of Central Baptist Seminary (Toronto); V. Raymond Edman, chancellor of Wheaton College; Carl F. H. Henry, editor of *Christianity Today;* Peter Eldersveld of "The Back to God Hour" (international broadcast voice of the Christian Reformed Church); David Hubbard, president of Fuller Theological Seminary; J. Theodore Mueller of Concordia Seminary; Harold John Ockenga of Park Street Church (Boston); W. Stanford Reid of McGill University; and John Wenger of Goshen Biblical Seminary.

21. See note 8.

22. For example, Daniel 11:31 and 12:11 refer to "the abomination that makes desolate," but in Matthew 24:15 and Mark 13:14, though they clearly refer to these Daniel passages (expressly so in Matthew), the reader finds references rather to "the desolating sacrilege"—even though the relevant Greek noun is rendered "abomination(s)" in Luke 16:15; Revelation 17:4–5; 21:27.

23. For other accounts of the conference see Goddard, *The NIV Story,* 15–19, and "Brief Report of the Activities of the Bible Translation Conference Held at Trinity Christian College, Palos Heights (Chicago), Illinois on August 26 and 27, 1965," by John Stek and Marten Woudstra (mimeographed, four pages, single-spaced). The "more comprehensive digest of the conference" to which this report refers was never written because the Committee of Fifteen decided that the Stek-Woudstra report was sufficient (see Paine, "Background of This Bible Translation Report," 5–6).

24. Paine, "Background of This Bible Translation Report," 5–6.

25. Minutes of the Committee on Bible Translation (CBT), 25–26 March 1966.

26. Minutes of the CBT (26–27 August 1966), minute 13.

27. Minutes of the CBT (25–26 March 1966).

28. For brief accounts of this conference, see Goddard, *The NIV Story,* 20–27; "Summary of Proceedings: Conference on Bible Translation: Moody Church, Chicago" (26–27 August 1966 [mimeographed, four pages, single-spaced]).

29. Minutes of the CBT (26–27 August 1966), minute 24.

30. Meanwhile, the Bible Society underwrote the cost of the CBT's meetings during 1967, up to $5,000 (Minutes of the CBT [24–25 March 1967], minute 19).

31. Minutes of the CBT (29 July–8 August 1968), minute 20. For the process through which this basis of cooperation was developed, see Minutes of the CBT (24–25 March 1967), minute 25; Minutes of the CBT (10–14 July 1967), minutes 16, 38, 39, 42; Minutes of the CBT (24–25 November 1967), minute 8; Minutes of the CBT (12–13 April 1968), minutes 19, 22, 29.

32. Minutes of the CBT (24–25 November 1967), minute 13; Minutes of the CBT (29–30 December 1967), minute 6. The committee had a vacancy to fill due to the resignation of Robert Mounce (Minutes of the CBT [26–27 August 1964], minute 7).

33. Minutes of the CBT (26–27 August 1966), minute 5(c).

34. Minutes of the CBT (28 December 1966), minute 10; see also Goddard's attached report (as temporary executive secretary).

35. Minutes of the CBT (24–25 November 1967), minute 33; cf. Minutes of the CBT (24–25 March 1967), minute 40 (1), (2).

36. Minutes of the CBT (24–25 March 1967), minute 47 (1); Minutes of the CBT (10–14 July 1967), minutes 31–34, 46.

37. Minutes of the CBT (10–14 July 1967), minute 10.

38. Minutes of the CBT (24–25 November 1967), minute 37.

39. Minutes of the CBT (12–13 April 1968), minute 2.

40. Minutes of the CBT (29–30 November 1968), minute 22. Many policy matters still required later consideration, and the manual grew as the years passed.

41. Minutes of the CBT (29 July–8 August 1968), minutes 12–17.

42. Minutes of the CBT (29–30 November 1968), minute 12.

43. Minutes of the CBT (5–6 August 1969).

44. See "Report on Experiment with the New Bible Translation at Masconomet Regional High School, Boxford, Massachusetts" (5 March 1969), attached to the Minutes of the CBT (1–5 April 1969).

45. Minutes of the CBT (28 December 1966), minute 12.

46. Minutes of the CBT (24 March 1967), minute 37.

47. Minutes of the CBT (10–14 July 1967), minute 40.

48. Minutes of the CBT (24–25 November 1967), minute 28.

49. Minutes of the CBT (29 July–8 August 1968), minute 25.

50. Minutes of the CBT (4–7 August 1969).

51. Minutes of the CBT (21 June–9 July 1971), minute 56.

52. Minutes of the CBT (22 June–2 July 1970), minute 32.

53. Minutes of the CBT (21 June–9 July 1971), minute 21.

54. Ibid., minute 25.

55. Minutes of the CBT (5–9 April 1971), minutes 22, 27, 28; minutes 15, 16: Minutes of the CBT (27–31 March 1972), minutes 15, 16.

56. Minutes of the CBT (5–9 April 1971), minute 21.

57. Minutes of the CBT (28 December 1972–1 January 1973), minute 24.

58. Ibid., minute 7.

59. Minutes of the CBT (28 December 1966), minute 27.

60. See budget attached to the Minutes of the CBT (10–14 July 1967).

61. As it turned out, the pace of initial translation varied considerably, depending on the makeup of each translation team and the book for which it was responsible. On the editorial levels, the intermediate editorial committees averaged five verses per hour, the general editorial committees averaged eight verses per hour, and the CBT averaged twelve verses per hour. See communication of the executive secretary to potential donors, dated February 1974.

62. Minutes of the CBT (5 February 1976).

63. The cost per person for room and board per day was $6.00 (St. Andrews), $8.00 (Athens), $5.50 (Salamanca), and $9.50 (Heverlee).

64. Minutes of the CBT (19 June–17 July 1974), minute 10.

65. Minutes of the CBT (28 August 1974), minutes 4, 8.

66. September 28–November 16; November 28–December 23; December 27–January 20; February 3–March; March 13–25; April 3–May 11; May 27–June 2.

67. Those who contributed are listed in Goddard, *The NIV Story,* 119–24; for an even more complete list, see Barnard, *God's Word in Our Language,* 191–98.

68. Zondervan's release date was 27 October1978. Because of the wide acceptance of the New Testament, Zondervan's first pressrun of the whole Bible was 1,200,000 (see Goddard, *The NIV Story,* 112).

69. Minutes of the CBT (18 March 1977).

70. The CBT's membership had changed somewhat since 1978. Charles Ryrie had resigned in 1977 (Minutes of the CBT [April 1977]), and Ronald Youngblood (Bethel Seminary, San Diego) was added in 1979 (Minutes of the CBT [28 May 1979]). In the spring of 1980 Bill Martin died and was replaced that same year by Bruce Waltke of Regent College, Vancouver (Minutes of the CBT [November 1980], minute 3). At the CBT's meeting in 1983, Youngve Kindberg resigned and his place was taken by Donald Wiseman of the University of London (Minutes of the CBT [2–3 August 1983]). Wiseman had for many years chaired the committee that Anglicized the text of the NIV for the Commonwealth edition published by Hodder & Stoughton, and he was present for part of the CBT's review of the NIV in 1983.

71. "The proposed revision may be adopted in committee if at least eight members are present and if the following majorities for the proposed revision are attained: 6 votes from 8 members, 7 from 9, 7 from 10, 8 from 11, 9 from 12, 9 from 13, 10 from 14, or 11 from 15" (Minutes of the CBT [1 November 1980], minutes 4–5).

72. This story has been told in part by Goddard and Barnard in their cited works.

Meetings of the CBT 1965–1983

1. 29 December 1965, Nashville, Tennessee
2. 25–26 March 1966, Moody Bible Institute, Chicago, Illinois
3. 26–27 August 1966, Moody Memorial Church, Chicago, Illinois
4. 28 December 1966, The King's College, Briar Cliff Manor, New York, New York
5. 24–25 March 1967, Moody Bible Institute, Chicago, Illinois

6. 10–14 July 1967, Calvin Theological Seminary, Grand Rapids, Michigan
7. 24–25 November 1967, Moody Bible Institute, Chicago, Illinois
8. 29–30 December 1967, New York Bible Society Headquarters, New York, New York
9. 12–13 April 1968, Philadelphia College of the Bible, Philadelphia, Pennsylvania
10. 29 July–8 August, Calvin College, Grand Rapids, Michigan
11. 29–30 November 1968, New York Bible Society Headquarters, New York, New York
12. 1–5 April 1969, Covenant Theological Seminary, St. Louis, Missouri
13. 4–7 August 1969, Wheaton College, Wheaton, Illinois
14. 28–29 November 1969, Moody Bible Institute, Chicago, Illinois
15. 23–27 March 1970, Houghton College, Houghton, New York
16. 22 June–2 July 1970, Covenant College, Lookout Mountain, Georgia
17. 5–9 April 1971, St. Paul's School of Theology, Kansas City, Missouri
18. 21 June–9 July 1971, Calvin College, Grand Rapids, Michigan
19. 27–29 December 1971, Trinity Christian College, Palos Heights, Illinois
20. 27–31 March 1972, Bibletown, Boca Raton, Florida
21. 19 June–25 August 1972, Pension Kuebler, Martinsmoos, West Germany
22. 24–25 November 1972, Trinity Evangelical Theological Seminary, Deerfield, Illinois
23. 28 December 1972–1 January 1973, Bethel Seminary, St. Paul, Minnesota
24. 9–19 July 1973, The Firs, Bellingham, Washington
25. 31 December 1973–4 January 1974, Wheaton College, Wheaton, Illinois
26. 8–15 April 1974, St. Paul's School of Theology, Kansas City, Missouri
27. 19 June–22 August 1974, David Russell Hall, University of St. Andrews, St. Andrews, Scotland
28. 27 December 1974–11 January 1975, Bibletown, Boca Raton, Florida
29. 24–29 March 1975, St. Paul's School of Theology, Kansas City, Missouri
30. 18 June–21 August 1975, Metsovian Polytechnical Institute, Athens, Greece
31. 9 November 1975, St. Paul's School of Theology, Kansas City, Missouri
32. 5 January–7 February 1976, Bibletown, Boca Raton, Florida
33. 23 February–27 March 1976, Fort Worth, Texas
34. 12 April–15 May 1976, Liberty Corners, New Jersey
35. 25 June–27 August 1976, Salamanca University, Salamanca, Spain
36. 10 January–12 February 1977, Bibletown, Boca Raton, Florida
37. 28 February–2 April 1977, Euless, Texas
38. 18 April–21 May 1977, Liberty Corners, New Jersey
39. 13 June–19 August 1977, Belgium Bible Institute, Heverlee, Belgium
40. 26 September–16 November 1977, Liberty Corners, New Jersey
41. 28 November–23 December 1977, Cape Coral, Florida
42. 27 December 1977–20 January 1978, Bibletown, Boca Raton, Florida
43. 13 February–3 March 1978, Wycliffe International Linguistic Center, Dallas, Texas
44. 13–25 March 1978, Wycliffe International Linguistic Center, Dallas, Texas

45. 3 April–11 May 1978, Liberty Corners, New Jersey
46. 27 May–2 June 1978, Liberty Corners, New Jersey
47. 28–31 March 1979, Liberty Corners, New Jersey
48. 2 November 1980, Ramada Inn O'Hare, Rosemont, Illinois
49. 20 June 1981, Ramada Inn O'Hare, Rosemont, Illinois
50. 26 June 1982, Ramada Inn O'Hare, Rosemont, Illinois
51. 23 June–6 August 1983, Spanish Bible Institute, Castelldefels, Spain

11

THAT FABULOUS TALKING SNAKE[1]

Ronald A. Veenker

Let me first comment on the intentional redundancy in the title of this address. I am using the word *fabulous* literally—that is, pertaining to a fable. Any story about a talking snake is, of course, a fable. I have spent much of the last thirty years poring over the texts of the early chapters of Genesis seeking to understand them better in terms of their ancient Near Eastern analogs.[2] But in this study I want to look at the garden of Eden story from the standpoint of its context within the traditions of the Hebrew Bible and set aside Near Eastern connections for a moment.

The opening chapters of the book of Genesis contain the first attempt at a monotheistic creation story. Therefore, in these two stories we encounter but one powerful deity creating this and creating that without violent conflicts with other cosmic beings in order to use their body parts for the construction of the cosmos. In other words, when compared with the Mesopotamian creation traditions, it's a bit dull. In the biblical story there is no suggestion of the darker side of the universe—only a benign sovereign bringing order out of chaos, filling the world with living creatures who are to be governed by human beings, the *pièce de résistance* of this solitary deity. What a contrast to the mythopoeic intrigues and murders of *Enuma Elish*. Our narrators have created a kind of nice, squeaky-clean Walt Disney world and, in so doing, have invented, perhaps unintentionally, the "problem of evil"—that is to say, if Yahweh is benign and at the same time sovereign in the universe, just where does evil come from? It's striking that immediately following the first monotheistic creation story, the author moves directly to work out the problem of evil. All of us know just how complex the garden of Eden story is—how many layers and levels of meaning it contains from the ancient to the last redactor. And on this final level—the arrangement of the first three chapters in their canonical form—I believe we are dealing with theodicy.

Now these creationist narrators are not in the slightest naive. They know exactly what they have done by positing a monotheistic scheme and move immediately to address the problem of evil by telling a story about a snake, a man, and a woman. The focal point of this etiological narrative is the poetic section (Gen 3:14–19), which contains a list of seven primal evils touching the whole natural world—fauna, flora, and human alike. Each etiology about evil is prompted by ancient man's most casual reflection on the world around him:

- "You will crawl on your belly."—Why is the serpent missing its legs?
- "He will crush your head."—Why do humans loathe serpents?
- "With pain you will give birth to children."—Why are birth pains necessary?
- "Your husband ... will rule over you."—Why on earth should men dominate women?
- "Through painful toil you will eat."—Why must we be food cultivators rather than food gatherers?
- "It will produce thorns and thistles."—Working the ground is hard, and what good are weeds, anyway?
- Finally, the big number seven: "Dust you are and to dust you will return."—Why must we die?

Each of these addresses one of the seven evils, while the earlier narrative of chapter 3 explains how it came to be.

If I am catching something intended by those who arranged and edited these opening chapters of the Bible and not simply reading in my own ideas, I am surprised to find reflection on the problem of evil in texts that I had always casually assumed to be products of an earlier editorial process. Perhaps not, then. Perhaps the final editing of the primal history occurred a little later than I suspected, since the whole enterprise of separating Yahweh from evil and focusing on his total goodness is usually assigned to the last two or three centuries BCE and to those authors who gave us apocalyptic dualism and a Satan who is co-ruler of the universe. And thus I find myself taking another look at the work of the melancholy Danish school of historical criticism (or "minimalists," as they are known in current discussions) and asking myself whether they may be correct in their dating of the literature.[3]

The Fall of Humanity

What about the story itself? The characters are familiar: God, the first human couple, and the serpent. We know them so well. God, Adam, Eve—no problem. But just exactly who or what is this snake creature? The most fascinating aspect is its ability to converse with Adam and Eve. How could this snake talk? Well, my students have no problem with this question. They all know that the serpent is really the Devil. Or the story is about Satan the ventriloquist. Every English speaker has known this since the publication of *Paradise Lost.* To suggest otherwise is a lost cause.[4]

But if the biblical narrator's strategy is to remove Yahweh from any association with evil, then there is a problem in identifying the serpent with Satan. The opening verse of Genesis 3 says quite simply, "The serpent was more crafty than any of the wild animals the LORD God had made." If the goal of theodicy is to remove Yahweh from any moral culpability, what sense does it make for Yahweh to create Satan? No, this serpent is surely not Satan.

Having said that, however, I am left with an animal that Yahweh created when he was populating the earth—a reptile who, in the beginning of the story at least, had legs and could talk. What sort of fable do we have here? Why does this snake talk? The church fathers and John Milton did not bother to answer this question. It was a simple matter for them. Having identified the serpent as Satan, it is a small step to ascribe to Satan godlike powers.

Let us look at the text again. Man, woman, and serpent. Upon each of them is delivered punishment. One by one they are cursed; evil is forced on the very core of their existence. The goal of theodicy is to believe simultaneously in a righteous, benign, and omnipotent deity who has created us and our world but is not culpable for the presence of what is commonly identified as "evil" in that world. Therefore, one must somehow exonerate Yahweh from any blame in this matter of the legs of the serpent, the woman's birth pains, and weeds in our garden.

From the beginning of civilization when the first cities were built and people began to experience urban density, laws regulating human behavior were established. The most rudimentary laws of behavior were those that recognized a person's right to protection from capricious malevolence initiated by another individual. In the Bible, *talion law* prescribes an "eye for an eye, a tooth for a tooth," and so forth. Other Near Eastern law codes offer compensation in place of talion. For example, in the Middle Assyrian laws, a man who slaps another's young wife loses a finger; if he kisses her, his lips are cut off.

Lurking in the Eden narrative is the implication that the benign and righteous nature of Yahweh demands justice for his world. The God who created mankind as moral must himself possess at least that same morality and, likely, a greater morality manifesting itself in a sense of justice that transcends that of his human creation. So this is how theodicy works in the narrative. God makes laws, others break the laws, and punishment ensues. God himself does not create evil, but it is necessitated by the actions of free moral agents living within his domain. It's not just a good idea, it's the law. The woman went her own way and enjoyed the fruit of the tree of the knowledge of good and evil. The man followed her and did the same. For these rebellious actions, God is justified in meting out punishment. The curses are necessitated by such behavior. We all recognize the fact that our actions are not without consequences.

But when we turn to the serpent, we encounter a serious problem. Humans, made in the image of God, owe their sense of justice to the creator. While God must in all ways be more just than humans, they, in turn, are a higher created order than the animals. Adam named those animals and in so doing participated in some way in the creative process and held a place of dominion over them.[5] They do not have a moral nature but are of a lower order of being. One does not blame them or praise them for their behavior, for they do not reason but follow their instinctual nature. Animals simply are not moral agents in the traditional thought of the Western world.[6] Now, if humans do not hold animals morally responsible for their actions, why would they expect that God would do so? For the Creator God to punish a dumb and innocent reptile—to which he gave life—by taking its legs is unthinkable. That would place God on a moral plane beneath that of his humble humanity. He cannot be less moral than humankind. Our storyteller has a problem: How can God be exonerated for cursing what the storyteller sees as an innocent animal? For literally picking on a dumb beast?

The Day They Hung the Elephant

Although I am operating from the assumption that humans throughout history have not considered animals to be moral agents and therefore neither praiseworthy nor blameworthy for their behavior, I have recently reread Jack Finkelstein's monograph *The Goring Ox,* published posthumously through the great labor of Maria D. Ellis.[7] The legal history of Western civilization is dotted with strange cases and juridical deliberations on the topic of beastly morality and behavior.[8] I am aware that this is no simple matter in the history of jurisprudence. But please allow me to relate one puzzling anecdote from American culture:

> History sometimes produces bizarre and instructive incidents that rival fiction. On September 11, 1916, the Sparks Circus conducted its afternoon performance in Kingsport, Tennessee, and eager hill people filled most of the five thousand seats under the big top. The show's star elephant, Mary, advertisements embellished, was "The Largest Living Land Animal on Earth," three inches taller than Barnum's Jumbo. It

was not just Mary's bulk that was important but also her skill. She could play a series of horns, hit baseballs at a .400 average, and even argue with the umpire. Only two days earlier, Walter Eldridge, a young man from nearby St. Paul, Virginia, had joined the circus and was assigned to handle the elephant, and as the show progressed, he proudly straddled the world's largest land animal.

At some point in the performance, things went suddenly wrong when the inexperienced mahout hit Mary to correct her course. Mary smashed Eldridge to the ground, gored him, and then tossed his remains into the crowd amid screams, panic, and a scattering of pistol shots aimed at the pachyderm by alarmed spectators. The bullets, the press reported, did not take effect. The Kingsport city fathers decided that Mary had to pay for this crime with her life, and after rejecting further gunplay and poison, they agreed to hang Mary from The Clinchfield and Ohio Railroad crane located in nearby Erwin. On September 13, there were five thousand people waiting in Erwin for the execution, as many as had attended the circus and watched Eldridge's death. Before her burial, a doctor helped saw off her tusks and noticed several abscessed teeth, and he speculated that Eldridge's blow to her head may have hit the sore teeth and provoked her rampage.

On first glance, the hanging of Mary seems so bizarre as to preclude analysis; yet there are elements that provide insight into Southern psychology. Obviously, a number of spectators attended the circus armed, and one can only speculate why they carried pistols into a circus tent for an afternoon performance or why they felt compelled to fire their weapons at Mary, even though the tent was crowded with women and children. Mary's death sentence came from the eye-for-an-eye sense of justice that pervaded the South, but the decision to hang Mary instead of shooting her was more puzzling. Fourteen years earlier, the police chief of Valdosta, Georgia, killed Gypsy, another circus elephant, with his rifle when she trampled her keeper to death and ran wild through the streets. [A photograph shows chief of police Calvin Dampier sitting atop the slain elephant, with his rifle prominently displayed.] The argument that a rifle would be ineffective on Mary seemed lame among a people who were descendants of Daniel Boone. No doubt the prospect of a hanging intrigued the Kingsport city fathers; it would be a spectacle far more gripping than a firing squad or death by poison.[9]

Trying to Discern the Mind of the Narrator

Our response to this story is to laugh incredulously—to laugh at the absurdity of it. We can scarcely imagine ourselves party to such goings-on. We simply do not regard animals as moral equals. Likewise, our ancestors' natural intuition was to regard themselves as benignly disposed toward and superior to the animal world. For them to imagine that a serpent angered the gods to the extent that they took away its legs may have been as mystifying as the elephant-hanging in East Tennessee. Humans do not enter into moral discourse with the animal kingdom. We are not able to do so, because they are dumb. They do not speak. And this is precisely the point in the garden narrative. By means of *deus ex machina,* the narrator takes charge of this microcosmic world and creates a talking snake—a serpent with human intelligence and the gift of speech. The narrator's story requires a talking serpent in order to remove from God himself a charge of unjustified cruelty to an innocent animal. For the theodicy to be complete, the snake must be given rationality like a human being. Then and only then can he become responsible for his own actions and bear his own punishment fairly. The serpent does not talk because Satan manipulates him. The serpent *must* speak, or God will be guilty of acting unjustly by human standards. The goals of the theodicy will always be served.

There is no need to summarize the simple points of this short address, but in conclusion, I wish to point out that the ideas contained in it are a result of an attempt to read the story as its earliest narrators understood it. Whether I have been successful will depend on the wisdom and judgment of the reader. I think this is a very important way to approach Scripture, especially for the Bible translator. It is so easy to find interpretations we have been taught since our youth in the text of the stories of early Genesis. I have never understood why these very sophisticated narratives, sometimes in a very difficult genre to identify, have so frequently become the focus of Sunday school presses when preparing materials for the primary grades. Have we not all seen more than once Noah and his cute little ark with its friendly animals dancing about on a flannelgraph board?

The story of the garden does not mention Satan, nor does it seek to identify this serpent as anything other than an exceptional animal that God created. Of course, the "serpent as Satan" identification grew out of the work of Hellenistic exegetes and found its way into the church fathers. From there it was further elaborated by John Milton in our English tongue, and nothing further need be said. I would not for a second presume that the meaning of the story for its original narrator is the only valid and appropriate message to be extracted from the garden narrative or any other. But I think it is important for the task of translation, and even of annotation, that scholars try as much as possible to free themselves from leading the reader to their own personal perspective on the matter. There is, after all, plenty of time after translation for unlimited hermeneutical adventure. And let me conclude by saying that I stand admonished by my own exhortations.

Notes

1. This manuscript was delivered as the presidential address for the Middle West Branch of the American Oriental Society at Wheaton College (Wheaton, Illinois) on 17 February 1997. I offer it with gratitude to Professor Youngblood as it was read on that date.

2. It is a great honor to be included in a volume honoring Ronald F. Youngblood. He was my mentor when I was a young student at Bethel Theological Seminary in the early 1960s. It was his fascination with Genesis that set me on my lifelong desire to read, study, and reread these amazing biblical stories. I have yet to plumb the actual depths of any and am continually aware of how much more there is to learn and understand, especially in the enigmatic chapters 1–11. Professor Youngblood was a great inspiration to his students, who continue to hold him in the highest esteem.

3. What I mean to say here is that the minimalist historians are placing the formation of the Hebrew Scriptures later and later, encroaching on the Hellenistic period. The Stoic philosophers were talking about the problem of evil about this same time. I do not think that the writers and editors of Hebrew Scripture had to be privy to Greek philosophical discourse in order to think about the problem of evil, nor do I think that this concomitance is an obvious coincidence. For an example of this sort of thinking, see Seneca's opening sentence to Lucilius: "You have asked me, Lucilius, why, if a Providence rules the world, it still happens that many evils befall good men" ("To Lucilius on Providence," in John W. Basore, ed., *Seneca Moral Essays,* vol. 1, Loeb Classical Library 214 [Cambridge, Mass: Harvard Univ. Press, 1928]: 3–47). For examples of the minimalist reconstructions of Israelite history, note especially Niels Peter Lemche, *The Israelites in History and Tradition,* Library of Ancient Israel (Louisville, Ky.: Westminster/John Knox, 1998); Thomas L. Thompson, *The Bible in History: How Writers Create a Past* (London: Pimlico, 1999); Philip R. Davies, *In Search of Ancient Israel,* JSOTSup 148 (Sheffield: Sheffield Academic Press, 1995); and the works of others who are pushing the dates of biblical literature later and later.

4. On the historical development of the figure "Satan" in the Hebrew Bible, see Jeffrey Burton Russell, *The Devil: Perceptions of Evil from Antiquity to Primitive Christianity* (Ithaca, N.Y.: Cornell Univ. Press, 1977), and Elaine Pagels, *The Origin of Satan* (New York: Random House, 1995).

5. "In a way which defies precise rational clarification, every word contains something of the object itself. Thus, in a very realistic sense, what happens in language is that the world is given material expression. Objects are only given form and differentiation in the word that names them. This idea of the word's power of mastery was very familiar in the ancient world. Even in J's story of the Garden of Eden, the word of the man is

noticeably given precedence over the world of objects. It was only when man gave the animals their names that they existed for him and were available for his use (Gen 2:19–20)." Gerhard von Rad, *The Message of the Prophets* (London: SCM Press, 1968), 61.

6. "In primitive law, animals and even plants and other inanimate objects are often treated in the same way as human beings and are, in particular, punished. However, this must be seen in its connection with the animism of primitive man. He considers animals, plants, and inanimate objects as endowed with a 'soul,' inasmuch as he attributes human and sometimes even superhuman mental facilities to them. The fundamental difference between humans and other beings, which is part of the outlook of civilized man, does not exist for primitive man." Hans Kelsen, *General Theory of Law and State,* trans. A. Wedberg (Cambridge, Mass.: Harvard Univ. Press, 1945), 3–4.

7. Jacob J. Finkelstein, *The Ox That Gored,* Transactions of the American Philosophical Society, 71, no. 2 (Philadelphia: 1981).

8. See especially Finkelstein, *The Ox That Gored,* part 2, section 11, for examples of a disorderly mule in Knoxville, Tennessee, in 1956; a sheep-killing dog in Virginia, 1961; and a German Shepherd that attacked a woman in New Canaan, Connecticut, in 1960.

9. Pete Daniel, *Standing at the Crossroads: Southern Life Since 1900* (New York: Hill & Wang, 1986), 52–54. Note also Charles Edwin Price, *The Day They Hung the Elephant* (Johnson City, Tenn.: Overmountain, 1992), a forty-page monograph with pictures.

12

SLIP OF THE EYE: ACCIDENTAL OMISSION IN THE MASORETIC TRADITION

David Noel Freedman and David Miano

The first step in Bible translation is the determination of the text. To be sure, ascertaining the precise wording of an original document can often be a daunting, sometimes impossible task, but it is nevertheless an important one. Great strides have been taken recently in the area of biblical textual criticism and are beginning to manifest themselves in the production of new critical texts—most notably the new Oxford Hebrew Bible, which promises to provide the best readings from all the available manuscripts and evidence.

On the other hand, we have noted that even the best textual critics are still reluctant to acknowledge the consequential role of accidental omission in the copying of ancient manuscripts. There seems to be a fascination with the concept of expansions and intrusions in the biblical text, to the point where various (sometimes complicated) scenarios are contrived to explain why a copyist may have made certain additions to a sacred text in his charge. The problem with this sort of exercise is that it requires a scholar to become a psychologist. How can we really know what a scribe's sentiments were or whether he was motivated to make an alteration? Under what circumstances did a copyist have authority or permission to make changes to the text? Reproduction was a scribe's chief task. Sentence after sentence, page after page, book after book, manuscript after manuscript, he would have found it impractical to pay attention to the meaning of every word. It is sometimes forgotten that the most common causes of textual corruption are *accidental,* not intentional, and we should always look first for possible mechanical errors when analyzing a text's history before delving into the intangible.

We have recently begun a systematic study of the most malignant of all mechanical errors—haplography—and we wish to share some of our preliminary findings to illustrate our point about the causes of textual divergence. Strictly defined, ***haplography*** ("single writing") refers to writing only once something that occurs two or more times in the original. Repeated sequences that instigate haplography may range from one character to a whole string of characters. When a cluster of letters is repeated in a text, the tendency is for a copyist's eye to skip ahead from one of these incidences (what we call the "trigger sequence") to a later one. This phenomenon is known as *parablepsis* ("looking aside"). We prefer to use this term strictly for horizontal shifts, and a coordinate term—*katablepsis* ("looking down")—for vertical shifts. Both sorts of visual error are quite common in the handwritten duplication of manuscripts. *Parablepsis* results in the loss of letters and words; *katablepsis* results in the loss of one or more lines. Sometimes *parablepsis* may occur across a column, in which case an entire section may be omitted. We thus can see the potential in haplography for serious damage to the text.

The most basic form of haplography is the omission of a single letter instigated by *homoiogrammaton* ("similar character"), a situation in which a letter occurs two or more times in a row; we call this type of misduplication "simple haplography." It may be illustrated by an error made during the copying of the Great Isaiah Scroll (1QIsa[a]) at Isaiah 1:2. In the Masoretic Text, the word ורוממתי ("and I have raised up") appears; however, the copyist of the Dead Sea Scroll accidentally wrote ורומתי, omitting one of the *mems*. We know this happened, because either he or someone else later caught the error and wrote a *mem* just above the word to correct the mistake.[1]

Because Hebrew words do not often contain two identical consonants in a row, simple haplography is relatively rare. Most cases of omission, unfortunately, are more serious. Whole-word haplography may occur when a word in the master text is written twice in a row (*homoiologon*—"similar word"). Such a sequence may trigger *parablepsis,* and the result is that only one of the words gets copied. An example of this sort of mistake can also be found in the Qumran Isaiah scroll at Isaiah 57:19, where the word שלום, written twice in the Masoretic Text, appears only once. The reading of the former witness is probably the result of *parablepsis* caused by *homoiologon.*

We must point out that two words in sequence that might instigate whole-word haplography need not be identical, only similar. Thus the omission of the word כן *(kn)* at 2 Samuel 18:20, a mistake recognized by the Masoretes, occurred because it sat immediately to the right of the word בן *(bn),* which resembles it closely.

MT *(Qere)* כי על כן בן המלך מת

MT *(Kethiv)* כי על בן המלך מת

The scribe skipped over כן and continued right along, as though nothing had happened. This sort of visual misjudgment, mistaking one letter or word for another, is called "graphic confusion." Note that it is equally possible that בן could have been left out and כן preserved. The result depended on the precise moment at which the scribe's eye moved ahead. In this case, it did so *before* he wrote the first letter. Had he succumbed to *parablepsis after* he transcribed the *ken,* then the word בן would have disappeared. When the first occurrence of the repeated element is omitted, we call it "anterior exclusion"; when a subsequent occurrence of the repeated element is omitted, we use the phrase "posterior exclusion." In the above example, there is a clear case of anterior exclusion, but it is only discernible because the repetition of letters is inexact. In most cases, one cannot determine which occurrence of the repeated segment has been left out, because the repetition is identical and there is no indication of the precise spot within the sequence where the scribe's eye skipped ahead.

In the types of haplography considered thus far, losses are restricted to members of a repeated sequence. An omission of this sort is reclaimable, since a representative reading still exists in the text. The third and final form of haplography is more damaging for the following reason: identical or similar elements are not always consecutive. Sometimes two similar segments may have material between them. In such scenarios, the copyist, when his eye is somewhere in the trigger sequence, skips ahead to the repetition of that sequence and fails to copy whatever happens to lie in between. The intervening material consists of unrepeated elements, which makes the loss beyond recall unless an unaffected manuscript can be found. However, this error may still be considered a form of haplography, since a geminate element is involved and is only written once in the finished text. We call this "concomitant haplography," because a portion of text accompanies one of the repeated elements into oblivion.

Repetitions may be short or long, ranging from a single letter to a lengthy phrase. The longer the repetition, the more likely that an error will occur. *Homoiologon* and *homoiogrammaton* may come into play in these situations, but there are other forms of homoiography, too. *Homoioarkton* describes a situation in which two words have a similar beginning, and the repetition may consist of one or more letters. To illustrate an omission caused by *homoioarkton,* we might refer to Ruth 3:17, where the Masoretes noted a missing word in the phrase כי אמר אל תבואי ("because he said, "Don't come ... "). The proper reading, as indicated in the margin, is כי אמר אלי אל תבואי ("because he said to me, "Don't come . . . "). The *homoioarkton* is seen in the words אלי and אל; they both begin with the same two letters *(aleph-lamed)*. *Parablepsis* occurred as a result of the repetition, and everything between the two *aleph-lamed* clusters (in this case, a *yod*), plus one of the geminate elements, was lost.

When two words have a similar ending, we dub this *homoioteleuton.* It instigates haplography in much the same way as *homoioarkton* and may also include one or more letters. An omission caused by *homoioteleuton* is seen at Jeremiah 31:38 in the Masoretic Text. The phrase should read הנה ימים באים נאם יהוה, but the word באים was lost in transmission. The Masoretes recognized the error and made a note in the margin. The *homoioteleuton* is seen in the words ימים and באים; they both have the same two final letters *(yod-mem)*. The copyist's eye jumped from one *yod-mem* to the next, omitting one of the geminate elements and the intervening letters.[2]

Sometimes *homoioarkton* and *homoioteleuton* work in conjunction with one another or with *homoiologon,* or they may not fit a given circumstance at all. It has been common among scholars to attribute every given instance of haplography either to *homoioarkton* or *homoioteleuton,* even when the repeated sequence includes whole words. Their reasoning is that the definitions can be expanded to apply not only to *words* with similar beginnings and endings but also to *phrases* with similar beginnings and endings. Here is an example:

Lev 4:25
MT על קרנת מזבח העלה ואת דמו ישפך אל יסוד מזבח העלה ואת כל חלבו
CG על קרנת מזבח העלה ואת כל חלבו

The reading of the Cairo Genizah appears to have suffered an omission. The repeated element is made up of three words: מזבח העלה ואת. The manner in which the variant readings are presented above would seem to indicate that the first occurrence of מזבח העלה ואת was left out while the second was retained (anterior exclusion). Some might perceive this as a case of *homoioarkton,* i.e., מזבח העלה ואת occurs at the beginning of the phrase מזבח העלה ואת דמו ישפך אל יסוד and at the beginning of the phrase מזבח העלה ואת כל חלבו. However, the variants could also be presented in this manner:

MT על קרנת מזבח העלה ואת דמו ישפך אל יסוד מזבח העלה ואת כל חלבו
CG על קרנת מזבח העלה ואת כל חלבו

The readings of the witnesses are no different here, but now it would seem that the second occurrence of מזבח העלה ואת was left out while the first was retained (posterior exclusion). Thus we might attribute the omission to *homoioteleuton,* i.e., מזבח העלה ואת occurs at the end of the phrase על קרנת מזבח העלה ואת and at the end of the phrase דמו ישפך אל יסוד מזבח העלה ואת. The error could be charted several other ways as well, and our view depends on which words we choose to place on either side of the gap. The fact is that we do not know precisely where the scribe's eye skipped ahead. Was it somewhere in the word מזבח? Or was it in העלה or ואת? *Parablepsis* may have occurred at any one of the eleven letters in these three words. We thus see that however useful the terms *homoioarkton* and *homoioteleuton* may be, on their own they are insufficient to describe every encountered situation. We therefore have opted to add the technical term *homoiologon* to our vocabulary, as indicated above. In this case we have a repetition of three complete words, so we may attribute the omission to triple *homoiologon*. Semantics aside, the important part of the analysis is to ascertain the number of repeated letters, so that we may identify the trigger sequence and its length. The longer the repetition, the more likely that it would have caused haplography.

Other forms of accidental omission are non-haplographic in nature. In other words, portions of a text may be left out, even when there is no obvious repetition of letters. There are many examples of this sort of error in the Great Isaiah Scroll. In a future study we will explore this important subject in more detail. For now, we will concentrate only on omissions for which we are able to find a graphic rationale. Fortunately, haplography often leaves fingerprints.

So far, the only representative illustrations of haplography we have provided have been from the Dead Sea Isaiah Scroll, which exhibits unmistakable signs of scribal error, from the Cairo Genizah texts, which were deemed inappropriate for use in the synagogue for one reason or other, or from places in the Masoretic Text where the Masoretes duly noted the discrepant reading. The truth is, in every manuscript there are many instances of accidental omission that were never noticed by the scribes who copied them or recognized by others afterward. The Received Text is no exception. It too has suffered losses. What is surprising about haplography is how widespread it is. Even the most careful scribes were subject to it. No section of text—no matter how important—is immune from its touch. Ironically, many modern biblical scholars still have a tendency to prefer shorter readings and attribute longer ones to scribal expansions, *even when there is evidence of haplography.* We must keep in mind that, where there is an indication of accidental omission, the longer, not the shorter, text is preferable. However, in order to make our point clear, we have decided to examine a biblical text and its transcriptional history. The first creation account (Gen 1:1–2:3) makes an excellent case study, as its formulaic structure and repetitions are a breeding ground for *parablepsis.* An examination of the text will reveal a considerable number of variations attributable to haplography in the Masoretic recension, most of which have remained unacknowledged by modern scholarship. We encourage you to use the accompanying charts for easy reference (see pp. 288–99).

TEXTUAL ANALYSIS: GENESIS 1

GENESIS 1:5

We'll begin with a small example—what appears to be the accidental omission of a single letter in the accepted text. In Genesis 1:5, the word יום ("day") in MT and SP is spelled יומם ("daytime") in 4QGen[g]. James Davila attributes the latter reading to dittography of the *mem*.[3] Ronald Hendel suggests either dittography or explication.[4] Explication can be ruled out in favor of a mechanical error. However, even though an error of dittography is a strong possibility here, it is not the only explanation. Surely יומם could represent the original reading, and יום could be the result of a haplographic loss when a copyist skipped from the first *mem* to the second.[5] (See table H1.)

GENESIS 1:6–7

An interesting variant is found between the Masoretic Text and the Septuagint with regard to the second day of creation. The typical formulaic phrase ויהי כן ("and it became so") appears at the end of verse 7 in the Hebrew version but at the end of verse 6 in the Greek. The reading of the Greek tradition is consistent with the order of events on the other creative days, while that of MT is not. Because the Masoretic Text has the more difficult reading, many have concluded that it represents the archetype.[6] However, the placement of ויהי כן at the end of verse 7 makes no sense, and no convincing explanation has been given as to why the author would have put the phrase there, particularly when it is at variance with his established modus operandi and disturbs the flow of the discourse.[7] LXX's testimony, therefore, is to be preferred here. How, though, can the difference between the versions be explained? The most reasonable conclusion is that ויהי כן originally appeared at the end of verse 6 in the earliest sources but during copying was repeated at the end of verse 7 by an error of dittography. It may be significant that some Greek cursive manuscripts contain the formula at the end of *both* verses. Some time during MT's transcriptional history, the ויהי כן at the end of verse 6 was lost by an error of omission. A scribe's eye accidentally skipped from the *waw-yod* of ויהי to the *waw-yod* of ויעש (a *homoioarkton* of two letters), and he failed to copy the phrase in question. (See table H2.)

Genesis 1:8

The frequency of a *waw-yod* combination at the beginning of words greatly encouraged *parablepsis,* and we see its pernicious product again in verse 8. The LXX preserves the familiar phrase וירא אלהים כי טב ("and God saw that it was good") immediately before the evening-morning formula. MT does not contain the clause. The two-letter *homoioarkton* caused the copyist's eye to skip ahead (from וירא to ויהי), and the phrase was lost. Hendel argues that the reading in LXX is a harmonizing addition, because he envisions the author using the formula only seven times, including all variations.[8] To limit the repetitions to this number because of some preconceived notion about number play is unwise. After all, there are *eight* acts of creation. We would expect a וירא אלהים כי טב formula (or one of its variations) to coincide with each one of them.[9] (See table H3.)

Genesis 1:9

In verse 9, we find an omission of eight words in MT. Both the Septuagint and 4QGen[k] give evidence of a lengthy clause reading ויקוו המים מתחת השמים אל מקויהם ותראה היבשה ("and the waters under the skies were collected into their collections, and the dry ground became visible") immediately before ויקרא אלהים, but MT, 4QGen[b], and SP do not. There can be little doubt that a three-letter *homoioarkton (waw-yod-qoph)* is responsible for the shorter reading.[10] (See table H4.)

Genesis 1:11

Although it is not a clear-cut case, haplography seems to have occurred in verse 11. The Hebrew source of the LXX apparently read למינהו ("according to its kind") immediately after the words אשר זרעו בו ("the seed of which is in it"). Now, it is true that the Greek has more than one κατα γενος that does not appear in MT, and dittography may be responsible for some of these; however, in this instance, there is a rationale for the variant. Three consecutive words—זרעו, בו, and למינהו—all end with a *waw,* so single-letter *homoioteleuton* may have caused *parablepsis.* (See table H5.)

Genesis 1:14

Verse 14 is very tricky, and we need to ascertain the true Greek reading before we can evaluate MT. There is some disagreement among the versions as to what words follow Γενηθητωσαν φωστηρες εν τω στερεωματι του ουρανου ("Let luminaries come to be in the firmament of the skies"). Note the variations:

1. εις φαυσιν της γης	A D M e h j q Ath ½
2. εις φαυσιν επι της γης	a b c d f g i k l m o p s t u v w x y z a_2 b_2 c_2 d_2 arm Theoph Ath ½ Chr Thd Cyr
3. εις φωτισμον της γης	v (in margin)
4. ωστε φαινειν επι της γης	E n eth(uid) aram Or-lat Eus Thd-syr de-P-C
5. εις φαυσιν της ημερας του φαινειν επι της γης	R

If we had a corresponding clause in the Hebrew, it would be much simpler to ascertain the correct reading. MT, however, lacks the difficult phrase altogether. SP has להאיר על הארץ ("to shine upon the earth") in this spot, which would seem to parallel reading #4 in the above chart (or the second half of reading #5). However, the majority of the Greek versions favor φαυσιν (Heb. למאורת) over φαινειν (Heb. להאיר). A simple explanation is that reading #5 is the original reading and that early in the Greek manuscript history a copyist skipped from της to της *(homoiologon),* thereby creating the new wording εις φαυσιν της γης (reading #1). In another tradition, a two-letter *homoioteleuton* instigated a skip from φαυσιν to φαινειν, resulting in a phrase reading εις φαυσιν επι της γης (reading #2). (See table G20.) True, only a single cursive manuscript attests to the longer reading, but sometimes obscure texts of this sort represent early forms, particularly if they originated in remote or impoverished communities that had no other comparable manuscripts at their disposal. If our hypothesis is correct, a manuscript in the proto-SP tradition originally would have read למאורת היום להאיר על הארץ ("for the illumination of the day, to shine upon the earth") and subsequently suffered a haplographic loss. The string of short phrases beginning with *lamed* made the chance of *parablepsis* quite high. In this case, the guilty *lameds* were in the words למאורת and להאיר (single-letter *homoioarkton*). Further encouraging the error is a single-letter *homoioteleuton* (the *mems* at the ends of השמים and היום). Thus we have a repetition of two consecutive letters (–ם ל-) that may be responsible for the scribal error in SP. (See table H6.)

A second clause in verse 14, also missing from MT and immediately following the last clause, appears in several witnesses of LXX. The wording corresponds to Hebrew ולממשלת היום והלילה ("and for the domination of the day and the night"). Its lack in SP is easily explained as haplography caused by the repetition of *waw-lamed* (two-letter *homoioarkton*). MT is lacking the entire phrase למאורת היום להאיר על הארץ ולממשלת היום והלילה ו- due to a scribal slip from the *lamed* in למאורת to the *lamed* in [ו]להבדיל (single-letter *homoioarkton*). There is no need, therefore, to resort to a theory based on scribal harmonization to explain the variants. (See table H6.)

Genesis 1:20–21

In LXX, we find evidence of another ויהי כן in verse 20 that is not in MT or SP. We would naturally expect the formula to appear in this position, and a double-letter *homoioarkton* (*waw-yod* in ויהי and ויברא) urges us to accept the longer reading (cf. analysis of Genesis 1:6–7 above).[11] (See table H7.)

Genesis 1:24

In verse 24, a longer reading is preserved in a number of Greek manuscripts that we feel is original. The words και τα κτηνη κατα γενος και παντα τα ερπετα της γης κατα γενος ("and the domestic animal according to its kind, and everything that crawls on the earth according to its kind") or portions thereof may easily have dropped out of some manuscripts accidentally. A quintuple *homoiologon* instigated the omission in most cases (see table G32). Similarly, MT's loss of the corresponding Hebrew phrase והבהמה למינה וכל הרמש האדמה למינה can be explained by a *homoiologon* plus a single-letter *homoioarkton* (למנהו ו- / למנהו ו-). (See table H8.) With the lost phrase restored, a greater correspondence exists between verse 24 and verse 25. Although the expression בהמה ורמש already appears in verse 24 of MT, its appearance does not preclude the existence of the restored fragment, since רמש and בהמה are being used in an appositional sense to modify נפש חיה and therefore take on a slightly different meaning than they do in the missing clause. They refer to the two main types of land animals—walkers and crawlers. That each occurrence of בהמה has a different meaning in this verse is seen in the Greek, where it is translated τετραποδα the first time and κτηνη the second. As it stands, MT only preserves one of the three animal types created in verse 25. The other two have probably fallen out. This section of the text is filled with all sorts of repetition, and whole-word repetitions all but guarantee *parablepsis* on the part of a careless scribe.

Genesis 1:26

The difficult reading ובכל הארץ (verse 26) in all manuscripts may be the result of *parablepsis* caused by single-letter *homoioarkton* (ח and ה) in an early period of transmission. The omission of the word חית is probable, considering the immediate context of the phrase. (See table H9.)

Genesis 1:26–27

At the end of verse 26, we are surprised not to find another ויהי כן. Could it be that the formula was lost through haplography? A two-letter *homoioarkton (waw-yod)* could have caused it. (See table H10.) There is a twelfth-century Greek manuscript that contains the expected reading. Whether or not it is a survival of an uncorrupted text is difficult to determine; a repetition of five letters (-ς και ε-) could easily have produced an omission in the Greek (της γης και εγενετο ουτως και εποιησεν > της γης και εποιησεν). However, the weight of the manuscript evidence is against it. If the phrase was lost through haplography, then it must have occurred at a very early date. (See table G37.)

Genesis 1:28

LXX and MT differ considerably in verse 28, the former giving a longer list of creatures over which the humans were to have dominion. In typical fashion, Ronald Hendel interprets the Greek version as a harmonizing addition.[12] However, we feel the differences are best explained as the result of accidental omission. The repetition of the word ובכל *(homoiologon)* is to blame for MT's lack of the phrase ובכל בבהמה immediately before ובכל היה. The next animal listed is not fully preserved in either LXX or MT, but a comparison of the two texts seems to indicate an original that read ובכל צית הארץ (as in verses 25 and 30). In LXX's Hebrew source, a single letter *homoioarkton* instigated the omission of the word חית (cf. analysis of Genesis 1:26 above). In MT, the word הארץ was omitted, along with the words ובכל הרמש (as preserved in the LXX's source), when a scribe's eye jumped from the *hê* in הארש to the *hê* in הרמשת (single letter *homoioarkton*). Sometime later, the awkward reading ובכל חית הרמשת was "corrected" to ובכל חיה הרמשת by a scribe who was unaware of the haplography. (See table H12.)

Genesis 1:30

In verse 30, MT appears to be missing the word רמש before the word רומש, as is indicated by the testimony of LXX. The shorter reading can be explained as the result of *parablepsis* caused by the repetition of the letter *resh* (single-letter *homoioarkton*). However, it is more likely that the mistake was made in early times, when both words were still written defective. In that case, *homoiologon* would have been responsible for the error (רמש / רמש). (See table H13.)

Conclusion

While from ancient times there has been an excessive or inordinate regard for the received Hebrew text, as though it somehow escaped the pitfalls that other manuscripts experienced, it is readily apparent that it, too, was affected by the imperfection of the individuals who copied it. True, in later times, the Masoretes were quite meticulous, but this is not to say that they were perfect or that the manuscripts they received were devoid of error.[13] No text is *the* text. We can only approximate the true biblical text by studying its history, by comparing the many variants, and, most important, by fully understanding the nature of transcriptional error. We believe that, although haplography is recognized conceptually by all textual critics, when it comes to the analysis of specific passages, it is largely dismissed. This attitude is understandable—as appeal to mechanical errors does not allow a biblical scholar to realize his full potential as an original thinker and theorist—but is it wise? Because of the prevalence of mistakes in every known manuscript, we feel that due consideration should be given to the possibility of scribal oversight when explaining a variant *before* resorting to any theory based on intentional alteration.

In his book on textual criticism, P. Kyle McCarter defends the principle that *shorter* readings are preferable by taking the stance that many have taken in the past, namely, that expansions are very common. However, while we do have evidence that certain explicative glosses have been added to various parts of the text, the number of additions is not easily determinable. The view that there are so many of them that we must accept the shorter reading as a matter of principle cannot be upheld. McCarter, perhaps too incautiously, justifies shorter readings by appealing to the argument that "the ancient scribes were careful to reproduce their texts fully" and that "in their concern to preserve the text they were reluctant to omit anything."[14] We agree that this is what the ancient copyists had every intention of doing, but did they always succeed? The evidence indicates that, although they tried hard to avoid making mistakes, mistakes were nevertheless made. Moreover, while McCarter acknowledges that "where haplography—or any accident that shortens the text—is suspected, the shorter reading may not be superior,"[15] his prime example illustrating the superiority of the shorter reading (Joshua 4:5a) exhibits clear signs of haplography:

MT	ויאמר להם יהושע עברו לפני ארון יהוה אלהיכם אל תוך הירדן
LXX^H	ויאמר להם עברו לפני לפני יהוה אל תוך הירדן

The word אלהיכם—"your God"—is not, as McCarter asserts, a simple expansion in MT. On the contrary, the word was left out in LXX^H because the repetition of the letters *aleph-lamed* (two-letter *homoioarkton*) encouraged *parablepsis.* The word "the ark" probably fell out in Greek due to a two-letter *homoioteleuton* (προσωπου του κιβωτου κυριου > προσωπου κυριου). The second לפני in LXX is either the result of dittography, or, more probably, MT lost it through haplography *(homoiologon).*[16] Finally, the subject, Joshua, was lost in Greek because of a single-letter *homoioteleuton* (αυτοις Ιησους Προσαγαγετε > αυτοις Προσαγαγετε). We do not see any signs of deliberate expansion. The longer reading is preferable here, and with the second לפני, it would be even longer.

Emmanuel Tov rightly calls into question the rule that the shorter reading is better and highlights its impracticality.[17] Since the principle does not take into account accidental omissions, it cannot be used without justification. We urge biblical scholars to avoid appealing to this rule when choosing the shorter reading. Any preference should be defended with the usual scholarly tools. Furthermore, mechanical errors, particularly errors of omission, must be given greater consideration in textual analysis, not least when dealing with the Masoretic recension.

Abbreviations and Signs

MT	Masoretic Text (citations are from the St. Petersburg [Leningrad] Codex, reproduced in Freedman et al., eds., *The Leningrad Codex: A Facsimile Edition* [Grand Rapids: Eerdmans, 1998])
LXX	The Greek Septuagint (the major edition used here is Alan Brooke and Norman McLean, *The Old Testament in Greek: Genesis* [Cambridge: Cambridge Univ. Press, 1906])
LXX^{H}	Hebrew retrotranslation from the Greek
A	Codex Alexandrinus
D	Codex Cottonianus (*D* = Grabe's collation)
E	Codex Bodleianus
M	Codex Coslinianus
U$_2$	Amherst Papyri
a	Paris, Bibl. Nat., Coislin Gr. 2
b	Rome, Chigi, R. vi. 38
c	Escurial, Y. II. 5
d	Zittau, A. I. 1
e	Florence, Laur., Acq. 44
f	Paris, Bibl. Nat., Reg. Gr. 17^{a}

g	Paris, Bibl. Nat., Reg. Gr. 5
h	Rome, Vat., Regin. Gr. 1
i	Paris, Bibl. Nat., Reg. Gr. 3
j	Rome, Vat., Gr. 747
l	Glasgow, Univ. Libr., BE. 7^b. 10
m	Oxford, Bodl., Canon. Gr. 35
n	Oxford, Bodl., Univ. Coll. 52
o	Paris, Bibl. Nat., Coislin Gr. 3
p	Ferrara, Bibl. Com., Gr. 187
q	Venice, St. Mark's, Gr. 4
r	Rome, Vat., Gr. 1252
s	Vienna, Imp. Libr., Theol. Gr. 1
t	Florence, Laur., v. 1
u	Jerusalem, Holy Sepulchre, 2
v	Athos, Pantocrator, 24
w	Athens, Bibl. Nat. 44
x	London, Brit. Mus., Curzon 66
y	Venice, St. Mark's, Gr. 3
z	Rome, Vat., Gr. 2058
a_2	St. Petersburg, Imp. Libr., 62
b_2	Venice, St. Mark's, Gr. 2
c_2	Bale, AN. III. 13 (Omont 1)
d_2	Oxford, Bodleian, Laud Gr. 36
14	Rome, Vat., Pal. Gr. 203
16	Florence, Laur., Plut. V 38
17	Moscow, S. Synod, Cod. gr. 385
71	Paris, Bibl. Nat., Reg. Gr. 1
73	Rome, Vat., Gr. 746
74	Florence, Laur., Aquisti da S. Marco 700
76	Paris, Bibl. Nat., Reg. Gr. 4
78	Rome, Vat., Gr. 383
79	Rome, Vat., Gr. 1668
83	Lisbon, Archivio da Torre do Tombo 540 ff.
107	Ferrara, Gr. 188
125	Moscow, S. Synod, Gr. 30
127	Moscow, S. Synod., Gr. 31
392	Grottaferrata, Bibl. della Badia, A. g. I.
508	Oxford, Bodl. Libr., F. 4. 32

509	Oxford, Bodl. Libr., T. 2. 1
527	Paris, Bibl. de l'Arsenal 8415
664	Rome, Vat., Pii II 20
707	Sinai, Cod. Gr. 1; Leningrad, Gr. 260
730	Venice, St. Mark's, Gr. 15
Ath	Athanasius
Chr	John Chrysostom
CyrJ	Cyril of Jerusalem
Eus	Eusebius
Heb	Letter to the Hebrews (NT)
Or	Origen (Or-gr = works extant in Greek; Or-lat = works extant only in Latin)
Phil	Philo
Sev	Severianus Gabalitanus
Thdt	Theodoret
Theoph	Theophilus
arm	Armenian version
bo	Bohairic version
eth	Ethiopic version
aram	Palestinian Aramaic version
de-P-C	De Pascha Computus
Hil	Hilary (Latin)
Iren	Irenaeus (Latin)
Thd-syr	works of Theodore of Mopsuestia extant in Syriac
DSS	Dead Sea Scrolls (4QGen^{b-k} are cited from *editio princeps* by James R. Davila in *Qumran Cave 4, Vol. VII: Genesis to Numbers* [Discoveries in the Judaean Desert 12; Oxford: Clarendon, 1994: 31–78])
SP	Samaritan Pentateuch (citations are from L.F. Giron Blanc, ed., *Pentateuco Hebreo-Samaritano: Genesis. Edición crítica sobre la base de Manuscritos inéditos* [Madrid: Instituto Arias Montano, 1976])
Codd	two or more manuscripts
ed	according to the text of the edition used
uid	*ut uidetur*
⅓	one out of three occurrences
*	original writing of a scribe
]	separates word in text (to the left) from a variant (to the right)
#	fragmentary reading

Notes

1. Jacob Weingreen, *Introduction to the Critical Study of the Text of the Hebrew Bible* (Oxford: Clarendon, 1982), 59–60.

2. See P. Kyle McCarter Jr., *Textual Criticism: Recovering the Text of the Hebrew Bible* (Philadelphia: Fortress, 1986), 40. Jacob Weingreen attributes the error to *homoiologon* (באם / נאם) at a time before medial vowels were added, with graphic confusion between the *nun* and the *bet,* 61–62 (see also footnote in *BHS*).

3. James R. Davila, "New Qumran Readings for Genesis One," in *Of Scribes and Scrolls: Studies on the Hebrew Bible, Intertestamental Judaism, and Christian Origins,* eds. Harold W. Attridge, John J. Collins, and Thomas H. Tobin (Lanham, Md.: University Press of America, 1990), 5–6; *Discoveries in the Judean Desert* XII (1994), 59.

4. Ronald S. Hendel, *The Text of Genesis 1–11: Textual Studies and Critical Edition* (New York: Oxford Univ. Press, 1998), 120.

5. Interestingly, several Aramaic targums and the Syriac version contain the reading with the extra *mem.* They testify to the use of יומם also at Genesis 1:14, 16, and 18. Whether 4QGen[g] carried the same spelling in these instances, however, cannot be determined, since that part of the text is not preserved.

6. See John W. Wevers, *Notes on the Greek Text of Genesis* (Atlanta: Scholars Press, 1993), 5; Hendel, *The Text of Genesis 1–11,* 20–22.

7. True, it is well within the writer's style to create slight variations in his pattern—but never at the expense of precision and intelligibility.

8. Hendel, *The Text of Genesis 1–11,* 23–24.

9. On the significance of the number eight, see David N. Freedman, *Psalm 119: The Exaltation of Torah* (Winona Lake, Ind.: Eisenbrauns, 1999), 28–29.

10. On this point, both Davila ("New Qumran Readings," 9–11) and Hendel (*The Text of Genesis 1–11,* 25–27) agree.

11. We are confused by Hendel's statement that "there is no obvious motive, either accidental or intentional, for a scribe to omit ויהי כן on the fifth day" (*The Text of Genesis 1–11,* 22). *Homoioarkton* is readily apparent.

12. Hendel, *The Text of Genesis 1–11,* 30–31.

13. Emmanuel Tov, *Textual Criticism of the Hebrew Bible* (Minneapolis: Fortress, 1992), 8–12; Hendel, *The Text of Genesis 1–11,* 3–5; McCarter, *Textual Criticism,* 13–15.

14. McCarter, *Textual Criticism,* 73.

15. Ibid., 74.

16. LXX indicates a reading where they were vocalized differently (לְפָנַי לִפְנֵי).

17. Tov, *Textual Criticism,* 305–7.

VARIANT READINGS OF GENESIS 1:1-2:3 IN HEBREW SHOWING POSSIBLE INSTANCES OF HAPLOGRAPHY

(H1) 1:5

אלהים לאור יומם ולחשך	4QGen^{g}
אלהים לאור יו ם ולחשך	MT SP

MT SP=*homoiogrammaton* (מ/מ)

(H2) 1:6

מים למים ויהי כן ויעש אלהים	LXX^{H}
מים למים ויעש אלהים	MT SP 4Qgen

MT SP 4QGen=*homoioarkton* (-וי/-וי)

(H3) 1:8

לרקיע שמים וירא אלהים כי טוב ויהי ערב	LXX^{H}
לרקיע שמים ויהי ערב	MT SP 4QGen

MT SP 4QGen=*homoioarkton* (-וי/-וי)

(H4) 1:9

ויהי כן ויקוו המים מתחת השמים אל מקויהם ותראה היבשה ויקרא אלהים	LXX^{H} 4QGen$^{k\#}$
ויהי כן ויקרא אלהים	MT SP 4QGen^{bg}

MT SP 4QGen^{bg}=*homoioarkton* (-ויק/-ויק)

(H5) 1:11

אשר זרעו בו למינהו על הארץ	LXX^{H}
אשר זרעו בו על הארץ	MT SP 4Qgen

MT SP 4QGen=*homoioteleuton* (-ו/-ה)

(H6) 1:14

השמים למאורת היום להאיר על הארץ ולממשלת היום והלילה ולהבדיל	LXX^{H}
השמים להאיר על הארץ ולהבדיל	SP
השמים להבדיל	MT

SP=*homoioteleuton+homoioarkton* (-ם ל/-ם ל-) and *homoioarkton* (-ול/-ול)|MT=*homoioarkton* (-ל/-ל)

(H7) 1:20-21

LXX^{H}	רקיע השמים ויהי כן ויברא אלהים
MT SP	רקיע השמים ויברא אלהים

MT SP=*homoioarkton* (-וי/-וי)

(H8) 1:24

LXX^{H}	נפש היה למינה בהמה ורמש וחית הארץ למינה והבהמה למינה וכל הרמש האדמה למינה ויהי כן
SP	נפש היה למינה בהמה ורמש וחית הארץ למינה ויהי כן
MT	נפש היה למינה בהמה ורמש וחיתו ארץ למינה ויהי כן

SP MT=*homoiologon+homoioarkton* (למינה ו-/למינה ו-)

(H9) 1:26

proposed original reading	ובבהמה ובכל חית הארץ ובכל הרמש
MT LXX^{H} SP	ובבהמה ובכל הארץ ובכל הרמש

MT LXX^{H} SP=*homoioarkton* (-ח/-ה)

(H10) 1:26-27

LXX^{H}	על הארץ ויהי כן ויברא אלהים
MT SP	על הארץ ויברא אלהים

MT SP=*homoioarkton* (-וי/-וי)

(H11) 1:27

MT	ויברא אלהים את האדם בצלמו בצלם אלהים ברא אתו
LXX^{H}	ויברא אלהים את האדם בצלם אלהים ברא אתו

LXX^{H}=*homoioarkton* (בצלם-/בצלם)

(H12) 1:28

ובעוף השמים ובכל בבהמה ובכל חית הארץ ובכל הרמש הרמשת על הארץ	proposed original reading
ובעוף השמים ובכל בבהמה ובכל הארץ ובכל הרמש הרמשת על הארץ	LXX[H]
ובעוף השמים ובכל חיה הרמשת על הארץ	MT

LXX[H]=*homoioarkton* (-ה/-ח)|MT=*homoiologon* (ובכל/ובכל) and *homoioarkton* (-ה/-ה)

(H13) 1:30

ולכל רמש רמש על הארץ	LXX[H]
ולכל רמש על הארץ	MT
ולכל הרמש על הארץ	SP

MT=*homoiologon* (רמש/רמש)| SP=*homoioteleuton* (-רמש/רמש)or *homoiologon* (הרמש/הרמש)

Leningrad word count = 469
Reconstructed original word count = 509
40 missing words from Leningrad codex (7.8%)

VARIANT READINGS IN THE GREEK VERSIONS OF GENESIS 1:1-2:3 SHOWING POSSIBLE INSTANCES OF HAPLOGRAPHY

(G1) 1:3

Γενηθητω φως και εγενετο φως και ιδεν	common reading
Γενηθητω φως και ιδεν	q*

q*=*double homoiologon* (φως και/φως και)

(G2) 1:4

και ιδεν ο θεος το φως οτι καλον	common reading
και ιδεν ο θεος οτι καλον	b 125 664 Eus

b Eus=*homoioteleuton* (-ς/-ς)

(G3) 1:4-5

του σκοτους και εκαλεσεν ο θεος το φως ημεραν και το σκοτος εκαλεσεν νυκτα και εγενετο	common reading
του σκοτους και εγενετο	U_2

U_2=*homoiologon*+*homoioarkton* (και ε-/και ε-)

(G4) 1:6-7

του υδατος και εστω διαχωριζον ανα μεσον υδατος και υδατος και εγενετο ουτως και εποιησεν	common reading
του υδατος και εστω διαχωριζον ανα μεσον υδατος και εγενετο ουτως και εποιησεν	eth
του υδατος και εγενετο ουτως και εποιησεν	w 664
του υδατος και εστω διαχωριζον ανα μεσον υδατος και υδατος και εποιησεν	i

eth=*double homoiologon* (υδατος και/υδατος και)|w=*double homoiologon*+*homoioarkton* (υδατος και ε-/υδατος και ε-)|i[b]=*homoioteleuton*+*homoiologon*+*homoioarkton* (-ς και ε-/-ς και ε-)

(G5) 1:6-7

και εγενετο ουτως και εποιησεν ο θεος το στερεωμα και διεχωρισεν	common reading
και εγενετο ουτως και διεχωρισεν	e*

e*=*homoiologon* (και/και)

(G6) 1:7

το στερεωμα και διεχωρισεν ο θεος ανα μεσον του υδατος ο ην υποκατω του στερεωματος και ανα	common reading
το στερεωμα και ανα	m

m=*homoiologon* (και/και)

(G7) 1:7-8

υποκατω του στερεωματος και ανα μεσον του υδατος του επανω του στερεωματος	και εκαλεσεν	common reading
υποκατω του στερεωματος	και εκαλεσεν	664

664=*homoioteleuton+double homoiologon* (-ω του στερεωματος/-ω του στερεωματος)

(G8) 1:8

το στερεωμα ουρανον και ιδεν ο θεος οτι καλον	και εγενετο	common reading
το στερεωμα ουρανον	και εγενετο	y* arm-codd

y* arm-codd=*homoioteleuton+homoiologon* (-ον και/-ον και)

(G9) 1:8

οτι καλον και εγενετο εσπερα	και εγενετο πρωι	common reading
οτι καλον	και εγενετο πρωι	664 707

664 707=*double homoiologon* (και εγενετο/και εγενετο)

(G10) 1:9

συναχθητω το υδωρ το υποκατω του ουρανου εις συναγωγην... συνηχθη	το υδωρ το υποκατω του ουρανου εις τας	comn reading
συναχθητω	το υδωρ το υποκατω του ουρανου εις τας	392

392=*septuple homoiologon* (το υδωρ το υποκατω του ουρανου εις/το υδωρ το υποκατω του ουρανου εις)

(G11) 1:9

εις τας	συναγωγας	common reading
εις	συναγωγας	107*

107=*homoioteleuton* (-ς/-ς)

(G12) 1:9-10

η ξηρα και εγενετο ουτως και συνηχθη ... και ωφθη η ξηρα	και εκαλεσεν	common reading
η ξηρα και εγενετο ουτως	και εκαλεσεν	i
η ξηρα	και εκαλεσεν	n

i=*homoiologon* (και/και)|n=*triple homoiologon+homoioarkton* (η ξηρα και ε-/η ξηρα και ε-)

(G13) 1:11

σπειρον σπερμα	κατα γενος	και καθ ομοιοτητα	και ξυλον	common reading
σπειρον σπερμα		και καθ ομοιοτητα	και ξυλον	Eus $^1/_3$
σπειρον σπερμα	κατα γενος		και ξυλον	Eus $^2/_3$ Cyr-hier-codd

Eus $^1/_3$=*homoioarkton* (κα-/κα-)|Eus $^2/_3$ Cyr-hier-codd=*homoioarkton* (και/και)

(G14) 1:11

ποιουν καρπον	κατα γενος αυτον	ου το σπερμα αυτου	78
ποιουν καρπον		ου το σπερμα αυτου	Common reading

common reading=*homoioteleuton* (-ον/-ον)

(G15) 1:11

το σπερμα αυτου	εν αυτω	κατα γενος	εις ομοιοτητα	επι της γης και	A 16 730
το σπερμα αυτου		κατα γενος	εις ομοιοτητα	επι της γης και	q
το σπερμα αυτου	εν αυτω	κατα γενος		επι της γης και	b d f g i* m n p w y c_2 bo eth Or-gr Eus Chr-ed Thd-syr
το σπερμα αυτου	εν αυτω	κατα γενος		και	508

q=*homoiologon* (αυτου/αυτω)|b *et al*=*homoioarkton* (ε-/ε-)|508=*homoioteleuton* (-ς/-ς)

(G16) 1:11-12

επι της γης	και εγενετο ουτως και εξηνεγκεν ... κατα γενος επι της γης	και ιδεν	common reading
επι της γης		και ιδεν	b d

b d=*quadruple homoiologon* (επι της γης και/επι της γης και)

(G17) 1:12

κατα γενος	και καθ ομοιοτητα	και ξυλον	common reading
κατα γενος		και ξυλον	Theoph

Theoph=*homoiologon* (και/και)

(G18) 1:12

και ξυλον καρπιμον	ποιουν καρπον	ου το σπερμα αυτου	Common reading
και ξυλον καρπιμον		ου το σπερμα αυτου	i*

i*=*homoioteleuton* (-ον/-ον)

(G19) 1:12-13

και ιδεν ο θεος οτι καλον και εγενετο	common reading
και ιδεν ο θεος οτι και εγενετο	l*

l*=*homoioarkton* (κα-/κα-)

(G20) 1:14

του ουρανου εις φαυσιν της ημερας του φαινειν επι της γης	R
του ουρανου εις φαυσιν της γης	A D M e h j q Ath ½
του ουρανου εις φαυσιν επι της γης	a b c d f g i k l m o p s t u v w x y z a_2 b_2 c_2 d_2 arm Theoph Ath½ Chr Thd Cyr

A *et al=homoiologon* (της/της)|a *et al=homoioteleuton* (-ιν/-ιν)

(G21) 1:14

της γης και αρχειν ... της νυκτος και διαχωριζειν ανα μεσον της ημερας και ανα μεσον της νυκτος και	A D n r
της γης και διαχωριζειν ανα μεσον της ημερας και ανα μεσον της νυκτος και	common reading
της γης και αρχειν ... της νυκτος και διαχωριζειν ανα μεσον της ημερας και	71
της γης και αρχειν ... της νυκτος και	l Ath½
της γης και αρχειν ... της νυκτος και διαχωριζειν ανα μεσον της νυκτος και	16
της γης και	Eus Ath½

common reading=*homoioteleuton+homoiologon* (-ς και/-ς και)|71=*homoioteleuton+homoiologon* (-ς και/-ς και)|Ath ½=*triple homoiologon* (της νυκτος και/της νυκτος και)|16=*triple homoiologon* (ανα μεσον της/ανα μεσον της)|l Eus Ath½=*homoioteleuton+homoiologon* (-ς και/-ς και)

(G22) 1:14-15

νυκτος και εστωσαν εις σημεια και εις καιρους και εις ημερας και εις ενιαυτους και εστωσαν εις φαυσιν	common reading
νυκτος και εστωσαν εις σημεια και εις καιρους και εις ημερας και ενιαυτους και εστωσαν εις φαυσιν	D 14 127 392
νυκτος και εστωσαν εις σημεια και εις καιρους και εις ενιαυτους και εστωσαν εις φαυσιν	346 Cyr-hier Hil
νυκτος και εστωσαν εις φαυσιν	d p 107 125

D 14 127 392=*homoioarkton* (ε-/ε-)|346 Cyr-hier Hil=*homoioteleuton+double homoiologon* (-ς και εις/-ς και εις)|d p 107 125=*homoioteleuton+triple homoiologon* (-ς και εστωσαν εις/-ς και εστωσαν εις)

(G23) 1:16

τον μεγαν εις αρχας της ημερας και τον φωστηρα τον ελασσω εις αρχας της νυκτος	common reading
τον μεγαν εις αρχας της νυκτος	n*

n*=*triple homoiologon* (εις αρχας της/εις αρχας της)

(G24) 1:16-18

της νυκτος και τους αστερας και εθετο αυτους ο θεος	εν ... της νυκτος	και διαχωριζειν	common reading
της νυκτος και τους αστερας και εθετο αυτους	εν ... της νυκτος	και διαχωριζειν	d p 125 527
της νυκτος		και διαχωριζειν	f

d p 125 527=*homoioteleuton* (-ς/-ς)|f=*triple homoiologon* (της νυκτος και/της νυκτος και)

(G25) 1-18-26

της ημερας	και της νυκτος ... οτι καλον	και ειπεν ο θεος	Common reading
της ημερας		και ειπεν ο θεος	73

73=*homoiologon* (και/και)

(G26) 1:20

τα υδατα	ερπετα	ψυχων ζωσων και πετεινα	common reading
τα υδατα		ψυχων ζωσων και πετεινα	B

b=*homoioteleuton* (-τα/-τα)

(G27) 1:20-21

του ουρανου	και εγενετο ουτως	και εποιησεν	common reading
του ουρανου		και εποιησεν	Chr

Chr=*homoiologon*+*homoioarkton* (και ε-/και ε-)

(G28) 1:21

υδατα κατα γενη αυτων	και παν	πετεινον	πτερωτον	κατα γενος	και ιδεν	common reading
υδατα κατα γενη αυτων	και	πετεινον	πτερωτον	κατα γενος	και ιδεν	Sev
υδατα κατα γενη αυτων	και παν	πετεινον		κατα γενος	και ιδεν	r bo
υδατα κατα γενη αυτων					και ιδεν	d g p

Sev=*homoioarkton* (π-/π-)|r bo=*homoioteleuton* (-ον/-ον)|d g p=*homoiologon* (και/και)

(G29) 1:22

τα μεγαλα	και πασαν ψυχην ζωων ερπετων α εξηγαγεν τα υδατα κατα γενη αυτων	και παν	common reading
τα μεγαλα		και παν	a 16 17 76

a 16 17 76=*homoiologon*+*homoioarkton* (και πα-/και πα-)

(G30) 1:22

επι της γης	common reading
επι γης	P

p=*homoiologon* (της/γης)

(G31) 1:24

κατα γενος και τα κτηνη και παντα τα ερπετα της γης κατα γενος τετραποδα	76
κατα γενος τετραποδα	common reading

common reading=*double homoiologon* (κατα γενος/κατα γενος)

(G32) 1:24

της γης κατα γενος και τα κτηνη κατα γενος και παντα τα ερπετα της γης κατα γενος και	d j n(ερπετα] τετραποδα)
της γης και τα κτηνη κατα γενος και παντα τα ερπετα της γης κατα γενος και	a b d h i o p t w c_2 d_2 Chr ½
της γης και παντα τα ερπετα της γης κατα γενος και	74
της γης κατα γενος και τα κτηνη κατα γενος και	83
της γης κατα γενος και	most others

a *et al*=*homoioteleuton*+*homoioarkton* (-ς κα-/-ς κα-)|74= *homoioteleuton*+*homoioarkton* (-ς κα-/-ς κα-)|83=*triple homoiologon* (κατα γενος και/κατα γενος και)|most others=*quintuple homoiologon* (της γης κατα γενος και/της γης κατα γενος και)

(G33) 1:24-25

θηρια της γης κατα γενος και εγενετο ... θηρια της γης κατα γενος και τα κτηνη κατα γενος και παντα	common reading
θηρια της γης κατα γενος και τα κτηνη κατα γενος και παντα	b
θηρια της γης κατα γενος και τα κτηνη και παντα	w
θηρια της γης κατα γενος και εγενετο ... θηρια της γης κατα γενος και παντα	E i l m d_2
θηρια της γης κατα γενος και παντα	aram

b w=*sextuple homoiologon* (θηρια της γης κατα γενος και/θηρια της γης κατα γενος και)|w=*homoioarkton* (κα-/κα-)|E *et al*=*triple homoiologon* (κατα γενος και/κατα γενος και)| aram=*triple homoiologon* (κατα γενος και/κατα γενος και)

(G34) 1:24-25

γενος και εγενετο ... κατα γενος και τα κτηνη κατα γενος και παντα ... της γης κατα γενος αυτων και ειδεν	cmn reading
γενος και εγενετο ... κατα γενος και τα κτηνη κατα γενος και παντα ... της γης και ειδεν	Theoph
γενος και εγενετο ... κατα γενος και ειδεν	d f n o p
γενος και εγενετο ... κατα γενος και τα κτηνη κατα γενος και ειδεν	e j y
γενος και ειδεν	g(spat relict)

Theoph=*homoioarkton* (κα-/κα-)|d f n o p=*homoiologon* (και/και)|e j y=*homoiologon* (και/και)|g=*homoiologon*+*homoioarkton* (και ε-/και ε-)

(G35) 1:25-26

αυτων	και ιδεν ο θεος οτι καλα	και ειπεν	common reading
αυτων		και ειπεν	74

74=*homoiologon* (και/και)

(G36) 1:26

του ουρανου	και των κτηνων και πασης της γης	και παντων	common reading
του ουρανου		και παντων	m

m=*homoiologon* (και/και)

(G37) 1:26-27

της γης	και παντων	των	ερπετων	των ερποντων επι της γης	και εγενετο ουτως	και εποιησεν	n 508
της γης	και παντων	των	ερπετων	των ερποντων επι της γης		και εποιησεν	common reading
της γης	και παντων		ερπετων	των ερποντων επι της γης		και εποιησεν	*D* (uid)
της γης	και παντων			των ερποντων επι της γης		και εποιησεν	Or-lat
της γης						και εποιησεν	f o c_2

common reading=*homoioteleuton*+*homoiologon*+*homoioarkton* (-ς και ε-/-ς και ε-)|D=*homoioteleuton* (-των/των)|Or-lat=*homoiologon* (των/των)|f o c_2=*homoioteleuton*+*homoiologon* (-ς και/-ς και)

(G38) 1:28

και ευλογησεν αυτους	ο θεος	λεγων	common reading
και ευλογησεν αυτους		λεγων	508

508=*homoioteleuton* (-ς/-ς)

(G39) 1:28

του ουρανου	και παντων των θηριων	και παντων των κτηνων	f m aram
του ουρανου		και παντων των κτηνων	common reading

common reading=*triple homoiologon* (και παντων των/και παντων των)

(G40) 1:28

των κτηνων	και πασης της γης	και παντων	των ερπετων	των ερποντων	common reading
των κτηνων		και παντων	των ερπετων	των ερποντων	q 509 eth aram
των κτηνων		και παντων		των ερποντων	E

q eth aram E=*homoiologon*+*homoioarkton* (και πα-/και πα-)|E=*homoiologon* (των/των)

(G41) 1:28-29

επι της γης και ειδεν οτι καλον	και ειπεν ο θεος Ιδου	1
επι της γης	και ειπεν ο θεος Ιδου	common reading
επι της γης	Ιδου	a

common reading=*homoiologon+homoioarkton* (και ει-/και ει-)|a=*homoioteleuton* (-ς/-ς)

(G42) 1:29

σποριμον σπειρον σπερμα ... σπερματος σποριμου	υμιν εσται	common reading
σποριμον σπειρον σπερμα ... σπερματος σποριμον	υμιν εσται	Thdt
σποριμον	υμιν εσται	1*

1*=*homoiologon* (σποριμον/σποριμου), or σποριμον/σποριμον – cf. Thdt

(G43) 1:30

της γης και πασι τοις πετεινοις του ουρανου	και παντι	Common reading
της γης	και παντι	N

n=*homoiologon+homoioarkton* (και πα-/και πα-)

(G44) 1:30

και παντα χορτον	χλωρον εις βρωσιν	common reading
και παντα	χλωρον εις βρωσιν	79

79=*homoioarkton* (χ-/χ-)

(G45) 1:30-31

βρωσιν και εγενετο ουτως	και ιδεν	common reading
βρωσιν	και ιδεν	127

127=*homoiologon* (και/και)

(G46) 2:1

συνετελεσθησαν ο ουρανος και		common reading
συνετελεσθησαν	ουρανος και	n*

n*=*homoioarkton* (ο/ο-)

(G47) 2:1

ο ουρανος και η γη και πας	common reading
ο ουρανος και πασαι	Phil-cod

Phil-cod=*homoiologon* (και/και)

(G48) 2:2

τα εργα αυτου α εποιησεν	common reading
τα εργα α εποιησεν	f m

f m=*homoioarkton* (α-/α)

(G49) 2:2

και κατεπαυσεν εν τη ημερα	M b e f g h j l m t u v w x c_2 Phil ½ Heb Theoph Or-gr ½ Or-lat Eus Chr ½ Thd Thdt Iren Hil
και κατεπαυσεν τη ημερα	most others

most others=*homoioteleuton* (-εν/εν)

(G50) 2:2

απο παντων των εργων αυτου ων	common reading
απο παντων εργων αυτου ων	F

f=*homoioteleuton* (-των/των)

(G51) 2:2-3

απο παντων των εργων αυτου ων εποιησεν και ηυλογησεν ... απο παντων των εργων αυτου ων ηρξατο	cmn reading
απο παντων των εργων αυτου ων ηρξατο	m

m=*sextuple homoiologon* (απο παντων των εργων αυτου ων/απο παντων των εργων αυτου ων)

(G52) 2:3

ο θεος την ημεραν την εβδομην και ηγιασεν αυτην οτι εν	Common reading
ο θεος την εβδομην και ηγιασεν αυτην οτι εν	73
ο θεος την ημεραν την εβδομην οτι εν	X

73=*homoiologon* (της/της)|x=*homoioteleuton* (-ην/-ην)

(G53) 2:3

απο παντων των εργων αυτου ων	common reading
απο παντων των αυτου ων	E

E=*homoioteleuton* (-ων/ων)

PART THREE

THE PRACTICE OF BIBLE TRANSLATION

13

AGUR'S APOLOGIA FOR VERBAL, PLENARY INSPIRATION: AN EXEGESIS OF PROVERBS 30:1–6[1]

Bruce K. Waltke

In this essay I aim to lay the epistemological foundation for Dr. Ronald Youngblood's outstanding scholarship and ministry as Bible translator, educator, and editor.[2] Professor Youngblood established his ministry on the conviction that the Bible is God's special revelation for humanity's salvation and that God inspired its words. The ancient sage Agur, probably a proselyte to Israel's faith, confesses that he, along with all humanity, could not find salvation apart from Israel's special revelation. In this essay I will first translate his confession, then exegete it—and in this way I hope to achieve my objective.

Translation: Proverbs 30:1–6

30:1 The sayings of Agur[3] son[4] of Jakeh.[5] An[6] oracle.[7]

The inspired utterance[8] of the man[9] to Ithiel:[10]
"I am weary, O God,[11] but I can prevail.[12]

30:2 Surely[13] I am too stupid to be a man;[14]
indeed,[15] I do not have the understanding of a human being.
30:3 Indeed,[16] I have not[17] learned[18] wisdom,
but I want to experience[19] the knowledge of the Holy One.[20]
30:4 Who has ever ascended to heaven and come down?
Who has ever gathered up the wind[21] in his fists?[22]
Who has ever wrapped up the waters in his robe?[23]
Who has established all the ends of the earth?
What is his name? and what is his son's[24] name?
Surely you know!

30:5 Every[25] word[26] of God[27] is purified;
he is a shield to those who take refuge in him.
30:6 Do not add[28] to his word,[29]
lest he convict[30] you and you be proved a liar."[31]

Exegesis

Agur's confession in Proverbs 30:1–6 partially introduces his unified sayings. Here we limit the discussion about its overall structure to a brief outline.

I. Introduction: Agur's autobiographical confession	1–9
A. Superscription	1
B. His confession	2–9
1. His sayings are inspired	2–6
2. His two petitions: for truthfulness and for modesty	7–9
II. Main Body: Seven numerical sayings	10–31

Superscription (30:1)

The superscription (v. 1) is craftily sewn into the autobiographical confession by shifting references to Agur from third person in 1A to first person in 1B. In the superscription Agur claims his sayings are inspired (v. 1) and then shows the necessity that God reveal truth and how it is attained (vv. 2–6). His vulnerable petitions in verses 7–9 reveal him as a pure channel of God's revelation.

Verset A of the superscription presents the literary genre and author of this collection of sayings. **Agur son of Jakeh,** who is otherwise unknown,[32] represents his **sayings** as inspired (i.e., divine-human speech, originating with God and invested with his authority) by placing the prophetic genre term **oracle** (or "burden"[33]) in apposition to the wisdom genre term **sayings.**[34] His claim matches Solomon's claim for the inspiration of his words (see 2:6). Verset B underscores his inspiration by another apposition, **the inspired utterance of the man** (see note 8; Prov 6:34; 29:5). Hans Kosmala[35] notes that *geber* in this formula signifies a man who stands in a special relationship with God. Kosmala also connects Agur's inspired utterances with Agur's assertions in verses 5 and 6 about the permanence and sufficiency of God's word. Agur addresses his inspired saying to **Ithiel,** but in its canonical context the editor of Proverbs addresses the universal people of God (see 1:1).[36] Finally, verset B summaries Agur's tension as a sage. He explains his statement **I am weary, O God** (see note 11)[37] in verses 2–3 as his quest for wisdom by natural reason, and its antithesis **but I can prevail**[38] in verses 5–6 as due to divine revelation. Agur is "weary," humanly speaking (vv. 2–4), but he can "prevail," since God and his canonical word is his refuge (vv. 5–6). Admittedly, an autobiography in a superscription is unusual, but the logical particle "surely"/"for" that introduces his autobiographical confession in verse 2 validates the emendation, for as such *kî* occurs medially in a discourse.[39]

AGUR'S CONFESSION: HIS SAYINGS ARE INSPIRED (30:2–6)

Many critics (e.g., W. O. E. Oesterley,[40] Otto Plöger[41]) deny a structural unity between verses 5–6 and verses 1–4. R. B. Y. Scott[42] and James Crenshaw[43] think the text consists of a dialogue between Agur the skeptic (verses 1–4) and an orthodox Jew's response (verses 5–6). However, the superscription credits Agur with authoring the entire unit, and nothing in the text—or, for that matter, in the whole chapter—suggests a change of speaker. Rather, one discerns a structural unity in the verses, and parallels in Baruch 3:29–4:1 and Job 28:12–28 validate its thematic unity.

The decision about whether or not the text is a unity is decisive in its interpretation. Those who deny its unity interpret Agur's questions in verse 4 as buttressing his skepticism in verses 2–3 about the inability of humanity to know wisdom. According to them, the answer to all his questions about who sustains the universe in 4A is "no man," and his questions in 4B—"what is his name? and what is his son's name?"—are biting sarcasm. Accordingly, the assertions in verses 5–6 about the purity and perfection of God's word are out of place, tacked on to correct—or to put into proper perspective—Agur's skepticism.

However, Jerry Pauls,[44] building on the work of Paul Franklyn,[45] establishes the structural unity of verses 1–6 as follows:

A. Human Confession (vv. 2–3)
  1. Statement # 1 (v. 2)
  2. Statement # 2 (v. 3)
    B. Rhetorical Questions (v. 4)
      1. "Who . . ." (v. 4A)
      2. "What . . ." (v. 4B)
A.' Scriptural Quotations (vv. 5–6)
  1. Counterstatement # 1 (v. 5)
  2. Counterstatement # 2 (v. 6)

Agur's thematic movement from human ignorance of wisdom to the possession of it follows the same logic as that of Baruch 3:29–4:1 and of Job 28:12–28. All three sages move from confessions that they could not find wisdom on their own (vv. 2–3) to assertions through rhetorical questions that God alone possesses it (4A) and that he has a "son"/*ʾādām* whom he teaches (4B). Agur's scriptural quotations establish that the words God gives Israel are pure (v. 5) and canonical (v. 6). Accordingly, verse 4, instead of being a redundant reinforcement of skepticism, plays a pivotal role, a Janus verse pointing to a personal relationship with the wise Sovereign as the means to overcome the human predicament of ignorance and death. The "inspired" sayings of Agur (v. 1) are part of canon and, as truth, not to be tampered with (v. 6).

2–3 The initial emphatic, logical particle of verse 2 **surely** binds Agur's autobiographical confession with verse 1, and the initial conjunctive **indeed** of verse 3 binds the autobiography of verse 2 with that of verse 1. Agur confesses that, in spite of his desire to know the Holy One and his wisdom, he failed. His confession suggests that his original statement "I am weary, O God" means that he grew weary in his quest to know wisdom. Agur makes no claim to wisdom *qua* a human being. If he is to know wisdom, he must be taught by God, who alone possesses it. His confession functions today as a polemic against the rationalism of the so-called Enlightenment, which thought that unaided human reason could attain truth. Two centuries later their enterprise proved a colossal failure.[46] Having failed in the enterprise, their heirs have drawn the perverse conclusion that there are no absolutes—except that one! Agur, however, points the way out of this nihilism. Verse 2 presents the earthbound predicament of a human being; verse 3 points the way out, namely, "the knowledge of the Holy One" (cf. Prov 3:5–6).

Agur structures his confession of verse 2–3 chiastically. In the outer frame he confesses his dilemma. On the one hand, he is less than human (2A); on the other hand, he wants to know the Holy One (3B). The connection implies that to be truly human one must know the person and the will of God. In the inner core, by means of two negative clauses, he explains he is less than human because he lacks understanding of the divinely established moral order, and though presumably instructed, because he has not learned wisdom (see 1:2).

In this confession Agur shows clearly that he writes within the wisdom tradition, using the same three words Solomon used to introduce his book—*insight, wisdom,* and *knowledge* (Prov 1:2–7)—plus "knowledge of the Holy One" (in Solomon's conclusion to the prologue in 9:10). However, whereas Solomon made them known, Agur failed to learn them, presumably from his pagan teacher. Although probably a proselyte to Israel's faith, Agur stands in the spiritual and intellectual line of Solomon (2:6).

2 Agur wearied himself to find wisdom and came up with what Qoheleth calls *hebel* ("a vapor," cf. Eccl 1:2; 12:8). In the synthetic parallelism of verse 2, verset B clarifies verset A. **Too stupid** [or brutish] **to be a man.** The psalmist uses a similar hyperbole: "But I am a worm and not a man" (Ps 22:5 [6]; cf. Ps 73:21–22; Job 25:4–6). "These are examples," says Richard Clifford, "of 'low anthropology,' self-abasement as an expression of reverence."[47] Agur qualifies his hyperbole by admitting he is without understanding—**I do not have the understanding of a human being,** as in Psalm 73:22 and Psalm 92:6. The parallelism infers that true humanity consists in having insight *(bînâ)* into the religio-ethical realm (see 1:2). To realize its true identity and destiny, humanity needs a divine revelation of the moral order. Arndt Meinhold comments: "These two nominal clauses express at the beginning what Job achieved only at the end of his long wrestling (Job 40:4; 42:3, 6)."[48] Agur begins where Job signed off. He also employs irony. With a mock ruefulness he implies that others seem to know all about God and wisdom, whereas he, poor fellow, is apparently subhuman, since for him both are shrouded in mystery.[49] Yet, this is his true wisdom. Robert Alden insightfully comments: "A man devoid of intelligence could never have written these words."[50] By confessing that he has no wisdom apart from revelation (vv. 5–6), he displays his wisdom and his becoming a true human being. His confession is also a polemic against sages who claim wisdom through their own efforts (cf. Isa 5:21; 19:11–12; 29:14; 44:25; Jer 8:8–9; 9:12, 23; 29:14; 44:25). In fact, however, they are so stupid that they don't even know they fall short of being human.

Agur's use of *baʿar* ("stupid," or "brutish") with reference to divine thought and ethics (see Prov 12:1) resembles its use in Psalm 73:21–23. Paul Franklyn notes, "The dying psalmist's confession of ignorance [is] followed by immediate affirmation of God's presence and rescue.... Here, as in Proverbs, the weary and embittered person confesses ignorance of God, and, in the same breath, he seizes the outstretched hand of the divine presence."[51] The biblical wisdom tradition often notes the limitation of human knowledge and the need of divine revelation. J. Luyten notes, "In classical wisdom books we meet this theme in the warning against trusting one's insight (Prov 3:5–7), in sentences on the opposition between man's proposal and God's disposal ..., and in the saying and poem expressing the transcendence of divine wisdom and man's ignorance (Prov 30:1b–3; Job 11:8–9)."[52] Agur, however, does not relieve his intellectual inadequacy so quickly. Instead, he develops, step by step, a way out of the human dilemma.

3 In 3A Agur continues to explain why he considers himself brutish. Although taught by a sage, he had **not learned wisdom.** As a human being, Agur does not possess the wisdom that can fathom the depths of the enigma with which the Creator confronts the human being (cf. Job 28:12–22), and without that ability to interpret the human situation, he cannot reach certainty about living skillfully. Moreover, the imprecise parallelism between *wisdom* and *knowledge of the Holy One* implies that wisdom as defined in this book is dependent on a personal relationship with God, who stands apart from the restrictions of finitude and depravity (cf. Prov 2:1–5). Gerald T. Sheppard comments, "Within the presupposition of Wisdom's original status in the heavenly domain of God, the questions of Baruch 3:29–30; Deuteronomy 30:12–13; Proverbs 30:3–4 satirize any pretense of grasping her by mere earthly genius and agility."[53]

Gerhard von Rad rightly noted that Israel's "thinking had to operate within spheres of tension indicated by the prior knowledge of God."[54] One cannot live in accordance with the divinely established moral order and find a refuge against death (cf. Prov 30:5) unless one can enter into the mind and will of God. God alone sees *ontologically* (i.e., the whole of what actually is). To be wise, a person must transcend the relativity and depravity of human epistemology. Henri Blocher argued, "If the whole of reality comes from one wise and sovereign Lord, who has ordered all things, reality is all of one piece; nothing is independent of God, and nothing can be truly interpreted independently of God."[55] Humanity can only know absolutely if it knows comprehensively. To make an absolute judgment on their own, human beings must usurp God's throne. Cornelius Van Til made this observation:

> If one does not make human knowledge wholly dependent upon the original self-knowledge and consequent revelation of God to man, then man will have to seek knowledge within himself as the final reference point. Then he will have to seek an exhaustive understanding of reality. He will have to hold that if he cannot attain to such an exhaustive understanding of reality, he has no *true* knowledge of anything at all. Either man must then know everything or he knows nothing. This is the dilemma that confronts every form of non-Christian epistemology.[56]

Earthbound mortals cannot find transcendent wisdom apart from the transcendent LORD. Real wisdom must find its starting point in God's revelation; in his light we see light (see Ps 36:9 [10]).

4 Agur now shifts his attention from his own ignorance of wisdom to confront Ithiel, who represents all Israel, with the call to know wisdom. By two sets of rhetorical questions—a form of strong assertion (cf. Ruth 3:1)—Agur challenges his audience to bridge the unbridgeable gulf between the LORD's knowledge of wisdom and human helplessness by personally identifying itself as a *son* of the Holy One. In verset A, he employs the animate interrogative pronoun **who** four times; in verset B, he uses the inanimate interrogative pronoun **what** [is his/his son's name]. The answer to the first is "no human being, but only God."

All the ends of the earth brings this set of questions to its climatic conclusion (see Prov 3:17). The answers to the second set of two questions are the names "the LORD" and "Israel"—God's son.

Agur's first four questions exhibit a chiastic pattern. The outer core presents the merism **heaven** (4Aaa) and **earth** (4Abb) to denote the whole universe (see 3:19). **Ascended to heaven** represents its vertical axis, and **ends of the earth** its horizontal axis. The inner core presents the two parts of a thunderstorm—**wind** (4Aab) and **waters** (4Aba) that sustain life on earth (see 3:20). By restraining them the LORD inflicts a drought (cf. 26:8; 28:25). The answer to these questions, standing between humanity's inability to know wisdom (vv. 2–3) and the presence of God's word with his people (vv. 5–6), explains the paradox of the way in which inaccessible wisdom becomes accessible to earthlings. Striking parallels in Baruch 3:29–37—which, as Gerald Sheppard has shown, reinterprets Deuteronomy 30:12[57]—and in Job 28:12–28 clarify that the first question ("Who has ever ascended to heaven and come down?") excludes the earthling as able to obtain wisdom. Parallels in two ancient Near Eastern texts infer that only a god, not even a superhuman being, can ascend into heaven (cf. Gen 11:7; 35:13).[58] In the hymnic literature, the LORD ascends his throne, perhaps in the symbolic form of Israel's king ascending the throne, to exercise dominion over the earth (Ps 47:5 [4] [cf. Num 23:21; 2 Sam 15:10; 2 Kgs 9:13]; 68:9).[59] In the prophetic literature the LORD sends to the lowest depths earthlings who in hubris resolve to become god by ascending to heaven to assume dominion (Isa 14:13–20; Jer 51:53). The remaining three questions, which ask who is sovereign over the cosmic elements, infer that the LORD has access to it. He created **all the ends of the earth,** implying that nothing is hidden from him (cf. Job 28:23f), and he controls **the wind** and **the waters** that sustain it, implying that nothing is beyond his ability. Michael Grisanti notes that "God's sovereignty is often emphasized by means of his control over water [cf. Gen 1:9–10; chs. 6–9; Ps 104:6–7, 10–13; Amos 5:8]."[60] God's total sovereignty over the universe expresses his wisdom. Walter Brueggemann, in speaking of Jeremiah 9:23, says that wisdom is not simply about "the power to discern, but the capacity to manage and control."[61]

Baruch (3:29–37) develops the same argument:

3:29 Who has gone up into heaven and taken her [wisdom],
    and brought her down from the clouds? . . .
3:31 There is neither one who knows her way,
    nor one who comprehends her path.
3:32 But he who knows [sees?] all things knows her.
    He found her out in his understanding.
He established the earth for evermore. . . .

3:36This is our God,
with whom none can be compared.
3:37He found the way of understanding
and gave it to Jacob his servant
and to Israel, whom he loved.

Similarly, Job 28:12–28 develops the argument, moving from human inability to obtain wisdom (vv. 12–19) to the LORD's finding and testing of it (vv. 20–27) to the LORD's revealing it to human beings (v. 28).

Agur's four questions in 4A proceed along the same line of reasoning. The first question establishes the unbridgeable gap between the earthling and heaven, which is presumably where wisdom dwells. The last three establish that God must possess wisdom because he demonstrates it. In Job 38 the LORD asks Job questions similar to Agur's and implies the answer "not you, Job, but God" (Job 38:5, 25, 29, 36–37, 41; 39:5).

Verset Ba asks both for the name of the one who is sovereign over the cosmos and for the name of his son. The inanimate interrogative **what is his name?** asks not merely for identification but for the circumstances attached to the person's name.[62] From the rest of the Old Testament the answer must be "the LORD"—or its equivalent. The parallel texts in Job 28 and 38 name the LORD. Jerry Pauls notes that the question "What is his name?" resonates with Israel's foundational question—"what is his name?" (Exod 3:13) and comments that the question "can produce but one answer—Yahweh."[63] The Midrash also responds, "His name is the Lord."[64]

The answer to **what is his son's name?** must be based on the lexical foundation that in Proverbs *son* always elsewhere refers to the son whom the father teaches (see 1:8). If Ithiel is Agur's son, who is the LORD's son? In the Old Testament, the LORD brought Israel into existence (cf. Exod 4:22; Deut 14:1; 32:5–22; Isa 43:6; 45:11; 63:16; 64:7; Jer 3:4, 19; 31:9, 20; Hos 11:1; Mal 2:10). The LXX reads "his son" as plural—"his children"—apparently interpreting "his son" as "the children of Israel." This is also the interpretation in the Midrash Yalkut Shimoni.[65] The striking parallel in Baruch 3:37 confirms the interpretation. Gerald Sheppard, commenting on Baruch 3:37b, says: "In the end the author concludes that created humanity can know the way only if God gives it by his elective will and that he has so chosen Israel (v. 37b)."[66] If it should be objected that the name *Israel* (see Prov 1:1) as the son of God is derived from outside the wisdom tradition, note Agur's use of intertextuality. The question "what is his name?" probably echoes Exodus 3:14; in verse 5 Agur quotes Psalm 18:30 [31], and in verse 6 he probably quotes Deuteronomy 4:2. Baruch 3:29–30 is certainly based on

Deuteronomy 30:12, and Agur's question "who ascended to heaven?" may be. Although neither Agur nor Baruch explain how the LORD gave wisdom, we may assume that he mediated it through his inspired sages (see Prov 30:1; cf. Exod 24:1, 9–12; Isa 6:1–11; 40:1–3; Dan 7:13–14, 27).

In Christian theology Jesus Christ is the fulfillment of typical Israel, for he alone was perfectly obedient to his father (see Matt 2:15; Heb 5:7–10). But he is more than a son. He identifies himself as the *Son of Man* who comes on the clouds, the biblical symbol of divine transcendence. In Luke he is the *incarnate Son of God* by virgin birth (Luke 1:29–33), and in John he is the *eternal Son of God* (John 17). As such he speaks with an immediate authority (cf. Matt 7:28; 9:1–8; 12:8, 42; Heb 3:3–6; Rev 5:1–14) and through the Holy Spirit guided his disciples into all truth (John 16:12–15).

In 4Bb Agur escalates his implied challenge that Ithiel embrace his opportunity to possess wisdom by asserting, in direct address, **Surely you know!** In addition to forming an inclusio with "I do not have the understanding" (v. 2), it probably intentionally echoes God's challenge to Job in a similar context (see Job 38:3). Both assertions challenge the son to name the LORD as the Sovereign One over creation and to receive from him his inheritance. Jerry Pauls says, "The second question represents a dramatic shift in our text. It is hardly a sarcastic comment about the 'unbridgeable gulf' between men and God, but rather, a small part of a larger invitation to bridge that very gulf. It does not merely assert impossibility but affirms possibility in that [the] wisdom [of the LORD] is accessible [to the son]."[67] Pauls then draws this conclusion: "It is this dual movement of the text—inaccessible/accessible, impossible/possible, hidden/made known, despair/hope—that Agur's opening words—weary/able—gain substance."[68]

Moreover, Pauls notes that by asking the questions "who ... ?" and "what is his name?"—not "how do you know?"—Agur "radically reshapes the crisis of knowing ... as a crisis of relationship. The preeminent rhetorical question, 'No one but Yahweh' and the dual request for personal names, shapes the passage in a radical way, suggesting that the resolution to the epistemological crisis is defined in relational rather than intellectual categories.... True wisdom is found in a responsive and receptive relationship with Yahweh, who is wisdom's sole possessor."[69] Similarly, Job's epistemological angst was relieved only when he humbled himself before the transcendent Sovereign. He replaced his prior state of being "without knowledge" with "I know that you can do all things" (Job 42:2–3).

5–6 Verses 5–6 are united by **his word** in 6A, having as its antecedent **every word of God** in 5A, and the threat of death in 6B complements the promise of life in 5B. The "Holy One" who is otherwise unknown (vv. 2–3), in spite of his revealed wisdom in the general revelation of creation (v. 4), is known through his inspired special revelation. Brevard Childs says, "As an answer to the inquirer's despair at finding wisdom and the knowledge of God, the answer offered is that God has already made himself known truthfully in his written word."[70] Rick Moore agrees: "Knowledge of the Holy One depends not on a human search for truth but a humble acceptance of the divine disclosure through inspired spokespersons."[71] Agur has brought his audience back full circle to the claim of the superscription—namely, that his words are an inspired "oracle." "The sayings *[dibrê]* of Agur" (30:1) are "his [God's] words *[dᵉbārāyw]*" (30:6A).

In verse 5 Agur cites David's confession of the reliability of God's word (Ps 18:30 [31]) and, in verse 6, Moses's assertion of its canonical status (Deut 4:2; 12:32; 13:13). Agur's line of reasoning again follows that of Moses and Baruch. After rejecting the notion that Israel needs to ascend to heaven to obtain the Law, Moses asserts, "No, the word is very near you; it is in your mouth and in your heart so you may obey it" (Deut 30:14). Likewise, after saying that the LORD found wisdom and gave it to Israel, Baruch immediately adds, "This is the book of the commandments of God and the law which endures forever" (Baruch 4:1). So also Agur implicitly admonishes his audience to seek their refuge in God by appropriating God's word, including his own sayings. Agur makes no attempt to validate by human reason Scripture's absolute claim for its reliability and canonical authority and perfection. If such an attempt were made, it would make limited human reasoning the final arbitrator of truth, turning the argument back on itself and, of necessity, once again ending in skepticism. The finite mind can neither derive nor certify infinite truth. Certain truth is found in the Scriptures themselves as the Holy Spirit certifies them to obedient children (cf. Matt 11:25–27; 16:13–17; John 5:45–47; 8:47; 10:2–6; 2 Cor 3:14–4:6; 1 Thess 1:13).

5 Verse 5 is an adaptation of David's victory song, celebrating his escape from his enemies and from death (2 Sam 22:31 [= Ps 18:30 (31)]; cf. also Pss 105:19; 119:4). Agur's changes of David's text suggest he is employing the trope of *metalepsis,* a rhetorical and poetic device in which a later text alludes to an earlier one in a way that draws on resonances of the earlier text beyond the explicit citation.[72] Immediately after the text quoted by Agur, David gives God's name: "Who is God besides the LORD?" (Ps. 18:31 [32]), the anticipated answer to Agur's question in verset 4B. Also, David celebrates the LORD as the one who soars on the wings of the wind and who made the dark rain clouds his covering (Ps 18:10–11 [11–12])—a thought similar to Agur's in 4A.

The synthetic parallels **word of God** in verset A and **he** in verset B suggest that God and his word are inseparable. In verset A the refiner's imagery of **purified** precious metal asserts the truthfulness of God's teachings (cf. Pss 12:6 [7]; 19:9b, 10A; 105:19B; 119:140).[73] All of God's inspired teachings perfectly represent the divinely established nexus of cause and effect, a knowledge that is wisdom's foundation. In verset B the imagery of God as a **shield** represents him as a warrior who protects his faithful ones from all their enemies, including death. The imprecise parallelism implies that **those who take refuge in him** do so by committing themselves to his inspired words (see Prov 3:5–6). The revelation aims to promote trust in the Speaker, not to give bare knowledge.[74] God's revealed word and the disciples' humble trust in him to keep it are the fundamental aspects of "the fear of the LORD" (1:7).

6 In 6A, a variation of Deuteronomy 4:2 and 12:32 [13:1], Agur asserts the canonical status of his sayings (see Rev 22:18–19). Since the Hebrew canon was not completed until around 165 B.C., Agur refers to them as part of a developing canon.[75] **Do not add to his word,** the so-called *canon formula,* "was intended to prompt Israel's obedience ..., not simply define the canonical status of divine utterances."[76] The formula emphasizes the authority of Agur's sayings, reinforces their purity, and safeguards them against an apostate form of human authority that would tamper with them. Anyone who alters it by adding to it is not seeking refuge in the LORD but arrogantly conforming him to his own inspiration (cf. 1 Cor 4:6).[77] Verset B provides the motivation for recognizing the canonical status of Agur's sayings. Since a human being by nature cannot know wisdom (Prov 30:2–3), anyone who adds to these sayings will falsify them. In contrast to an empirical epistemology, which is accustomed to proving everything else, Agur argues that it is *our word,* not God's, which finally must be proven.[78] God will **convict** the offender. It can be inferred that the crime of adulterating Agur's sayings is a capital offense, since those who trustfully obey his word find salvation from death. This interpretation is validated by its *metalepsis* with Deuteronomy 4. To the canon formula in Deuteronomy 4:2–3 Moses attached life for obedience and death for disobedience. To this promise and threat Moses added the additional motivation that observance of his words will establish Israel, God's son, as a wise and understanding people, set apart in the sight of all nations (Deut 4:6–8). Agur's intention for this "son" is the same.

CONCLUSION

To my knowledge, Agur's confession is the most sustained argument in the Bible for the necessity of *special revelation* (through Israel's Scripture) to bridge the gulf between the infinite and the finite—to make the inaccessible accessible, the impossible possible, and the hidden known; and to transform humanity's epistemological despair to hope. But his argument is an enigma, intended to both conceal and reveal. He demands of his reader an intuitive grasp to understand his argument. Those willing to invest their total person to understand his argument will internalize it, but this cannot be achieved by those unwilling to commit themselves.

Without a translation into lucid English, however, Agur's enigmatic confession cannot be understood by even the most devoted reader of English. In other words, the translator *also* aims to make the inaccessible accessible, the impossible possible, and the hidden known. The translator also transforms the human epistemological despair over not knowing God's special revelation into hope.

Notes

1. This essay is adapted from Bruce K. Waltke's commentary on *Proverbs* in the New International Commentary on the Old Testament series, forthcoming from Wm. B. Eerdmans Pub. Co. in 2003. Used with permission.

2. Ron joined the NIV project a year before me and also became a member of the CBT a year before me. I had the exceptional privilege of serving with Ron on every committee to which I was assigned and learned much from him, but I could never pick up his keen sense of humor.

3. The LXX renders *ʾāgûr* by *phobētheti*—"reverence"—derived from a jussive of *gzr*—"dread, fear." "This is problematic because it involves the rejection of an *aleph*" (Paul Franklyn, "The Sayings of Agur in Proverbs 30: Piety or Scepticism?" *ZAW* 95 [1983]: 239). The change is part of the LXX's fiction that Solomon authored these sayings.

4. For the rare pointing *bin,* see *Gesenius' Hebrew Grammar,* §96.

5. The LXX renders *yāqeh* by *dexamenos*—"receive"—(from *lāqaḥ*) as part of its Solomonic fiction.

6. Interpreting the article to signify class, see Bruce Waltke and Michael O'Connor, *An Introduction to Biblical Hebrew Syntax* (Winona Lake, Ind.: Eisenbrauns, 1990), 244, §13.5.1f.

7. Franz Delitzsch (*Biblical Commentary on the Proverbs of Solomon,* trans. M. G. Easton [Grand Rapids: Eerdmans, 1970; preface 1872], 262) and others think the prophetic term *maśśāʾ* is unfitting in Wisdom literature, especially in a context where Agur confesses his weakness. They emend the text to either *mimmaśśāʾ*—"from Massa," or *hammaśśāʾ î*—"the Massaite," which was "a district in N.W. Arabia ... attested for the early to middle 1st millennium B.C. in Assyrian texts [see Prov 25:14]." See K. A. Kitchen, "Proverbs and Wisdom Books of the Ancient Near East," *TynBul* 28 (1977): 101. However, the *neʾum haggeber*—"the inspired utterance of the man," is also prophetic, so that the two terms reinforce the prophetic interpretation.

8. The lexeme *neʾum*—"an inspired utterance"—occurs 365 of 376 times in the formula *neʾum yhwh* (D. Vetter, *TLOT* 2:93, s.v. *neʾum*). That construction designates the words that follow originated with the LORD and carry his authority. One time (Jer 23:31) it occurs absolutely with the same sense (L. Coppes, *TWOT* 2:541f, s.v. *neʾum*). Its ten other uses occur in construct with a human author to denote the heavenly origin of his utterance and its divine authority: six times of Balaam's oracles (Num 24:3 [twice], 4, 15

[twice], 16), and twice of David's inspired hymns (2 Sam 23:1 [twice]), and of Agur's sayings. Remarkably, both Balaam and David use exactly the same formula as Agur: *nᵉʾūm haggeber*—"the oracle of the man." Agur's claim for divine inspiration should not be dismissed as "very odd" (William McKane, *Proverbs: A New Approach* [Philadelphia: Westminster, 1970], 644) or "unexplained" (R. N. Whybray, *Proverbs,* New Century Bible Commentary [Grand Rapids: Eerdmans, 1994], 407). Franklyn ("The Sayings of Agur," 241) forces the interpreter to chose between Agur's sayings as either "part of the formal prophetic tradition, or a self-assertive human revelation in the prophetic mode." Jerry Pauls ("Proverbs 30:1–6, 'The Words of Agur' as Epistemological Statement [Th.M. thesis, Regent College, 1998], 65) rightly rejects the second option: "Given the explicit claims of vv. 2–3, which denigrate the claims of human wisdom, the second option appears hardly tenable." Rick Moore ("A Home for the Alien: World Wisdom and Covenant Confession in Proverbs 30:1–9," *ZAW* 106 [1994]: 97) draws the right conclusion that in Agur's sayings there is "a striking confluence of sapient and prophetic traditions."

9. Edward Lipinski ("Peninna, Itt'el et l-Athlete," *VT* 17 [1967]: 73) reads here the personal name Gab(b)ru, according to the Assyrian form of the name, which is also attested in Arabic (cf. Gaber in the LXX of 1 Kings 4:13, 19). He understands this to mean "The Athlete." Franklyn ("The Sayings of Agur," 240) rightly objected: "the combination of *nʾm hgbr* in Numbers 24:3, 15 and 2 Samuel 23:1 decisively overrules a nominal [sic! proper noun] usage."

10. Numerous emendations have been unnecessarily proposed. MT is supported by Theodotus and Aquila.

11. Although Targ., Aquila, Theodotus read with MT, the text should be emended by redividing and repointing *lᵉʾîtîʾēl* as *lāʾ îtî ʾēl* (cf. Num 12:13; Ps 83:2). Charles Torrey ("Proverbs, Chapter 30," *JBL* 73 [1954]: 93–103), followed and modified by R. B. Y. Scott (*Proverbs, Ecclesiastes: Introduction, Translation, and Notes,* Anchor Bible [Garden City, N.Y.: Doubleday, 1965], 176), James Crenshaw ("Clanging Symbols [Proverbs 30:1–14]," in *Justice and the Holy,* eds. Douglas A. Knight and Peter J. Paris [Atlanta: Scholars Press, 1980]: 51–64) interpret *lʾytyl* as a scribal cover-up in Aramaic for a blasphemy. Torrey (cf. NAB) thinks the text should read *lʾ ʾty ʾl*—"I am not God, I am not God." The others essentially read *lâʾ ʾîtay ʾēl* (cf. Dan 3:29)—"there is no god, there is no god." However, they arbitrarily dissect 30:1–6 into the words of skeptical Agur (vv. 1–4) and the words of an orthodox response (30:5–6) and overlook or dismiss too easily Agur's claim of inspiration. Finally, one must raise a skeptical eye that either the writer or a scribe inserted Aramaic into a passage otherwise expressed in Hebrew. Emil Joseph Dillon (*Skeptics of the Old Testament: Job, Koheleth, Agur,* with English text [London: Isbister, 1895], 269), R. B. Y. Scott (*The Way of Wisdom in the Old Testament* [New York: Macmillan, 1971], 60) et al. regard the phrase as a descriptive clause. Scott (in "Solomon and the Beginnings of Wisdom in Israel," VTSup 3 [1969]: 262–79) emended the text into *lōʾ ʾittō ʾēl lōʾ lôʾ ʾitî ʾēl*—"with whom God is not, I have not God." The proposal finds some support in the grammar of the Vulgate (*vir cum quo est deus*—"with whom is God") but not in its content. The LXX also reads a relative clause but with very different content: *tois pisteuousin theō*—"to those who believe God." However, although *nᵉʾūm haggeber* in Numbers 24:3, 15 and 2 Samuel 23:1 is followed by a relative clause, it is not necessary. Moreover, Scott adds consonants to the text in addition to redividing them. Finally, he

mishandles the parallels in Numbers 24:3, 15 and 2 Samuel 23:1, which strongly support Agur's inspiration. In sum, the proposed and most widely accepted emendation is best from a text-critical, exegetical, and canonical point of view. In 1669 Johannes Cocceius proposed the reading "I have labored on account of God, and I have obtained" (cited by Crawford Toy, *The Book of Proverbs,* ICC [Edinburgh: T. & T. Clark, 1977], 519). In modern times he has been accepted by Berend Gemser, *Sprüche Salomos,* HAT 16 (Tübingen: Mohr, 1963; preface 1937), 102. Taking God as vocative is favored by many, e.g., Otto Plöger, *Sprüche Salomos (Proverbia),* BKAT 27, nos. 2–4 (Neukirchen-Vluyn: Neukirchener Verlag, 1984), 354; also NEB, REB, NIV [text note], NRSV.

12. There is little consensus about the meaning of *ʾuḳāl.*

13. The emphatic adverb *ḳî*—"surely"—should not be radically separated from its logical use, "for" (*IBHS,* p. 665, §39.3.4e).

14. Understanding *min* as a comparative of capability, marking "man" as the object or goal Agur wishes to attain (*IBHS,* p. 266, §14.4ff.; NRSV). Delitzsch (*Proverbs,* 272) understands it as a comparative of exclusion—"not a man" (cf. *IBHS,* p. 265, §14.4e), and Franklyn ("The Sayings of Agur," 244, note 24) thinks the *min* is privative (i.e., "separated from other men by his beastly nature"). All agree, however, that the expression makes a sharp distinction between man and God (cf. Hos 11:9; see N. P. Bratsiotis, *TDOT* 1:229, s.v. *ʾsh*]). The NIV renders it as a superlative—"most ignorant"—but the predicate adjective lacks the necessary article for that sense. The LXX supplies the missing element of another superlative construction, *hapantōn anthrōpōn*—"of all men" (cf. *IBHS,* p. 267, §14.5c).

15. *Waw* has an epexegetical function (*IBHS,* p. 652, §39.2.4a).

16. See note 14.

17. Johannes Fichtner *(BHS)* attractively but unnecessarily emends the text to *lûʾ*—"would that I had learned." The chiastic structure of the MT, with two negatives in the inner core (2B and 3A), argues against it.

18. LXX reads *theos dedidaxen me sophian* (> *ʾēl limmad ʾōtî ḥokmâ*—"God taught me wisdom"), which is favored by Marvin Pope, *El in the Ugaritic Texts,* VTSup 2 (Leiden: Brill, 1955), 14. But Franklyn ("The Sayings of Agur," 245) notes, "Most reject the LXX because it imputes more piety into the text than is necessary." The *waw* conjunctive in MT links verse 3 with verse 2, but the LXX, which omits the conjunctive, puts the verses into tension with each other. The LXX anticipates the resolution in verses 5–9 (i.e., wisdom is dependent on God's revelation [vv. 5–6] and on piety [vv. 7–9]) but provides no transition by way of verse 4 to the resolution of the tension.

19. Literally, "know."

20. Understanding *qᵉdōšîm* as an objective genitive and an honorific plural (*IBHS,* p. 122, §7.4.3; see 2:5; 9:10), not a genitive of inalienable possession and a countable plural (i.e., "the knowledge that is proper to the holy ones" [*IBHS,* p. 145, §9.5.1h]). "The adjective *qādôsh* (holy) denominates that which is intrinsically sacred or which has been admitted to the sphere of the sacred.... It connotes that which is distinct from the common or profane" (Thomas E. McComiskey, *TWOT* 2:788, s.v. *qādôsh*).

21. The wind has the power to set other things in motion (cf. Prov 25:23; 27:26). Here it refers to the thunderstorm. "He who rules [the movement of wind] has, as it were, the north or east wind in one fist, and the south or west wind in the other, to let it forth according to his pleasure from this prison (Isa. xxiv.22)" (Delitzsch, *Proverbs,* 273).

22. Kevin Cathcart ("Proverbs 30.4 and Ugaritic Ḥpn, 'Garment,'" *CBQ* 32 [1970]: 418–20) argues that *en kolpō* in the LXX does not render *bᵉḥiṣnô* (= "bosom of his garment") but represents the same reading as MT—only singular—because Ugaritic *ḥpn* denotes some sort of garment. This interpretation provides a nice parallel to "robe" in v.4Aba), but elsewhere the Hebrew word denotes "hollow of hand" (i.e., "fist"; see HALOT 1:339, s.v. *ḥōpen*).

23. A metaphor for the clouds (see Job 26:8).

24. LXX renders by plural *teknois autou* apparently to refer to the children of Israel.

25. Agur varies David's thanksgiving song (Ps 18:30 [31]) in several ways. First, he omits David's initial "As for God, his way is perfect; the word of God . . ." because David features the reliability of God's word in connection with God's protection, but Agur features the reliability of God's word as revelation. Second, by transferring *kol* from verset B (= "to all who seek refuge in him") to "every word of God" in verset A, Agur shifts the emphasis "from an all-embracing protectorship to a total reliability of divine words" (Crenshaw, "Clanging Symbols," 58).

26. "The verb *ʾmr* [the root here] directs attention to the contents of the speech, but *dbr Piel* indicates primarily the activity of speaking" (G. Gerleman, *TLOT* 1:327, s.v. *dabar*).

27. Psalm 18:30 [31] reads *yhwh,* not *ʾᵉlôah.*

28. Plural of Deuteronomy 4:2 is replaced by singular to accommodate the shift of addresses from all Israel to Ithiel in particular.

29. "The word which I [Moses] am commanding you" (Deut 4:2 NASB) becomes "his word" in order to bind verse 6 to verse 5, to fit the restraints of the poetic line, and to replace Moses' words with Agur's words.

30. HALOT 2:410, s.v. *ykḥ*.

31. Or, "be found guilty of a lie" (see Job 41:1 for its other occurrence in *Niphal*). Agur gaps the other half of the canonical formula—"do not take away from his word"—to replace it with a threat for not guarding the sacred word.

32. The Midrash on Proverbs allegorized the name to retain Solomonic authorship: "The words—these are the words of Solomon; Agur—he who girded (*ʾāgûr*) his loins for wisdom; son of Jakeh (Yakeh)—a son who is free (*nāqîʾ*) from all sin and transgression" (Burton L. Visotzky, *The Midrash on Proverbs,* Yale Judaica Series [New Haven, Conn.: Yale Univ. Press, 1997], 117). Ammon Cohen ("Proverbs," in *Soncino Books of the Bible* [London: Soncino, 1946], 200) notes that some later Jewish commentators rejected the identification of Agur with Solomon. Abraham ben Meir ibn Ezra held that Solomon incorporated into his book the words of a contemporary. Jerome interprets the proper names as substantives: *verba congregantis filii vomentis* (= "words of G/gatherer son of V/vomiter"), which Crawford Toy (*Proverbs,* 518) interprets to mean "the gatherer of people for instruction" and "who pours out words of wisdom." Patrick Skehan ("Wisdom's House" [Studies in Israelite Poetry and Wisdom, Catholic Biblical Quarterly Monograph Series I; Washington: Catholic Biblical Association of America, 1971], 27–45) interpreted "Agur son of Jakeh" as a riddle. According to him *Agur* means "I am a sojourner" and *Jakeh* is an acronym for *Yahweh qādôš hûʾ* ("Yahweh is holy"). In this way, "Agur, in association with Jacob/Israel, is the Lord's son" (see v. 4B). It is best, however, to take it as a proper name. The formula *proper noun + "son of" + proper noun* occurs over

1500 times in the Old Testament. It parallels the superscription in 31:1, which also combines "words of" with a proper noun. In ancient Near Eastern Wisdom literature, the real author is named (Kitchen, "Proverbs and Wisdom Books of the Ancient Near East," 93, 95). Finally, *Agur* and *Jakeh* show up as proper personal names in the cognate Semitic languages. This may suggest that he is a proselyte to Israel's faith. Even if verse 4 parodies Job 38–41, Agur cannot be dated, for the date of that text is also questionable.

33. Fritz Stolz (*TLOT* 2:773, s.v. *nś*ʾ) says *hammaœœā*ʾ is "a prophetic technical term meaning 'judgment proclamation,'" but he broadens the term to a prophetic address in general in Zechariah 9:1; 12:1 and Malachi 1:1 (cf. Hab 1:1). The specific genre—"judgment oracle"—is not inappropriate in connection with the single proverbs that introduce the two parts of the collection of numerical sayings and threaten judgment for violating the established order (vv. 10, 17). Perhaps, however, in Wisdom literature the term is modified to mean simply "oracle," even as *qesem* in Proverbs 16:10 and *ḥāzôn* in 29:18 are nuanced differently from prophetic literature.

34. He also infers his inspiration by joining his sayings with God's words to David and to Moses in verses 5–6.

35. Hans Kosmala, *TDOT* 2:378–79, s.v. *gābhar.*

36. Heb. *lᵉ*ʾ *îtîēl* is usually emended in connection with the following words. However, the proper name is attested in Nehemiah 11:7 and, as documented by Lipinski ("Peninna," 72) and Franklyn ("The Sayings of Agur," 241ff., note 14), has possible analogues in ancient Near Eastern texts. Moreover, it supplies the necessary antecedent to the implied "you" in verses 4 and 6. Commenting on the addressees in ancient Near Eastern "instructional" texts, K. A. Kitchen ("Proverbs and the Wisdom Books," 76) says, "Frequently the author addresses his son, the latter often being named." In 31:1, a parallel to this superscription, Lemuel is inferentially the one addressed by his mother.

37. "I am weary, O God" (Heb. *lā*ʾ *îtî* ʾ*ēl*) is an emendation of the MT *lᵉ*ʾ*îtîēl* (see note 11), which repeats "to Ithiel." The repetition of the addressee's name would be abnormal. Furthermore, if it were a proper name, the conjunction "and" with ʾ*ukāl* demands that it, too, be taken as a proper name. However, ʾ*ukāl* is a verb and never attested as a proper name in any Semitic language. Moreover, if ʾ*ukāl* is a proper name, then we are left with the bizarre situation of an oracle addressed twice to one person and once to another, without reason. Finally, if these are all personal names, the emphatic and logical particle "surely/because" that introduces verse 2 is nonsensical. The transparent pun, *l*ʾ*yty* ʾ*l* and *l*ʾ*yty*ʾ*l,* readily explains the confusion in the MT. The verbal root has been identified as (1) *l*ʾ*h*—"to be weary"—which is favored by most (see HALOT 2:512, s.v. *l*ʾ*h*), or (2) *l*ʾ*h*—"to be strong"—which is favored by Dahood (*Proverbs and Northwest Semitic Philology* [Rome: Pontificum Institutum Biblicum 1963], 57) and Lipinski ("Peninna," 74). The second root, however, is otherwise attested only in the cognate languages. Moreover, the notion of weariness, rather than power, better suits Agur's confession of weakness in verse 2, which is syntactically connected with verse 1 by *kî*—"surely."

38. The interpretation of *w*ᵉ ("but") as an antithetical disjunctive depends on interpreting ʾ*ukāl* as "I am able" or "I can prevail"—the opposite of "to be weary." Without emending the consonants, ʾ*ukāl* can be read as a defective *Pual* participle of ʾ*kl* (= "and [I am] one who is consumed/destroyed"—cf. Exod 3:2), but a *daghesh* has to be supplied, and one expects the pronoun ʾ*ānōkî*. Franklyn ("The Sayings of Agur," 244) repoints it

as *wāʾēkal, waw*-consecutive with apocopated short prefix conjunction of *klh*—"and I am spent," which Franklyn refers to old age. The LXX probably also read it thus: *kai pauomai*—"and I cease" (i.e., "cease speaking"); similarly, Delitzsch (*Proverbs,* 271): "and I have withdrawn" (i.e., from a troubling pursuit of wisdom). Kuhn (cited by Franklyn, "The Sayings of Agur," 243, note 18) repointed it as *ʾākîl* (defective *Hiphil* imperfect of *kûl*—"but I will endure"—investing the form with a positive tone, not negative). Brown, Driver, and Briggs (BDB 408, s.v. *yâkôl*), Theodotus, Cocceius, and Plöger (*Sprüche,* 354) et al. read MT as a defective form of *ʾukāl* from the root *yākōl* = "I am able/I can prevail." Jerry Pauls ("Proverbs 30:1–6," 82f.) defends this reading exegetically, for it holds in tension the notions of human weakness in verses 2–3 and divine enabling in verses 5–6. He also supports it textually by noting the defective form of this root in 3d masculine plural in Joshua 7:12; Jeremiah 20:11; and Psalm 18:39 and by noting that the root occurs without an object in Exodus 1:23 or a complementary verb in Isaiah 1:13 and Psalm 101:5. However, the absolute use is unique. Finally, he maintains it lexically by noting that *lʾh* and *ykl* joined together also in Isaiah 16:12 and Job 4:2.

39. See *IBHS,* p. 655, §39.3.4e.

40. W. O. E. Oesterley, *The Book of Proverbs* (London: Methuen, 1929), 270.

41. Plöger, *Sprüche,* 359.

42. Scott, *Proverbs,* 176; idem, *The Way of Wisdom* (New York: Macmillan, 1971), 165.

43. Crenshaw, "Clanging Symbols," 58.

44. Pauls, "Proverbs 30:1–6," 48–51.

45. Cf. Franklyn, "The Sayings of Agur," 238–52.

46. See Alister MacIntyre, *After Virtue* (Notre Dame, Ind.: University of Notre Dame Press, 1984).

47. Richard J. Clifford, *The Book of Proverbs and Our Search for Wisdom* (Milwaukee, Wis.: Marquette Univ. Press, 1995), 26.

48. Arndt Meinhold, *Die Sprüche* (Zrich: Theologischer Verlag Zürich, 1991), 2:497.

49. Adapted from McKane, *Proverbs,* 646f.

50. Robert Alden, *Proverbs: A Commentary on an Ancient Book of Timeless Advice* (Grand Rapids: Baker, 1984), 208.

51. Franklyn, "The Sayings of Agur," 244–45.

52. Cited in Franklyn, "The Sayings of Agur," 245.

53. Gerald T. Sheppard, *Wisdom as a Hermeneutical Construct: A Study in the Sapientializing of the Old Testament,* BZAW 151 (New York: Walter de Gruyter, 1980), 91.

54. Gerhard von Rad, *Wisdom in Israel,* trans. James D. Martin (London: SCM Press, 1972), 68.

55. Henri Blocher, "The Fear of the Lord as the 'Principle' of Wisdom," *TynBul* 28 (1977): 23.

56. Cornelius Van Til, *A Christian Theory of Knowledge* (Philadelphia: Presbyterian & Reformed, 1969), 17.

57. See Sheppard, *Wisdom as a Hermeneutical Construct,* 90–99.

58. In the Epic of Gilgamesh (III. iv [3]), the heroic superman Gilgamesh asks his counterpart Enkidu, "Who, my friend, can scale he[aven]? Only the gods [live] forever under the sun" (*Ancient Near Eastern Texts,* 79b). In the Dialogue of Pessimism, the servant asks his master, "Who is tall enough to ascend to heaven? Who is broad enough to embrace the earth?" (ibid., 438b).

59. Cited in G. Wehmeier, *TLOT* 2:887, s.v. *ʿlh*.

60. Michael A. Grisanti, *NIDOTTE* 2:929, s.v. *mayim*.

61. Walter Brueggemann, "The Epistemological Crisis of Israel's Two Histories (Jer. 9:22–23)," in *Israelite Wisdom: Theological and Literary Essays in Honor of Samuel Terrien,* eds. John G. Gammie et al. (New York: Union Theological Seminary, 1978), 94.

62. See *IBHS,* pp. 319ff., §18.2d.

63. Pauls, "Proverbs 30:1–6," 117.

64. Visotzky, *The Midrash on Proverbs,* 118. Paul Franklyn ("The Sayings of Agur," 247), drawing on James Crenshaw's *Hymnic Affirmation of Divine Justice,* Society of Biblical Literature Dissertation Series 24 (Missoula, Mont.: Scholars Press, 1975), 75–92, suggests that the question has a striking affinity with the hymnic refrain "The LORD [of Hosts] is his name" (cf. Exod 15:3; Isa 48:2; Jer 10:16; 31:35; 32:18; 33:2; Amos 4:13; 5:8, 27; 9:6; cf. Pss 83:18; 91:9; 113:3). "Accordingly," he suggests, "the answer to the first *mâ* … would most appropriately be 'Yahweh is his name' or 'Yahweh of Hosts is his name.'"

65. Visotzky, *The Midrash on Proverbs,* 118.

66. Sheppard, *Wisdom as a Hermeneutical Construct,* 93.

67. Pauls, "Proverbs 30:1–6," 122.

68. Ibid.

69. Ibid., 124.

70. Brevard Childs, *Introduction to the Old Testament as Scripture* (Philadelphia: Fortress Press, 1979), 556.

71. Moore, "A Home for the Alien," 100ff.

72. For a discussion of the trope in ancient and modern literature, see John Hollander, *The Figure of Echo: A Mode of Allusion in Milton and After* (Berkeley: University of California Press, 1981); for the Old Testament, see Michael Fishbane, *Biblical Interpretation in Ancient Israel* (Oxford: Clarendon, 1985); for the New Testament, see Richard B. Hays, *Echoes of Scripture in the Letters of Paul* (New Haven, Conn.: Yale University Press, 1989), 14–21.

73. The metaphor "is purified"—*ṣᵉrûpâ*—implicitly likens God's word to a precious metal such as silver or gold from which dross has been removed. The purified, molten precious metal is now ready to be poured from the crucible or cupel into the cast. Free from impurities, the cast figure both endures and radiates beauty. The removed dross in this metaphor refers to falsehood.

74. Derek Kidner, *Proverbs: An Introduction and Commentary,* Tyndale Old Testament Commentary (Downers Grove, Ill.: InterVarsity Press, 1981), 179.

75. See Roger T. Beckwith, *The Old Testament Canon of the New Testament Church and Its Background in Early Judaism* (Grand Rapids: Eerdmans, 1985).

76. Andrew E. Hill, *NIDOTTE* 2:476, s.v. *ysp;* cf. Gunnel André, *TDOT* 6:122, s.v. *yāsap*.

77. Raymond Van Leeuwen thinks verse 5 (better, vv. 4–6) aims to exclude apocalyptic speculation. Pseudepigraphal Enoch claimed, "I know everything; either from the lips of the Lord, or else my eyes have seen from the beginning even to the end.… I know everything.… I measured all the earth … and everything that exists.… And I ascended to the east, into the paradise of Eden [i.e., into heaven]" (2 Enoch 40, 41; cited by Raymond Van Leeuwen, *The Book of Proverbs, NIB* 5 [Nashville: Abingdon, 1997], 252).

78. See Moore, "A Home for the Alien," 101.

14

JUSTICE AND/OR RIGHTEOUSNESS: A CONTEXTUALIZED ANALYSIS OF *ṢEDEQ* IN THE KJV (ENGLISH) AND RVR (SPANISH)[1]

Steven M. Voth[2]

It is a well-known fact that translations of any text are never neutral or objective. This is equally true of translations of the Bible. For many years the Christian church lived under the illusion that the translations of the biblical text it was using were free from biases, ideologies, and interpretation. It is now recognized that, minimally speaking, every translation is *interpretation*. And yet others would even go so far as to argue that every translation is *treason,* as suggested by the Italian saying *traduttore traditore*—"A translator is a traitor."[3]

Eugene Nida has alerted us to the three basic principles of semantic correspondence that must underlie all adequate semantic analysis: First, no word (or semantic unit) ever has exactly the same meaning in two different utterances; second, there are no complete synonyms within a language; and third, there are no exact correspondences between related words in different languages. In other words, perfect communication is impossible, and all communication is one of degree.[4]

It is also recognized that every translation of the Bible is a serious attempt to provide a profoundly accurate translation of the ancient text. The translator or team of translators makes every effort to transmit the meaning of the ancient text into a modern target language. However, this translation process does not take place in a vacuum. It is part of a historical process, carried out in a particular context at a particular time. Thus, a number of factors come into play in the exercise of translation. I suggest that the more critical factors are realities of race, class, gender, life histories, theological persuasions, political alliances, cultural distinctives, and, last but not least, marketing issues. These specific factors contribute to the *ideology* as well as to the *worldview* of a translator or team of translators. It can be safely assumed that every translation of the biblical text exhibits a definite ideology, whether conscious or unconscious—which means, then, that there is no such thing as an "immaculate" translation of the Bible. Having participated on two translation teams for two different Bibles in the Spanish language,[5] I am thoroughly convinced, both on theoretical and experiential grounds, that neutral, objective translations are an impossibility—and, to a degree, undesirable. At best, I can speak of honest translations when and if the presuppositions, preunderstandings, theological agendas, and marketing pressures are explained clearly in the preface of the translation offered. Whatever philosophy of translation one adopts, whether it is formal equivalency, dynamic/functional equivalency, or some variation of these, one cannot escape the fact that ideology will play an important role in the process of translation, as well as in the final product. As Stanley Porter has observed, "The history of Bible translation is charged with ideological issues."[6]

Once the presence of ideology is acknowledged, the next step is to suggest a theory of translation that will help in addressing the problem I describe below. Perhaps one of the fundamental areas of concern in any translation is that of achieving a healthy degree of cultural equivalence—so that the "receptor language" can communicate as accurately as possible the intended meaning in the "source language." Ernst Wendlund's theory is very helpful and insightful in this regard. He argues that the formal and functional acceptability of translations may be determined on the basis of the interaction of four closely related and mutually interacting variables—fidelity, intelligibility, idiomaticity, and proximity:[7]

1. *Fidelity* addresses the issues concerned with the accurate communication of the author's intended message in the source-language text.
2. *Intelligibility* focuses on the understanding of the message by hearers in the receptor language.
3. *Idiomaticity* attends to our concern with the "naturalness" of the message received by hearers in the receptor language.
4. *Proximity* considers the structure of the message in the source language and the desirability of preserving its distinctiveness.

These four variables need to be present at all times; yet, no single solution can claim complete equivalence in translation, that is, in all functional aspects of the message—form, meaning, impact, connotation, naturalness, history, lifestyle, and worldview. The translator accepts the responsibility to utilize every available heuristic "so that the receptors can participate much more fully in the communication process whereby the seed of the Word is sown and takes root in the soil of a new linguistic and cultural setting."[8]

The Problem

Having offered a theory of translation and having established that ideology is an integral part of any process used to translate the biblical text, I will now introduce the problem I wish to address in this essay. The problem has many facets to it and thus needs a multifaceted approach to address it. One of the facets has to do with two modern languages—Spanish and English. Another has to do with the understanding of a specific Hebrew term as it appears in a variety of contexts in the biblical text, and yet another has to do with the consequences of translation choices for the theology embraced by the Christian church.

The issue becomes readily apparent when one compares the most influential Bible translations for the English-speaking and Spanish-speaking worlds—the King James Version for the English-speaking world and the Reina Valera Revisada for the Spanish speaking world. Anyone who is familiar with both translations immediately becomes aware of a significant difference between the two texts.[9] Reading the Reina Valera Revisada, one is struck by the number of times the word *justicia* ("justice") appears in the text. A more careful comparison reveals that in the majority of the cases where Reina Valera Revisada (hereafter RVR) uses *justicia,* the King James Version (hereafter KJV) uses *righteousness.* Two examples, one from the Old Testament and one from the New, will suffice as illustrations of the apparent innocent difference:

- In Jeremiah 33:16 the KJV reads, "In those days shall Judah be saved, and Jerusalem shall dwell safely; and this is the name wherewith she shall be called, The LORD our righteousness." By contrast the RVR reads, *"Jehová, **justicia** nuestra,"* which means, "Jehova, our justice."
- In Matthew 5:6 the KJV reads, "Blessed are they which do hunger and thirst after righteousness; for they shall be filled," whereas the RVR reads, *"Bienaventurados los que tienen hambre y sed de **justicia**, porque ellos serán saciados,"* which means, "Blessed are they which do hunger and thirst for justice, for they shall be satisfied."

A more comprehensive reading of both texts will reveal that initial impressions can be corroborated by a simple statistical search. A computer search for the word *justice* in the KJV finds that it appears only 28 times in the entire Bible.

A further interesting fact is that of those 28 uses of the term *justice,* none are to be found in the New Testament translation of the KJV; all occurrences are in the Old Testament. To express this another way, people who during their entire lifetime have read the New Testament of the KJV would never have come across the word *justice* in their reading. More will be said about the meaning and consequences of this reality later on.

The same search carried out in the RVR reveals that the word *justicia* ("justice") appears a total of 370 times. The term can be found 101 times in the New Testament—which means that the term is used more than 13 times as often in the RVR as in the KJV. Once again, I will deal later with the theological implications of this contextual difference in translation.

A further comparison can be done by looking at the use of *justice/justicia* in other English and Spanish translations:

English		**Spanish**	
KJV	28*x*	RVR	370*x*
JPS:	80*x* (only OT)	DHH	277*x*
TEV:	103*x*	NVI	426*x*
ASV:	116*x*		
RSV:	125*x*		
NKJV:	130*x*		
NRSV:	131*x*		
NIV:	134*x*		
NAB:	221*x*		
NJB:	253*x*		

The Spanish translation Nueva Versión Internacional (NVI) represents the most recent translation done by a team of evangelical Latin American scholars. This translation (released in February 1999) demonstrates that an even wider gulf exists between the English and Spanish translations regarding the use of the term *justice/justicia.* This is further substantiated by a look at two standard translations in German and French. The Revised Martin Luther Text (1985) has the word *gerechtigkeit* ("justice") 306 times. The French Nouvelle Version Segond Révisée has *justice* 380 times, and the Latin Vulgate (including the Apocryphal books) utilizes *iustitia* over 400 times.

This simple illustration of the difference in translation between the KJV and the RVR (as well as in Latin, German, and French translations) raises a number of questions. These questions cannot be answered by merely looking at the translations or by relying on statistical analysis. The problem needs to be considered from many different angles.

A Proposed Course of Action

The contextual differences between translations cannot be addressed exclusively from the point of view of the modern English and Spanish languages. It is necessary, first of all, to ascertain the significant Hebrew and Greek words that have a direct impact on the way a translation is completed. For this particular case, I've chosen to concentrate on one particular Hebrew word—*ṣedeq*. There are many other Hebrew words that could be analyzed, especially as they appear together with *ṣedeq*.[10] That, however, would be fertile ground for a doctoral dissertation. The limits of this essay prevent us from spreading our wings so widely. The primary reason for choosing *ṣedeq* is that it is precisely this term that the KJV consistently translates as "righteousness," whereas the RVR translates it as *justicia* ("justice"). So our first task is to try to define the meaning, or range of meanings, of the Hebrew *ṣedeq*.

A second step will be to try to ascertain the history and meaning of the term *righteousness* as it developed in the English language. Questions of usage over time need to be considered: How was the term understood when the translators of the KJV utilized it? Did the translators inherit the term from previous translations? Did the meaning of the term change over time? What connotations does the word have today? These and other matters need to be considered when one attempts to understand the contextual differences of two translations and the implications of these differences for the Christian church.

A third step will be to analyze some key texts in which the term *ṣedeq* is used in the Hebrew Scriptures. The purpose of this study is to offer what would be the most relevant and accurate contextual interpretation of the term in its given context. As these texts are analyzed, a constant comparison will be made between the KJV and the RVR, with a view to understanding the theological implications of each translation.

A final step will be to offer preliminary suggestions based on the analysis done thus far. These suggestions will also consider the present state of understanding of these terms and how the theology of the church has been influenced by the use of either *righteousness* or *justice*.

Meaning of the Term *Ṣedeq*

The scholarly literature on *ṣedeq* is, as might be expected, quite vast. This Hebrew term has been the subject of many studies.[11] These studies demonstrate a wide variety of suggestions about the most original and accurate meaning of the term in question. This is, of course, due to a number of factors, including the particular biases of each scholar. However, it is important to point out at the outset that *ṣedeq* is used in a number of different contexts and in many different literary genres. Thus, the range of semantic meanings of the term can be quite wide. It should come as no surprise, then, that the term can be understood, interpreted, and translated in a variety of ways.

A cursory look at the standard dictionaries reveals the following understandings of the term *ṣedeq:*[12]

- BDB:[13] rightness, righteousness; 1. what is right, just, normal; rightness, justness. 2. righteousness. 3. righteousness, justice in a case. 4. rightness, in speech. 5. righteousness, as ethically right. 6. righteousness as vindicated.
- K-B:[14] 1. the right, normal thing. 2. righteousness, rightness (of law). 3. justice.
- K-B–1996:[15] 1. a. accuracy, what is correct; b. the right thing, what is honest. 2. equity, what is right. 3. communal loyalty, conduct loyal to the community. 4. salvation, well-being.
- Schökel:[16] Justice, right (legal); honesty, innocence; merit; victory. a. As a noun: Justice.

It is interesting to note that there are definite similarities among the suggestions offered by these dictionaries, but there are also differences. The most notable difference is that the dictionary produced in Spain by Luis Alonso Schökel, a most distinguished biblical scholar, uses the word *justice* as the first and primary meaning for the Hebrew term *ṣedeq*. In fact, I wish to draw attention to the fact that, in a more extended explanation of the term, the dictionary mentions that, as a noun, *ṣedeq* means primarily "justice."[17]

One cannot, of course, limit oneself to "dictionary meanings" of words. Eugene Nida has also reminded us that it is necessary to look at the sum total of the contexts in which a given word is used in order to arrive at a more accurate meaning or meanings of a particular lexical unit.[18] For this I can resort to the many excellent theological wordbooks, which make a serious attempt at understanding the range of semantic fields in which a word is used.

The many comprehensive theological articles written on the word *ṣedeq* obviously treat the entire range of cognate words that stem from the root *ṣ-d-q*. As mentioned in note 12, however, I agree with those scholars who see no significant difference in meaning between *ṣedeq* and *ṣᵉdāqâ*. Reimer has correctly asserted that "*ṣedeq* and *ṣᵉdāqâ* are completely synonymous terms."[19] Therefore, the following discussion will concentrate primarily on the term *ṣedeq* but will not exclude *ṣᵉdāqâ*.

Research has demonstrated that the semantic range of the word *ṣedeq* is quite wide. No one English word is able to capture the many and varied uses and meanings of this word. Though one can, based on morphology, suggest some generalizations regarding the term, it is much more advisable to derive the various semantic nuances from the different contexts in which the word is used. For example, the idea of *legitimate* or *just* with regard to weights and measures is present in the Pentateuchal literature—a meaning that is also present with respect to ordinances and sacrifices in the psalms. This immediately suggests that *ṣedeq* often carries a forensic sense—which is quite evident in the use of *ṣedeq* in the book of Job, particularly as Job argues for his innocence.[20]

Another meaning that surfaces is the idea of proper order and right behavior. This can be applied both to individual situations and to communal contexts. *Sedeq* is often used to describe proper conduct and the kind of behavior that is socially acceptable. It can also depict Yahweh's order and the kinds of social disorders that occur when the order of Yahweh is not followed. There is a real sense in which the right behavior of a human being must be commensurate with divine *ṣedeq*.

A significant use of the term *ṣedeq* relates to the concept of salvation, liberation, victory, and deliverance. This is especially true of God's saving action. In the psalms, God's *ṣedeq* comes to the aid of cities, the oppressed, the abandoned, the afflicted, and the like. This divine intervention on behalf of those in need is expressed through the word *ṣedeq*. This is also true in Isaiah 40–55. John Scullion has drawn this conclusion:

> In Isaiah 40–55 *ṣedeq-sedaqah* are constantly used for Yahweh's saving activity and its effects in the life of his covenant people. And one of the most important of these effects was the peace, harmony, and well-being of the community. *Ṣedeq-ṣedaqah* very often connote prosperity in these chapters. This conclusion fits in well with that of H. H. Schmid in his detailed study of *ṣedeq:* "*ṣ-d-q* in Second Isaiah, then, means Yahweh's world order in salvation history, an order that is based on creation and extends over the proclamation of the divine will, the rousing of Cyrus and the 'servant' right up to the coming of the salvation of the future."[21]

In other words, it is evident from various contexts that *ṣedeq*'s meaning goes beyond a forensic and proper conduct domain and includes a salvific connotation that must be recognized in any translation of the Hebrew Bible.

Finally, a related meaning to the ones discussed above is that of *justice*. There are many contexts in which the best rendition of *ṣedeq* is achieved through the word or concept *justice*. This is especially true when *ṣedeq* is used in parallelism with *mišpāt*—a rich Hebrew term meaning, among other things, "decision," "legal decision," "legal case," "justice," "right" (i.e., the right of an individual). When these two terms are used together, they often express the obligation of the king to be just and to ensure that justice is meted out in the community. In the prophets, there is a constant concern that justice is practiced, both by royalty and by the religious leaders. It is in these contexts that a right relationship between God and the people needs to be maintained on the basis of the existence of *ṣedeq*.

Social justice is also at the heart of the meaning of *ṣedeq*. In such contexts as Isaiah 1, it is clear that the prophet insists that *ṣedeq* needs to be present in order for restoration to take place on behalf of the dispossessed and the marginalized. Listen to the words of the prophet, as he cries out:

> See how Jerusalem, once so faithful, has become a prostitute. Once the home of justice and righteousness, she is now filled with murderers.... Your leaders are rebels, the companions of thieves. All of them take bribes and refuse to defend the orphans and the widows....
>
> Afterward I will give you good judges and wise counselors like the ones you used to have. Then Jerusalem will again be called the Home of Justice and the Faithful City.
>
> ISAIAH 1:21, 23, 26 NLT

As will be seen in specific key passages discussed below, the concern for social justice is expressed many times in the Hebrew text by the use of the hendiadys formed by *ṣedeq* and *mišpāt*. David Reimer is correct to suggest that "together they represent the ideal of social justice, an ideal lauded by the Queen of Sheba concerning Solomon's kingship in 1 Kings 10:9, forming part of the excellence of his impressive administration."[22]

The evidence presented thus far, albeit incomplete, demonstrates that there is no single meaning for the word *ṣedeq*. It is quite impossible to reduce the term to a linear, flat, one-dimensional meaning. This is what makes the translation of the term quite difficult. At the same time, one must embrace the rich multiple-meanings reality of *ṣedeq* and allow the translation of the Hebrew text of the Bible to reflect this. For this reason I will not propose at this time a single, overarching suggestion regarding *ṣedeq*. One could, I suppose, come close by suggesting something like "communal responsibility" or "being faithful to the community." These phrases are attempts at encompassing the semantic range of the term. And yet I wouldn't be willing to venture that they can cover all contexts. There is, however, in the evidence presented a clear indication that the Hebrew term has more of a *relational* and *communal* flavor than a moral, individualistic sense.

In light of this, the question regarding the KJV's overwhelming choice of "righteousness" as the translation for *ṣedeq* must be addressed. For example, the word *ṣedeq* appears in the Old Testament a total of 119 times. Of these 119 instances, the KJV has translated it "righteousness" 82 times, "righteous" 10 times, and "right" 3 times. The percentages are much higher if one includes *ṣᵉdāqâ* and other cognate words of the root *ṣ-d-q*. Consequently, as I stated in my introductory comments, before any judgments are made or conclusions reached it is necessary to delve into questions of the original meaning of "righteousness," the history of the translation of the KJV, and current understandings of the term.

History and Meaning of the Term *Righteousness*

The meaning of the term *righteousness* found in contemporary English language dictionaries is generally tied to a theological or religious context. In one dictionary the main entry states that righteousness is the "quality or condition of being righteous; conformity of life or conduct to the requirements of the divine or moral law; *spec.* in *Theol.* applied e.g. to the perfection of the Divine Being, and to the justification of man through the Atonement."[23] Another dictionary adds the ideas of purity of heart and rectitude of life. It also underscores the concept of conformity of life to divine law. Matters of holiness and holy principles are also mentioned in conjunction with righteousness.[24] Still another work emphasizes the quality or state of "being righteous." The idea of uprightness and rectitude come into play in this nuance. And in a third entry it includes "the state of being rightful or just."[25]

It is quite clear that the modern understanding is that which suggests, first of all, a state of being—meaning that righteousness has more of a stative connotation than an active connotation. Second, the various definitions always portray the term in relationship to divine and moral law. Therefore a righteous person, or one who demonstrates righteousness, is one who is in right standing with God, who is justified by God, and who exhibits the qualities of holiness, purity, uprightness, and rectitude. Finally, the definitions suggest a highly individualistic meaning for the term. There doesn't seem to be present in this contemporary understanding of the term a corporate element or a community emphasis. In summary, to state the ideas in terms of opposite categories:

- Righteousness is not active but passive;
- it is theologically bound;
- it is not secularly relevant;
- it is individualistic rather than community oriented.

I recognize that casting the term in these black-and-white categories may lead to an overstatement of the conclusions. Nevertheless, I would contend that the popular contemporary understanding of the term falls within these categories.

The question that must still be addressed is whether this was the way the translators of the KJV used and understood the term. This, of course, is not easy to determine, since we cannot ask them directly. We can also suspect that the different men involved in the translation process had slightly different views on how to use the term and how to best translate the word *ṣedeq*. We are indeed once again faced with a variation of the well-known biblical hermeneutical problem of "authorial intent."

One of the first problems we encounter as we try to uncover the meaning of "righteousness" and how it was used in the late sixteenth and early seventeenth centuries is that, up until 1604, the English language did not have English dictionaries as we know them today. What was available were glossaries, vocabularies, and a number of bilingual dictionaries. These cannot be equated to a monolingual dictionary that arranges words in alphabetical order and tries to systematically define the meaning of a word by using other words in the same language. In this sense the English language was quite far behind other languages such as French, Italian, and German. It is astonishing to think that William Shakespeare did not have access to a full dictionary while he was composing some of the most outstanding English literature of all time. Because dictionaries as we know them didn't exist at that time, Simon Winchester observed, "If the language that so inspired Shakespeare had limits, if its words had definable origins, spellings, pronunciations, *meanings*—then no single book existed that established them, defined them, and set them down.... The English language was spoken and written—but at the time of Shakespeare it was not defined, not *fixed*."[26]

The lack of a systematic treatment of any given word makes it doubly difficult to discern its meaning at any given time. As Ian Lancashire noted—referring to the English-speaking world in the sixteenth century—"Most persons alive at this time would not have understood the question 'what does this word *mean?*' as anything other than a request for a translation, an etymology, or gesture pointing to something in the world denoted by that word."[27]

Some help in this regard can be sought in a modern reconstruction of the English language. A project undertaken by the University of Michigan has developed what is called a *Middle English Dictionary*.[28] This dictionary attempts to discover the meaning of English words as they were used from approximately 1100 to 1500. Numerous sources of English literature from that time period are taken into consideration in order to create lexical meanings of a given word. This dictionary suggests that the word *righteousness* most likely comes from the term *right-wisnesse.* According to this modern attempt to reconstruct the meaning of a term from several texts, *right-wisnesse* meant "justice; fairness, impartiality." What still remains unclear, it seems to me, is the transition from *right-wisnesse* to *righteousness* as used in the biblical text. As I'll contend below, the Puritan understanding of the term *righteousness* seems to have determined how the reader of the late sixteenth and earlier seventeenth centuries internalized the term.

Not having a precise source to turn to with regard to the meaning and usage of the term *righteousness* in the sixteenth and seventeenth centuries, our next step is to look at some of the factors that had an influence on the production of the magnificent literary piece we know as the King James Version.

The political and social scene during the early seventeenth century in England was quite tumultuous. By 1603, when Queen Elizabeth I died, England had established itself as the major player in the concert of nations in Europe. One clear symbol of this reality is the fact that the Church of England had severed all ties with the Church of Rome. This didn't mean, however, that total unity among the religious parties existed in England. In fact, one of the urgent tasks King James I had to confront was the division that existed over which version of the Bible was going to be the so-called "authorized version" legitimized by political authority. At that time people were using neither the Bishops' Bible (1568) nor the Great Bible (ca. 1535) that had been installed in the churches. The people had turned their attention toward and were buying the editions of the Geneva Bible (1560) being produced copiously by the presses of England and the Netherlands.

At the suggestion of Dr. John Reynolds, president of Corpus Christi College in Oxford and spokesman for the Puritan group, King James I decided to support the production of a new translation and proposed that "this bee done by the best learned in both Vniuersities, after them to be reuiewed by the Bishops, and the chiefe learned of the Church; from them to bee presented to the Priuie-Councell; and lastly to bee ratified by his Royall authoritie, and so this whole Church to be bound vnto it, and none other."[29]

From this we can conclude that a very important agenda item in the production of the KJV was to have one—and only one—legitimized version that would unite all the people under a single text. As is typical in any translation project, certain rules and guidelines have to be established and then adhered to. For our present study, the following guidelines for the translators of the KJV are pertinent:

1. The ordinary Bible read in church, commonly called the Bishops' Bible, to be followed and as little altered as the truth of the original will permit.

2. The old ecclesiastical words to be kept, viz. the word "church" not to be translated "congregation." (The Greek word can be translated either way.)
3. When a word hath divers significations, that to be kept which hath been most commonly used by most of the ancient fathers.
4. No marginal notes at all to be affixed, but only for the explanation of the Hebrew or Greek words, which cannot without some circumlocution be so briefly and fitly expressed in the text.[30]

Moreover, it is important for our purposes to recognize the influence of the Bishops' Bible as well as other versions such as Tyndale's, Matthew's, Coverdale's, Whitchurch (Great Bible), and the Geneva Bible. Translations in other languages were also consulted, including the Valera's Spanish Bible (1602), the precursor to the RVR.[31] Recognizing the fact that the Bishops' Bible was used as the basic text, it is generally agreed that the changes incorporated into the KJV were most influenced by the Geneva Bible.

Regarding the translation of the Hebrew *ṣedeq,* the Bishops' Bible never uses the word *justice* to translate this term. Therefore, since this text was to serve as the basis for the KJV translators, it is not surprising that *justice* or other cognates were hardly ever used to translate *ṣedeq*. It is also interesting to note that the Geneva Bible does use the word *justice* a few times. In fact, *ṣedeq* is translated by the word *justice* twelve more times in the Geneva Bible than in the KJV. I believe that the Geneva Bible made a genuine effort to express the wider range of meaning of *ṣedeq*. So I suggest that the KJV translators had the opportunity to build on the work of the Geneva Bible and to incorporate some of the advances regarding the meaning of *ṣedeq,* but they did not do so. The instructions were clear: The Bishops' Bible was to be followed as much as possible and altered as little as possible.

A number of other factors contributed to the lack of flexibility in the translation process of the KJV as well. First and perhaps foremost, the production of the new translation was a project ordered by the king. One can't help but suspect that any so-called questionable translations or any translations that would call into question political policies would be avoided. Walter Wink has alerted us to an example of how translators working in the hire of King James were conditioned. We know that one of the reasons King James commissioned a new translation was to counteract the "seditious ... dangerous, and trayterous" ideas expressed in the marginal notes printed in the Geneva Bible, which included endorsement of the right to disobey a tyrant.[32] Wink argues that the translation of Jesus' words in Matthew 5:38–41 is more than a translation from Greek into English. It resulted in the translation of nonviolent resistance into docility. By translating *antistēnai* in verse 39 as simply "resist not evil," the clear message is that total submission to any monarchical power is what Jesus intended. And yet Jesus often opposed unjust political powers. Therefore the preferred translation would take this into account, and Wink proposes neither passivity nor violence but a *third way*—one that is at once assertive and yet nonviolent. For example, a translation such as TEV's "Do not take revenge on someone who wrongs you" would not have represented enough insurance for the king against assertive nonviolent resistance.

Along the same lines, I suggest that one of the reasons the translators hired by King James didn't even consider incorporating the latest changes introduced by the Geneva Bible with regard to *ṣedeq* was that *justice* was not an issue the king wanted people to think about or even consider as part of their spiritual responsibility. Powerful words such as *justice, just, rights,* and *communal faithfulness* were not in the king's best interests. A religious word such as *righteousness,* which speaks of a state of being and not of an active, intentional responsibility towards others—especially the poor and the marginalized—is a much safer term. It's also a term that speaks more of an individual state than a societal or communitarian *shalom.* It is my contention that the term *righteousness* fit the royal agenda and served the purposes of the monarchy quite well.

A third factor that exercised a significant influence on the KJV was the Puritan worldview. It's important to remember that it was Dr. John Reynolds, the spokesman for the Puritan group, who convinced King James of the need to produce a new translation that would have the approval of the whole church and bring everybody under the authority of the new version. The Puritan concern for individual holiness, purity, and moral stature was not a significant problem for the king. However, their strong emphasis on *social justice* and an antagonistic attitude toward the luxurious lifestyle of the court were no doubt reasons for concern.[33]

Years later, in 1644, Puritan Samuel Rutherford published his famous manifesto *Lex, Rex, or The Law and the Prince.* In this treatise Rutherford openly challenged the king's right to stand above the law and oppress the poor. Throughout the document there are numerous places where a call is issued to the king to ensure justice.[34] The Puritan agenda clearly didn't seem to be in the best interests of the king. I suggest, on this basis, that a highly politicized context certainly determined how a translation would be rendered. Once again, *righteousness,* which we've noted to be almost exclusively a religious term, would fit the king's agenda and ideology quite well. Issues of social justice, transformation of the evil structures of society, and civic responsibility were not priorities for the king at the time.

Still another factor that had an influence, albeit tangentially, on the final outcome of the KJV was the decision to eliminate marginal notes. This began a practice in Bible translation that ultimately led to the notion that a "clean, plain, unadorned" text was free from biased subjectivity and therefore absolutely objective and true. On the one hand, there were valid reasons for eliminating some of the more extreme ideologically infused marginal notes such as they existed in the Geneva Bible. On the other hand, the ultimate consequence of such a practice was the development of another ideology that set the translation on a pedestal that was untouchable. Whereas marginal notes could have explained or illustrated the various nuances of the term *ṣedeq,* a plain and, to a degree, "flat" concordance-type translation served the king's purposes quite well.

Thus, as far as can be determined, the meaning and usage of the term *righteousness* emphasized personal piety, individual holiness, and moral purity. These connotations served the king well and supported the Puritan worldview and theological framework.

Analysis of Critical Texts

As I noted earlier, the word *ṣedeq* appears in the Old Testament 119 times—not including, of course, the number of times its cognates occur in the Hebrew text. As I've analyzed various texts, I have become convinced that my contention would be strengthened if I included as evidence the 157 times the term *ṣᵉdāqâ* is used. However, in order for this study to stay within certain reasonable parameters, I've limited my arguments to contexts where just *ṣedeq* appears. Of the 119 occurrences of *ṣedeq*, I've chosen a sample from different literary genres in order to expose the problem at hand.

The Deuteronomic Literature

A critical text from the Deuteronomic literature for consideration is Deuteronomy 16:20. The KJV reads, "That which is altogether just shalt thou follow, that thou mayest live, and inherit the land which the LORD thy God giveth thee." The RVR reads, *"La justicia, la justicia seguirás, para que vivas y heredes la tierra que Jehová tu Dios te da"* ("Justice, and only justice, you will follow, so that you may live and inherit the land which Jehovah your God gives to you"). Other English translations have captured what the RVR suggests by translating as follows:

- "Follow justice, and justice alone" (NIV)
- "Justice, and only justice, you shall follow" (RSV)
- "Let true justice prevail" (NLT)
- "Justice, and justice alone" (NEB)

The entire context of this particular verse is concerned with *communal* responsibilities. The previous verse speaks clearly about not perverting justice, not showing partiality, and not taking a bribe. To the modern reader of the biblical text, "follow justice" carries with it a slightly different connotation from merely something "altogether just." It states clearly that the covenantal relationship with God requires that justice is exercised and nurtured in society. The KJV translation waters down the impact of the repetition of the Hebrew *"ṣedeq ṣedeq"* placed at the very beginning of the verse. Of course the context for the KJV is already set in the previous verse by translating it "Thou shalt not wrest judgment" (Deut 16:19). To my own surprise the New Scofield Reference Bible (1967) has seen fit to correct the Authorized King James Version by introducing the phrase "Thou shalt not distort justice" in the text and placing the KJV translation in the margin.

If one of the basic requirements of a translation is to produce a similar response, I suggest that the RVR translation elicits a much more similar response to that of the original hearers of Deuteronomy. It is a translation that mobilizes a communal responsibility in the direction of seeking justice for "the other." And it is precisely this concern for communal justice that will enable the original hearers to live and to inherit the land. Jeffrey Tigay makes this observation about this verse:

> The injunctions of the previous verse [v. 19] have all been stated earlier in the Torah. Characteristically, Deuteronomy adds an exhortation pleading for the basic principle of justice and seeks to persuade its audience to follow it by emphasizing the benefits it will bring.... The pursuit of justice is an indispensable condition for God's enabling Israel to endure and thrive in the promised land.[35]

THE POETIC LITERATURE

Moving on to the poetical genre, I wish to consider Psalm 4:5, especially as it relates to 4:1 and the entire poem. The KJV reads, "Offer the sacrifices of righteousness, and put your trust in the LORD." The RVR reads, *"Ofreced sacrificios de justicia, Y confiad en Jehová"* ("Offer sacrifices of justice, and trust in Jehovah").

Two preliminary matters must be emphasized. First, the verbs "to offer" and "to trust" are in the imperative mood—something that is clear in both translations. In other words, these are not suggestions; they are *commands* that must be taken seriously. The second matter is not readily clear in English translation because of the nature of the English language. The commands are plural, that is, they are addressed not to the individual but to the *community*. This, of course, is evident in the English from verse 2 ("ye sons of men"). Nevertheless, it is worth underscoring, if for no other reason than the fact that so many of the verses in the psalms are lifted out of context and quoted individually in church life.

The psalm depicts the situation of a person who is being accused and persecuted. The poet begins the poem with a strong plea, and given the context, it seems much more appropriate to translate *ṣedeq* in verse 1 as justice: "Hear me when I call, God of my justice." I concur with Hans-Joachim Kraus that verse 5 needs to be read in light of verse 1, and therefore I would argue that "sacrifices of justice" fits the communal context much better. Kraus states the following:

> If now *z-b-hṣ-d-q* may be connected with *ʾ-l-hṣ-d-q* (v. 1)—and that is obvious—then we are dealing with sacrifices by means of which the ***justice*** proceeding from Yahweh is acknowledged.... In this connection it can only have been the meaning of *z-b-hṣ-d-q* to bring the persecutors and the persecuted into a new social relation at a sacrifice after Yahweh's declaration of ***justice*** and into a social relation that corresponds to the bestowal of *ṣ-d-q* by Yahweh.[36] (emphasis mine)

The issue is more about doing justice than about offering sacrifices that will bring about a kind of individual morality or a state of individual holiness. Certainly these concerns are present in *ṣedeq,* but by translating in or incorporating the concern for justice, the message once again is more dynamic and more communal, and it results in the transformation of social relationships, which in turn affects all of society.

In Psalm 50:6 the KJV reads, "And the heavens shall declare his righteousness: for God is judge himself." The RVR reads, *"Y los cielos declararán su justicia, Porque Dios es el juez"* ("And the heavens shall declare his justice, for God is the judge"). Once again Kraus alerts us to the fact that "*ṣedeq* here leans toward the meaning 'actual sense of justice.'"[37] If indeed God is the judge, then it follows that the heavens will proclaim his justice. This justice will certainly have a moral dimension—it will include holiness, proper conduct, and all that the word or idea of *righteousness* includes. But more important, it also declares and requires that relationships are based on a kind of justice that enables men, women, and children to relate to God and thus to each other. Without the justice that *ṣedeq* bespeaks, no real relationship can develop.

A final example from the poetic literature deserves mention, at least in passing. Perhaps the most popular and influential psalm in the church over the centuries has been Psalm 23. It is quoted over and over again in different contexts and memorized in Sunday schools all over the world. Language has been transcended by this psalm, and people from different ethnic groups, social classes, and educational backgrounds have found inspiration and comfort in Psalm 23. In the KJV, Psalm 23:3 reads, "He restoreth my soul: he leadeth me in the paths of righteousness for his name's sake." The RVR reads, *"Confortará mi alma; Me guiará por sendas de justicia por amor de su nombre"* ("He will comfort my soul; he will guide me through paths of justice for the love of his name"). Given the context of the entire psalm, perhaps one could argue that *justice* is not the best rendering for *ṣedeq*. It is entirely possible that the poet, in thinking of his situation, might have been thinking more along the lines of *victory* or even *salvation,* which are semantic possibilities for *ṣedeq*. However, my point here is not so much to argue for one specific translation over another but to state that the reader/hearer comes away with a significantly different feeling and understanding when she/he reads "paths of justice" instead of "paths of righteousness." Given that this is such a popular poem in the church, it is important to understand these differences. More will be said about this in the final section of this essay.

The Prophetic Literature

Although we could consider a number of examples from the wisdom literature in the Hebrew Bible, I'll conclude this section with a couple of examples from the prophetic genre. Of all the prophets, Isaiah uses the term *ṣedeq* the most: a total of 25 times. As I noted earlier, the prophet is constantly concerned about the right communal relationships, where concern for the marginalized is not overlooked.

In Isaiah 1:21 the KJV reads, "How is the faithful city become an harlot! it was full of judgment; righteousness lodged in it; but now murderers." The RVR reads, *"¿Cómo te has convertido en ramera, oh ciudad fiel? Llena estuvo de justicia, en ella habitó la equidad; pero ahora, los homicidas"* ("How have you become a harlot, O faithful city? It had been full of justice, equity inhabited it, but now murderers"). I've chosen this verse in order to show, first of all, that *ṣedeq* here is used in parallelism with *mišpāṭ* ("justice," "right")—and RVR has taken this into account and introduced a different nuance for *ṣedeq*—and then, secondly, to suggest that the KJV is somewhat off the track when it translates *mišpāṭ* as "judgment." The context of the verse clearly indicates that what is being communicated is that at one point Jerusalem was full of justice, not judgment (cf. RSV, NIV, NLT, NEB). Therefore, since the first term (*mišpāṭ*) used is best translated as "justice," *ṣedeq* takes on a slightly different connotation. The RVR uses the word *equity* in the sense of "impartial, equitable, and fair." In other words, it is almost synonymous with justice in the sense that all are treated fairly according to the covenant stipulations. Walter Brueggemann has this comment about the scene described by Isaiah:

> The city is remembered as having been faithful in some time past, filled with justice and righteousness, and fully permeated with covenantal practices that enhance the entire community. But now the city is likened to a whore—fickle, self-indulgent, unprincipled.... Everyone seeks self-advancement, and no one cares anymore for the public good. When there is such self-serving and self-seeking, moreover, the needy of society predictably disappear from the screen of public awareness. Widows and orphans are the litmus test of justice and righteousness (cf. 1:17). On this test, Jerusalem fails completely and decisively. *The large theological issues of life with Yahweh boil down to the concreteness of policy toward widows and orphans.*[38] (The emphasis here is mine.)

The context of the passage is better understood by employing words that speak more to a communal concern for justice rather than by using words that suggest an individual moral state of being.

The same scenario is evident when one compares the different translations of Isaiah 1:26. The implications present, and the responses elicited in readers or hearers, are not the same when one reflects on the naming of Jerusalem as "city of righteousness" (KJV) or "City of justice" (RVR—*Ciudad de justicia*).

The final passage I'll comment on is Isaiah 61. This text is well-known because Jesus quotes the first two verses as he announces his ministry and validates it with the words of the prophet (see Luke 4:18–19). In Isaiah 61, the word *ṣedeq* occurs in verse 3 and *ṣᵉdāqâ* in verses 10 and 11. I will take the liberty in this last passage to include two uses of *ṣᵉdāqâ* to support my argument.[39]

Following the first two verses where there is a definite concern for the less privileged of society—the afflicted, the brokenhearted, the captives, the prisoners, and the like—we read that the result of the words and actions of the Servant-Messiah will be that the people will be called "trees of righteousness" (KJV), or "trees of justice" (RVR). Given the theme of the first two verses I would argue strongly that the context demands that *ṣedeq* here refers to justice being done on behalf of those who do not have the power to alter their situation.

If this meaning is accepted for verse 3, then it follows that the speaker in verse 10, which I take to be Zion herself,[40] having experienced the justice offered by the Messiah, is now able to incarnate that justice—"clothed with a robe of justice," "wrapped in a mantle of justice" *(ṣᵉdāqâ)*. And then it follows that verse

11 speaks of God making justice *(ṣ^e^dāqâ)* and praise spring forth through Zion before and on behalf of all the nations. Michael Crosby states this in his comments on the fourth Beatitude ("blessed are those who hunger and thirst for justice; they shall be satisfied"):

> Constituted in God's justice, God uses us to "make justice and praise spring up before all nations" (Isa 61:11).... Justice is God's authority, which must be manifested in the world.... When God intervened in the life of the community that suffered injustice of its clerical class (Jer 23:1–4), the community experienced Yahweh as "our justice" (Jer 23:6; 33:16; cf. Isa 11:1–11). In the power of that experienced justice, Israel was called to a similar ministry of justice. Since Israel's religious experience and ministry is the archetype of our spirituality, *when the world sees our ministry of justice it should also be able to say of us "our justice."*[41] (The emphasis here is mine.)

If the world is ever going to experience our ministry of justice, the primary meaning of *ṣedeq* must come to light in English translations of the Bible. The "religious and moral state of being" elicited by the term *righteousness* has not and will not mobilize the church to "do justice."

Preliminary Suggestions

Let me first underscore again that all translation is interpretation. For translation to take place, a given text must be understood. Understanding implies interpretation—which means that translation choices indeed have a direct bearing on theology and "theologizing." Thus, I offer the following suggestions based on the above discussion.

First, I suggest that the evidence presented has pertinent implications for the way theologizing is done (or not done) in the church and how it is put into practice through discipleship in the church. The evangelical church in general, particularly in the Western world, is predicated on an individualistic worldview. The ideology of discipleship is one marked by a heavy emphasis on personal and individual holiness, purity, moral uprightness, and rectitude. This extreme individualism tends to promote individual theologies that often result in withdrawing from the real world and retreating into a comfort zone where spirituality is measured primarily by my "righteous state of being."

Many years ago Émile Durkheim, the noted French sociologist, warned against this phenomenon. He pointed out that religion was occupying a smaller and smaller portion of social life. Originally, religion played a significant role in all areas of life. However, slowly but surely, the political, economic, and scientific worlds separated themselves from their religious functions. Durkheim observed that "God, if in fact we can express ourselves this way, who at the beginning was present in all human relations, now progressively withdraws, abandoning the world to men and their conflicts."[42] The result is that religion is then reduced to the private life of individuals. In evangelical terms, the transforming power of the gospel is taken away from the public sphere and is reduced and limited to a privatized expression.

My first major suggestion, then, is that the evangelical church, if it is serious about making the Ancient Book relevant, needs to *de-privatize* the faith. A first step is to nuance the traditional English translations of *ṣedeq* and incorporate the communal challenge present in the biblical understanding of justice that is fundamental to the meaning of *ṣedeq* and its cognates.

If this is done, two profoundly important things can begin to happen. First, change can take place from a passive state of being—where what matters is my *personal righteousness*—to an active *communal* concern whereby "covenant life" affects all of life. Instead of an emphasis on a self-centered, ethnocentric spirituality that is static, a dynamic, imaginative, unselfish concern for "the other" can emerge. This then can have an impact on all aspects of life and begin to break down the escapist ideological paradigm in which the "secular" and "spiritual" spheres of life are totally separated. Rather than withdrawing from the contemporary needs of the world, a different translation can challenge the church to an *active engaging* of the world with a relevant message of hope. Second, a more communal, horizontal model for ministry and leadership can emerge. The privatistic, individual paradigm for ministry tends to foster a theology of leadership that is hierarchical, which in turn nurtures desires for power, self-aggrandizement, and success that play into the mercantilistic and narcissistic values of society in general. I submit that what society needs is not for the church to imitate the hunger and thirst for power that is so prevalent in human nature but to offer a redemptive alternative based on the hunger and thirst for justice that is communally faithful.

My second and final major suggestion is that the "needs of the world" will be addressed much more faithfully by a church that understands the communal aspects of justice as expressed in the *ṣedeq* word family. I wish to emphasize *understand,* for I am fully aware that a mere change in translation will not be enough. I suggest, however, that if the word *justice* appears more often in English Bibles, the richest church in the world may get the message and begin to take seriously the biblical mandate to pursue justice—and justice only.

The needs of the world in which we live are indeed overwhelming. Realities such as hunger, oppression, increasing numbers of poor people, injustice, broken families, broken relationships, natural disasters, violence, and many other devastating situations threaten to drown us in anguish and despair. Oftentimes the "righteous response" to these realities has been one of relative indifference rooted in the premise that one cannot solve all of the problems of the world. Consequently, privatized spirituality concentrates on individual righteousness and well-being without a true "conscientization" of the call to be the salt and light of this world. However, if the church really takes seriously the communal practice expressed by *ṣedeq,* whereby all members of the human community have the right to a life of decency and respect, then real hope will be proclaimed to the world.

Two examples of world needs will suffice to illustrate what can happen if the church embraces the command to "do justice." And, I might add in passing, this constitutes a command, not an option. This is not an elective among many. *Doing and practicing justice* is gospel (cf. Luke 4:18–19).

Globalization is a term that now has many meanings. In terms of economics, those who have economic power have taken advantage of the "global village" concept and have imposed a "free market" economy that in Latin America is known as "neoliberalism." This system or worldview assumes that free markets—free from any government intervention—provide the solution to the economic and social needs of the world. This has led to what is called in many Third-World countries "savage capitalism," where there are no controls over fierce and deadly competition.

This extreme form of "free market economy" has been studied carefully by Ulrich Duchrow, who concludes that the consequence of this economic libertarianism is "that the accumulation of money assets is now the absolute, immutable yardstick for all economic, social, ecological, and political decisions. It is no longer just an aim but a concrete mechanism."[43] The result of this "concrete mechanism" imposed on the world by those with economic power is that the disadvantaged, the poor, the handicapped, the elderly, and the children of the world are living in subhuman conditions and are becoming increasingly more vulnerable. As the accumulation of wealth becomes the primary concern, all other concerns rapidly fade into the distance. This context of "global pillage" cries out for *ṣedeq*. This reality represents an enormous challenge to the church to be proclaimers of hope by taking seriously the communal and relational demands of *ṣedeq*. The total absence of justice in so many places around the globe has created an enormous void in God's creation that God's people can fill only if they truly understand and practice the meaning of *ṣedeq*.

Political and military oppression should also be the concern of the church. Many in the United States are not aware of the past existence of a place in Fort Benning, Georgia, called "The U.S. Army School of the Americas"—a school that closed in December 2000 and reopened in January 2001 under a new name (Western Hemisphere Institute for Security Cooperation). This school trained Latin American soldiers in combat, counterinsurgency, and counternarcotics. It is significant that 90 percent of the literature in the Amos Library of the School of the Americas is in Spanish.[44] It is also a well-known fact that graduates of this infamous institution have been responsible for some of the worst human rights abuses in Latin America. I have been a personal witness to the atrocities committed by the military regime in Argentina from 1976 to 1983.[45] Argentine dictators Leopoldo Galtieri and Roberto Viola were both trained at the School of the Americas, and they are among those responsible for the murders or disappearances of over 30,000 civilians. The same is true of other graduates of SOA responsible for terrible acts of violence in Central America.[46]

Many have raised their voices in efforts to get this school closed down. If the church were to put on the mantle of justice, it, too, would raise its voice on behalf of those who are oppressed and who suffer injustice. If we who call ourselves followers of Jesus of Nazareth are truly going to help restore the voiceless, the faceless, the marginalized, the downtrodden, the disadvantaged, we will need to be agents of justice as well as righteous beings. And a good place to start is by offering the church a more balanced translation of the Hebrew and Greek texts of God's revelation when his revelation issues a call to "do justice."[47]

A Hasidic tale will serve to conclude this study:

A rabbi asked his students, "When, at dawn, can one tell the light from darkness?"

One student replied, "When I can tell a goat from a donkey."

"No," answered the rabbi.

Another said, "When I can tell a palm tree from a fig."

"No," answered the rabbi again.

"Well, then, what is the answer?" his students pressed him.

"Not until you look into the face of every man and every woman and see your brother and your sister," said the rabbi. "Only then have you seen the light. All else is still darkness."[48]

NOTES

1. A note of special appreciation is due my assistant, Ms. Janice Raymond, for her help in the research process and the collecting of statistical data, and to my colleague, Dr. Tom Correll, for his constant stimulating comments on this theme.

2. It is with a deep sense of appreciation that I offer this study to my professor and friend Ron Youngblood. His example of serious scholarship and commitment to the biblical text will forever be an inspiration for me.

3. See Randall C. Bailey and Tina Pippin, eds., *Race, Class, and the Politics of Bible Translation,* Semeia 76 (Atlanta: Scholars Press, 1996); Stanley Porter and Richard Hess, eds., *Translating the Bible—Problems and Prospects,* JSNTSup 173 (Sheffield: Sheffield Academic Press, 1999); Mark Strauss, *Distorting Scripture? The Challenge of Bible Translation and Gender Accuracy* (Downers Grove, Ill.: InterVarsity Press, 1998); D. A. Carson, *The Inclusive-Language Debate* (Grand Rapids: Baker, 1998); David Jobling and Tina Pippin, eds., *Ideological Criticism of Biblical Texts,* Semeia 59 (Atlanta: Scholars Press, 1992); and William Smalley, *Translation as Mission* (Macon, Ga.: Mercer Univ. Press, 1991).

4. Eugene A. Nida, "Analysis of Meaning and Dictionary Meaning," *International Journal of American Linguistics* 24 (1958): 281.

5. Nueva Versión Internacional, sponsored by International Bible Society and released in February 1999, and La Biblia en lenguaje sencillo, sponsored by Sociedades Bíblicas Unidas, to be published in 2003.

6. Stanley Porter, "The Contemporary English Version and the Ideology of Translation," in *Translating the Bible—Problems and Prospects,* 18.

7. Ernst R. Wendland, "Culture and the Form/Function Dichotomy in the Evaluation of Translation Acceptability," in *Meaningful Translation,* ed. Johannes P. Louw (Reading, UK: United Bible Societies, 1991), 8–40. See also Ernst R. Wendland, *Language, Society, and Bible Translation* (Cape Town: Bible Society of South Africa, 1985).

8. Wendlund, "Culture and the Form/Function Dichotomy," 40.

9. This was recognized as early as 1978 by my former colleague in Argentina, Dr. Sidney Rooy. See Sidney Rooy, "Righteousness and Justice," in *The Responsibility of Christian Institutions of Higher Education to Justice in the International Economic Order* (Grand Rapids: Calvin College, 1980), 1–16.

10. The translation of *mišpāt* ("justice") in the KJV has been questioned by Frank Gaebelein, "Old Testament Foundations for Living More Simply," in *Living More Simply: Biblical Principles and Practical Models,* ed. Ron Sider (Downers Grove, Ill.: InterVarsity Press, 1980), 27–39.

11. See, for example, H. G. Reventlow and Yair Hoffman, eds., *Justice and Righteousness,* JSOTSup 137 (Sheffield: Sheffield Academic Press, 1992); Ahuva Ho, *Ṣedeq and Ṣᵉdāqâ in the Hebrew Bible,* American University Series VII, vol. 78 (New York: Peter Lang, 1991); J. Krasovec, *La Justice (ṢDQ) de Dieu dans la Bible Hebraïque et L'Interprétation Juive et Chrétienne,* Orbis Biblicus et Orientalis 76 (Freiburg: Unviversitätsverlag Freiburg Schweiz, 1988); John J. Scullion, "*Ṣedeq and Ṣᵉdāqâ* in Isaiah cc. 40–66," *Ugarit-Forschungen* 3 (1971): 335–48; K. Koch, *"ṣedeq, Ser fiel a la comunidad,"* in E. Jenni and C. Westermann, *Diccionario Teológico Manual del Antiguo Testamento,* vol. II (Madrid: Ediciones Cristiandad, 1985), 640–68; David J. Reimer, *"ṣ-d-q"* in *NIDOTTE* 3:744–69; Harold Stigers, *"ṣedeq,"* in *TWOT* 2:752–55; and Moshe Weinfeld, *Social Justice in Ancient Israel and in the Ancient Near East* (Minneapolis: Fortress Press, 1995).

12. A word of clarification is necessary with regard to the cognate words. Terms such as the verb *ṣādaq,* the feminine noun *ṣᵉdāqâ,* the masculine noun *ṣaddîq,* and the adjective *ṣaddîq* will not be considered as part of this study. There is much disagreement

as to whether there is in fact any difference in meaning between *ṣedeq* and *ṣᵉdāqâ*. It is my contention that if there is any difference, it is not significant enough to affect the general argument presented in this particular study.

13. F. Brown, S. R. Driver, and C. A. Briggs, *A Hebrew and English Lexicon of the Old Testament* (Oxford: Clarendon Press, 1975), 841–42.

14. L. Koehler and W. Baumgartner, *Lexicon in Veteris Testamenti Libros* (Leiden: Brill, 1985), 794–95.

15. L. Koehler and W. Baumgartner; revised by W. Baumgartner and J. Stamm, *The Hebrew and Aramaic Lexicon of the Old Testament* (New York: Brill, 1996), 1004–5.

16. Luis Alonso Schökel, *Diccionario bíblico hebreo-español* (Madrid: Editorial Trotta, 1994), 632–33 (my translation).

17. Ibid., 632.

18. Nida, "Analysis of Meaning and Dictionary Meaning," 282.

19. Reimer, "*ṣ-d-q*," in *NIDOTTE* 3:767.

20. The forensic sense of *ṣᵉdāqâ* can also be found in 2 Samuel 8:15; 15:4.

21. Scullion, "*Ṣedeq and Ṣᵉdāqâ* in Isaiah cc. 40–66," 341; cf. H. H. Schmid, *Gerechtigkeit als Weltordnung* (Tbingen: Mohr, 1969), 134.

22. Reimer, "*ṣ-d-q*," in *NIDOTTE* 3:750.

23. *The Shorter Oxford English Dictionary on Historical Principles,* vol. 2 (Oxford: Clarendon Press, 1933), 1739.

24. *Webster's Universal Dictionary of the English Language,* vol. 2 (New York: The World Syndicate Publishing Company, 1936), 1430.

25. *Webster's New International Dictionary of the English Language,* 2d ed. unabr. (Springfield, Mass.: G. & C. Merriam Company, 1935), 2148.

26. Simon Winchester, *The Professor and the Madman* (New York: HarperCollins, 1995), 82–83.

27. Ian Lancashire, *What Renaissance Dictionaries Tell us about Lexical Meaning* (on the Web at http://www.chass.utoronto.ca/epc/chwp/lancash2/lan2_3.htm).

28. *Middle English Dictionary* (Ann Arbor: University of Michigan, 1984).

29. Cited in *A Ready-Reference History of the English Bible* (New York: American Bible Society, 1971), 22.

30. For a complete list of guidelines, see Gustavus S. Paine, *The Men Behind the KJV* (Grand Rapids: Baker, 1977), 70–71.

31. The Spanish Valera of 1602 is a revision done by Cipriano de Valera of the 1569 Spanish version done by Casiodoro de Reina. The Spanish Valera of 1602 was then revised again in 1862, 1909, and 1960. The RVR is the 1960 revision. There is now a Reina-Valera 1995 revision.

32. Cited in Walter Wink, *The Powers That Be* (New York: Doubleday, 1998), 98–101.

33. See H. G. Alexander, *Religion in England, 1558–1662* (London: University of London, 1968), 135.

34. See Samuel Rutherford, *Lex, Rex, or The Law and the Prince* (Harrisonburg, Va.: Sprinkle Publications, 1982), 54–57, 89, 96–97.

35. Jeffrey Tigay, *Deuteronomy,* The JPS Torah Commentary (Philadelphia: Jewish Publication Society, 1996), 161.

36. Hans-Joachim Kraus, *Psalms 1–59: A Commentary* (Minneapolis: Augsburg, 1988), 148–49.

37. Ibid., 492.

38. Walter Brueggemann, *Isaiah 1–39* (Louisville, Ky.: Westminster John Knox, 1998), 21–22.

39. Moshe Weinfeld has drawn the parallel between the Hebrew word-pair *mišpāt/ṣᵉdāqâ* and the Akkadian word-pair *kittum u misharum,* where the Akkadian pair as well as the Hebrew pair refer to a "sense of justice." Moshe Weinfeld, "'Justice and Righteousness'—*mišpāt and ṣᵉdāqâ*—The Expression and its Meaning," in H. G. Reventlow and Yair Hoffman, eds., *Justice and Righteousness,* JSOTSup 137 (Sheffield: Sheffield Academic Press, 1992), 230.

40. There is considerable debate over who the speaker is in verse 10. The arguments in favor of considering Zion to be the speaker rather than the Servant-Messiah are, in my opinion, much more convincing. Cf. John Oswalt, *The Book of Isaiah Chapters 40–66* (Grand Rapids: Eerdmans, 1998), 574–75.

41. Michael H. Crosby, *Spirituality of the Beatitudes* (Maryknoll: Orbis, 1982), 118–19.

42. Émile Durkheim, *De la división del trabajo social* (Buenos Aires: Schapire, 1967), 145–46 (my translation).

43. Ulrich Duchrow, *Alternatives to Global Capitalism: Drawn from Biblical History, Designed for Political Action* (Utrecht: International Books, 1995), 71. See also Jeremy Brecher and Tim Costello, *Global Village or Global Pillage,* 2d ed. (Cambridge, Mass.: South End Press, 1998); Wes Howard-Brook and Anthony Gwyther, *Unveiling Empire* (Maryknoll, N.Y.: Orbis, 1999).

44. See the information on the Web at http://www.benning.army.mil/whinsec/.

45. For a detailed report on these atrocities see *Nunca Más,* Informe de la Comisión Nacional Sobre La Desaparición de Personas (Buenos Aires: EUDEBA, 1984).

46. For detailed reports, see http://www.soaw.org/ and http://www.soawne.org/. You can also find interesting facts on the Web at http://www.ciponline.org/facts/soa.htm. In all fairness, it is necessary to point out that U. S. Army Secretary Louis Caldera is attempting to make significant changes at the school. Caldera's postition is that the school continues to be strategically very important for the United States and that it can be instrumental in the control of drug traffic. See the debate between Louis Caldera and U. S. Representative Joseph Moakley on the Web at http://www.pbs.org/newshour/bb/military/july-dec99/sotamericas_9-21a.html.

47. We encounter the same problem in the New Testament regarding the translation of *dikaios* and *dikaiosyne.* See the excellent analysis offered by C. H. Dodd, "Some Problems of New Testament Translation," *The Bible Translator* 13 (July 1962): 157; David Bosch, *Transforming Mission* (Maryknoll, N.Y.: Orbis, 1991), 70–73, 400–8; Michael H. Crosby, *Spirituality of the Beatitudes* (Maryknoll, N.Y.: Orbis, 1982), 118–39; Elsa Tamez, *The Amnesty of Grace: Justification by Faith from a Latin American Perspective* (Nashville: Abingdon, 1993). Although the problem has been recognized and addressed carefully, modern English translations of the New Testament have been reluctant to go against tradition and have for the most part chosen "righteousness" and "justification" to render the Greek words in question.

48. Cited in Johann C. Arnold, *Seeking Peace* (Farmington, Pa.: Plough, 1998), 103.

37. Ibid., 49.

38. [illegible] *Introduction to* [illegible] (Louisville: Westminster John Knox, 1999), 11–22.

39. M. [illegible] Westerfeld [illegible] the parallel between the Hebrew [illegible] and the [illegible] word [illegible] where the [illegible] as well as the Hebrew [illegible]. Again Westerfeld: "[illegible]"—[illegible] and [illegible] Hoffman, eds., [illegible] (Sheffield: Sheffield Academic Press, 1992), 36.

40. There is [illegible] whether the speaker is [illegible] in [illegible] rather than the [illegible] John Oswalt, *The Book of Isaiah, Chapters 40–66* (Grand Rapids: Eerdmans, 1998), 374–75.

41. [illegible]

42. [illegible] (my translation).

43. [illegible] *Global Christianity* [illegible] International Books, 1999) [illegible] and [illegible] *Global Christianity* [illegible] (Cambridge, Mass.: South End [illegible] and [illegible] (New York: [illegible], 1999).

44. See [illegible] information on the Web at http://www.[illegible].

45. For a detailed report on [illegible] National [illegible] (Nairobi [illegible]).

46. For [illegible] see [illegible] can also find [illegible] on the Web at http://www.[illegible]. In all fairness, it is necessary to point out that [illegible] is attempting to [illegible] at the school [illegible] continues to [illegible] the [illegible] States [illegible] mentioned in the [illegible] See the [illegible] between [illegible] and U.S. [illegible] on the Web at http://www.[illegible] [illegible].html.

47. We encounter the same problem in the New Testament regarding the translation of [illegible]. See the excellent analysis offered by C. H. Dodd, "Some Problems of New Testament Translation," *The Bible Translator* 13 (July 1962): [illegible] [illegible] (Grand Rapids: Zondervan, 1983), [illegible] [illegible] (Edinburgh: T. & T. Clark, 1955), 148–49; [illegible] *Righteousness in the Old Testament* [illegible] (Nashville: Abingdon, 1998). Although this problem has been recognized and addressed extensively, modern English translations of the New Testament have been reluctant to go against tradition and use [illegible] rather than "righteousness" and "justification" to translate the Greek words in question.

48. [illegible] *Second Isaiah* (Birmingham: [illegible] Press, 1998), 116.

15

TRANSLATING JOHN'S GOSPEL: CHALLENGES AND OPPORTUNITIES

Andreas J. Köstenberger

New translations continue to proliferate at an astonishing pace, and there is a growing need for translators to develop both linguistic and exegetical sophistication in order to be adequate to their task.[1] The present essay focuses on particular challenges—and opportunities—in translating John's Gospel. These include textual issues, questions of background or chronology, and ideological, exegetical, and stylistic matters. The following discussion may serve as a survey and brief for the translator of a biblical book that, in terms of influence and significance, is second to few.[2] To make things a bit more interesting, the essay concludes with an attempt at rating the quality and accuracy of nine major English translations of the Gospel of John.

TEXTUAL ISSUES

The first difficult textual issue in translating John's prologue—pertaining to punctuation—is the proper rendering of 1:3–4. Should the phrase *ho gegonen* ("that has been made") be construed with what precedes or with what follows? If we choose the former, "without him nothing was made that has been made" can easily be seen to bring closure to the thought expressed in verse 3 by way of emphatic restatement of the converse. If the latter, on the other hand, it is unclear what the statement "that [which] has been made in him was life" would mean.[3] Also, John frequently begins a sentence or clause with *en* and a demonstrative pronoun (e.g. 13:35; 15:8; 16:26). Johannine theology elsewhere likewise favors taking the phrase with what precedes (cf. 5:26, 39; 6:53). Among the translations that construe *ho gegonen* with what precedes are the NASB, NIV, NKJV, ISV, NLT, HCSB, ESV, and TNIV; among the major translations only the NRSV favors the alternative.

One of the most important textual issues affecting translation in John's Gospel is the reading of 1:18. With the acquisition of p[66] and p[75], however, both of which read *monogenēs theos,* the preponderance of the evidence now leans in the direction of "one and only God" as the probable original wording. This is not only the earlier but also the more difficult reading. Most likely, *monogenēs huios* represents a scribal assimilation to John 3:16 and 18.[4] This evidence convinced the NIV, NASB, ISV, and ESV, though not the NKJV and HCSB. The NRSV ("God the only Son"), NLT ("his only Son, who is himself God"), and TNIV ("the one and only [Son], who is himself God") also appear to accept *theos* as the original reading, though render *monogenēs* "only *Son,*" with the latter two versions taking *theos* to be in apposition to *monogenēs.*

Murray J. Harris expresses a strong preference for *monogenēs theos,* for at least four reasons: (1) its superior manuscript support; (2) it represents the more difficult reading; (3) the phrase serves as a more proper climax to the entire prologue, attributing deity to the Son by way of *inclusio* with verses 1 and 14; and (4) this reading seems best to account for the other variants.[5] In this he follows Westcott and Hort and an impressive list of commentators, including R. E. Brown, L. Morris, B. Lindars, F. F. Bruce, and G. R. Beasley-Murray.[6] A translation such as "one-of-a-kind [Son, himself] God" is to be preferred.[7]

Another knotty issue is the reading "Bethzatha" vs. "Bethesda" in 5:2. While "Bethzatha" is preferred by Nestle-Aland (followed by Newman and Nida), "Bethesda" is attested much more widely and clearly constitutes the superior reading. After an extended discussion, the eminent German historian Martin Hengel states categorically, "One should by all means read 'Bethesda.'"[8] Hengel considers the reading "Bethzatha" to be a scribal emendation (*pace* Josephus). "Bethesda" is favored by the NASB, NIV, ISV, NLT, NKJV, HCSB, and TNIV. "Bethzatha" is adopted by the NRSV and the ESV. In light of the very sparse external attestation of "Bethzatha" (א 33 Eusebius), "Bethesda" is to be preferred.

Also the subject of much discussion is the pericope of the adulterous woman in 7:53–8:11. The literature on this passage is substantial, with most scholars favoring noninclusion.[9] Virtually every verse in 8:1–11 (the sole exception being 8:5) contains words not otherwise found in the Gospel or even in the other Johannine writings.[10] Perhaps most notable is the occurrence of the term "elders" *(presbyteroi)* only here in John's Gospel, since one may surmise that John would have had occasion to use the expression elsewhere. Several other words occur elsewhere only once or twice. To this should be added the conspicuous absence of standard Johannine vocabulary (such as *alla, ean, ek, hēmeis, hina mē, mathētēs, oida, hos, hoti, ou, hymas, hymeis*) and syntactical differences with the rest of the

Gospel.[11] The penchant for verbs with a *kata* prefix in the present pericope *(katagraphō, katakyptō, kataleipō, katakrinō)* seems unusual as well.

For reasons such as these, the United Bible Societies committee unanimously rejects inclusion, considering the evidence for the non-Johannine origin of the pericope to be "overwhelming"—citing lack of early manuscript support as well as stylistic considerations—and the case against its Johannine authorship "conclusive."[12] Newman and Nida likewise state categorically, "This passage was doubtless not an original part of the Gospel of John.... It is not found in the earlier and better Greek manuscripts, it differs in style and vocabulary from the rest of John's Gospel, and it interrupts the sequence of 7.52 and 8.12 and following."[13] Nevertheless, most of those who prefer noninclusion affirm the probable authenticity of the event. This raises interesting questions of both a doctrinal and pragmatic nature.

On the doctrinal level, if inspiration is not attributed to the pericope, one deals here with a possibly authentic yet nonetheless fallible account composed at a time subsequent to the writing of John's Gospel. More pertinent still in the present context are pragmatic considerations. In the case of the pericope of the adulteress, Bible translators (and publishers) are faced with a dilemma—either not to include an account that has the ring of authenticity (though not inspiration) or to include it in a qualified fashion, be it within square brackets with an explanatory footnote or in a footnote. Most translations, such as the NIV, NASB, NLT, NRSV, HCSB, ESV, and TNIV opt for the former alternative—in which case the boundaries between the presumed original inspired text and material added later (no matter how interesting or possibly authentic) may be blurred.[14] In order to avoid such compromise, I personally favor not including the pericope in the text (even in square brackets) but rather putting the entire section in a footnote, thus indicating its doubtful inclusion in the original Gospel.

Of more than academic interest is the translation of 12:32. Will Jesus draw "all people" or "all things" to himself? Both external and internal considerations weigh decisively in favor of the former. Since I have elsewhere provided a detailed discussion of this issue, I need not do so again here.[15] Suffice it to say that the best contextual understanding of the phrase holds that the exalted Jesus will draw, not literally *all* people, but all *kinds* of people to himself, including Gentiles such as the Greeks who had, in the preceding pericope (12:20–23), just requested to see him.

The major English translations struggle, not so much with the textual issue—all construe the underlying text as *pantas* (masculine plural), not *panta* (neutral plural)—but with the potentially implied universalism of the passage (see also 1:7, 9). The NIV and NASB have "all men," which is in our age unduly gender specific (women, too, are included); the NRSV, HCSB, ISV, ESV, and TNIV have "all people"; the NLT has "everyone"; the NKJV has "all peoples." In light of the above exegetical comments, my preference is "all *kinds* of people," with a footnote indicating that this means both Jews and Gentiles, with reference to 12:20–23 and 11:52. By this standard, the NKJV seems to come closest.

Yet another difficult issue that continues to puzzle interpreters is the reading of 20:31. Both the present subjunctive *pisteuēte* and the aorist subjunctive *pisteusēte* have early support.[16] It is ironic that, of the evangelists, only John provides us with a purpose statement, and yet this statement is sufficiently ambiguous to make ascertaining his purpose difficult. In any case, there is widespread consensus that the form of the subjunctive, whether present or aorist, is by itself insufficient to indicate John's purpose.[17] In translation, "that you may believe" or a similar translation adequately renders the Greek without prejudging the textual issue. The rendering "continue to believe" is problematic.

Beyond this there are several other textual uncertainties facing the translator, yet only few have a bearing on significant theological or interpretive issues.[18]

Background Issues

Several items pertaining to first-century background or chronology affect the translation of particular passages in John's Gospel. One such issue is the proper construal of the Greek term *Hebraisti,* which is variously rendered "in Hebrew" or "in Aramaic" in the major versions. Translations of Hebrew or Aramaic terms are provided in 1:38 and 20:16 ("rabbi"); 1:41 and 4:25 ("Messiah"); 1:42 ("Cephas"); 9:7 ("Siloam"); 11:16, 20:24, and 21:2 ("Didymus"); and 19:17 ("Golgotha"). A study of the linguistic background of the translated terms yields the following results:

- "Rabbi" derives from the Hebrew/Aramaic term *rabbi,* which literally means "my great one."
- "Messiah" is a transliteration of a Hebrew or Aramaic word meaning "anointed one."
- Underlying "Cephas" in 1:42 is Aramaic *k̂êpaʾ*—"rock."
- In 9:7, "Siloam" is the translation for Hebrew *šilôaḥ* (itself derived from the verb "to send").
- As to 11:16, 20:24, and 21:2, both Hebrew *tʾōm* and Aramaic *tʾōmā* mean "twin."
- In 19:17, the underlying word is Aramaic *gulgoltâ*, which means "skull."

On the whole, therefore, it seems preferable to render *Hebraisti* in 19:17 as "in Aramaic" (NIV, TNIV), not "in Hebrew" (NASB, NLT, ISV, NKJV, HCSB, ESV; also NRSV, but see footnote—"That is, Aramaic").[19] Currently, the NIV and TNIV (with the partial exception of the NRSV) stand alone over against all other major English translations.

Decisions must also be made regarding the rendering of the Johannine time references. John provides time markers in 1:39 ("tenth hour"), 4:6 ("sixth hour"), 4:52 ("seventh hour"), and 19:14 ("sixth hour"). While it is sometimes argued that Roman reckoning of time commenced at midnight—so that "tenth hour," for example, would mean "ten in the morning"—the preponderance of evidence suggests that time in first-century Palestine was counted from sunrise to sunset (i.e., from about 6 A.M. until about 6 P.M.; cf. John 11:9).[20] Moreover, the day was divided into three-hour intervals, with people approximating the estimated time to the next full three-hour segment.

As to current translations, some opt for a literal translation of, for example, John 1:39, such as "the tenth hour" (so the NIV, ESV, NKJV, and NASB), in some cases with explanatory footnotes.[21] Other translations choose to spell out the modern-day equivalent, be it along the lines of time reckoning outlined above—NRSV, NLT, ISV, and TNIV ("about four o'clock in the afternoon"; ISV footnote: Lit. *the tenth hour*)—or on the basis of presumed Roman time (HCSB: "about ten in the morning").[22] By way of evaluation, little is to be said for the Roman time theory (disqualifying the HCSB rendering and the NASB footnote). "Tenth hour" (NIV et al.) is literal, but hardly helpful. Most satisfying are those translations that give the modern-day equivalent, with first prize in this category going to the ISV, where the literal rendering is noted in a footnote.

Another interpretive crux affecting translation is the proper construal of 2:20. Renderings such as those found in the NIV, ESV, NKJV, and TNIV—"It has taken [NASB = NLT: 'took'] forty-six years to build this temple"—suggest, almost certainly incorrectly, that the temple building was still under reconstruction at the time of Jesus' cleansing of the temple.[23] Historical records indicate, however, that Herod the Great (37–4 B.C.) began restoring the temple *(naos)* in the eighteenth year of his reign, that is, 20/19 B.C. (Josephus, *Ant.* 15.380), with completion a year and a half later in 18/17 B.C. (*Ant.* 15.421). It is true that the restoration of the entire temple area *(hieron)* was not completed until A.D. 63/64 under Herod Agrippa II and the governor Albinus (*Ant.* 20.219). But John's consistent use of *naos* for the temple building proper and *hieron* for the temple area precludes taking *naos* in 2:20 as referring, not to the temple building, but to the entire temple area.[24] A better rendering is therefore, "This temple *has stood for forty-six years,* and you will raise it up again in three days?"[25] In this case, the contrast would be between the lasting nature of the temple ("stood for forty-six years") and the quickness of both its destruction (cf. v. 19: "Destroy this temple") and rebuilding ("three days").

Even more important are issues relating to the chronology of the Last Supper and the dating of Jesus' crucifixion. The primary passages affected are 13:1; 18:28; 19:14, 31, 42. By way of background, the Synoptic Gospels clearly present the Last Supper as a Passover (Matt 26:17, 19 and parallels). Certain references to the "Day of Preparation" for the Passover in John's Gospel seem to suggest that, for John, the Passover is still future from the vantage point of Jesus and his followers at the time of the Last Supper, so that the latter cannot be a Passover meal but must have taken place earlier. Before involving John and the Synoptists in factual contradiction, however, it is important to investigate closely the most likely meaning of the crucial phrases *tēs heortēs tou pascha* (John 13:1), *phagōsin to pascha* (18:28), and *paraskeuē tou pascha* (19:14; cf. vv. 31, 42).

The best evidence suggests that John, as did other writers, used the term "Passover" *(pascha)* with reference to the entire Passover week, including the Feast of Unleavened Bread (see especially Luke 22:1: "the Feast of Unleavened Bread, called the Passover"; see also John 18:39). Moreover, Matthew, Mark, Luke, and Josephus alike use *paraskeuē* ("Day of Preparation") to refer to the day *preceding the Sabbath* (Matt 27:62; Mark 15:42; Luke 23:54; *Ant.* 16.163–64).[26] If so, 13:1 indicates that Passover week was at hand; "eat the Passover" in 18:28 probably means simply "to celebrate the Feast" (2 Chr 30:21), that is, the eight-day Feast of Unleavened Bread, not necessarily the Passover more narrowly conceived; and 19:14, 31, 42 refer to the Day of Preparation, not for the Passover in a narrow sense, but to the Day of Preparation *for the Sabbath of Passover week.* If so, there is no actual conflict between John and the Synoptics; all four evangelists portray Jesus as observing the Passover proper with his disciples on Thursday evening and place Jesus' crucifixion on Friday afternoon, the Day of Preparation for the "special Sabbath" of Passover week.[27]

A look at the major translations yields the following picture:

	John 13:1	18:28	19:14
NIV	Passover Feast	eat the Passover	day of Preparation of Passover Week
NASB	Feast of the Passover	eat the Passover	day of Preparation for the Passover
ISV	Passover Festival	eat the Passover meal	Preparation Day for the Passover
HCSB	Passover Festival	eat the Passover	Preparation Day for the Passover

NKJV	feast of the Passover	eat the Passover	Preparation Day of the Passover
NLT	Passover celebration	celebrate the Passover feast	day of preparation for the Passover
NRSV	Passover Feast	eat the Passover	day of Preparation for the Passover
ESV	Feast of the Passover	eat the Passover	day of Preparation of the Passover
TNIV	Passover Feast	eat the Passover	day of Preparation of the Passover

As to the translation of 13:1 and 18:28, the NLT probably does greatest justice to the exegetical conclusions arrived at above. "Passover celebration" and "celebrate the Passover feast" are sufficiently broad to encompass, not just the Passover meal in a narrow sense, but the entire week of festivities. With regard to the Day of Preparation referred to in 19:14, the NIV alone brings out the presumed true meaning of the phrase "Day of Preparation of Passover *Week*." All other major English translations, while not literally incorrect, seem to convey the notion that the Passover referred to is the actual Passover meal in a narrow sense—which, if the above argumentation is correct, it is not. The alternatives in this case are to resort to paraphrase (as the NIV does by adding "Week") or to provide a more formally equivalent translation with a misleading effect. The choice must be the former.[28]

Ideological Issues

Clearly the most important ideological issue facing the translator of John's Gospel today is the rendering of the expression *hoi Ioudaioi.*[29] The consistent translation of this term with "the Jews" in a given version renders John open to the charge of anti-Semitism.[30] Once again, since I commented on this issue previously, I can limit myself to a few summarizing comments.[31] First, it is true that John, like the other Gospels, places ultimate responsibility for Jesus' crucifixion squarely on the shoulders of the Jewish people as represented by their religious leadership—the Jewish ruling council called the Sanhedrin. Yet, importantly, the thrust of John's use of the term "the Jews" in this context is not ethnic but salvation-historical. For Jesus, and John, the Jews in their day wrongly presumed upon their religious heritage by claiming Abraham and Moses as their ancestors and the Scripture as their own, while at the same time rejecting their God-sent Messiah. Just as Peter, in his Pentecost sermon, told his Jewish audience that "God has made this Jesus, whom *you* crucified, both Lord and Christ" (Acts 2:36, emphasis mine) and later confronted the same group, chillingly, with their guilt by saying, "*You* handed him [God's servant Jesus] over to be killed, and *you* disowned him before Pilate, though he had decided to let him go. *You* disowned the Holy and Righteous One and asked that a murderer be released to you. *You* killed the author of life" (Acts 3:13–15, emphasis mine). John, too, held the Jewish people responsible for the death of their Messiah. Yet, like Peter, John did so, not to condemn them, but to proceed to tell them the good news of salvation in Jesus—yet this was good news not for them only but for "whoever believes" (John 3:16). Thus the general charge of anti-Semitism is refuted.

A study of the major English translations yields the following picture (the relevant passages are 1:19; 2:18, 20; 5:10, 15, 16, 18; 6:41, 52; 7:1, 11, 13, 15, 35; 8:22, 31, 48, 52, 57; 9:18, 22; 10:19, 24, 31, 33; 11:8, 19, 31, 33, 36, 45, 54; 12:9, 11; 13:33; 18:14, 20, 31, 33, 36, 38, 39; 19:3, 7, 12, 14, 19, 20, 31, 38; 20:19):

- The NIV, NASB, NRSV, NKJV, ISV, and ESV render all major instances of *hoi Ioudaioi* with "the Jews."[32]
- In addition, the ISV provides explanatory footnotes in order to distinguish references to the Jews in general from references to the Jewish leaders. The footnote "I.e. Jewish leaders" is placed at the following passages: 5:15, 16, 18; 6:41; 7:1, 11, 13, 15, 35; 8:48, 52; 10:19, 31; 11:45, 54; 13:33; 18:36, 38. While the practice of retaining the general reference "the Jews" in the text and of placing explanatory comments in footnotes has much to commend it, there seem to be several instances where the label "Jewish leaders" is questionable (see 6:41; 10:19, 31; 11:45, 54). Also, there are some problems with consistency (If 10:31, why not 11:8? If 18:36, 38, why not 19:7?).
- In the HCSB, one finds at 1:19 the global footnote, "In John *the Jews* usually indicates the Jewish authorities who led the nation." At 7:1, 11, 13, 15, and 35, footnotes refer back to 1:19. This is a halfhearted solution at best. Does "the Jews" in John "usually" refer to the Jewish authorities? This is a doubtful assertion. Moreover, why are footnotes placed only at the above-mentioned five instances in chapter 7 and nowhere else? This hardly exhausts the possible references to the Jewish authorities.
- The NLT translates "Jewish leaders" at 1:19; 2:18; 5:10, 15, 16, 18; 7:1, 11, 13, 15, 35; 8:22; 9:19, 22; 10:24, 31; 11:8; 13:33; 18:14, 31, 36; 19:7, 12, 31, 38; 20:19. At 6:41, 52; 9:31, 48, 52, 57; 10:19; 11:19, 31, 33, 36, 45, 54; 12:9, 11; 18:20, 38; 19:14, 20, the chosen translation is "the people" (footnote: Greek *Jewish people*). A comparison with the ISV indicates that, on the whole, the NLT construes a larger number of references to be to the Jewish leaders (ISV: 18; NLT: 26). At the same time, several passages

taken by the ISV as referring to the Jewish leaders are taken by the NLT as referring to the Jewish people at large (6:41; 10:19; 11:45, 54; 18:38). Thus it is interesting to note that in two recent translations with a similar orientation there remains a certain degree of variance as to which references are construed as referring to the Jewish leaders and which are construed as referring to the Jewish people at large.

- The TNIV, finally, renders the term as "Jewish leaders" in 1:19; 5:10, 15, 16; 7:1, 11, 13; 9:22; 18:14, 28, 36; 19:12, 31, 38; 20:19 (15 instances—less than the 18 in the ISV and the 26 in the NLT; see above). At other places, the added epithet "there" limits "the Jews" to those present at a given instance. On the whole, the committee showed commendable restraint.

By way of evaluation, it seems necessary to go beyond the earlier practice of simply translating *hoi Ioudaioi* with "the Jews"—at the very least by adding appropriate explanatory footnotes (as in the ISV). Better still, translators may infer from the context which nuance of *Ioudaioi* is invoked in a particular instance and then provide the appropriate gloss. While this procedure may open the door to ideology (minimizing general references to Jews in order to avoid anti-Semitism)—thus necessitating exegetical restraint along the cautions registered above—such an approach is both responsible and most sophisticated and satisfying linguistically. It is responsible in that it refuses to choose the easy path of an alleged functional equivalence where Greek *hoi Ioudaioi* equals "the Jews" in English. It is most sophisticated and satisfying linguistically because it recognizes the determinative role played by context, which may limit the scope of reference either locally or otherwise.

Exegetical Issues

In other cases, the translation of a particular passage in John's Gospel is dependent on interpretive judgments. One such instance is 1:5. Does *ķatelaben* there mean "understand" or "overcome"—or both? Again, I need not repeat what I've said elsewhere.[33] In short, in light of the close parallel at 12:35—"Walk while you have the light, before darkness overtakes *[ķatalambanō]* you" (see also 16:33)—I advocate "overcome" as the superior rendering. The major translations divide more or less evenly between the two options, usually mentioning in a footnote the one not chosen: (1) NIV: "understood"; NASB = NKJV: "comprehend"; (2) NLT: "extinguish"; NET: "mastered"; ISV: "put out"; HCSB, ESV, NRSV: "overcome." Notably, the TNIV changed the NIV's "understood" to "overcome." I believe a strong case can be made for the second group of translations having captured the force of the original better than the first.

Another interesting issue is that of the Johannine intersentence connections, specifically, *oun, de, kai,* and asyndeton. As Randall Buth and Stephen Levinsohn observe, John seems to be using these connectors differently than the Synoptics.[34] While in the Synoptics (and Acts) *kai* serves as an unmarked connector, John employs a simple asyndeton. The Synoptic "development marker" *de* is frequently replaced by the Johannine *oun.* After a preliminary analysis of the four above-mentioned intersentence connections, Buth concludes that John's usage revolves around the two coordinates "significant change" and "close connection":

- *oun* is used for significant change and close connection (logical, resumptive, new unit, change of subject; analyzed are 1:39; 4:28–34, 40; 6:3–5; 11:46–47, 54)
- *de* occurs for significant change but loose connection (background, new unit, change of subject; 2:8; 6:71; 11:45–46, 54–55)
- *kai* indicates coordinated sameness (same subject, continuity with previous subject; 1:19–21; 2:9; but see comments on instances of an adversative *kai* in John below)
- asyndeton is unmarked regarding both significance and connection (1:17, 39; 2:6–7, 17; 4:22; 9:9; 12:12, 22)

The implications for translators of John's Gospel can be sketched as follows:

- As to *kai,* no translation will often be necessary; the English asyndeton will suffice. Care should be taken, however, to identify instances of an adversative *kai,* which should be rendered "yet" or the like (cf. 1:10, 11; 3:6, 19, 32; 5:39; 7:19, 30; 8:52; 9:27; 10:25, 39; 12:34, 35, 47; 18:11; 20:29).[35]
- The connector *oun* may be translated with "now" (conveying the beginning of a new unit or resumptive force).
- Finally, *de* will need to be treated on a case-by-case basis to determine if the change is significant enough to warrant an explicit English rendering that reflects such a change.[36]

While a comprehensive evaluation of the nine major translations regarding their rendering of intersentence connections is beyond the scope of this essay, their translation of three instances of adversative *kai* in John 1:10 ("though the world was made through him, the world did not recognize him"), 1:11 ("He came to that which was his own, but his own did not receive him"), and 3:19 ("Light has come into the world, but people loved darkness instead of light") may serve as a test case for their sensitivity to these kinds of issues. The picture is as follows:

	1:10	**1:11**	**3:19**
NIV	though	but	but
NASB	and	and	and
NKJV	and	and	and
NRSV	yet	and	and
NLT	although	even	but
ISV	yet	yet	but
HCSB	yet	and	and
ESV	yet	and	and
TNIV	though	but	but

This survey suggests that the NASB and NKJV are insufficiently sensitive to instances of adversative *kai* (and perhaps other intersentence connection issues), while the NIV, NLT, ISV, and TNIV display an appropriate awareness of this important nuance that ought to have translational implications. The NRSV, HCSB, and ESV get mixed reviews in the present spot check. One wonders if a commitment to a formal equivalence approach in translation has led—in the present case, misled—the translators of the NASB and NKJV to translate *kai* with "and" even when the conjunction demonstrably conveys an adversative force in the Johannine context.

In conclusion, a related—indeed foundational—issue that can merely be noted is that of the determination of what constitutes a (Greek) sentence. Vern Poythress, following Robert Longacre and Kenneth Pike, defines a sentence as a "maximal clause," including relative and dependent clauses.[37] Consequently, the question arises regarding the legitimacy of breaking up Greek sentences into smaller English sentences for the sake of greater readability in English. This procedure may result in the loss of connection between related units in the Greek original—a considerable price to pay for greater clarity in the receptor language.

Stylistic Issues

In yet other instances, there are stylistic decisions to be made. One such instance is the rendering of Johannine passages that are generic in import but have traditionally been rendered in English by the use of masculine language. Vern Poythress and Wayne Grudem cite John 14:23 as an example.[38] The NIV renders this verse as follows: "If anyone loves me, he will obey my teaching. My Father will love him, and we will come to him and make our home with him."

In the NRSV, the verse reads, "Those who love me will keep my word, and my Father will love them, and we will come to them and make our home with them." In order to avoid masculine pronouns and to render the passage generically, singulars have been changed to plurals. According to Poythress and Grudem, this attempted remedy of one perceived problem introduces a problem that is even more severe, namely, the shift of focus from individuals to groups.

How valid is this argument? To begin with, to make this an issue of doctrinal fidelity and orthodoxy (inerrancy)—as Grudem and Poythress continue to insist on doing[39]—is erroneous and fails to appreciate the complexities involved in Bible translation. As D. A. Carson rightly contends, translation is an exercise in the impossible—in that sense, translation is "treason," because of necessity it will always fall short of perfection. While there is clearly a trade-off in the kind of shift that has taken place from the NIV to the NRSV in the above example, this does not mean that the motive for such translation is a low view of Scripture or that inerrancy is in fact compromised.[40]

Thus Grudem's contention that in the NIVI rendering of John 14:23 "six singular Greek words which John wrote as part of Scripture are mistranslated in this one text"[41] is sheer populism, reflecting naïveté concerning the types of trade-offs needing to be made in the "inevitable and impossible task" of (Bible) translation.[42] Also, Grudem's argument that John's use of the singular in the original obliges the faithful translator to use a singular in translation misconstrues the relationship between donor and receptor languages by conceiving of it in unduly rigid, wooden terms.[43] It is true that the shift from singular to plural in the case of John 14:23 may have the (doubtless unintended) effect of diluting the believer's personal relationship with each of the persons of the Godhead and thus is less than ideal. Yet it is also true that the immediate context does in fact suggest a collective reference on Jesus' part to the disciples as a group.[44] Note the question of Judas (not Iscariot) that triggered Jesus' response: "But, Lord, why do you intend to show yourself to *us* and not to the world?" (14:22, emphasis mine). It is *those disciples* whom Jesus addresses in 14:23ff. Moreover, to charge, as Poythress and Grudem do, that a plural translation in this instance "mutes the masculinity of God's words,"[45] since it suppresses the sense of male representation present in the original, is hardly accurate.

Much of the discussion revolves around the use of generic "he" in English. Carson says that many have stopped using generic "he" and have begun to use alternatives. Poythress and Grudem agree, but they contend that generic "he" should still be considered as a possible alternative in translation, together with other options.[46] To some extent, the difference is over perceptions to what degree the English language has in fact shifted or is expected to shift. While I am no expert in this area, I believe that translation committees should consider all the available options—including generic "he"—and then choose the best overall translation that presents the least amount of difficulties. In my consulting work I have seen a fair share of instances where translation committees were so intent on avoiding generic "he" that they chose inferior options instead.[47]

Nevertheless, to say that generic "he" is still being used and understood is not the same as saying that it is widely accepted by all audiences. Just as Poythress and Grudem criticize Carson for appearing to exclude generic "he" as an option, they should be open to other possibilities—including those that entail changes from singular to plural, from third to second person singular, and so forth. They should not claim divine sanction for English generic "he," as though it were somehow intrinsically superior to possible alternatives. I am also not so sure that the latent masculinity Poythress and Grudem claim underlies certain generics is as widespread as they allege.[48]

Summary and Conclusion

For easy reference, it may be helpful to summarize the conclusions reached in the preceding discussion in chronological order of appearance in John's Gospel. The recommended translations were as follows:

1:3	"without him nothing was made that has been made"
1:5	"overcome" or synonym
1:10, 11; 3:19; etc.	"but" or "yet"
1:18	"one-of-a-kind [Son, himself] God" or the like
1:19; etc.	"the Jews," with appropriate explanatory footnote or contextually sensitive gloss
1:39; 4:6, 52; 19:14	based on time reckoning, starting day at around 6:00 A.M.
2:20	"this temple has stood for forty-six years"
5:2	"Bethesda"
7:53–8:11	put in footnote, not in square brackets in the text
12:32	"all *kinds* of people" (that is, Jews as well as Gentiles)
13:1; 18:28	"celebrate the Passover"; 19:14: "the Day of Preparation [for the Sabbath] of Passover Week"
19:17 (cf. 1:38, 41, 42; 4:25; 9:7; 11:16; 20:16, 24; 21:2)	"in Aramaic"
20:31	"believe"

It is now time to rate the existing translations with regard to translation accuracy in John's Gospel. A plus rating is awarded in case of a superior translation of above average accuracy; a minus rating is assigned for a rendering of doubtful accuracy; no rating is given for an average translation with nothing particularly to commend or disqualify it. Pluses and minuses offset each other.

The ratings are as follows:

	NIV	**NASB**	**NKJV**	**ISV**	**NLT**	**HCSB**	**ESV**	**NRSV**	**TNIV**
1:3	+	+	+	+	+	+	+	–	+
1:5	–	–	–	+	+	+	+	+	+
1:10, etc.	+	–	–	+	+				+
1:18	+	+	–	+		–	+		+
1:19, etc.				+	+	–			+
1:39, etc.		–		+					
2:20	–	–	–	–	–	–	–	–	–
5:2	+	+	+	+	+	+	–	–	+
7:53ff			–	–			–		
12:32			+		–				
18:28					+				
19:14	+								
19:17	+	–	–	–	–	–	–		+
Total	4	–2	–3	4	3	–1	–1	–2	6

Hence, in our unscientific case study, the TNIV comes out on top with a superior "6" rating. The NIV and ISV also receive a very favorable rating (+4 each), as does the NLT (fourth at +3). A distant fifth are the HCSB and ESV (both at–1), followed by the NASB and NRSV (tied at–2), and the NKJV (–3). While the above comparison of translations of John's Gospel is admittedly less than comprehensive—not to mention my postulation of exegetical and other judgments with which other scholars may differ—I believe the comparison is nevertheless revealing as to the translation philosophy and quality of translation of these nine major English translations. This, of course, still allows for the possibility that the quality of a given version may be uneven with regard to the various books of the Bible, in which case the above results would be representative of the translation of John's Gospel but not necessarily the rest of Scripture.

NOTES

1. I offer this essay as a token of appreciation and respect to my predecessor as *JETS* editor, Ronald Youngblood, with best wishes for his continuing ministry and scholarship.

2. On the translation of John's Gospel, see also Barclay M. Newman and Eugene A. Nida, *A Handbook on the Gospel of John* (New York: United Bible Societies, 1980).

3. Ibid., 168: "...—whatever that may be supposed to mean." In Bruce Metzger's dissenting opinion (the majority of the United Bible Societies committee favors taking the phrase with what follows), "Despite valiant attempts of commentators to bring sense out of taking *ho gegonen* with what follows, the passage remains intolerably clumsy and opaque."

4. This is the judgment of the majority of the UBS committee; see Bruce M. Metzger, *A Textual Commentary on the Greek New Testament,* 2d ed. (Stuttgart: United Bible Societies, 1994), 169–70, for discussion and a more extended rationale.

5. Murray J. Harris, *Jesus as God: The New Testament Use of* Theos *in Reference to Jesus* (Grand Rapids: Baker, 1992), 78–80.

6. Note that C. K. Barrett changed his position between the first and second edition of his commentary. Cf. *The Gospel According to St. John* (London: SPCK, 1955), 141, and *The Gospel According to St. John,* 2d ed. (Philadelphia: Westminster, 1978), 169: "The added evidence of the two recently discovered papyri may seem to swing the verdict this way." See also Daniel B. Wallace, *Greek Grammar Beyond the Basics* (Grand Rapids: Zondervan, 1996), 360: "the unique One, God."

7. See my forthcoming commentary on John's Gospel in the BECNT series. Cf. TNIV: "one and only [Son], who is himself God."

8. Martin Hengel, "Das Johannesevangelium als Quelle für die Geschichte des antiken Judentums," in *Judaica, Hellenistica et Christiana. Kleine Schriften II* (Tübingen: Mohr-Siebeck, 1999), 309. Hengel also refers to the discussion in Barrett, *The Gospel According to St. John,* 252–53, and notes that the United Bible Societies committee was divided on this point.

9. See Frederick A. Schilling, "The Story of Jesus and the Adulteress," *AThR* 37 (1955): 91–106; Ulrich Becker, *Jesus und die Ehebrecherin,* BZNW 29 (Berlin: Alfred Töpelmann, 1963), 8–74; Gary M. Burge, "A Specific Problem in the New Testament Text and Canon: The Woman Caught in Adultery (John 7:53–8:11)," *JETS* 27 (1984): 141–48; and Bart D. Ehrman, "Jesus and the Adulteress," *NTS* 34 (1988): 24–44, critiqued by J. Ian H. McDonald, "The So-called *Pericope de Adultera,*" *NTS* 41 (1995): 415–27. See also Metzger, *A Textual Commentary,* 187–89 and commentaries. Dissenting voices are John Paul Heil, "The Story of Jesus and the Adulteress (John 7,53–8,11) Reconsidered," *Bib* 72 (1991): 182–91—but see the convincing critique by Daniel B. Wallace, "Reconsidering 'The Story of Jesus and the Adulteress Reconsidered,'" *NTS* 39 (1993): 290–96—and Maurice A. Robinson, "Preliminary Observations regarding the *Pericope Adulterae* based upon Fresh Collations of nearly all Continuous-Text Manuscripts and over One Hundred Lectionaries" (paper presented at the 50th annual meeting of the Evangelical Theological Society, 19–21 November 1998). Gail O'Day, "John 7:53–8:11: A Study in Misreading," *JBL* 111 (1992): 631–40, unconvincingly construes the canonical marginalization of the pericope as the result of an attempt "to marginalize not only the woman but her story as well."

10. The evidence pertaining to vocabulary statistics is set forth in Robert Morgenthaler, *Statistik des neutestamentlichen Wortschatzes,* 2d ed. (Zürich: Gotthelf, 1958), 60–62.

11. Cf. Morgenthaler, *Statistik,* 61–62; Wallace, "Reconsidering," 291; Burge, "A Specific Problem," 144.

12. See Metzger, *A Textual Commentary,* 187–88. A reassessment of the available evidence is beyond the scope of the present essay and, in light of the preceding comments, hardly necessary in any case. The following discussion is therefore devoted to pragmatic challenges facing the translator.

13. Newman and Nida, *A Handbook on the Gospel of John,* 257. On the external evidence, see William L. Petersen,"ουδε εγω σε [κατα]κρινω. John 8:11, the *Protevangelium Iacobi,* and the History of the *Pericope Adulterae,*" in *Sayings of Jesus: Canonical and Non-canonical. Essays in Honour of Tjitze Baarda,* ed. William L. Petersen et al.; NovTSup 89 (Leiden: Brill, 1997), 191–221, who claims to have found an allusion to John 8:11 in the *Protevangelium Iacobi,* an apocryphal Christian romance dating from the second half of the second century A.D. He thinks that the pericope originated in Egypt (probably Alexandria) in the first half of the second century A.D. (p. 220, note 99).

14. The ISV simply includes the pericope without any indication (such as square brackets) that the text may not have been part of the original Gospel (though it does include a footnote at the end of the pericope). The NKJV places an asterisk at 7:53, noting that the Nestle-Aland and UBS texts bracket the pericope as not in the original text, but noting that these verses are present "in over 900 mss."

15. *Encountering John: The Gospel in Historical, Literary, and Theological Perspective* (Grand Rapids: Baker, 1999), 134.

16. In the parallel at 19:35, the preponderance of witnesses have *pisteusēte,* with the notable exceptions of ℵ and B.

17. As D. A. Carson, *The Gospel According to John,* PNTC (Grand Rapids: Eerdmans, 1991), 662, rightly notes, "John elsewhere in his Gospel can use *either* tense to refer to *both* coming to faith and continuing in the faith." Carson goes on to advocate the rendering, "that you may believe that the Christ, the Son of God, is Jesus." See also, idem, "The Purpose of the Fourth Gospel: John 20:31 Reconsidered," *JBL* 106 (1987): 639–51; and the critiques by Gordon D. Fee,"On the Text and Meaning of John 20,30–31," in *The Four Gospels 1992: Fs. Frans Neirynck,* ed. F. van Segbroeck et al.; BETL (Leuven: University Press, 1992), 3:2193–2205; and Wallace, *Greek Grammar Beyond the Basics,* 46–47.

18. An interesting instance is the reading "Son of God" in John 1:34 (cf. 1:49; the reading adopted by the NIV, NASB, NRSV, NKJV, ISV, ESV, NLT, and HCSB) versus "God's Chosen One" (cf. Isa 42:1; notably adopted by the TNIV). While some early manuscripts have "Son of God," "God's Chosen One" is found in ℵ*, p^{5vid}, and a recently published papyrus (p^{106}; *The Oxyrhynchus Papyri* Vol. LXV [Egypt Exploration Society, 1998], 12–13), which renders the latter—harder—reading marginally more likely (contra, in part, P. R. Rodgers, "The Text of John 1:34," in *Theological Exegesis. Essays in Honor of Brevard S. Childs,* eds. C. Seitz and K. Greene-McCreight [Grand Rapids: Eerdmans, 1999], 299–305, who prefers a combination of both [!] readings). On textual issues surrounding John 3:13, see David Alan Black, "The Text of John 3:13," *Grace Theological Journal* 6 (1985): 49–66, who advocates including the final clause—"who is in heaven" *(ho ōn en tō ouranō)*. Currently, only the NKJV and the ISV follow this reading. Personally, I favor "God's Chosen One" in 1:34 and not including "who is in heaven" in 3:13.

19. Similarly, Newman and Nida (*A Handbook on the Gospel of John,* 585) state, "*In Hebrew* . . . means 'in Aramaic.'"

20. D. A. Carson, *The Gospel According to John,* 156–57, points out that the primary support for the Roman time-reckoning theory comes from Pliny the Elder, who notes that Roman authorities (like Egyptian ones) counted the official, civil day from midnight to midnight—in case of leases and other documents that expired at day's end. But Pliny himself says that "common people everywhere" conceive of the day as running "from dawn to dark" (*Nat. Hist.* 2.188 LCL). See the discussion in Leon Morris, *The Gospel According to John,* NICNT (Grand Rapids: Eerdmans, 1971), 800–801, note 34.

21. NASB: "Perhaps 10:00 A.M. (Roman time)"; ESV: "That is, about 4:00 P.M."

22. A footnote contends that John probably used a different method of reckoning time from the other three Gospels, adding that if he used the same method, the translation would be "about four in the afternoon."

23. Similarly, ISV = NRSV: "has been under construction for forty-six years"; HCSB: "took forty-six years to build."

24. This reading of John 2:20 and a date of A.D. 30 for Jesus' first Passover and the temple cleansing are advocated by Harold W. Hoehner, *Chronological Aspects of the Life of Christ* (Grand Rapids: Zondervan, 1977), 38–43; idem, "Chronology," in *Dictionary of Jesus and the Gospels,* ed. Joel B. Green et al. (Downers Grove, Ill.: InterVarsity Press, 1992), 119; C. J. Humphreys and W. G. Waddington, "The Jewish Calendar, a Lunar Eclipse, and the Date of Christ's Crucifixion," *TynBul* 43 (1992): 351; and Andreas J. Köstenberger, "John," in *Zondervan Illustrated Bible Backgrounds Commentary,* ed. Clinton E. Arnold (Grand Rapids: Zondervan, 2002), 2:28–33.

25. It should be acknowledged that currently no major English translation renders the passage this way.

26. See in greater detail Köstenberger, "John," in *ZIBBC,* 2:130, 164, 173.

27. For this reconstruction, see Carson, *The Gospel According to John,* 455–58; idem, *Matthew,* EBC 8 (Grand Rapids: Zondervan, 1983), 530–32; Craig L. Blomberg, *The Historical Reliability of the Gospels* (Downers Grove, Ill.: InterVarsity Press, 1987), 175–80; Köstenberger, *Encountering John,* 146.

28. Regrettably, the TNIV changes the NIV's "day of Preparation of Passover Week" to "day of Preparation of the Passover," thus aligning itself with a more literal but overall less accurate and potentially misleading rendering. On the limitations of functional equivalence, see the essay by D. A. Carson in the present volume.

29. For a discussion of all the instances of "the Jews" in John's Gospel, see Robert G. Bratcher, "'The Jews' in the Gospel of John"; also see appendix 1 in Newman and Nida, *A Handbook on the Gospel of John,* 641–49.

30. See especially the massive volume edited by Reimund Bieringer et al., *Anti-Judaism and the Fourth Gospel* (Assen: van Gorcum, 2001). Cf. Glenn Balfour, "Is John's Gospel Anti-Semitic?" *TynBul* 48 (1997): 369–72 (abstract of Ph.D. thesis, University of Nottingham, 1995).

31. See my *Encountering John,* 248–49.

32. A solitary footnote in the ESV at 7:1 has, "Or *Judeans*" (cross referenced at 7:11).

33. *Encountering John,* 55.

34. Randall Buth, "Οὖν, Δέ, Καί, and Asyndeton in John's Gospel," in *Linguistics and New Testament Interpretation: Essays on Discourse Analysis,* ed. David Alan Black

(Nashville: Broadman, 1992), 144–61; Stephen H. Levinsohn, *Discourse Features of New Testament Greek* (Dallas: SIL, 1992), 39–48 (cf. 159–60); cf. the second edition (2000), 81–90 and 247–60. See also Vern S. Poythress, "The Use of the Intersentence Conjunctions δέ, οὖν, καί and Asyndeton in the Gospel of John," *Novum Testamentum* 26 (1984): 312–40. For further literature on the subject, see Buth, page 144, note 1, and his bibliography on page 161.

35. Levinsohn, *Discourse Features,* 2d ed., 124–26 (esp. 124), would probably agree that these kinds of passages ought to be translated adversatively: "Thus, although conjunctive *kai* can generally be translated 'and' [i.e., it is 'connective'], there are times when it seems that 'but' would be more appropriate [i.e., it would appear to be 'adversative']" (p. 72). Yet he seeks to make the technical distinction that, even in cases of an "adversative" use of *kai,* there remains an underlying continuity. Buth ("Οὖν, Δέ, Καί, and Asyndeton in John's Gospel"), in his discussion on pages 152–54, fails to deal with adversative instances of *kai.*

36. It is beyond the scope of the present essay to evaluate existing translations as to their accuracy in rendering intersentence connections. The general comments above and below are designed to register important issues in the translation of John's Gospel and to suggest basic guiding principles for the rendering of conjunctions that mark intersentence connections.

37. Poythress, "The Use of Intersentence Conjunctions," 315.

38. Vern S. Poythress and Wayne A. Grudem, *The Gender-Neutral Bible Controversy: Muting the Masculinity of God's Words* (Nashville: Broadman & Holman, 2000), 117–20, 154–55.

39. Ibid, chapter 3.

40. See chapter 3 ("Translation and Treason") in D. A. Carson, *The Inclusive-Language Debate: A Plea for Realism* (Grand Rapids: Baker, 1998), 47–76.

41. Wayne Grudem, in *World* magazine 12, no. 5 (19 April 1997): 16, quoted in Carson, *The Inclusive-Language Debate,* 31–32.

42. The quote is from the subtitle of Carson's chapter 3.

43. Cf. Carson, *The Inclusive-Language Debate,* 38; Mark L. Strauss, *Distorting Scripture? The Challenge of Bible Translation and Gender Accuracy* (Downers Grove, Ill.: InterVarsity Press, 1998), 120, who charges Grudem with an "overly wooden approach."

44. So Grant R. Osborne, "Do Inclusive-Language Bibles Distort Scripture?" *Christianity Today* (27 October 1997): 38, cited in Strauss, *Distorting Scripture?* 120.

45. Poythress and Grudem, *The Gender-Neutral Bible Controversy,* 155.

46. Much of the discussion is chronicled in Carson, *The Inclusive-Language Debate,* chapter 9: "But Is the English Language Changing?" and Poythress and Grudem, *The Gender-Neutral Bible Controversy,* appendix 6: "The Evaporation of an Argument: D. A. Carson's Lack of Evidence for the Unusability of Generic 'He' in English." See also chapters 5 and 6 in Strauss, *Distorting Scripture?*

47. An example is a contemplated change of John 6:65 to read, "no one can come to me unless the Father has enabled them" or for 7:38 to read, "Whoever believes in me, . . . streams of living water will flow from within them."

48. See the example of John 14:23 discussed above, or substantival masculine participles such as *ho pisteuōn* in 14:12.

16

"FLESH" IN ROMANS: A CHALLENGE FOR THE TRANSLATOR

Douglas J. Moo

The decision of the original New International Version (NIV) translators to render the Greek *sarx,* when it had its distinctively negative connotation in Paul, with the phrase *sinful nature* has been widely criticized. I was one of those critics. Every time I taught on passages in which the phrase occurred, I insisted that students heed the marginal note indicating the alternate rendering "the flesh" and criticized the translators for their decision. Along with many others, I worried that the introduction of the notion of "nature" would further encourage the questionably biblical focus on contrasting "natures" as a framework for conceptualizing the contrast between pre-Christian and Christian experience.[1] Then, in 1995, I was asked to join the Committee on Bible Translation (CBT), the group charged with oversight of the NIV text. As we comprehensively reviewed the NIV text with a view to needed revisions, we came to Romans—and I was asked to serve on a subcommittee that would recommend alternatives to the existing NIV rendering of *sarx* in Paul. As we did our work—based on a comprehensive review of the translation alternatives by my colleague Walter Liefeld—it quickly became apparent to me that the translator had to consider factors that the exegete and teacher did not. The committee as a whole decided in the end to retain "sinful nature" as the usual rendering for the negative use of *sarx* in Paul. I am not sure that I agree with this decision—but the point of this article is not to reopen the debate. Rather, I want to analyze the situation from the point of view of the translator. I will begin with a brief survey of the distinctively Pauline usage of *sarx.* To make the task manageable, I will focus on Romans and especially on Romans 7–8. With this survey of usage in mind, I will then consider the options and issues facing the translator.[2]

SARX IN THE WRITINGS OF PAUL

Paul uses the word *sarx* proportionately more than any other New Testament author: Of the 147 occurrences of *sarx* in the NT, 91 are found in the Pauline letters. The complexity of Paul's use of this word is reflected in Today's New International Version (TNIV), where twenty-eight different words or phrases are used to translate *sarx*.[3] Only sixteen times does the TNIV render *sarx* as "flesh." As Anthony Thiselton has pointed out, *sarx* in Paul is a "polymorphous concept," and its meaning is very much context dependent.[4] The large number of different renderings of *sarx* in the TNIV simply reflects this fact. Critics of "sinful nature" in the NIV will not be appeased by the TNIV: in all thirty places where the NIV translates *sarx* "sinful nature" the TNIV has done the same (only two of these do not come in Paul: 2 Peter 2:10 and 2:18 ["sinful human nature"]). In fact, the TNIV introduces remarkably few changes in the NIV translation of *sarx*. Apart from four inclusive-language changes (Rom 8:3b, 3c; Gal 1:16; 2:16) only five texts have been changed—Romans 1:3, where "human nature" has been replaced with "earthly life"; Galatians 6:12, where "outwardly" has been replaced with "flesh"; Galatians 4:23 and 29, where "ordinary way" has been changed to "human effort"; and Philemon 16, where "man" has been changed to "fellow man."

Many scholars and lexicographers have attempted to categorize Paul's uses of *sarx*. For the sake of the argument of this article, five basic senses can be distinguished. The most basic meaning of *sarx*—and the most common in secular Greek—is (1) "the material that covers the bones of a human or animal body."[5] Paul occasionally uses the word with this sense. The clearest example is 1 Corinthians 15:39: "All flesh is not the same: Human beings have one kind of flesh, animals have another, birds another and fish another" (see also Eph 2:11; Col 2:13; cf. Gal 6:13).[6] Following precedents in secular Greek, Paul also (2) applies *sarx* to the human body as whole: e.g., 2 Corinthians 7:1: "Since we have these promises, dear friends, let us purify ourselves from everything that contaminates body *[sarx]* and spirit, perfecting holiness out of reverence for God" (see also 1 Cor 5:5 [?]; 6:16; 2 Cor 12:7; Gal 4:13; Eph 5:31). But more often, Paul (3) uses *sarx* to refer not to the human body narrowly but to the human being generally. First Corinthians 1:28–29 illustrates this use of the word: "He chose the lowly things of this world and the despised things—and the things that are not—to nullify the things that are, so that no one *[sarx]* may boast before him" (see also Gal 1:16; 2:16; 1 Cor 1:29). This sense of the word merges almost imperceptibly into a bit broader concept, namely, (4) the human state or condition. While debated, 1 Corinthians 10:18, where Paul refers to Israel *kata sarka* ("according to the flesh"), probably falls into this category. Finally (5), in a usage that is distinctively (though not uniquely) Pauline, *sarx* can designate the human condition in its fallenness.

As Timo Laato has neatly put it, the difference between meanings (4) and (5) is the difference between the human being in *distinction* from God and the human being in *contrast* to God.[7] The latter is often called the "ethical" use of *sarx,* in contrast to the "neutral" use of meaning (4).[8] A clear example of the "ethical" use is Galatians 5:16–17: "So I say, walk by the Spirit, and you will not gratify the desires of the sinful nature *[sarx].* For the sinful nature *[sarx]* desires what is contrary to the Spirit, and the Spirit what is contrary to the sinful nature *[sarx].* They are in conflict with each other, so that you are not to do whatever you want." This sense of *sarx* is quite common in Paul (anywhere from 25 to 30 occurrences, depending on how one interprets several notoriously difficult texts) and is, of course, the point of special controversy in the NIV translation.

The Meaning of *Sarx* in Romans

Paul uses *sarx* proportionately more often in Romans than in any other letter; the word occurs 26 times. Four of the five meanings we have isolated above are found among Paul's uses of *sarx* in Romans. *Sarx* in the first sense occurs in Romans 2:28, which contrasts the "outward" *(phaneros)* circumcision "in the *sarx*" with circumcision of the heart carried out in (or by *[en]*) the Spirit. The TNIV rendering of *sarx* here is "physical." No instance of *sarx* with the second meaning—the human body as a whole—is found in Romans. Paul uses *sarx* to refer to the human being generally (meaning 3) once: "Therefore no one *[sarx]* will be declared righteous in his sight by observing the law; rather, through the law we become conscious of our sin" (3:20). Another instance is difficult to categorize, but may belong here also, namely, Romans 11:14, where Paul denotes his fellow Jews simply with the word *sarx* (TNIV "my own people"). Paul uses *sarx* here to stress his sense of solidarity, at the level of human relationships, with his fellow Jews.

Clearly, then, instances of the fourth and fifth meanings dominate, but some contentious interpretive issues make it difficult to determine the exact number that falls into each category. Pretty clearly belonging to the fourth (or "neutral") meaning are Romans 1:3, 8:3b and c, and 9:5. All use *sarx* to refer to the human condition with which Jesus Christ identified as the incarnate Son. Jesus, affirms Paul, was descended from David *ḳata sarḳa* (1:3; "as to his earthly life"), took on *homoiōmati sarḳos hamartias* ("the likeness of sinful humanity") so that he might condemn sin *en sarḳi* ("in human flesh"—8:3), and traces his human lineage back to Israel *ḳata sarḳa* (9:5; "human ancestry"). Romans 4:1, 9:3, and 9:8 similarly use *sarx* to denote human ancestry: Abraham is the father of the Jews *kata sarka* (4:1; untranslated in TNIV); the Israelites are Paul's kinsfolk *kata sarka* (9:3; untranslated in TNIV); and the Israelites who inherit the promise given to Abraham are not the *ta tekna tēs sarkos* (9:8; TNIV "natural children"). Falling equally clearly into the fifth category—"human beings in conflict with God"—are Romans 7:5, 8:8, and 8:9, which describe unbelievers as being *en sarki* ("in the flesh"); 8:3a, where the inability of the law to rescue from sin is attributed to the *sarx;* 8:4, 5a, 5b, 6, 7, where *sarx* denotes the orientation of non-Christian behavior and thinking; 8:12a, 12b, 13, which warn Christians of the danger of living *kata sarka* ("according to the flesh"); and 13:14, where believers are exhorted to make no provision for the *sarx.* The TNIV translates each of these instances of *sarx* with "sinful nature," except for 8:7, where the rendering is simply "sinful," describing the "mind" mentioned earlier in the verse (in 8:5 and 12, "sinful nature" is alluded to by an abbreviation ["that nature"] and a pronoun ["it"]).

Difficult to categorize are Romans 6:19, 7:18, and 7:25. In 6:19, Paul explains that he uses the imagery of the slave as an analogue to the believer because of *tēn astheneian tēs sarkos hymōn* ("the weakness of your flesh"). C. E. B. Cranfield, citing Galatians 4:13, takes *sarx* here in its ethical sense: "What is meant is the incomprehension, insensitiveness, insincerity, and proneness to self-deception, which characterize the fallen human nature even of Christians."[9] C. K. Barrett, on the other hand, argues for the neutral sense: *sarx,* he claims, has no special theological sense here "but simply refers to the frailty of human nature."[10] By translating the phrase "human limitations," the TNIV translators have opted for Barrett's "neutral" interpretation. This is probably closer to Paul's intention, although it must be said that a certain negative nuance seems to be unavoidable. There is something about *sarx* that creates a "weakness" in understanding the things of God.

Romans 7:18 and 25, because of some ambiguous syntax in verse 18 and the debate surrounding the general meaning of the passage, are even more difficult. Commenting on his vivid depiction of the "divided *egō*" in verses 15–17, Paul claims in verse 18 that "good does not dwell in me, *tout estin en tē sarki mou*—"that is, in my flesh." Advocates of the view that Paul is here describing his struggle with sin as a Christian often take "that is" in a restrictive sense and conclude that Paul here confesses that, even as a Christian, he continues to be influenced by "the whole fallen human nature."[11] Scholars who think that Paul describes unregenerate human experience also often give *sarx* its ethical meaning but take "that is" as definitional—the fallen human nature characterizes "me."[12] The TNIV, translating "sinful nature," also takes *sarx* in its ethical sense, while leaving open the precise syntactical function of "that is." But a good case can be made for taking *sarx* in what we have to this point been calling its "neutral" sense. Romans 7:14–25 is remarkable, among other things, for the very unusual degree to which Paul depicts the human being dualistically. Verses 15–17 and 18b–20 describe a conflict within a person between willing and doing, which is then in verses 21–23 attributed to a conflict between "the law of my mind" and "the law of sin at work within my members" (NIV). The reference of these phrases is debated, but they probably refer, in turn, to the law of God—the Torah (cf. v. 22), which the *egō* honors in his mind (cf. v. 16)—and an opposite compulsion, or force, namely, the bent toward sin that prevents the *egō* from putting the will to do the law into practice. In this context, then, "flesh" in verse 18 probably is equivalent to the "members" of verse 23. And *sarx* in verse 25, where it is contrasted with "mind" *(nous),* will then have the same basically "neutral" sense.[13] Just where in our categorization of Paul's uses of *sarx* we should place these verses is not clear. They come closest to the third usage—the human body—but stand out from the other occurrences of the word with this meaning in Paul by virtue of their focus on the concrete, even physical, part of the human being.

In what we have said about Paul's use of *sarx* in Romans thus far, we have followed the traditional distinction between Paul's "neutral" and "ethical" uses of the term. James D. G. Dunn, however, has called into question this distinction. He argues that the meanings of *sarx* in Paul do not fall into separate, watertight categories but occupy a spectrum of meaning. In contrast to scholars who suggest that Paul may have derived his more neutral sense of *sarx* from the Old Testament and the Jewish world and the more negative sense from the Greek world, Dunn, along with many others before him, traces the spectrum of Paul's usage to the Hebrew *bāśār,* with its sense of "human mortality."[14] One implication of this conclusion is that a certain negative nuance often clings to *sarx,* even when Paul uses it in apparently neutral senses.

Dunn has a point, as can be seen from a closer look at several of the neutral occurrences of *sarx* in Romans. In Romans 1:3–4, the claim that Jesus is descended from David *kata sarka* is balanced by the claim that he has been appointed the Son of God in power *kata pneuma hagiōsynēs* ("according to the spirit of holiness"). The rarity of this latter phrase (it does not occur elsewhere in the NT) has led some commentators to deny a reference to the Holy Spirit here. But the phrase is a literal rendering of a Hebrew phrase that refers to the Holy Spirit,[15] and the unusual language is probably due to the influence of a source or tradition on which Paul depends.[16] However we understand the contrast between Jesus "according to the flesh" and Jesus "according to the Spirit" (on which see below), the implication is that one has not fully comprehended the significance of Jesus unless *both* perspectives are included. Paul in no way minimizes the fact that Jesus was a descendant of David and therefore the one who fulfilled the OT promises about a "greater son of David." But he also suggests that understanding Jesus only in these terms is deficient.

A similar mildly negative nuance attaches to *kata sarka* in the other Christological passage where this phrase occurs, namely, Romans 9:5. Culminating a list of privileges and promises granted to Israel is the fact that "the Messiah" comes from among the Israelites—*to kata sarka.*[17] Though strongly contested, it is quite likely that the verse goes on to call this Messiah "God" *(theos).*[18] As in 1:3–4, therefore, Paul hints that considering Jesus to be the promised Messiah of Israel, as true and as valuable as this role may be, falls short of a full and robust Christological understanding. The qualifier "according to the flesh" underlines the incompleteness of the assertion. Falling into the same general category, though not Christologically oriented, is the addition of the phrase *kata sarka* to Paul's introduction of Abraham in 4:1 as "our forefather" (NIV).[19] One can understand why the TNIV translators did not explicitly render this phrase *(kata sarka)* in English, since it adds nothing material to the verse. But the phrase does add a certain tone, or nuance, suggesting that designating Abraham only as the ancestor of the Jewish people ultimately falls short of appreciating his full significance. And, of course, Paul elaborates just this point in the following verses, claiming that Abraham is, in fact, the "father of all who believe"—Gentile and Jew alike (vv. 11–12).

Very similar, though more clearly negative because of the presence of an explicit contrast, is 9:8. Paul is here developing biblical support for his contention that there exists throughout salvation history an "Israel" within Israel—a spiritually alive remnant within the nation as a whole. He appeals to Genesis 21:12, which promises that it would be through Isaac that "offspring [seed]" would be "reckoned" to Abraham. Those familiar with the biblical account will immediately detect the implied contrast with Abraham's firstborn son Ishmael. It is this contrast to which Paul alludes in Romans 9:8. Ishmael represents "the natural children [the children of the flesh]"—those who can claim descent from Abraham only through physical generation. But Isaac represents "the children of the promise"—those who are not only physically descended from Abraham but also have been "called" by God, as Isaac was. (And note the somewhat parallel argument in Galatians 4:21–31, where Ishmael is designated the one born according to the flesh, in contrast to Isaac, the one born according to the promise/Spirit [vv. 23, 28–29].)

In these four passages, then—Romans 1:3, 4:1, 9:5, and 9:8—we have validated Dunn's suggestion that some negative nuance clings to the word *sarx,* even when it seems to be used in a "neutral" sense. We might then wonder whether the other "neutral" occurrences of the term in Romans—8:3b, 3c; 9:3; 11:14—

carry a similar connotation. But before looking at these verses, an important methodological point should be made. The negative nuance attaching to *sarx* in the four verses we have examined comes by way of an explicit *contrast* in the context. No such contrast exists in the remaining four verses. Moreover, such contextual nuancing does not necessarily affect the meaning of *sarx* in itself. Indeed, in 8:3b and 3c, any negative nuance is difficult to discern. *Sarx* occurs three times in the verse: "What the law could not do in that it was weakened through the *sarx,* God did:[20] by sending his own son in the likeness of sinful *sarx* and as a sin offering,[21] he condemned sin in the *sarx*" (my own rendering). The first occurrence falls toward the negative end of the spectrum of meaning; the TNIV accordingly translates "sinful nature." This opening phrase recapitulates the argument of Romans 7:14–25, where Paul demonstrates that God's good law is incapable of rescuing human beings from the ravages of sin because of their inability to obey this law. The spiritual nature of the law is opposed by and ultimately defeated by (cf. v. 23) the "fleshiness" *(sarkinos)* of human beings—their ingrained tendency toward sin (see v. 14). But it was into just this arena of "flesh" that God sent his own Son. The cumbersome phrase *homoiōma sarkos hamartias* attempts to preserve the fine balance between the reality of Jesus' complete identification with the human condition—he really "became *sarx*"—and his unprecedented conquering of that condition by preserving faithfulness to God as a human being—he took on the *likeness* of "sinful flesh." *Sarx,* then, denotes the human condition, and this condition is, of course, one of weakness, mortality, and susceptibility to sin. But any negative nuance in *sarx* here is very muted at best, and the very fact that Paul has to qualify it with "sinful" suggests that the word itself is neutral. The occurrence of *sarx* at the end of the verse is similar. God has himself "condemned" sin so that those who identify with that Son need not be condemned (v. 1). And he accomplished this by invading, through his Son, the very arena in which sin held sway, namely, the flesh.

The two remaining "neutral" occurrences of *sarx* (Rom 9:3 and 11:14) are closely related. In both, Paul uses *sarx* to emphasize his identification with his fellow Jews from an earthly, or human, perspective. Paul's strong emotional attachment to his kinsfolk (9:1–3; 10:1) and his assertion of their genuine divine privileges and blessings (9:4–5; 11:28–29) make clear that being Jewish is, indeed, an "advantage" (3:1–2) and is, in itself, hardly a negative thing. Nevertheless, by qualifying his relationship to his fellow Jews with the phrase *kata sarka* (9:3; untranslated in the TNIV), Paul may imply that he values even more highly his relationship to another "family"—his brothers and sisters in Christ. However, Paul never elsewhere uses *syngenēs* (in the plural here, translated "my own race" in the TNIV) in a spiritual sense.[22] Any hint of a contrast with his true spiritual family is therefore quite remote from this context. The same is true in 11:14, where Paul accentuates his commitment to his fellow Jews by calling them "my own people *[sarx]*."

The evidence of Romans suggests, then, that Paul uses *sarx* theologically to refer to the human condition or sphere. In distinction from *sōma*—"body"—which will be resurrected and enjoy the life to come, *sarx* is earthbound; "flesh and blood cannot inherit the kingdom of God" (1 Cor 15:50). The word need have no negative connotations; to be *human* is not itself evil or sinful (Rom 8:3b, 3c); and one's earthly relationships may be worthy and even valuable (9:3; 11:14). On the other hand, to be human is also to be weak and prone to ignore or misunderstand the things of the world to come (6:19; cf. 7:18, 25). And, when one regards matters from this human perspective, one may not get the full picture (1:3; 4:1; 9:5, 8). It is as a takeoff from this sense that the strongly negative (or "ethical") use of *sarx* develops. The natural human condition is to be "in the flesh," that is, to be fundamentally determined by the perspective of this world in contrast to the world to come. The natural person therefore cannot please God (8:8); he or she sins and dies (7:5), thinking and acting as a person who takes no account of the divine realm (8:4–7). Christians, because they are still in this world, must strive to avoid falling into such patterns of thought and activity (8:12–13; 13:14).

The Redemptive-Historical Framework for Paul's Concept of *Sarx*

One more important dimension of Paul's concept of *sarx,* hinted at in the previous paragraph, remains to be considered, namely, the redemptive-historical framework that provides the critical context for the idea. We may begin by returning to the first occurrence of *sarx* in Romans—1:3. As noted earlier, the TNIV made one of its few material translational changes with respect to *sarx* here, changing the NIV's "human nature" to "earthly life." The move reflects a change in interpretation from a "two natures" view of 1:3–4 to a "two stages" view of the text. In the NIV, Jesus, the Son, is a descendant of David "as to his human nature" (v. 3) and was "declared" to be Son of God by his resurrection from the dead (v. 4). The focus is on two eternal natures of Christ—his human and his divine, the one manifested in his being a Davidic descendant and the other proclaimed at his resurrection. This view of the passage has some supporters,[23] but their numbers are steadily dwindling. For one thing, the word translated "declared" in the NIV *(horizō)* does not have this meaning in first-century Greek.[24] The verb has the sense of "appoint," and any taint of adoptionism is avoided if we understand the phrase *en dynamei* to qualify "Son of God": The eternal Son (v. 3) became, at the time of his resurrection, the "powerful Son of God," able to dispense the salvation that he had won on the cross (cf. v. 16). More important and more relevant to our purposes, however, is the nature of the "flesh"/"Spirit" contrast in verses 3–4. We have already seen reason to take *pneuma hagiōsynēs* in verse 4 as a reference to the Holy Spirit. And Paul sets his understanding of the Holy Spirit decisively in his foundational redemptive-historical scheme of two eras. This scheme, probably borrowed from Jewish apocalyptic, presents the salvific work of God as a historical progression, divided into two eras—the old era of sin and death and the new era of righteousness and life. The flesh belongs to the old era; the Spirit to the new era.[25] Understood within this framework, the flesh/Spirit contrast of verses 3–4 reveals that Paul presents, as the core of his gospel (see v. 2), the two stages of Jesus' ministry—his birth and work as Son of David in the old era (the flesh), climaxed by his elevation in the new era to powerful Son of God via his resurrection.

It is no accident that the flesh/Spirit antithesis is resumed and developed precisely in those chapters that also depend most heavily on the redemptive-historical scheme of the two eras, namely, in Romans 5–8. Dominating the chapters is the contrast between the powers of the old era and the powers of the new—Adam versus Christ, sin versus righteousness, death versus life, law versus grace, flesh versus Spirit. In speaking of "powers," we do not intend to subscribe to the idea that the "flesh" is a cosmic power of the same nature as the Spirit, to which it is opposed.[26] "Flesh" is always ***human*** flesh in Paul, never a power separate from the human being. Paul presses into service the rhetoric of opposing powers to make clear the radical opposition between the old era and the new. Or perhaps, with respect at least to Romans 5–8, it would be better to use the language of opposing "realms," for Paul uses the language of power structures and domination throughout these chapters to conceptualize the contrast between the new life and the old. The person who is "in Christ" rather than "in Adam" has been transferred from the old realm to the new. "Flesh," that aspect of the human being separate from—and therefore often hostile to—God, dominated the old era and brought in its train sin and death (8:6–8). But dominating the new realm is God's own Spirit, bringing to all those who belong to Christ (8:9) the benefits of that new realm, namely, life and peace (8:6). Nevertheless, as Paul's imperatives make clear, the transfer into the new realm does not mean a complete separation from the negative influence of "flesh." As long as we live in unredeemed bodies (cf. 8:10–11), the flesh will remain an aspect of being human that will seek to pull Christians back into the sinful habits of the old realm. Hence, in his typically balanced way, after rehearsing the benefits of no longer being "in the flesh" but instead being "in the Spirit" (8:4–11), Paul goes on to insist that it is absolutely necessary for Christians to continue to battle against the influence of the flesh if they expect to gain eternal life (8:12–13; cf. 13:14).

The Translation of *Sarx*

With this brief sketch of the meaning of *sarx* in Romans behind us, we can now turn to the question of translation. Most of the scholars who have protested against the NIV/TNIV rendering "sinful nature" would probably agree with James D. G. Dunn: "A much more satisfactory rule of translation would be to recognize that *sarx* is an important technical and linking term in Paul's letters and is therefore best translated consistently by the same term, 'flesh.'"[27] Among the English translations, the NASB, as one might expect, comes closest to following this philosophy, translating *sarx* in Romans as "flesh" in every verse except 11:14. Indeed, one might think that Dunn would also make this verse an exception to the rule. To render "I magnify my ministry, so that in some way I might move to jealousy my flesh and save some of them" would make little sense to the English reader. However, one way to retain "flesh" while avoiding nonsense is to paraphrase in another direction, as does the NKJV (following the KJV), which renders 11:14 "those who are my own flesh." Indeed, KJV and NKJV use "flesh" to translate *sarx* in all its Romans occurrences with the exception of 8:6 and 7, where they translate, respectively, "carnally" and "carnal." The RSV makes exceptions to the translation of "flesh" for *sarx* only in 2:28 ("physical"), 3:20 ("human being"), 6:19 ("natural"), 9:3 ("race"), and 11:14 ("my fellow Jews"). The NRSV changes the RSV only in 9:3 ("flesh") and 11:14 ("my own people"), while the ESV, which is also built on the RSV, changes the RSV only in 9:3 ("flesh"). The NAB avoids "flesh" only in 3:20 ("human being"), 6:19 ("nature"), and 11:14 ("my race"). These exceptions to the general rule should be no surprise, since we have identified these occurrences as those falling outside the sphere of Paul's distinctive theological usage.

At the other end of the spectrum are those versions that move almost entirely away from using "flesh" to render *sarx*. The NIV and NLT never use "flesh" to translate *sarx* in Romans, while the TNIV, NJB, and TEV use "flesh" once, but in each case as part of a larger phrase—"flesh and blood" (9:3, both NJB and TEV); "human flesh" (8:3b; TNIV). Why do these versions avoid the translation "flesh"? I cannot speak for all these versions, but the translators of the TNIV thought that the word *flesh* in contemporary English would either connote "the meat on our bones" or (where context rendered that particular meaning impossible) the sensual appetites, and especially sexual lust. The former, of course, is never the meaning of *sarx* in Romans, while the latter is only a derivative part of Paul's meaning in most of the texts. Here, then, is a case in which the allegedly "straightforward rendering" of a word into English could, in fact, lead the English reader astray as to the real significance of the word. Nevertheless, the argument could be made, as Dunn suggests, that the best route is simply to render *sarx* with "flesh" every time it is conceivable to do so, and let the English reader, through careful contextual reading, build up for himself or herself a sense of this important technical term. The TNIV, of course, retains many such technical theological terms, in contrast to some modern versions that seek to avoid them. But the problem with technical terms is that it demands a great deal of the reader. A careful reader of the Bible would no doubt eventually acquire a sense of the significance of "flesh" in Romans. Yet, no matter what our hopes might be, how many readers of the Bible today are that careful? If one is translating for the well-read churchgoer—the person who goes to Bible studies where the Bible is really studied—then "flesh" is probably the best rendering of *sarx*. But the unpalatable fact is that only a minority of Christians anymore fall into that category—to say nothing of non-Christians, who, we hope, will pick up and read the Bible. For many readers, then, translating Paul's *sarx* as "flesh" would not effectively communicate.

Yet the problem with *sarx* is not only that it is a technical term but also, as we noted above, that it is a polymorphous term. While, as we have argued, the meaning of *sarx* in Paul occupies a continuous spectrum of meaning, the actual occurrences of the term fall in quite different places on this spectrum. Therefore, for instance, to translate *kata sarka* in both Romans 8:5 and Romans 9:3 with the same English phrase (as does the NKJV, NASB, NRSV, ESV, and NAB) could create a misapprehension about Paul's meaning in 9:3. "According to the flesh" in 8:4, in opposition to "according to the Spirit" as a standard for behavior, is a clearly negative concept. Finding this same phrase in 9:3, the English reader might conclude that Paul views his relationship with his fellow Jews in a negative light—emphatically *not* his intention. Most of these versions implicitly acknowledge the problem by shifting to other translations in 2:28, 3:20, and 11:14.

We turn finally to consider the difficulties facing translators who decide to contextually nuance their translation of *sarx*—for such a decision does come at a cost. First, a good English equivalent for Paul's theologically loaded use of *sarx* in a negative sense is difficult to find. The NIV/TNIV decision to go with "sinful nature" has, as noted at the beginning of this essay, been widely criticized. But the "nature" language is hard to avoid, as a glance at other translations reveals. The NLT follows the NIV and TNIV closely, rendering "sinful nature" in every passage that the NIV and TNIV do, with the exception of 7:5 ("old nature"), 8:3b ("human body like ours"), 8:3c (not translated), 8:5b ("sinful things"), and 13:14 ("evil desires"). The TEV sticks mainly with "human nature," varying only in 8:3c and 13:14 ("sinful nature"). The NJB pursues "elegant variation" to a fault: "natural inclinations" (7:5; 8:4, 5a, 8, 9), "human nature" (8:3a, b, c, 5b, 6, 12a, 12b, 13), "disordered nature" (7:25), "disordered human nature" (8:7), "disordered natural inclinations" (13:14). The "nature" language can indeed mislead English readers into thinking that Paul is describing component "parts" of the human being—and there is no doubt that it has been used to foster un-Pauline perspectives on the Christian life. But any *translation* runs such a risk, granted, as all recognize, that the Greek of Paul cannot be mechanically transferred into equivalent English terms. One could avoid the language of "nature" by translating "sinful impulse," but this rendering moves too far away from the idea of something that is the seat of sinful behavior. "Sinful aspect" might fit better with Paul's anthropology but is hardly understandable English. At the other end of the phrase, "sinful nature" is certainly preferable to "sinful self," since the latter would suggest that the person as a whole is irremediably sinful. And other possible variations—"evil nature," "lower nature," "old nature," "fallen nature"—are hardly improvements on "sinful nature." With all its problems, therefore, "sinful nature" is hard to improve on if one chooses to translate *sarx* in a contextually nuanced manner.

A second penalty one pays for such a translation procedure is the loss of explicit connections among Paul's various uses of *sarx*. Romans 8:3 is the best example. Paul uses the word *sarx* three times in this verse to make clear that the victory over *sarx* was ultimately determined in the sphere of *sarx* itself. God in the person of his Son entered fully into *sarx* in order to defeat it from within. This notion is clearly maintained in renderings such as the NRSV: "For God has done what the law, weakened by the *flesh,* could not do: by sending his own Son in the likeness of sinful *flesh,* and to deal with sin, he condemned sin in the *flesh*" (my emphases). Because the meaning of *sarx* within the verse varies, the TNIV renders the three occurrences with three different English expressions, thereby somewhat obscuring the connections: "For what the law was powerless to do because it was weakened by the *sinful nature,* God did by sending his own Son in the likeness of sinful *humanity* to be a sin offering. And so he condemned sin in *human flesh*" (my emphases). Critics of the NIV at this point should at least be grateful that the TNIV has smuggled one use of "flesh" into the translation of *sarx* in Romans (the NIV had "sinful man")! It should also be noted that "sinful nature" is footnoted (as it is everywhere this translation of *sarx* occurs in the NIV and TNIV), with the alternative "flesh" provided to the reader. And the conceptual relationship of these three occurrences is certainly still present in the TNIV. But it must be admitted that the different renderings make this connection less obvious.

The decision on whether to pursue a generally concordant translation or a dynamically equivalent translation of *sarx* depends, in the last analysis, on translation philosophy and intended audience. Neither decision is right or wrong apart from such variable considerations. Advocates of translations such as the NRSV and ESV will claim that their translations, following a more concordant approach, provide a better foundation for careful study. But, of course, these translations do not attempt to provide a consistently concordant approach—an impossible goal for any translation. Careful study will still require the use of a concordance to help the English reader identify the underlying Greek and Hebrew words. On the other hand, what the TNIV may sacrifice on this score may be more than made up for in contextual readability. Every indication is that the ability of people to read is steadily declining. If we are to hope for a Bible that an entire congregation can use, the readability of a more contextually nuanced translation such as the TNIV may be the best option.

Notes

1. For recent examples of this criticism, see J. D. G. Dunn, *The Theology of Paul the Apostle* (Grand Rapids: Eerdmans, 1998), 70; Thomas R. Schreiner, *Paul: Apostle of God's Glory in Christ* (Downers Grove, Ill.: InterVarsity Press, 2001), 143.

2. This article therefore brings together the two foci—exegesis and translation—that have marked the distinguished career of my CBT colleague Ron Youngblood. He has been a great encouragement to me—a relative newcomer to CBT and the art of translation—and he and his wife, Carolyn, have helped make our weeks of CBT work a true joy for me and my wife, Jenny. It is a distinct pleasure to dedicate this essay to Ron.

3. "Person" (1*x*); "personally" (1*x*); "one" (2*x*); "fellow man" (1*x*); "my own people" (1*x*); "human" (2*x*); "human being" (1*x*); "humanity" (1*x*); "human standards" (1*x*); "human effort" (3*x*); "human flesh" (1*x*); "world" (3*x*); "in a worldly manner" (1*x*); "worldly point of view" (2*x*); "standards of this world" (1*x*); "body" (10*x*); "physical" (2*x*); "birth" (1*x*); "natural" (1*x*); "earthly life" (1*x*); "this life" (1*x*); "earthly" (2*x*); "birth" (1*x*); "sensual" (1*x*); "unspiritual" (1*x*); "sinful nature" (27*x*); "flesh" (16*x*); nothing (5*x*). All statistics, here and elsewhere in the article, include pronouns that refer to the relevant English rendering.

4. Anthony Thiselton, *The Two Horizons: New Testament Hermeneutics and Philosophical Description with Special Reference to Bultmann, Heidegger, Gadamer, and Wittgenstein* (Grand Rapids: Eerdmans, 1979), 408–11.

5. BDAG, 914.

6. Except where indicated, the English translations in the article are from the TNIV.

7. Timo Laato, *Paulus und das Judentum: Anthropologische Erwägungen* (Åbo: Åbo Academy, 1991), 95.

8. See, e.g., W. D. Davies, *Paul and Rabbinic Judaism,* 4th ed. (Philadelphia: Fortress, 1981), 19; D. E. H. Whitely, *The Theology of St. Paul* (Oxford: Blackwell, 1964), 39.

9. C. E. B. Cranfield, *A Critical and Exegetical Commentary on the Epistle to the Romans,* ICC (Edinburgh: T. & T. Clark, 1975, 1979), 1:326 note 1.

10. C. K. Barrett, *The Epistle to the Romans,* HNTC (New York: Harper & Row, 1957), 132.

11. E.g., Cranfield, *Romans,* 1:361; Anders Nygren, *Commentary on Romans* (Philadelphia: Fortress, 1949), 300.

12. E.g., Ernst Käsemann, *Commentary on Romans* (Grand Rapids: Eerdmans, 1980), 204–5.

13. For more, see Robert H. Gundry, Sōma *in Biblical Theology with Emphasis on Pauline Anthropology,* SNTSMS 29 (Cambridge: Cambridge Univ. Press, 1987), 137; Douglas J. Moo, *The Epistle to the Romans,* NICNT (Grand Rapids: Eerdmans, 1996), 459, 467.

14. Dunn, *The Theology of Paul the Apostle,* 62–70; cf. also Dunn's "Jesus—Flesh and Spirit: An Exposition of Romans I.3-4," *JTS* 24 (1973), esp. 44–51; Walter David Stacey, *The Pauline View of Man: In Relation to its Judaic and Hellenistic Background* (London: Macmillan, 1956), 154–73.

15. The Hebrew *rûaḥ qodeš* refers to the Holy Spirit in Psalm 51:11 [13]; Isaiah 63:10, 11; Rule of the Community (1QS) 4:21; 8:16; 9:3; Thanksgiving Hymns (1QH) 15:7; 17:32; cf. *Testament of Levi* 18:7. See further Gordon Fee, *God's Empowering Presence: The Holy Spirit in the Letters of Paul* (Peabody, Mass.: Hendrickson, 1994), 478–84.

16. Some unusual language, the rough parallelism of verses 3 and 4, and the rhetorical situation (namely, Paul trying to establish common ground with a church he had never visited) have led most scholars to conclude that Paul is quoting an early creed or confession (e.g., K. Wengst, *Christologische Formeln und Lieder des Urchristentums* SNT 7 [Gütersloh: Mohn, 1972], 112–14). However, the evidence for such a preexisting tradition is not compelling; Paul may simply be using traditional language (Vern S. Poythress, "Is Romans 1:3–4 a Pauline Confession After All?" *ExpTim* 87 [1975–76]: 180–83; J. M. Scott, *Adoption as Sons of God: An Exegetical Investigation into the Background of ΥΙΟΘΕΣΙΑ in the Pauline Corpus,* WUNT 2.48 [Tübingen: Mohr Siebeck, 1992], 227–36).

17. The neuter article *to,* which does not agree with the masculine *Christos* ("Messiah"), stresses the limitation expressed in the prepositional phrase (BDF, 266[2]).

18. For a defense of this understanding of the punctuation (with a comma rather than a period after *sarka*), see esp. Bruce M. Metzger, "The Punctuation of Romans 9:5," in *Christ and the Spirit in the New Testament: In Honour of Charles Francis Digby Moule,* eds. B. Lindars and S. Smalley (Cambridge: Cambridge Univ. Press, 1973), 95–112; Murray J. Harris, *Jesus as "God":* Theos *as a Christological Term in the New Testament* (Grand Rapids: Baker, 1992), 144–72.

19. The phrase *kata sarka* probably qualifies *propatora* ("forefather")—"our forefather from a fleshly standpoint," rather than *heurēkenai* ("to have found")—"what did Abraham find by his own [fleshly] exertions?" (For the latter suggestion, see Robert Jewett, *Paul's Anthropological Terms: A Study of Their Use in Conflict Settings,* AGJU 10 [Leiden: Brill, 1971], 425–26.)

20. No Greek verb corresponding to the English "did" occurs, but the verb is implied in the syntax of the verse.

21. The meaning of *peri hamartias* (lit., "concerning sin") is disputed, but the occurrence of this phrase in the LXX to denote the sin offering (44 of the 54 LXX occurrences translate *ḥaṭāʾt, ḥaṭāʾâ,* or *ʾāšām*) renders this translation likely (both the NIV and TNIV have "sin offering"). See N. T. Wright, "The Meaning of *peri hamartias* in Romans 8.3," in *Studia Biblica* 1978 III: 453–59.

22. All three of his other uses are similar to Romans 9:3, denoting Paul's fellow Jews (Rom 16:7, 11, 21).

23. See, e.g., Charles Hodge, *Commentary on the Epistle to the Romans,* rpt. (Grand Rapids: Eerdmans, 1950), 18–19.

24. The word means "determine," "appoint," "fix," in its seven other NT occurrences (Luke 22:22; Acts 2:23; 10:42; 11:29; 17:26, 31; Heb 4:7).

25. A pioneer of this approach was Geerhardus Vos, "The Eschatological Aspect of the Pauline Conception of the Spirit," in *Redemptive History and Biblical Interpretation,* rpt. (Phillipsburg, N.J.: Presbyterian & Reformed, 1980), esp. 103–5; probably the most thorough presentation is found in Herman Ridderbos, *Paul: An Outline of His Theology* (Grand Rapids: Eerdmans, 1974), esp. 64–68.

26. This is the tendency in Rudolf Bultmann, *Theology of the New Testament* (New York: Charles Scribner's Sons, 1951, 1955), 1:197–200, 245 (although, as Dunn [*The Theology of Paul the Apostle,* 62 note 52] points out, Bultmann also makes clear that the language is "figurative").

27. Dunn, *The Theology of Paul the Apostle,* 70.

17

FAITH AS SUBSTANCE OR SURETY: HISTORICAL PERSPECTIVES ON *HYPOSTASIS* IN HEBREWS 11:1

James D. Smith III

I received a new Bible on my seventh birthday many years ago. Within its pages I was able to explore for myself the changeless truths and inspiring stories regularly presented at our church and by my parents. The Old Testament was huge. Aside from the book of Genesis, selected psalms, and the adventures of heroic people, there was a great deal that was beyond both my intellect and my interest. The New Testament was easier to navigate, for it was full of Jesus (with his words in red letters) and his contemporaries. Sometimes, people like Abraham and Moses were mentioned, and I began to sense a connection between the Testaments that was both reassuring and challenging.

Then, through a memory verse window opened by the Word of God being "quick, and powerful, and sharper than any twoedged sword," I encountered the Epistle to the Hebrews. It was wonderful! Here was Christian teaching presented in continual interaction with the Old Testament. I learned to use the cross references and to see the patterns of lives and ideas linked together. Eventually, Hebrews 11 became my favorite chapter. As a baseball fan, I liked the "Hall of Faith" idea and could think about what each one's plaque might look like—Joseph's coat, Samson's muscles, and so forth. There was even a definition of faith—in that familiar, "especially holy" old English language: "Now faith is the substance of things hoped for . . ." (Heb 11:1).

What could this mean? Well, I saw how those Bible heroes welcomed God being really present in their lives long before the "big events" began. When ill, I knew that St. Joseph's Aspirin, once inside me, would soon work to reduce my childhood fevers. Growing older, I was assured that the "peach fuzz" on my face was an indication that someday I could grow whiskers like my dad. These are theologically naive parallels, to be sure, but there was no doubt that the "real stuff" planted in my life by God was growing.

When I reached high school, a copy of the Good News New Testament was given to me. To the witness of the King James Version was now added that of Today's English Version (and cool stick-figure illustrations were added to impressive oil paintings). Eventually, I worked through the text until I arrived at Hebrews 11 and discovered there that to have faith is *to be sure* of the things we hope for. When asked about the difference in translation, a teacher said, "They just made it easier to understand." Several years later, in college, I received a New American Standard Bible. I turned to the same passage and read that faith is the *assurance* of things hoped for. When asked about the difference between the KJV and NASB, a different teacher responded that it was no doubt due to the discovery of earlier and better Greek manuscripts than were available in the seventeenth century.

Soon I knew better. Studying Greek in college and in seminary and plowing into the New Testament with the recommended scholarly apparatus, I learned that the manuscripts contained no significant variants. In Hebrews 11, faith is *hypostasis*—tangible reality, objective presence, essential substance.[1] What had changed was not the text to be translated but the "word culture" of the translators. To put it differently, growing up in a Baptist church, I had been taught that there was Scripture (God's authoritative Word) and tradition (humanity's fallible views). In the years that followed, I discovered a third reality, namely, traditions of Scripture translation and interpretation.[2] Thus, it was no surprise later to find the New International Version declaring, "Faith is *being sure* of what we hope for." The noun is rendered as a verb. The objective had become subjective. The philosophical root had given way to the psychological result. The divine substance was eclipsed by the personal surety.

The purpose of this essay is to address two questions: How did we get here from there? and, What may be the significance of this shift? To do so requires a historical survey that will include a foundational patristic figure, the development of perspectives on faith in the medieval Roman Catholic and Byzantine literature, and the description (after Luther) of two emerging traditions of the English translation of Hebrews 11:1 in the sixteenth century. One of these, eclipsed for centuries by the KJV, reemerged (for new reasons) to dominate in the twentieth century, paralleled by developments in Spanish translation as illustrated by editions of the Reina-Valera. Finally, we will note some missiological implications for the translation of Hebrews 11:1 in tribal situations today and then offer some concluding reminders.

The Patristic Perspective

John Chrysostom (347–407), the renowned exegete and preacher in Antioch and Constantinople, stands as the foremost representative of the Greek patristic tradition. Obviously *hypostasis* requires no translation in his New Testament text. But in his series of homilies on Hebrews, Chrysostom underlines its objective character in 11:1 by comparing the nature of faith with the human faculty of eyesight: "Faith, then is the seeing of things not plain, and brings things not seen to the same full resolution as those that are.... For since the objects of hope seem to be unsubstantial, faith gives them substantiality *(hypostasis),* or rather, does not give it but is itself their substance *(ousia).*"[3]

For Chrysostom, faith manifests the tangible reality of its objects, revealing the very essence of ultimate things. He uses the example of Jesus' resurrection, maintaining that, while we have not yet been physically raised from death, yet it is at present already in our souls. This participation in divine realities lies at the heart of the believer's new life in Christ.

In this series of homilies and elsewhere, Chrysostom emphasizes the importance of Christian life beyond mere doctrinal conviction. His comments on Hebrews 6:1, for example, exhort the believer to be dedicated to truth and spiritual excellence in ways that go beyond the basics of the faith while yet building on them. This pursuit of practical virtue at no point diminishes the objective character of faith in the life of a child of God. It does, however, anticipate developments in which—both in East and West—the Christian discussion of faith will come to distinguish two varieties.

The patristic understanding is sustained and expanded in the Eastern Orthodox tradition throughout the Byzantine era. For example, Maximus the Confessor (580–662), the great Greek theologian and ascetic writer, underlines Chrysostom's insights:

> The Apostle gives the following definition of faith: "Faith makes real for us things hoped for, gives assurance of things not seen" (Heb 11:1). One may also justly define it as an engrained blessing or as true knowledge disclosing unutterable blessings.... Faith is a relational power or a relationship which brings about the immediate, perfect, and supernatural union of the believer with the God in whom he believes.... Faith is knowledge that cannot be rationally demonstrated.... The strength of our faith is revealed by the zeal with which we act.[4]

In classic Orthodox statement, Maximus held that union with God—and the purification that preceded it—was closely tied to this knowledge. Only divine revelation could lead to a holy confession of sacred truth. The faith of the church made hope and love possible as well. As such, it was the foundation underlying the deeds of piety—that which gives assurance that God is and that things divine are real. Faith, for Maximus, is not initially assurance. Rather, it *results* in an assurance that inspires life in the kingdom of God—that is, faith in action.

Two Kinds of Faith

By the twelfth century, however, Byzantine exegetes and theologians were talking about something quite different. They were talking about two distinct kinds of faith. Isaac the Syrian had earlier spoken of a faith received through baptism and the grace of Christ, which makes us God-fearers. Then, he says, a second kind of faith is born in us, the great faith of contemplation, which grows as a mustard seed and renders nothing impossible. In the Greek translations from Syriac, the first variety is called *psilē pistis*—thin, formal, implicit, or abstract faith. Later, with Peter of Damascus, who had read the work of Isaac the Syrian, this becomes *koinē pistis*—common faith. In either writer, this first faith is indispensable, but their larger discussions are devoted to what they consider the more glorious second variety. Peter of Damascus outlines the distinction:

> Thus there is, first, the ordinary faith of all Orthodox Christians, that is to say, correct doctrinal belief concerning God and His creation, both visible and invisible, as the Holy Catholic Church, by God's grace, has received it; and there is, second, the faith of contemplation or spiritual knowledge, which is not in any way opposed to the first kind of faith; on the contrary, the first gives birth to the second, while the second strengthens the first.... We acquire the first kind of faith through hearing about it, inheriting it from devout parents and teachers of the Orthodox faith; but the second is engendered in us by our true belief and by our fear of the Lord.... Because of this fear we have chosen to keep the commandments and so have resolved to practice the virtues that pertain to the body—stillness, fasting, moderate vigils, psalmody, prayer, spiritual reading ... so that the body may be purified of the worst passions. It is in this way that a man finds the strength to devote himself undistractedly to God.... He comes to believe that the Orthodox faith is truly glorious, and he begins to long to do God's will.[5]

In the face of widespread formalism, the greatest of Byzantine mystical writers, Symeon the New Theologian (949–1022), had addressed this issue as well, advocating what would be called in the tradition *zosa pistis*—full, living faith fired by the Holy Spirit.[6] His practice of Hesychasm, in which the prayers of the heart seek a vision of the Divine Light, was influential not only in monastic culture but in the larger Eastern Orthodox tradition reaching beyond the fall of Constantinople in 1453, with movement from Byzantine to Slavic soil. If the ground of Christian faith remained the Scriptures, the councils and creeds, and worship of the Holy Trinity, believers were also called to grow in union with Christ as "partakers of the divine nature" *(theosis)*.[7]

Maximus had once observed, "The strength of our faith is revealed by the zeal with which we act. Thus, our actions disclose the measure of our faith." What was stated by him as a quantitative issue had, centuries after, increasingly become a qualitative one—salvation exegetically pictured as involving two kinds of faith, their efficacy intertwined.

In the West, a similar development took place. The text tradition, of course was decisively established through Jerome's translation of Hebrews 11:1 in the Latin Vulgate: "Es autem fides sperandarum *substantia* rerum...." This rendering was almost universally received throughout the Middle Ages and into the sixteenth century, with vernacular translations not favored by the Roman Catholic hierarchy.

What did emerge, however, was a distinctive exegetical and homiletical tradition in which faith as "substance" was usually seen as the formal foundation, cause, or beginning of salvation. Necessary for the believer's salvation was both a faith in the content of Christian doctrine *(fides quae)* and faith formed by works of love *(fides formata)*.

Hugh of St. Victor (1096–1141), in his work *De Sacramentis,* devoted an entire section to the nature of faith. His treatment opens with the quotation of Hebrews 11:1, in which he declares that "the invisible goods which are not yet present though act presently through faith subsist in our hearts, and faith itself in these things is their subsistence in us." This, however, does not represent, in Hugh, the fullness of Christian life: "So the substance of those things is faith, since through faith alone they now subsist in us, and similarly the proof of those is faith, since through faith alone they are proven by us.... In this description not what faith is but what faith does is shown...." Positing a distinction between the believer and the knower, he carries the discussion a step further: "There are two things in which faith consists, this question and affection, that is, constancy or firmness in believing. For in affection the substance of faith is found, in cognition, the matter." The substance of faith, then, is located in the affection by which one embraces the doctrinal essentials.[8]

While a century later the influence of Thomas Aquinas (1225–74) on this matter cannot be overlooked, perhaps the most significant voice for our purposes belongs to the late-medieval Franciscan biblical expositor Nicholas of Lyra (1270–1349). His biblical commentaries *Postillae Litterales* and *Postillae Morales* were frequently used as Sunday sermons and, with the advent of printing, went into over one hundred editions from 1471–1600. Lyra continues the exegetical tradition in which, through interlinear and marginal notes (glosses) on the biblical text, medieval "study Bibles" were developed. With regard to our text, the consensus was that foundation-faith *(fundamentum)* was insufficient for salvation but represented a first step—after which hope and love (completing the triad of theological virtues) would advance the process of sanctification. To be "clear" and "just" was a fitting goal to be realized by life's end but not to be grasped in the present.

For Lyra, faith is a *prima virtus infusa,* a "habit of mind by which eternal life is begun in us, making the intellect assent to things not seen." He distinguishes between two levels of faith (and people). Certain doctrines, such as the incarnation, passion, and resurrection of Christ, could be embraced by common people under the church's teaching "explicitly through simple assent." However, the more subtle aspects of the faith, the rationale and the implications of the "mysteries of the faith," could be grasped by "only those who are *superiores* in the Church, and such things are not discussed with the simple."[9]

In summary, by the year 1500, the prevailing Roman Catholic position on *hypostasis* in Hebrews 11:1 was that its Latin rendering—*substantia*—indicated the foundation-faith upon which one could build through works of love in the hope of ultimate salvation.

The Reformers' Influence

The Augustinian *cum* Reformer Martin Luther (1483–1546) found this viewpoint wholly unsatisfactory, and he was aided by Philip Melanchthon (1497–1560) in developing an alternative position. Luther argued that, in our passage, *hypostasis* meant "possession." As Kenneth Hagen has noted, "In stark contrast, then, to medieval exegetes . . . , faith as 'possession' means for Luther that salvation is complete and full to one who has faith. Faith is the first, last, and only step to salvation," a personal and subjective response to an encounter with the Word of God. In translating *hypostasis* in Hebrews 3:14, Melanchthon advised a hesitant Luther to use the rendering "sure confidence."

In this, Luther knowingly differed from the *visio* theology of Chrysostom and the *intellectus* theology of Aquinas and Lyra and opposed the medieval understanding of faith as (mere) foundation of the virtues.[10] Drawing on the Latin, Luther invites the reader, "Let us follow the most common use of 'substance.' In Scripture, it almost always means possession and supply (Heb 10:34; Luke 8:43; 1 John 3:17). Since faith is nothing other than adherence to the Word of God, as in Romans 1, it follows that faith is ... the possession of the Word of God, of eternal goods." With this, Luther changed the course not only of subsequent exposition of this passage but of vernacular translations as well. Early editions of the English Bible demonstrate the interplay of factors—including lexical, traditional, and theological—in the rendering of our passage.

As a result of the work of William Tyndale (1494–1536), the first complete printed New Testament in English appeared toward the end of February 1526, and copies were beginning to reach England about a month later.[11] Being obliged to do most of his translation on the continent, spending the greater part of 1524 in residence in Luther's Wittenberg, Germany, it is no surprise that his own rendering of Hebrews 11:1 began as follows: "Faith is a *sure confidence* of things which are hoped for...." Through a faith encounter with the Word, one could be certain of his or her salvation.

Within a decade, Miles Coverdale (1488–1569), a Cambridge graduate and Augustinian friar who had left the order to join the Protestant Reformers, was able to produce the first complete printed Bible in English. *The Bible: That is, the holy Scripture of the Olde and New Testament, faithfully and truly translated out of Douche and Latyn into English* appeared in October 1535. Drawing his version from five others in print (notably Tyndale's and Luther's), our text reads, "Faith is a *sure confidence* of things which are hoped for...." He also edited the Great Bible of 1539, which was supported by Anglican bishop Thomas Cranmer for use by the clergy. That edition likewise read, "Fayth is a *sure confydence* of thynges, whych are hoped for...."

Thus, at the fountainhead of English translations is this evangelical rendering, which affirms the believer's subjective possession of the assurances of a saving faith. In the sixteenth century, however, a second tradition of English translations of Hebrews 11:1 would emerge in the next generation. England had no Bible translation activity during the reign of Mary Tudor, but a group of expatriates was active in Geneva.

The Christian community in Geneva had been profoundly shaped by the person and theology of John Calvin (1509–64), and by the biblical scholarship of Theodore Beza (1519–1605). The English congregation's pastor there was William Whittingham (1524–79), and his edition of the Scriptures appeared in 1560 as the Geneva Bible. Much of the New Testament portion reflected text based on Tyndale, but the Calvinist conviction that informed the famous notes also led to a distinctive translation of our text: "Now faith is the *ground* of things, which are hoped for...."

While readily adopted by Reformed congregations in Scotland and widely embraced in England, the Anglican prelates did not appreciate the notes and authorized a revision of the Great Bible by qualified bishops. This Bishops' Bible appeared in 1568, with the revisers charged to depart from the Great Bible only where it did not accurately represent the original languages. Interestingly, they altered the rendering of Hebrews 11:1, following instead the Geneva: "Fayth is the *grounde* of thynges hoped for...."

The King James Version and Subsequent English Developments

So in the sixteenth century, English translations of our text reflected both Tyndale's first-generation "Lutheran *confidence*" and Whittingham's second-generation "Reformed *ground*" as definitions of Christian faith. It remained for the Authorized Version (KJV) of 1611 to establish a long-standing text tradition. With the Greek text and a wealth of the other editions before them, their rendering was as already noted: "Now faith is the substance of things hoped for...." Given the option, the scholars had returned to the Latinized objective rendering (as did, predictably, the Roman Catholic Rheims translation from the Vulgate into English in 1582) and relegated both "confidence" and "ground" to the notes and marginal references of subsequent editions.

With the KJV, the English textus receptus would be settled for 250 years.[12] The exegetical and homiletical activity, however, went forward unabated. For example, almost concurrently published was William Perkins's (1558–1602) exposition of Hebrews 11 titled *A Cloud of Faithful Witnesses,* in which his notes on verse 1 distinguish between three meanings of faith—historical, miraculous, and saving/justifying. Admirers of Perkins took his sermon notes and posthumously (1609) published them as a biblical commentary. The result was that his influence was far-reaching on both sides of the Atlantic.[13] In the era that followed, scholastic Protestantism stirred movements varying from a warmhearted Pietism to an Enlightenment "turn to the subject," bringing a heightened emphasis on personal religion and shifting perspective on the nature of faith.

By the mid-nineteenth century, during what church historian Alec Vidler has called "an age of revolutions," both Roman Catholics and Protestants were revisiting their authoritative sources. Coincidentally, the year 1870 saw the close of the First Vatican Council, with a revised constitution on faith *(Dei Filius)* and the positing of papal infallibility *ex cathedra*—and Canterbury's bicameral call for a revision of the Authorized Version of the Scriptures. The rationale for any such new translation in the existing language is noteworthy, as was their aim: "We do not contemplate any new translation of the Bible, or any alteration of the language, except when in the judgement of the most competent scholars such change is necessary."[14]

Over the years that followed, this "necessity" spoke with many voices. On the New Testament team were such Cambridge textual scholars as B. F. Westcott and F. J. A. Hort, whose devotion to the ancient codices (Sinaiticus and Vaticanus) was influential. Moreover, the English-speaking cultures within which both the British and American teams pursued their work of translation had changed in notable ways from that of seventeenth-century England. Their worldview and readership influenced the judgments of these revisers in ways both recognized and unrecognized. Ultimately, the British Revised Version New Testament appeared in May of 1881, and the American text was published as the American Standard Version (ASV) in 1901. While there were minor differences in translation, and other differences in the extensive marginal notes, the RV and ASV agreed on a modern text rendering of Hebrews 11:1—"Now faith is the *assurance* of things hoped for...."

In the study notes of my ASV edition, the mind of scholarly contemporaries is revealed, as the catena of linked thematic verses is presented at 11:1. The lead definition of faith *(pisteuō)* provided there—namely, "a union of assurance and conviction"—is striking. While expressing the affirmation that faith is given by God, comes by hearing the Word of God, and so forth, the notes are soon clear on a particular point: "Facts produce feeling."[15] That the choice of the word "assurance" in our text helped heighten this shift toward the subjective (with "substance" marginalized) may be illustrated by a glance at the subsequent tradition of translations.

The renderings of the NASV, TEV, and NIV were noted at the outset of this essay. To this list, virtually every other popular (notably Protestant) twentieth-century translation may be added as examples. The objective has become subjective. The philosophical/ontological root has given way to the psychological result. The divine substance is eclipsed by the personal surety. By mid-century, this tradition of Scripture translation and interpretation held sway.

International Comparisons

Evidence of this translational tide does not only appear in English. In tracking another world language, the case of Spanish editions is instructive. Briefly, in 1569 La Biblia del Oso (Reina) appeared, declaring "Es pues la Fe, la *sustancia* de las cosas que se esperan...." The revision of Valera (1602) repeated this. Except for some minor orthographic variations, the Reina-Valera maintained this rendering through the revision of 1909—this in spite of the fact that the British and Foreign Bible Society had assumed proprietorship for this publication in the mid-nineteenth century. This translation of *hypostasis* as "substance," however, was changed to "certainty" *(certeza)* in the United Bible Societies' 1960 edition, and this is repeated in the 1995 revision as well. Five years earlier (to cite but one parallel), the Adventists' NRV had rendered "La fe es *estar seguros* de lo que...."[16] Faith had become a state of mind, a matter of "being sure."

The worldwide impact of the United Bible Societies' translational tendency in this matter cannot be ignored. The notes on Hebrews 11:1 in their translator's handbook on the Letter to the Hebrews (1983) are enlightening. "To have faith or to trust God shows that 'faith' is an event, not an object." They give a concise survey of the three ways in which the Greek word the RSV translates as "assurance" has been understood: (1) substance or underlying reality, (2) assurance or verbal expressions like "to be sure," and (3) guarantee, as favored by some French translations and the Jerusalem Bible. There follows a suggested translation: "Those who trust God are sure that he will give them what they hope for...."[17] Would John Chrysostom—or the apostle Paul—have confidently rendered it in this manner?

At this point, our great debt to the United Bible Societies and other missions organizations assisting in worldwide evangelization needs to be acknowledged—as does the difficulty of tribal translation work. Eugene Loos, a Wycliffe/SIL missionary-linguist in partnership for a half century with the congregation I pastor, makes this comment:

> As in almost all cases of abstract nouns, the noun has to be rendered as a verb. Like other primitive cultures, [Argentina's] Capanahua has a good inventory of verbs, but nouns are scarce.... Nouns are for naming plants and animals. Verbs are for naming events, and since most Greek abstract nouns have events as their semantic source, we have to use verbs in the rendering.[18]

Conclusion

What lessons for the challenge of Bible translation today may be gained from a survey such as this? As a pastor and historian, I would specifically suggest these four, none wholly original:

First, we must keep in mind that, while translation and exegesis are related, a distinction must be maintained, and the second should exercise no decisive influence on the first. *Hypostasis* had a distinctive, first-century cluster of meanings. In recent years, New Testament scholar William Lane assessed these and reached an apt conclusion: "It is imperative that the objective sense of the term be represented in translation.... Translations like 'confidence' or 'assurance' are untenable because they give to *hypostasis* a subjective value it does not possess."[19]

Second, while Scripture and tradition are useful topics for theological reflection, there are also traditions of Bible translation (as we have sought to demonstrate from Hebrews 11:1). We need to be aware of these, identify their origins and underlying rationales, consider the ways in which ostensibly neutral tools of the trade may perpetuate them, and evaluate their proper role in current projects.

Third, the challenge of translating the Scriptures into tribal languages and cultures is compelling, particularly in the area of faithfully conveying concepts of an abstract nature. That being said, the person rendering a new translation into English (or any language with rich literary resources) should fully avail themselves of both the original tongue and that particular language. A translation can be both readable and challenging to prevailing thought-forms.

Finally, in this essay our subject has been *faith,* which, according to Romans 10:17, comes by hearing the very Word of God. The vocation of translation, therefore, is a high calling. We have read the claim that "faith is an event." If so, what *kind* of event is it that we desire—even pray for—in the reader? My contention is that it includes, according to our text, not only faithful acts and godly virtues, not only personal surety and spiritual confidence, but an objective participation in divine realities already present, which will be someday fully manifest. To Corrie ten Boom—a woman of faith and a lover of Scripture—belongs the closing word:

> I was once a passenger aboard a ship that was being guided by radar. The fog was so dense we couldn't see even the water about us. But the radar screen showed a streak of light, indicating the presence of another ship far ahead. The radar penetrated the fog and picked up its image. So, also, is faith the radar that sees the reality through the clouds. The reality of the victory of Christ can be seen only by faith, which is our radar. Our faith perceives what is actual and real; our senses perceive only that which is limited to three dimensions and comprehended by our intellect. Faith sees more.[20]

Notes

1. Helmut Koester, *"hypostasis," TDNT* 8:572–84. Special thanks are due him, as teacher and Harvard adviser, for early lexical and historical insights. See also Harold

Attridge, *The Epistle to the Hebrews* (Philadelphia: Fortress, 1989), 205–14, and William L. Lane, *Hebrews* (Waco, Tex.: Word, 1991), 323–26.

2. Provocative in the rethinking of "tradition" is Heiko Oberman, "Quo Vadis, Petre? The History of Tradition from Irenaeus to Humaric Generis," *Harvard Divinity Bulletin* 26 (1962): 1–26.

3. John Chrysostom, *NPNF* (First Series, vol. 14), 462–64.

4. *The Philokalia: The Complete Text,* eds. G. E. H. Palmer, P. Sherrard, and K. Ware (London: Faber, 1984), 2:189–90, 218.

5. *Philokalia,* 3:213–16. Thanks to Ted Stylianopoulos of Holy Cross Greek Orthodox School of Theology in Brookline, Massachusetts, for his perspectives on the Byzantine tradition.

6. "Discourse 12," in *Symeon the New Theologian: The Discourses,* ed. C. J. de Catanzaro (New York: Paulist, 1980).

7. John Meyendorff, *Byzantine Theology* (New York: Fordham Univ. Press, 1974), 159–65.

8. "On Faith," in *Hugh of St. Victor on the Sacraments of the Christian Faith,* ed. R. J. Deferrari (Cambridge, Mass.: Medieval Academy of America, 1951), 165–69.

9. On Lyra's Hebrew exegesis here (and its influence), see Kenneth Hagen, *A Theology of Testament in the Young Luther: "The Lectures on Hebrews"* (Leiden: Brill, 1974), 84–85.

10. See Hagin, *A Theology of Testament,* 71–90. For Luther's Hebrews commentary, see *Luther's Works* (St. Louis, Mo.: Concordia, 1968), 29:229–31.

11. On a century of English translations beginning with Tyndale, see F. F. Bruce, *History of the Bible in English,* 3d ed. (New York: Oxford Univ. Press, 1978), 24–126. Thanks to Liana Lupas, curator of American Bible Society's text archives, and Michael Holmes of Bethel College (Minnesota) for help in accessing and evaluating these texts.

12. Note in this volume Walt Wessel's assessment of Alister McGrath's *In the Beginning: The Story of the King James Bible and How It Changed a Nation, a Language, and a Culture* (New York: Doubleday, 2001).

13. William Perkins, *A Commentary on Hebrews 11* (1609), ed. John H. Augustine (Boston: Pilgrim Press, 1991).

14. Cited in Bruce, *History of the Bible in English,* 135–36, among a citing of the Canterbury Committee's five resolutions. His larger discussion remains valuable.

15. *The Cross-Reference Bible,* ed. Harold E. Monser (New York: Cross-Reference Bible, 1910), 2284. Among the associate editors were I. M. Price, R. A. Torrey, A. T. Robinson, and J. R. Sampey.

16. Thanks to Esteban Voth and others in the Sociedades Biblicas Unidas for providing these texts.

17. UBS's translator's handbook, edited by Paul Ellingsworth and Eugene Nida (London: United Bible Societies, 1983), 251.

18. Personal correspondence (10 May 2001 and 16 May 2001).

19. Lane, *Hebrews,* 326.

20. Corrie ten Boom, *Amazing Love* (London: Christian Literature Crusade, 1953), 8–9.

18

THE USE OF CAPITAL LETTERS IN TRANSLATING SCRIPTURE INTO ENGLISH

Larry Lee Walker

The languages in which Scripture first appeared did not use capital letters in the same way they are used in modern English. Hebrew (and Aramaic) has no capital letters; the other languages of the literary world of the Old Testament didn't either. Greek has capital letters, but they are not used as they are in English. In fact, early Greek manuscripts are written entirely in capital letters. Latin, the language of the Vulgate (the longest-used translation) has capital letters, but they are not used as they are in modern English. Modern editions of Latin works will often capitalize names like Virgil or Cicero, but the earliest Latin did not make such distinctions between common nouns and proper nouns. The various modern languages that do use capital letters use them in a variety of ways. For example, German capitalizes all nouns, whereas English capitalizes only proper nouns.

The English language, unlike many other ancient and modern languages, uses capital letters in a deliberate and specific way that is designed to help the reader. English begins proper nouns with a capital letter in contrast to common nouns, which are written in all small letters. The degree to which this takes place has evolved somewhat through the centuries and varies greatly in the history of the English Bibles.

The following tables are intended to be representative and not exhaustive. They reveal general patterns in the different versions. It is extremely important to observe the *context* of each passage. The tables are designed as a quick reference; detailed literary analysis and exegesis of the cited passages are not appropriate in a survey of the kind presented in this study. The tables show in their first two columns the treatment found in the two most widely used English translations, followed by a sampling of other versions.

References to God

Divine names normally begin with a capital letter in English usage. This is true, regardless of whether the name is used of such deities as the one true God or of the various gods of the surrounding nations (Baal, Dagan, or Zeus, for example).

The issue of capital letters must be decided when the translator encounters the Bible's many ways of referring to God. General agreement is found in the case of the actual names of God, but the issue is more complicated when encountering various titles used of God.

Names

The various names for God, especially in the Old Testament, are understood as proper nouns and therefore appropriately begin with a capital letter. This is true of compound names (Almighty God, God Most High) as well as one-word names (God, Lord).

A special case involves the Hebrew personal name of God, a word used more often than any other Hebrew word in the Old Testament. It is expressed by the Hebrew letters *YHWH* (usually translated "the Lord") and is used over six thousand times in the Hebrew Bible. This must be distinguished from the Hebrew *ʾᵃdōnāy* (translated "the Lord"). Unfortunately, this difference in script can only be seen and not heard. Another unique situation arises when these two names are juxtaposed—*ʾᵃdōnāy YHWH*; Amos 3:11, which should logically and consistently be translated "the Lord Lord." To avoid this awkward sequence, some translators have put *YHWH* in capital letters but rendered it as GOD, with the resultant combination: "the Lord GOD."

The following table reflects how various translations have rendered some of the names of God:

Reference	KJV	NIV	Other
Gen 17:1	the Almighty God	God Almighty[1]	God Almighty (NRSV, REB, NASB, GW, NLT, NCV); the Almighty God (TEV, AMP); God All-Powerful (CEV)
Num 24:4	the Almighty	the Almighty[2]	the Almighty (NRSV, GW, NLT, NASB); the God All-Powerful (CEV)
Gen 14:18	most high God	God Most High	God Most High (NRSV, NLT, REB, CEV, GW, NCV); the Most High God (TEV)
Gen. 2:4	Lord God	Lord God[3]	Lord God (NRSV, NLT, REB, TEV, NCV)

Amos 3:11	Lord GOD	the Sovereign LORD	Lord GOD (NRSV, NASB, REB, NCV); LORD God (CEV); Sovereign LORD (NLT); Lord God (AMP, NL)
Isa 6:5	LORD of hosts	LORD Almighty	LORD of hosts (NRSV, JPS, NASB, NAB, AMP, BER); LORD of Hosts (REB); Yahweh Sabaoth (NJB); the Lord of All (NL); LORD All-Powerful (CEV, NCV); LORD of Armies (GW); LORD Almighty (NLT, TEV)

Table 1: Names of God

TITLES

In addition to specific names, various common terms used as titles or references to God are capitalized. Such common words as rock, king, name, shepherd, redeemer, savior, and even "one" are so used and capitalized. In many passages it is a matter of judgment whether a common noun is being used in this way. Study of the context and usage of the term elsewhere are the determining factors.

Rock

It should not be surprising to find God referred to as "Rock." Even the KJV capitalized this usage of the word in some places (cf. Deut 32:4, 15, and 31) but not in other places (Pss 18:31, 46; 28:1).

The table below displays how various modern English versions have treated this issue. In some cases, where many versions treat the word as a common noun, the NIV treats it as a proper noun (Gen 49:24; 2 Sam 22:32; Pss 18:31, 46; 28:1).

Notice that in Deuteronomy 32:31 "rock" is used in two different ways and that the different usage is reflected in English by the use of capital letters for the second time the word is used. The NIV is the most prone to capitalize this term, as the table reveals.

Reference	KJV	NIV	Common Noun	Proper Noun
Ps 18:31	who is a rock	who is the Rock	rock (NRSV, CEV, REB, NLT, GW, TNK, BER)	Rock (NCV)
Ps 18:46	blessed be my rock	Praise be to my Rock	rock (NRSV, NLT, GW, REB, CEV, TNK, BER)	Rock (NCV, NL, NCV)
Ps 28:1	O LORD my rock (Rock, NKJV)	O LORD my Rock	my rock (NRSV, NLT, GW, CEV, TNK, BER)	Rock (REB, NCV, NL)
Gen 49:24	the shepherd, the stone of Israel (Shepherd, Stone, NKJV)	The Shepherd, the Rock of Israel	rock (CEV)	Rock of Israel (NRSV, NCV, NLT, GW, TNK, NL, BER)

Deut 32:4	He is the Rock	He is the Rock	rock (CEV, NCV, GW)	Rock[4] (NRSV, NLT, TNK, NL, BER[5])
Deut 32:15	lightly esteemed the Rock of his salvation	rejected the Rock	rock (GW)	Rock (NRSV, CEV, REB, NCV, NLT, TNK, BER)
Deut 32:31	their rock *is* not as our Rock	their rock is not like our Rock	Their rock is not like our rock (GW)	Their rock is not like our Rock (NRSV, CEV, REB, NCV, NLT, TNK, BER)

Table 2: Rock

King

It should not be surprising to find "king" used in reference to God, but what is surprising is the variety of treatments found in the English translations. Much disagreement is seen in the English translations as to whether the word is used in such a divine sense or is only limited to the earthly king. It can, of course, in some cases refer in a sense to both—which poses a challenge for the English translator.

Reference	KJV	NIV	king	King
Ps 84:3	my King and my God	my King and my God	king (NRSV,[6] TEV, GW)	King (CEV, REB, NCV, NLT, RSV, NL, BER)
Ps 95:3	great King above gods	the great God, the great King above all gods	king (CEV, TEV, GW)	King (NRSV, REB, NCV, NLT, NL, BER)
Ps 145:1	My God, O king	my God, the King	king (GW, TEV)	King (NRSV, REB, NLT, CEV, NL, NCV, BER)
Ps 68:24	King of glory	God and King	my God, my king (GW, TNK); of God, my king (TEV)	Our God and King (CEV); my God, my King (NRSV, REB, BER); my God and King (NLT, NL); God my King (NCV)

Table 3: King

One

The word "one" is sometimes capitalized when it refers to God, and the NIV does this more than any other version. This is often the case when a modifier is found before it (Ps 132:2; Prov 9:10; 21:12; Isa 1:4). But it is also used in the absolute form in the NIV (Ps 144:10), NKJV (Ps 144:10), the NIrV (Rom 11:26), and in the NL (Amos 4:13). In some cases the NIV uses this form (e.g., Ps 144:10) where most other versions have a different syntax and therefore don't face the issue.

Notice the change of the RSV/NRSV from "Holy One" to "holy ones" in Proverbs 30:3.

Reference	KJV	NIV	one (or something else)	One
Isa 1:4	Holy One of Israel	Holy One of Israel[7]	holy God of Israel (CEV); holy God of Israel (TEV)	Holy One of Israel (GW, NRSV, NLT, REB, NCV, BER, JPS)
Prov 9:10	knowledge of the holy is understanding (Holy One, NKJV)	knowledge of the Holy One is understanding	knowledge of the Most Holy (BER); you must know the Holy God (CEV); the All-holy (JPS)	Holy One (NRSV, GW, NLT, NCV, TEV); Most Holy One (REB)
Prov 30:3	holy (Holy One, NKJV)	Holy One	holy ones (NRSV)	Holy One (RSV, GW, BER, NLT, JPS); Most Holy One (REB); God the Holy One (NCV); God (TEV)
Ps 132:2 (cf. v. 5)	the mighty *God* of Jacob (Mighty God, NKJV)	the Mighty One of Jacob	the Mighty God of Jacob (CEV, TEV, NCV)	the Mighty One of Jacob (NRSV, REB, NLT, GW, JPS)
Prov 21:12	the righteous *man* wisely considereth (righteous *God*, NKJV)	the Righteous One[8] takes note	righteous one (TEV); who is always right (NCV)	Righteous One (NRSV, NLT, JPS); Just One (REB)
Amos 4:13	he that formeth (he who, NKJV)	He who forms	He who (NASB, TNK); He Who (AMP); the one who (NRSV, NLT, TEV, NCV); he who (REB); He that formeth (JPS)	He is the One who (NL, BER)
Rev 1:18	he that liveth (am He who lives, NKJV)	the Living One	living one (NRSV, NLT, REB, CEV, GW, TEV)	the living One (NASB); Ever-Living One (AMP); the One who lives (NCV); Living One (GNC, JNT, NL, BER)

Table 4: One

Name

As the following table reveals, this term receives a variety of treatment in the versions. The NIV is the only version that uses capitals in all the passages listed here. Most versions don't use capitals, but it is noteworthy that the JPS of 1917 already uses capitals in Leviticus 24:16 and 2 Samuel 6:2.

Reference	KJV	NIV	name	Name
Ps 75:1	name	your Name	Thy name (JPS, BER); Your name (NASB); your name (REB); you (NLT, TEV, GW, NCV); presence (TNK)	Your Name (AMP)
Lev 24:16	the name of the LORD	the Name	name (NRSV, REB, NLT, GW,) NASB, NL, BER	Name (TNK, JPS, BER, RSV[9])
Deut 12:11	name	dwelling for his Name	name (NRSV, REB, NLT, GW, TNK, BER, NASB, JPS)	
2 Sam 6:2	called by the name	called by the Name	name (NRSV, REB, NLT, GW, BER)	Name (NASB, TNK, JPS, NCV)

Table 5: Name

Shepherd

The newer versions are prone to use capitals on this word. I found no exceptions to this on Genesis 49:24.

Reference	KJV	NIV	shepherd	Shepherd
Gen 49:24	from thence is the shepherd, the stone of Israel (Shepherd … Stone, NKJV)	the Shepherd, the Rock of Israel		the Shepherd … the Rock of Israel (NRSV, NL, TNK, NCV, AMP); Shepherd … Stone of Israel (NASB, JPS)
Ps 80:1	Give ear, O Shepherd of Israel	Hear us, O Shepherd of Israel	shepherd (TNK)	Give ear, O Shepherd of Israel (NRSV, NL, JPS)

Table 6: Shepherd

Redeemer

It is strange that the TNK capitalizes this word in Psalm 78:35 but not in Psalm 19:14 [15]. In Job 19:25 the TNK capitalizes it and translates it "Vindicator." The BER is also inconsistent in its treatment of this term when used of God. Surprisingly, the KJV never capitalizes this term, although it does capitalize King (Isa 44:6) and Holy One (Isa 41:14).

Reference	KJV	NIV	redeemer[10]	Redeemer
Job 19:25	I know that my redeemer liveth	I know that my Redeemer lives	defender (GW); vindicator (REB); someone in heaven who will come at last to my defense (TEV)	I know that my Redeemer lives (NRSV, NASB, NLT, AMP, BER, JPS); Vindicator (TNK); Defender (NCV); One Who bought me (NL); Savior (CEV)
Ps 19:14	my strength, and my redeemer	O LORD, my Rock and my Redeemer	O LORD, my rock and my redeemer (NRSV, TNK, BER); the one who saves me (NCV)	One Who saves me (NL); my Rock and my Redeemer (JPS)
Ps 78:35	God was their rock, and the high God their redeemer	that God Most High was their Redeemer	their redeemer (NRSV, NLT, REB); their defender (GW); who had saved them (NCV)	Redeemer (TNK, BER, JPS); the One Who set them free (NL)
Isa 44:6	the King of Israel and his redeemer	Israel's King and Redeemer	Israel's king and defender (GW)	King of Israel and his Redeemer (NRSV, JPS); the One Who saves (NL); Israel's King and Redeemer (NLT); the King of Israel and his Redeemer (NASB, AMP)

Table 7: Redeemer

Savior

The issue here is one of translation as much as capitalization. If the translation involves the abstract noun "salvation," the issue of capitalization disappears (cf. Deut 32:15; 2 Sam 22:47; 1 Chr 16:35 in the NRSV), but if translated "savior" the issue emerges—as seen in the NIV in the following table. Note the use of "savior" in Isaiah 43:11 in the phrase "apart from me there is no savior."

Reference	KJV	NIV	Other
2 Sam 22:47	God of the rock of my salvation	God, the Rock, my Savior	God, the rock of my salvation (NRSV, GW, NLT); who saves me (NCV); the Rock that saves me (NL); you are a mighty rock (CEV); the Rock who saves me (NCV); Rock of salvation (JPS)
Deut 32:15	lightly esteemed the Rock of his salvation	rejected the Rock his Savior	the Rock of his salvation (NRSV, JPS); Rock who saved them (NCV); the Rock of His saving power (NL); rock of their salvation (GW); Rock of their salvation (NLT, REB); mighty savior (TEV)
1 Chr 16:35	O God of our salvation	O God, our Savior	O God of our salvation (NRSV, NLT, JPS); our Savior (NCV); God our Savior (TEV, NCV, GW); God our savior (REB); God Who saves us (NL)

Table 8: Savior

Father

The use of "Father" for God in the Bible understandably matches the use of "son" (or "child") for believers in the family of God. "Father" in Ephesians 4:6 is found in all versions examined for this article—probably because it is in the context of "God and Father." Each of these references must be studied in context. The two oldest versions noted (KJV, JPS) are inconsistent. In general, the tendency is for newer versions to make more use of capitals in this usage.

Reference	KJV	NIV	father	Father
Isa 64:8	thou art our father	O LORD, you are our Father	father (TEV, NCV)	Father (NRSV, NASB, AMP, NL, CEV, GW, NLT, REB, TNK, JPS)
Jer 3:19	Thou shalt call me, My father	I thought you would call me 'Father'	father (TEV, JPS)	Father (NRSV, NASB, NLT, REB, GW, NL, NCV, TNK, AMP)
Mal 2:10	have we not all one father	have we not all one Father	have we not all one father (NRSV, REB, TEV, NCV, GW, NASB, JPS)	Father (CEV, NLT, NL, TNK, AMP, BER)

Table 9: Father

Miscellaneous Names and Titles

The NIV capitalizes a variety of other terms in reference to God—too numerous to be listed here. The following table reveals the variations among the versions on some of these.

Reference	KJV	NIV	Common Noun	Proper Noun
Heb 8:1	majesty	Majesty	majestic [God] (AMP); All-powerful God (NL); divine majesty (GNC); throne of majesty (GW)	The Majesty (NRSV, NASB); HaG'dulah in heaven (JNT); throne of the Majesty (BER)
Isa 51:13	maker	Maker	maker (REB); who made you (TEV, NCV, NL)	Maker (NRSV, NASB, TNK, AMP, JPS); Creator (CEV, NLT, GW)
Matt 19:4	he which made them	Creator	He who created them (NASB); He Who made them (AMP, NL); the one who made them (NRSV, PHILLIPS); creator (GNC); God (NLT, NCV); He who (BOL)	Creator (REB, TEV, CEV, GW, JNT)

Table 10: Miscellaneous Names and Titles

Pronouns

The following table displays the way a few versions have handled the issue of capitalizing pronouns referring to God. I know of only the following versions that do so: NKJV, NASB, AMP, NL, BER, BOL, JPS, and TNK. This feature is much more common in literature quoting the Bible than it is in the Bible itself. As the following table reveals, the KJV doesn't capitalize pronouns referring to God (contrary to what many think), although the NKJV does.

This practice is normally applied to personal pronouns (in all three persons) and also to relative (cf. Ps 18:31) and interrogative pronouns. In Hebrews 8:1 notice that the NL and AMP have capitals on both ("One Who"); the NASB doesn't capitalize "who" but does "His."

Reference	KJV	Others
Ps 31:2	Bow thine ear (Your, NKJV)	Bow down Your ear (AMP); incline Thine ear (NASB); Turn Your ear to me (NL); incline Your ear (TNK, JPS); incline Thy ear (BER)
Ps 31:3	For thou art my rock (You, NKJV)	Yes, You are my rock (AMP); be Thou to me a rock (NASB); For You are my rock (NL); For You (TNK); For Thou (BER, JPS)
Ps 18:22	his judgments (His, NKJV)	All His laws (NL, TNK, NASB); His ordinances (BER, JPS)
Ps 18:31	For who is God (who, NKJV)	For Who is God (NL); who is God (NASB, BER, JPS)

Ps 31:16	Make thy face (Your, NKJV)	Make Your face shine (NL); Make Thy face (NASB, JPS); show favor to Your servant (TNK); Cause Thy face (BER)
Ps 2:2	against his anointed	Against His anointed (TNK, NASB, BER, JPS); His Chosen One (NL)
Ps 2:5	in his wrath ... in his sore displeasure	Then He speaks ... His rage (TNK); Then He ... His anger (NL); He ... in His anger ... in His fury (NASB); His indignation (BER); in His wrath ... in His sore displeasure (JPS)
Ps 2:6	my king ... my holy (My king ... My holy, NKJV)	Installed My king (TNK); set My King (NL, BER); My king ... My holy (NASB, AMP, JPS)
Ps 2:12	when his wrath (when His wrath, NKJV)	of His anger (TNK); that He (NL); His wrath (NASB, AMP); He be angry (BER)
Ps 3:8	Thy blessing ... thy people (Your ... Your, NKJV)	Your blessing be upon Your people (TNK, NL, AMP); Thy blessing ... Thy people (NASB, BER)
Heb 8:1	who is set (who is seated, NKJV)	He is the One Who sits (NL, AMP); who has taken His seat (NASB)

Table 11: Pronouns

Messianic References

Since some passages in the Old Testament may refer specifically to the Messiah, the coming incarnate God, they are usually capitalized. The translator often faces a difficult question of interpretation in such passages—especially when some kind of double reference of the term may be involved. The reference may first be to the local king of the time but ultimately to the King of kings (cf. Ps 2:6).

Old Testament

Notice that the KJV, which uses capitalization sparingly, does use it in Psalm 2:7, 12. Although we would not expect the TNK or JPS (Jewish versions) to capitalize in such places, we are surprised at the reluctance of the CEV and NCV to capitalize. Notice the care and attempted consistency of the NIV to capitalize Messianic references in these passages.

Reference	KJV	NIV	Capitalized	Noncapitalized
Ps 2:2	his anointed	his Anointed One	His Chosen One (NL); Messiah (GW); His Anointed (NASB); His Anointed One (AMP)	anointed (NRSV, NAB, NJB, TNK, BER, JPS); anointed king (REB, NCV); chosen one (CEV); appointed one (NCV, NLT); the king he chose (TEV)
Ps 2:6	my king	my King[11]	King (NL, BER)	king (TNK, TEV, REB, NRSV, NAB, CEV, NCV, GW, NJB, JPS)
Ps 2:7	my Son	my Son	Son (NASB, AMP, BER)	son (NRSV, REB, NAB, NJB, TNK, CEV, NCV, JPS);

Ps 2:12	Kiss the Son	Son	Son (NASB, AMP, BER, GW)	kiss his feet (NRSV, NJB); bow down in homage (NAB); bow down to him (TEV); pay glad homage (REB); God's royal son (NLT); son (CEV); do homage (JPS)
Gen 49:10	Shiloh	to whom it belongs	Shiloh (NASB, AMP, GW, NCV, BER, JPS)	tribute comes to him (NRSV); tribute shall come to him (TNK); to whom it belongs (RSV, NLT); receives what is his due (REB)

Table 12: Messianic References in the Old Testament

New Testament Titles for Christ

The use of "son" in the NT in reference to the Messiah also requires the use of capitalization. In Matthew 3:17 all versions I analyzed capitalize "Son"—true also in "Son of Man" in Matthew 8:20, and in "Son of God" in Matthew 8:29 (cf. also Matt 17:5).

The tendency of the NIV to capitalize is noticeable in Ephesians 4:15, where only two other lesser-known versions use "Head"; all the other newer versions stay with "head."

Notice that the NKJV capitalizes the KJV's "shepherd" in Hebrews 13:20.

Reference	KJV	NIV	Common Noun	Proper Noun
Heb 13:20	that great shepherd of the sheep (Shepherd, NKJV)	the great Shepherd of the sheep	that great shepherd of the sheep (NRSV, JNT, GNC, BOL, GW)	great Shepherd (REB, BER); Good Shepherd (NL); Great Shepherd (TEV, CEV, NCV)
3 John 7[12]	his name's sake	sake of the Name	the one named Christ (GW); Christ's name (REB); love of Christ's name (REB); sake of the name (NJB); His name's sake (BOL)	Name (BER); Ha-Shem (JNT); "the name" (PHILLIPS); sake of the Name (NAB, NASB); the Name's sake (AMP)
1 Pet 5:4	when the chief Shepherd shall appear	when the Chief Shepherd appears	when the chief shepherd appears (NRSV); the shepherd who is set over all other shepherds (GNC)	Head Shepherd (NL); Great Shepherd (NCV); Chief Shepherd (JNT, BER, BOL)
Eph 4:15	head	Head	head (NRSV, NASB, NAB, REB, GNC, JNT, CEV, GW, NLT, PHILLIPS, TEV, NCV, BOL, NJB[13]); leader (NL)	Head (AMP, BER)
Eph 6:9	Master	Master[14]	master (GW, GNC)	Master (NRSV, NASB, NJB, NAB, REB, CEV, NLT, TEV, NCV, JNT, BER, AMP); Owner (NL)

Table 13: New Testament Titles for Christ

REFERENCES TO THE HOLY SPIRIT

Of special concern (and challenge) are the numerous references to the Spirit of God in both the Old and New Testaments. Christian translators, as Trinitarians, must capitalize the word when it refers to God the Holy Spirit. As the table below reveals, the versions differ widely on this issue. In general, the NIV tends to capitalize "spirit" more than other versions.

OLD TESTAMENT

The issue in the OT is especially difficult because of the culture and context—as well as the danger of reading back into it the theology more fully revealed in the New Testament. The following table reveals the clear differences of opinion on this issue. The NIV is undoubtedly the most aggressive in capitalizing "Spirit" in OT references.

We would not expect to find "Spirit" in the Jewish translations (JPS, TNK). Notice that in some versions the translators understood the reference to mean something other than either "spirit" or "Spirit."

Reference	KJV	NIV	Common Noun	Proper Noun
Isa 63:10–11	holy spirit	Holy Spirit	holy spirit (NRSV, REB, NAB)	Spirit (NASB, CEV)
Gen 1:2	spirit of God	Spirit of God	wind from God (TNK, NRSV[15]); spirit (REB, JPS)	Spirit (NCV, TEV,[16] RSV, CEV,[17] GW, NLT, NL, BER)
Gen 6:3	my spirit	my Spirit	spirit (NRSV,[18] RSV, REB, JPS); life-giving breath (CEV); My breath (TNK)	Spirit (NCV, GW, NLT, BER)
Num 11:17–29	spirit	Spirit	spirit (TEV, NRSV, REB, TNK, JPS); authority (CEV)	Spirit (NCV, GW, NLT, BER)
Judg 3:10	spirit of the LORD	Spirit	spirit (NRSV, TEV, REB, TNK, JPS)	Spirit (NCV, CEV, GW, NLT, BER)
1 Sam 19:20	spirit of God	Spirit of God	spirit (NRSV, TEV, JPS, REB)	the Spirit of God (RSV); Spirit (NCV, CEV, GW, NLT, BER)
1 Chr 28:12	spirit	that the Spirit had put in his mind	plan that he had in mind (NRSV, RSV, REB, NCV, TEV); he gave him plans (GW); plan of all he had by the spirit (TNK, JPS)	Spirit (BER)
Ps 104:30	thy spirit	Spirit	breathe (NCV); breath (TEV); spirit (NRSV,[19] REB, JPS)	Spirit (RSV, CEV, GW, NLT, BER)

Table 14: Spirit in the Old Testament

New Testament

In the New Testament, too, this particular issue can be difficult, as reflected in the way the various English versions treat different passages. The adjective form of a proper noun is especially frustrating in English, when the adjective "spiritual" is used for matters related to either "spirit" or the Holy "Spirit." There is a difference between the human spirit (or another spirit) and God the Holy Spirit.

The places where "spirit" in the NIV reads "Spirit" in the TNIV are noted in the NIV column.

Reference	KJV	NIV	Common Noun or Adjective[20]	Proper Noun
Col 3:16	spiritual songs	spiritual song (songs from the Spirit, TNIV)[21]	spiritual songs (NASB, NRSV, REB, NLT, GW, CEV, NCV, JNT, GNC, BER, BOL); sacred songs (TEV); Christian songs (PHILLIPS)	
Rom 8:10	Spirit	your spirit is alive (yet the Spirit gives life, TNIV)	spirits are alive (RSV, GW); spirit (NASB, GNC, BER)	the Spirit is life to you (TEV[22]); the Spirit is life (BOL); the Spirit gives you life (NCV); the Spirit is giving life (JNT); Spirit of God finds a home within you (PHILLIPS)
Rom 8:15[23]	spirit … Spirit	not receive a spirit … but the Spirit (the Spirit you received … rather the Spirit, TNIV)	spirit of slavery … spirit of adoption (NRSV); the Spirit you … is not a spirit of (REB); spirit … spirit (RSV, GW, NASB,[24] GNC); spirit … Spirit (NET, JNT, BER, BOL); Spirit … attitude (PHILLIPS)	God's Spirit (CEV); Spirit … Spirit (TEV, NCV)
1 Cor 2:15	spiritual	spiritual man (the person with the Spirit, TNIV)	spiritual (NRSV, GW,[25] NCV, NET, NASB, GNC, BER, BOL)	we who have the Spirit (NLT, TEV[26]); who has the Spirit (JNT); guided by the Spirit (CEV, PHILLIPS)
1 Cor 14:12	spiritual	spiritual gifts (gifts of the Spirit, TNIV)	spiritual gifts (NRSV, NASB, NLT, GW, CEV, GNC, BER, BOL)	gifts of the Spirit (REB, TEV); manifestations of the Spirit (RSV, NET); things of the Spirit (JNT)
1 Cor 14:16	spirit	praising God with your spirit (praising God in a tongue by the Spirit, TNIV)	spirit (NRSV, NASB, REB, NLT, GW, CEV, TEV, RSV, JNT, BOL); spiritual fashion (GNC)	
1 Cor 14:37	spiritual	spiritually gifted (gifted by the Spirit, TNIV)	spiritual powers (NRSV); inspired (REB); spiritual (NLT, NASB, CEV, RSV, BOL); spiritually gifted (GW, TEV); endowed with spiritual gifts (GNC); inspired (BER)	endowed with the Spirit (JNT)

Gal 6:1	spiritual	you who are spiritual (you who live by the Spirit, TNIV)	who are godly (NLT); spiritual (NASB, GW, CEV, TEV, RSV, BER, BOL); spiritually minded (GNC)	received the Spirit (NRSV[27]); live by the Spirit (REB); who have the Spirit (JNT)
2 Tim 1:7	spirit	not give us a spirit of timidity, but a spirit of power (the Spirit God gave us does not make us timid but gives us power, TNIV)	spirit ... spirit (NRSV, REB, GW); spirit (NASB, NLT, GNC, BER, BOL)	Spirit ... Spirit (CEV, TEV); Spirit (JNT)

Table 15: Spirit in the New Testament

References to Pagan Deities

The various deities of the OT world have traditionally been capitalized, since they are recognized as proper nouns. Many of these deities have been known since antiquity (e.g., Baal, Dagan, Ashtoreth[28]), and ongoing research continues to shed light on them. The following chart displays references to some deities already known but now recognized in additional places in the new English versions.

Molech

Molech is a deity known from early times of Bible translation for whom the spelling has varied greatly—some of which is due to textual variants in spelling in Hebrew. Molech was recognized already in the KJV, although spelled differently (Milcam in 1 Kgs 11:5 and Milcom in 11:33), but this deity has now been found in additional places in the new versions, as the table below reveals. Several of the versions have footnotes noting the variant spellings in various texts (these footnotes are not usually cited in the charts). Another example of a deity with various spellings in the versions, beginning with the KJV, is Ashtaroth/Ashtoreth/Astaroth.

Reference	KJV	NIV	Translation in Modern Versions
Jer 49:1	their king (Milcham, NKJV)	Molech[29]	Milcom (NRSV, NEB, JB, LB, TNK, CEV, REB, GW, BER); Molech (NCV, TEV, NLT); Malcam (NL, JPS)
Jer 49:3	their king[30] (Milcham, NKJV)	Molech	Milcom (NRSV, TNK, REB, GW, BER); Molech (NCV, TEV, NLT); Malcam (NL, JPS)
Zeph 1:5	Malcham (Milcom, NKJV)	Molech	Milcom (NRSV, NL); Molech (NCV); Malcam (TNK, JPS); Malcham (BER)

Table 16: Molech

ASHERAH

Asherah was a Canaanite deity not specifically recognized in the older versions (e.g., KJV) but now recognized by the great majority of new English versions (e.g., about forty times in the NIV). The table below reveals a sampling of the way "Asherah" is handled in the newer versions, most of which recognize the existence of this Canaanite deity in various passages.

It should also be noted that modern translations will update the names of pagan deities mentioned in Scripture (e.g., Jupiter [KJV] to Zeus [modern versions]).[31]

Reference	KJV	NIV	Common Noun	Proper Noun
1 Kgs 15:13	an idol in a grove	Asherah pole	an idol (LB)	Asherah (NRSV, NASB, NEB, JB, NL, BER, JPS); Asherah idol (NCV); idol of Asherah (CEV); idol of the fertility goddess Asherah (TEV); obscene object made for the worship of Asherah (REB); Asherah pole (NLT); goddess Asherah (GW)
Exod 34:13	groves	Asherah poles	sacred poles (NRSV[32]); false gods (NL)	Asherah idols (NCV); Asherim (RSV, NASB, JPS); poles dedicated to the goddess Asherah (GW); symbols of the goddess Asherah (TEV); carved images (NLT); sacred poles they use in the worship of the goddess Asherah (CEV); sacred poles (REB); sacred trees (BER)
Judg 3:7	groves	Asherahs	Asherahs	Asherahs (NRSV); idols of Asherah (NCV); Ashtaroth (BER); Asheroth (JPS)

Table 17: Asherah

PERSONAL NAMES

Whether a word in the original Hebrew or Greek is a common or proper noun is a matter of judgment based on context and usage. Hebrew has more examples of this phenomenon, not only because of the sheer length of the OT compared to the NT, but also because of inadequate knowledge of OT culture and various contexts where this issue emerges.

OLD PERSONAL NAMES MISSING IN THE NIV

Several personal names found in the KJV are missing in the NIV (and other new versions). More recent interpretation understands these to be common nouns instead of proper nouns. For example, the three terms in 2 Kings 18:17 have been found in Akkadian to refer to various personnel and therefore should not be transliterated and capitalized as though they were personal names (for some reason the NRSV seems to reject this).

In the case of Ish-tob (2 Sam 10:6, KJV), the NIV retains the last half (Tob) as a place name but then translates Ish as "men." In the KJV the word appears in such a context that readers could understand it either as a personal name or a place name.

Shiloh (Gen 49:10, KJV)—understood as a personal name—is missing in most of the new versions (see table 12); Belial in the KJV (Judg 19:22) is considered a personal name, it, too, is lost in the new English translations.

Reference	KJV	NIV	Common Noun	Proper Noun
Jer 39:3	Rabsaris	chief officer	chief eunuch (NEB); chief of the eunuchs (AMP); a chief officer (NCV)	Sarsechim the Rabsaris[33] (NRSV); the Rab-saris (NASB, NL, TNK, BER, JPS)
Jer 39:3 (cf. 39:13; 2 Kgs 18:17)	Rab-mag	high official	high official (JB); chief of the magicians (AMP); commander of the frontier troops (NEB[34]); an important leader (NCV)	the Rabmag (NRSV); Rabmag (BER); Rab-mag (NL, JPS); the Rab-mag (NASB, TNK)
2 Kgs 18:17	Tartan and Rabsaris and Rab-shakeh	supreme commander, chief officer, field commander	field marshall, chief treasurer, and the chief of staff (BER); general, lord chamberlain, and the commander (NAB); commander-in-chief, the chief eunuch, and the chief officer (REB); cupbearer-in-chief (NJB)[35]	Tartan, Rab-saris and Rabshakeh (NRSV, NASB, NL, JPS)
2 Sam 10:6	Ish-tob[36] (Ish-Tob, NKJV)	men of Tob	men of Tob (JB, AMP, RSV, NEB, NL, TNK, JPS, BER); men from Tob (NCV)	
Judg 19:22	sons of Belial	wicked men	base fellows (RSV); a perverse lot (NRSV); worst scoundrels (NEB); scoundrels (JB); sex perverts (LB); perverted men (BER); certain sinful men (NL)	

Table 18: Old Personal Names Missing in the NIV

New Personal Names Found in the NIV

Although a few personal names have been lost in the new versions, there is some compensation. A few new ones have been found! The following table reveals that several versions have found a personal name (Syzygus) in Philippians 4:3, which they put either in the text (NEB, CB, NL, NCV, NET) or in a footnote (NIV, JB, NRSV). Rapha (2 Sam 21:15) is a personal name or a designation of a people not recognized in the KJV, which translated it with the common noun "giant." By a redivision of letters in Jeremiah 39:3, the NIV creates a new name (Nebo-Sarsekim), and thus the old KJV name Samgar-nebo is now missing.

Reference	KJV	NIV	Common Noun	Proper Noun
2 Sam 21:16	giant	Rapha	giants (AMP, NRSV); very tall and strong people (NL); of the sons of the giant (JPS)	Rapha (JB, NCV); Rephaim (NEB); descendent of the Rapha (TNK[37]); the descendants of the giant (NASB)
Jer 39:3[38]	(1) Nergal-sharezer, (2) Samgar-nebo, (3) Sarsechim	(1)Nergal-Sharezer of Samgar, (2) Nebo-Sarsekim		
Phil 4:3[39]	yokefellow	Syzygus (in the footnote)	loyal yokefellow (NIV); loyal companion (NRSV); yokefellow (AMP; RSV, BER); true partner (CEV); fellow worker (NAB, BOL); partner (TEV); comrade (NASB); teammate (LB); loyal companion (NRSV); true companion (NASB); loyal comrade (GNC)	Syzygus (NIV footnote, NJB, JNT)

Table 19: New Personal Names Found in the NIV

PLACE-NAMES

As with personal names, new understanding of some words has caused some place-names in older translations to vanish, but also for this same reason new places appear in the text! The issue again is whether the original word is a common noun or a proper noun. Our increasing knowledge of the geography and topography of the Bible world helps us understand the patterns used in forming place-names.

NEW PLACE-NAMES FOUND IN THE NIV

Some terms understood by the KJV as common nouns are now being understood in many of the new translations as place-names. The NKJV reflects some of this new light (see Judg 11:33), but in most other cases it stays with the judgment of the KJV.

New place-names can be formed in two ways: (1) transliteration of the source language, or (2) capitalized translation. Examples of the former are found in "the Negev" (Gen 12:9), "Abel Keramim" (Judg 11:33), "Beth Haggan" (2 Kgs 9:27), and "Harmon" (Amos 4:3). Transliteration of the source language happens often in English place-names with regard to Indian or Spanish names—Los Angeles, San Diego, Mississippi, and Arkansas.

Examples of the capitalized translation pattern include "Dead Sea," "Red Sea," and "Fields of the Forest" (Ps 132:6). More often, the place-name is a combination of the two principles (translation plus transliteration)—"Desert of Ziph" (1 Sam 23:15) or "Beth Eked of the Shepherds" (2 Kgs 10:12). An example of a Hebrew term represented both ways in the new English versions is "Negev"/"Negeb" (NRSV, REB, GW, NLT, TNK) or "Southern Desert" (CEV). Versions that don't treat the Hebrew as a proper noun translate it variously. The TEV has "southern part of Canaan" in Genesis 12:9 but "dry river bed" in Psalm 126:4; the NCV has "southern Canaan" in Genesis 12:9 but "desert" in Psalm 126:4.

It is somewhat strange that some modern translations hesitate to accept "the Negev," which is common terminology today (and already used in the RSV of 1952). Notice that the transliteration (Negev/Negeb) varies, depending on whether the translators wish to represent the Hebrew letters or the phonetic equivalent.

In cases of compound names, the NIV usually capitalizes both words (Trans-Euphrates, Abel Keramim, Beth Haggan, Beth Eked). In some cases, if one of the words in a compound place-name is translated, it is understood as a common noun and not capitalized (wilderness of Ziph, fields of Jaar).

Reference	KJV	NIV	Common Noun	Proper Noun
Gen 12:9	south	the Negev	southern part of Canaan (TEV); southern Canaan (NCV); southland (BER)	the Negeb (NRSV, RSV, REB, TNK); the Negev (GW, NLT, NL); Southern Desert (CEV); South (JPS)
Ps 126:4	south	the Negev	dry river bed (TEV); desert (NLT, NCV); dry riverbeds (GW); dry land (JPS)	the Negeb (NRSV, REB, TNK); Southern Desert (CEV); Southland (BER)
Ezra 4:10	this side the river	Trans-Euphrates	west of the Euphrates River (NLT, GW); west of the River (BER); country beyond the River (JPS)	Beyond the River (NRSV, TNK); West-of-Euphrates (TEV); Beyond-Euphrates (REB); Western Province (CEV); Trans-Euphrates (NCV)
Judg 11:33	the plain of the vineyards	Abel Keramim		Abel-cheramim (NASB, BER, JPS); Abel-keramim (JB, NRSV, NEB, NL); Abel Keramim (CEV)
2 Kgs 19:24	besieged places	Egypt[40]	canals of the Nile (BER)	rivers of Egypt (JB, CB, NEB, NRSV, NL, JPS)
Isa 19:6	brooks of defense	streams of Egypt		streams of Egypt (CB, RSV, NEB, BER, JPS); canals of Egypt (AMP); Niles of Egypt (JB); Egypt's Nile (NRSV); rivers of Egypt (NASB)
Ezek 27:11	thine army	Helech	their army (JB); your army (NASB, NKJV)	Helech (NRSV,[41] NL, BER, JPS)

1 Sam 23:15	wilderness of Ziph in a wood	at Horesh in the wilderness of Ziph	at Horesh in the wilderness of Ziph (JB, NEB, TNK); Wilderness of Ziph in a forest (NKJV); wilderness of Ziph in the wood (JPS)	in the wood at Horesh (AMP); at Horesh in the Desert of Ziph (NCV); in the wilderness of Ziph at Horesh (NASB); desert of Ziph at Horesh (NL); Ziph desert at Horesh (BER)
Ps 132:6	fields of the wood	fields of Jaar[42]	field of the woods (NKJV); Fields-of-the-Forest (JB[43]); field of the wood (JPS)	fields of Jaar (RSV); Kiriath Jearim (CB); region of Jaar (NEB); field of Jaar (NASB)
2 Kgs 9:27	by way of the garden house	Beth Haggan[44]	garden house (NASB, NL); garden-house (JPS)	Beth-haggan road (JB); direction of Beth-haggan (RSV); road to Beth-haggan (NEB); road to Beth Haggan (NKJV)
2 Kgs 10:12	the shearing house in the way	Beth Eked of the Shepherds	shearing house of the shepherds on the way (AMP, JPS); a shepherd's shelter (NEB)[45]	Beth-eked of the shepherds (NL, NASB); Beth-eked of the Shepherds (JB, RSV); Beth Eked of the Shepherds (NKJV)
Amos 4:3	ye shall cast them into the palace	into Harmon[46]	garbage dump (NCV, GW); dunghill (REB); refuse heap (TNK); fortress	Hermon (JB); Harmon (NRSV, NASB, RSV, NKJV, CEV, JPS)
1 Kgs 10:28	received the linen yard at a price	Kue	received them in droves, each at a price (NASB)	Cilicia (JB, BER);[47] Kue (RSV, NL, TNK, NCV); Coa (NEB); Keveh (NKJV, JPS)
Ezek 27:19	going to and fro	Uzal	to and fro (NL); traversing back and forth (NKJV)	Uzal (NASB, TNK, NCV, CEV, NLT, GW, BER); Izalla (REB)
Ezek 27:18	white wool	wool from Zahar	white wool (NASB, NRSV, NL, TNK, NKJV, BER, JPS)	wool from Zahar (CEV, NLT); wool from Sahar (TEV, GW); Suhar wool (REB)

Table 20: New Place-Names Found in the NIV

Reference to names missing does not include corrected name changes, such as Ethiopia to Cush,[48] or Syria to Aram,[49] or Lybia to Put,[50] or Lydia to Lud.[51] These anachronisms were removed for the sake of accuracy in new translations. There are many examples of name changes for various reasons (cf. Hiddekel to Tigris;[52] Chittim to Cyprus;[53] the Red Sea to Yam Suph.[54]

FORMER PLACE-NAMES MISSING IN THE NIV

Some of the old place-names found in the KJV are missing in the NIV, where they are now understood as common nouns. The issue is a judgment call based on context, usage elsewhere (including outside the Bible), and other factors. Old place-names (in the KJV) such as Asuppim (1 Chr 26:15), Maktesh (Zeph 1:11), Pannag (Ezek 27:17), Hazerim (Deut 2:23), and others are missing in the new versions. The table reveals the differences in treatment in the newer English versions.

Reference	KJV	NIV	Proper Noun	Common Noun
Josh 19:33	from Allon to Zaanannim	large oak in Zaanannim	the Oak of Zanannim (JB); oak of Za-anan-nim (BER); Elon-bezaannannim (NEB)	the oak (NASB, NRSV); big tree (NL)
1 Chr 26:15	the house of Asuppim	storehouse		storehouse (NASB, JB, BER, NCV, NRSV); gatehouse (NEB); store-house (NL)
Zeph 1:11	Maktesh	market district	the Mortar (NASB, JB, NRSV)	market area (NCV); part of the city where people buy and sell (NL)
1 Kgs 10:22	ships of Tarshish	trading ships[55]	Tarshish (AMP, NASB, JB, NRSV, NL)	trading ships (NCV)
Ezek 27:17	Pannag	confections[56]		olives or early figs (AMP); cakes (NASB); wax (JB); early figs (RSV); millet (NRSV)
Deut 10:6	Beeroth	wells	Beeroth (NASB, RSV); Beeroth-bene-jaakan (NRSV)	wells (JB, NCV); wells of the sons Jaakan (NL)
Deut 2:23	Hazerim	villages		villages (NASB, RSV); encampments (JB); towns (NCV); settlements (NRSV)

Table 21: Former Place-Names Missing in the NIV

Special Places

Several places deserve special mention here. Although the places known as "heaven" and "hell" are not treated as proper nouns and capitalized, the place known as "Hades" is capitalized in the NIV and other versions (NRSV, NASB, AMP, BOL). Literature about the Bible will often capitalize Heaven and Hell—including references in theology books.

The Greek text in 2 Peter 2:4 does not use the usual Greek word for "hell," but the point is that in other places where the usual Greek word *is* used, the word "hell" is not capitalized in English. Only the NAB renders the Greek term here a proper noun (Tartarus)—a transliteration from 2 Peter 2:4.

"Sheol" can refer to either the place where the body was deposited or to the eternal place where the soul continues to live.[57] Context must determine. The NIV either has Sheol in the text or in a footnote in each place it is found.

In Isaiah 51:10 and Luke 8:31, only the NJB finds a proper noun ("Abyss"); most versions treat this term as a common noun.

Reference	KJV	NIV	Common Noun[58]	Proper Noun
Job 26:6	Hell[59] is naked before him, and destruction hath no covering	Death is naked before God; Destruction lies uncovered	the place of the dead . . . and the place that destroys (NL); nether-world . . . Destruction (JPS)	Sheol is naked before God, and Abaddon has no covering (NRSV, TNK); Sheol . . . Death (BER)
Prov 15:11	Hell and destruction	Death and Destruction lie open before the LORD	nether-world . . . Destruction (JPS)	Sheol and Abaddon lie open before the LORD (NASB, NRSV)
Prov 27:20	hell and destruction are never full	Death and Destruction are never satisfied	place of the dead is never filled (NL); nether-world . . . Destruction (JPS)	Sheol and Abaddon are never satisfied (NASB, NRSV, BER)
Matt 16:18	gates of hell[60]	gates of Hades	hades (BER); gates of hell (GW); death itself (CEV); powers of hell (NLT, NL); powers of death (RSV, REB, PHILLIPS); power of death (NCV); not even death (TEV); forces of hell itself (GNC)	Hades (NRSV, NASB, AMP, BOL); gates of Sh'ol (JNT)
Rev. 1:18	keys of hell and of death	death and Hades	of death and of Hades (NASB, REB, NJB); death and its realm (BER); death and the netherworld (NAB)	Death and Hades (NRSV, NASB, BOL)
2 Pet 2:4	hell	hell[61]	hell (NRSV, CEV, GW, NLT, PHILLIPS, TEV, NCV, NL, BOL, BER); dark pits of hell (REB); dark abyss (NJB); nethermost world (GNC)	Tartarus (NAB)
Luke 8:31	deep	the Abyss[62]	abyss (NRSV, NASB, NAB, REB, BER, GNC, BOL); bottomless pit (AMP); hole without a bottom in the earth (NL)	Abyss (NJB); Bottomless Pit (JNT)
Isa 51:10	great deep	great deep	great abyss (REB); great deep (NAB, NRSV, NASB, AMP, TNK[63]); great ocean (GW); deep ocean (NCV)	great Abyss (NJB)

Table 22: Special Places

MYTHOLOGICAL REFERENCES

In addition to the ever increasing new light on the specific deities of the ancient Near Eastern and OT world, much new light is being shed on the mythological elements in the religious literature of that world.

As expected, the KJV did not capitalize the transliterated term "leviathan." Notice that the NL gives in different contexts four different translations of the same word—Leviathan, crocodile, hippopotamus, and large sea animal. Perhaps this is by design in order to impress the reader with the concept of some large creature of any kind.

Leviathan

Reference	KJV	NIV	Common Noun	Proper Noun
Isa 27:1	leviathan	Leviathan	leviathan (JPS)	Leviathan (NRSV, REB, NLT, GW, CEV, TEV, NCV, NL, NCV, TNK)
Job 3:8	their mourning	Leviathan	sea monster (REB, NLT, NCV); leviathan (JPS)	Sea (NRSV[64]); Leviathan (NASB, RSV, GW, TEV, NL, NCV)
Job 41:1	leviathan	the leviathan	crocodile (NL); the leviathan (NCV); sea monster (CEV)	Leviathan (NASB, NRSV,[65] TEV, GW)
Ps 74:14	leviathan	Leviathan	leviathan (JPS)	Leviathan (NRSV, NL, NCV, TNK)
Ps 104:26	that leviathan	the leviathan	large sea animal (NL); leviathan (JPS)	Leviathan (NRSV, NCV, TNK)

Table 23: Leviathan

Rahab

Rahab is another term that can be a mythological reference, although it is sometimes used as a poetic name for Egypt (cf. Isa 30:7). The term is already used in the KJV (Isa 51:9) but is found in several additional places (Job 9:13; 26:12; Ps 87:4; Isa 30:7) in the newer versions, and it is found in all of them (except the KJV) in Ps 87:4; 89:10; and Job 26:12.

Reference	KJV	NIV	Common Noun	Proper Noun
Job 9:13	the proud helpers (allies of the proud, NKJV)	Rahab	the winds as messengers (JB); the pride of man (LB)	Rahab (NRSV, NASB, NEB, JPS, TNK, NL, NCV)
Job 26:12	the proud	Rahab		Rahab (NRSV, NJB, NAB, REB, NL, NCV, TNK, JPS)
Isa 30:7	I cried ... their strength is to sit still	call her Rahab the Do-Nothing	"they are a threat that has ceased" (TNK)	"Rahab-the-collapsed" (NJB); "Rahab quelled" (NAB); Rahab Subdued (REB); "Rahab who sits still" (NRSV).

Table 24: Rahab

Other Mythological References

Some versions now recognize the existence of several additional mythological references that could be treated as proper nouns and capitalized—Sea (TNK), Dragon (NJB, TNK, JPS), and Behemoth (NRSV, NASB, GW, TEV). However, newer versions are reluctant to accept these, as the following table reveals.

Reference	KJV	NIV	Common Noun	Proper Noun
Isa 51:9[66]	wounded the dragon	monster	dragon (NRSV, NAB, REB, NASB, AMP, NLT); serpent (GW); sea monster (NCV)	Dragon (NJB, TNK, JPS)
Isa 51:10	sea	sea	sea (NRSV, NAB, NJB, REB, JPS, NASB, GW, NLT, TEV, NCV)	Sea (TNK); Red Sea (AMP)
Job 3:8	the day	days[67]	the Sea[68] (NRSV); day (NASB, NL, NCV, TNK, JPS)	
Job 7:12	a sea or a whale (sea or sea serpent, NKJV)	The sea or the monster of the deep	the sea or the sea monster (NASB, NCV); the sea or a sea monster (CEV, GW, RSV, JPS); sea monster (TEV); monster of the deep ... sea monster (REB); the sea or a large sea animal (NL)	the sea or the Dragon (TNK)
Job 40:15	behemoth	the behemoth	hippopotamus (NL, CEV, NL; behemoth (NCV, TNK, JPS); crocodile (REB, NLT); whale (REB)	Behemoth (NRSV, NASB,[69] GW); monster Behemoth (TEV)

Table 25: Other Mythological References

Personification

Personification involves personalizing common nouns, which typically results in them being capitalized. Again, it's a matter of judgment for the translator, who must observe the use of the term elsewhere as well as in the immediate context. Although the versions agree on some passages (Isa 65:11), most passages received mixed treatments. Isaiah 14:12 is a good example, where the versions disagree on how to treat the special term formerly known as Lucifer.[70] Five of them treat the term as some kind of proper noun, but eight of them treat the term as a common noun.

Note that the NIV capitalizes Wisdom in Proverbs 7:4 but not in Proverbs 8:1, 12.

Reference	KJV	NIV	Common Noun	Proper Noun
Ps 88:11	thy faithfulness in destruction	your faithfulness in Destruction	how faithful You are in the place that destroys (NL); grave ... destruction (BER); thy faithfulness in destruction (JPS);	Your faithfulness in Abaddon (NRSV, NASB)
Isa. 14:12[71]	Lucifer	O morning star	bright morning star (REB); shining one (NL); shining star (NLT); star of the morning (NASB); morning star (NAB, GW); shining gleam (BER); day-star (JPS)	Day Star (NRSV, JB); Daystar (NJB); Lucifer (LB); Shining One (TNK)

Isa 65:11	troop ... number	Fortune ... Destiny		Fortune ... Destiny (NRSV, NASB, BER, JPS); Gad ... Meni (AMP); Fate ... Destiny (REB); Luck and Destiny (TNK); gods of Fate and Destiny (NLT); god of good fortune and goddess of destiny (GW); gods you call Good Luck and Fate (CEV); Gad and Meni, the gods of luck and fate (TEV); the god Luck ... the god Fate (NCV)
Prov 7:4	Say unto wisdom	Say to Wisdom	wisdom (NRSV, NASB, CEV, GW, NLT, NL, REB, TEV, NCV, BER)	Wisdom (NJB, NAB, AMP, TNK)
Prov 8:1	Doth not wisdom cry?	Does not wisdom call out?	wisdom (NASB, GW, NRSV, NLT, NL, BER)	Wisdom (AMP, CEV, NLT, TNK)
Prov 8:12[72]	I wisdom	wisdom	wisdom (NRSV, NASB, REB, NCV, NL, BER)	Wisdom (AMP, CEV, GW, TEV, TNK, NJB, NAB)

Table 26: Personification

Miscellaneous Items

Ceremonial Items

Several items connected with the religious ceremonies of ancient Israel are treated as proper nouns and capitalized. This was not the practice of the KJV translators (and those before them). This modern treatment in newer English versions helps the reader follow more easily the references to specific items in Israelite life.

The following tables reveal the variety of treatments by the newer English versions. Most of them appear to be satisfied with the older treatment of such items as common nouns, despite the specificity of their use in the various contexts. Some, such as the NRSV and NIV ("bread of the Presence"), treat some of these terms in a mixed way (cf. NIV's "Sea of cast metal"). Most of them treat the old "ark of the covenant" as a proper noun complex (NEB, TEV, NCV, TNK) although many do not (NASB, NRSV, NAB, NL). The JNT transliterates *menorah*—the Hebrew word for "lampstand."

When should specific items associated with the tabernacle or temple be capitalized? The versions disagree. The NIV uses "tabernacle," "lampstand," and "atonement cover" but also capitalizes "bread of the Presence" and "Sea of cast metal." The "ark of the testimony" of the RSV (1952) was changed to "ark of the covenant" in the NRSV, changing the wording but not the use of capitalization.

Places associated with worship in ancient Israel are usually capitalized in the NIV—Tent of Meeting, Holy Place, and Most Holy Place. As the following table reveals, these receive a mixed treatment in the new translations.

Reference	KJV	NIV	Common Noun	Proper Noun
Exod 26:1	tabernacle	tabernacle	tabernacle (NRSV, NASB, AMP, BER, JPS); sacred tent (CEV)	Tabernacle (NLT, REB); Dwelling (NAB, NJB); sacred Tent (TEV); Holy Tent (NCV)
Heb 9:8	first tabernacle	first tabernacle	outer tabernacle (NASB, GNC, NAB); former tabernacle (AMP); first tabernacle (BER, BOL); tent (CEV, GW); first tent (NRSV); first room (NLT); outer tent (REB, TEV, PHILLIPS); outside tent (NL); old tent (NJB)	old Holy Tent (NCV); first Tent (JNT)
Exod 26:33	ark of the covenant	ark of the Testimony	ark of the testimony (NASB, RSV, JPS); ark of the covenant (NRSV); ark of the commandments (NAB); box of the Law (NL)	Ark of the Tokens (NEB); Covenant Box (TEV); Holy Box (NCV); Ark of the Pact (TNK); ark of the Testimony (NJB); Ark of the Testimony (BER)
Exod 25:31	candlestick	lampstand	candlestick (JPS); lampstand (NRSV, NASB, NAB, AMP, CEV, NLT, REB, NCV, TNK, BER); lamp-stand (NL, NJB); lamp (GW)	
Heb 9:2	candlestick	lampstand	light (NL); lampstand (NRSV, NASB, CEV, GNC, NLT, TEV, REB, NAB, BER); lamp stand (GW); lamp-standard (PHILLIPS); lamp-stand (NJB); lamp (NCV)	*menorah* (JNT)
Exod 25:17	mercy seat	atonement cover	mercy seat (NRSV, NASB, AMP, BER); lid (CEV); throne of mercy to cover (GW); mercy-seat (NJB); cover (TNK); atonement cover (NLT); cover (REB); lid (TEV, NCV); propitiatory (NAB); ark cover (JPS)	
Exod 25:30	shewbread	bread of the Presence	sacred bread (TEV); show-bread (NAB, AMP, BER, JPS, NKJV); the bread that shows you are in my presence (NCV); loaves of permanent offering (NJB)	Bread of the Presence (NEB, REB); bread of the Presence (NRSV, NASB)

1 Kgs 7:23	molten sea (Sea of cast bronze, NKJV)	Sea of cast metal	Sea of cast metal (NEB, NJB); molten sea (NRSV); sea of cast metal (NASB); sea (NAB); tank of bronze (TEV); large round bowl from bronze (NCV); brass water pool (NL); tank of cast metal (TNK)	
Lev 3:2	tabernacle of the congre-gation	Tent of Meeting	meeting tent (NAB); tent of meeting (NASB, RSV, NRSV); meeting tent (NL)	Tent of Meeting (NJB, TNK); Tent of the Presence (NEB); Meet-ing Tent (NCV); Tabernacle (LB)
Exod 26:33	Holy Place/Holy of Holies	Holy Place/Most Holy Place	holy place/Holiest Place of All (NL); holy place/most holy place (NRSV); holy place/holy of holies (NAB)	Holy Place/Most Holy Place (TEV, NCV); Holy/Holy of Holies (TNK); Holy Place/ Holy of Holies (NJB)
Heb 9:2	sanctuary	Holy Place		
Heb 8:1	high priest	high priest	high priest (NRSV, REB, NASB, GNC, CEV, NCV, NAB, NJB); chief priest (GW)	High Priest (NLT, AMP, PHILLIPS, TEV, BOL); Religious Leader (NL); cohen gadol[73] (JNT)
Exod 28:6	ephod	ephod	ephod (NIV, NLT, NRSV, GW, REB, TEV, NAB, NJB); priestly vest (CEV); holy vest (NCV); linen apron (NIrV)	

Table 27: Ceremonial Items

Special Times

We would expect special designated times to be capitalized—as they are in English: Monday, January, Christmas. This issue has been handled in a wide variety of ways, as the following table indicates. The evolution of the increasing use of capitalization in this area is clearly manifest in the NIV and NCV. The KJV omits the use of capitalization in this category, with Sabbath being about the only exception.

It appears that the NIV leads in using capitalization to denote the special times on Israel's calendar (Day of Atonement, Jubilee, New Moon festivals). Only the more recent paraphrases have done this (CEV, TEV, NL). The exception is the Day of Atonement, which receives this use of capitals also in the REB, TNK, NAB, and NJB—although they don't do so for the other special times. Although "Sabbath" is capitalized by several versions (NIV, NLT, CEV, AMP, TEV, BER, NASB, NCV), only one version capitalized "Festival" (CEV) in addition to the NIV. Some form of reference to the "New Moon" is capitalized by three versions in addition to the NIV.

It is probably no accident that "Preparation Day" is used in the translations of Jewish background. The passage in Hebrews 10:25 is so cryptic that many translations felt that some kind of paraphrase is needed to help the English reader.

Reference	KJV	NIV	Common Noun	Proper Noun
Lev 25:9	day of atonement	Day of Atonement	day of atonement (NRSV, NASB, AMP); special day for the forgiveness of sin (GW); day to be made free from sin (NL); day when sin is paid for (NirV)	Great Day of Forgiveness (CEV); Day of Atonement (NLT REB, TEV, TNK, BER, NAB); Day of Cleansing (NCV); Day of Expiation (NJB)
Lev 25:33	*year of* jubilee	Jubilee	jubilee (NASB, AMP, GW, NRSV, REB, NAB, NJB, TNK, BER)	Year of Celebration (CEV); Year of Jubilee (NLT, NL); Year of Restoration (TEV); Jubilee (NCV)
Num 10:10	beginnings of your months	New Moon festivals	first *days* of your months (NASB); beginnings of months (AMP); new moons (JPS); first day of the month (GW); beginnings of your months (NRSV); beginning of each month (NLT); first day of every month (REB); new-moon feasts (NJB, NAB); first day of your months (BER); first days of your months (NL); new moon days (TNK)	New Moon Festival (CEV); New Moon Festivals (TEV); New Moon festivals (NCV)
Col 2:16	holyday	religious festival	festival(s) (NRSV, NASB, REB, BOL, GNC, BER); annual holy days (GW); holy days (TEV); religious feast (NCV); Jewish festival (JNT)	Festival (CEV)
Col 2:16	new moon	New Moon	new moon(s) (NRSV, NASB, AMP, REB, PHILLIPS, BOL, GNC, BER); new-moon festivals (NLT); new moon ceremonies (LB); new moon festivals (TEV); *Rosh-Chodesh* (JNT)	New Moon (CEV); New Moon Festival(s) (GW, NCV);
Col 2:16	Sabbath *days*	Sabbath Day	sabbath(s) (NRSV, REB, PHILLIPS, BOL, GNC); weekly worship days (GW); Shabbat (JNT)	Sabbath(s) (NLT, AMP, CEV, TEV, BER); Sabbath day (NASB, NCV)
Mark 15:42	preparation	Preparation Day[74]	preparation day (NASB, PHILLIPS); Friday, the day of preparation (NLT, REB, BER, NAB); the day before the Sabbath (LB)	day of Preparation (NRSV, AMP); Preparation day (TEV); Preparation Day (NCV, GNC, BOL, JNT, NJB)
Heb 10:25	the day approaching	see the Day approaching	day of the Lord (REB, GW, CEV, NCV); the day (NASB, AMP); day of his coming back again (NLT); the final day (PHILLIPS); the day of His return (NL); the great day (GNC)	the Day (NRSV, NJB, NAB, TEV, BER, BOL, JNT)

Table 28: Special Times

This brief overview displays the main categories involved in the use of capital letters in English Bible translation. Space does not indicate other uses of capitalization, for example in inscriptions (see Dan 5:25 and Rev 17:5). Translators who put Scripture into English face problems not encountered when putting Scripture into some other languages. Some of these are doctrinal and crucial, for example the "spirit" versus "Spirit" question. Others are simply a matter of style and preference. The decisions made are not mechanical but involve careful assessment of text and context. All are important in the task of communicating the message of Scripture to modern English readers. The goal should be to help the reader grasp the message of Scripture; as with matters of punctuation, capitalization can help the general reader of the Bible more quickly grasp the flow of the text and its meaning.

Notes

1. Hebrew *El Shaddai*.
2. Hebrew *Shaddai*.
3. Hebrew *Yahweh Elohim*.
4. The REB translates the Hebrew here as "Creator."
5. The BER has a footnote here noting that this is a frequent title for God and cites 2 Samuel 23:3; Isaiah 17:10; Psalm 31:3.
6. Notice the change from "King" to "king" in the NRSV revision of the RSV.
7. One of Isaiah's favorite titles for God.
8. Cf. Isaiah's frequent use of the "Holy One of Israel."
9. Notice this was dropped to lowercase "name" in the NRSV.
10. The point is common noun or proper noun, not necessarily the same word.
11. Footnote: Or *king*.
12. Many of the versions paraphrase this passage, thus avoiding the use of "name."
13. It is interesting to note that in the next verse this version capitalizes "Body."
14. Cf. the use of Master in 2 Timothy 2:21 and Colossians 4:1. Note its use of "Christ" in Luke's account (Luke 9:33, 49; 17:13).
15. The footnote gives the alternates "spirit of God, mighty wind."
16. The footnote gives the options of "power of God, wind from God, awesome wind."
17. The footnote gives the alternate "mighty wind."
18. With footnote: "Meaning of Hebrew uncertain."
19. With a footnote: Or "your breath."
20. The adjective can refer to either "spirit" or "Spirit" (there is a difference).
21. The TNIV is currently available only in the New Testament.
22. With a footnote offering the alternate "your spirit is alive."
23. Note that some versions find both uses (spirit/Spirit) in this passage (REB, NET, PHILLIPS).
24. With a footnote giving the alternate "the Spirit."

25. The word begins the sentence, so it is written "Spiritual."

26. The NLT and TEV do not have exactly the same wording but basically the same. Such minor differences are not usually indicated with a footnote.

27. Notice the change here in the revision of the RSV.

28. Although spelling varies, most versions have references to this deity.

29. With a footnote giving the alternate "their king."

30. With an alternate reading "Melcom."

31. See Acts 14:12–13.

32. With a footnote: "Hebrew *Asherim*."

33. Since the definite article is not used with proper nouns in English, this rendering is ambiguous. The fact that it is capitalized suggests a proper noun.

34. Plus a footnote.

35. The NJB uses only one English term for all three Hebrew terms.

36. Some editions of the KJV have Ishtob.

37. Footnote: "apparently a race of giants."

38. The KJV has two names: Nergal-sharezer and Samgar-nebo, but the NIV redivides the Hebrew to read Nergal-Sharezer of Samgar

39. This is a difficult decision, and many, like the NRSV and NIV, give the alternate in a footnote.

40. Obviously this is not a new place-name in the Bible—but it is in this place. See also Isaiah 19:6.

41. With a footnote: "and your army."

42. With footnote: "That is, Kiriath Jearim."

43. The entire phrase is taken as a proper noun, although the Hebrew for forest/woods is translated instead of transliterated.

44. Or "garden house."

45. Footnote: "Or Beth-eden of the Shepherds."

46. Plus footnote.

47. Plus footnote.

48. Genesis 2:13.

49. 2 Samuel 8:6.

50. Ezekiel 30:5.

51. Ezekiel 30:5.

52. Genesis 2:14.

53. Numbers 24:24.

54. Deuteronomy 1:1.

55. Footnote: "Hebrew *of ships of Tarshish*."

56. Footnote: "The meaning of the Hebrew for this word is uncertain."

57. The Watchtower Society and others deny this second meaning of the term.

58. In cases of parallel terms, if one of the terms is treated as a common noun, it is placed in this column.

59. This word begins the sentence; the same is true in Proverbs 15:11.

60. Footnote: "Or, hell."

61. Footnote: "Greek, *Tartarus*." (The NRSV has a similar footnote.)

62. The NIV also uses this proper noun in the book of Revelation—chapters 9, 11, 17, and 20.

63. In the next line the TNK refers to the "abysses of the Sea."

64. With footnote that indicates reading Hebrew *yôm* instead of *yām*.

65. Footnote: "Or crocodile."

66. Note the parallel in this verse between Rahab and Dragon.

67. With a footnote, giving the possible reading of "the sea."

68. With a footnote, giving the possible reading of "day."

69. Footnote: "Or the hippopotamus."

70. Although the Living Bible retained "Lucifer," its revision (NLT) uses "shining star."

71. This example is not necessarily one of personification but is treated here for convenience.

72. Some versions have a companion term here in capitals—Prudence (TNK); Common Sense (CEV).

73. Such transliterated terms are usually put in italics in this version.

74. Cf. also Matthew 27:62; Luke 23:54. But see also "day of Preparation" in John 19:31, 42

INDEX

CPSIA information can be obtained
at www.ICGtesting.com
Printed in the USA
LVHW102226180322
713857LV00004B/6

9 780310 246855